Germany 1914–1933

Germany, 1914–1933

Politics, Society and Culture

Matthew Stibbe

For John

Best wishes

Matthew

Longman
is an imprint of

Harlow, England • London • New York • Boston • San Francisco • Toronto • Sydney • Singapore • Hong Kong
Tokyo • Seoul • Taipei • New Delhi • Cape Town • Madrid • Mexico City • Amsterdam • Munich • Paris • Milan

Pearson Education Limited
Edinburgh Gate
Harlow CM20 2JE
United Kingdom
Tel: +44 (0)1279 623623
Fax: +44 (0)1279 431059
Website: www.pearsoned.co.uk

First edition published in Great Britain in 2010
© Pearson Education Limited 2010

The right of Matthew Stibbe to be identified as author of this work has been asserted by him in accordance with the Copyright, Designs and Patents Act 1988.

ISBN: 978-1-4058-0136-2

British Library Cataloguing in Publication Data
A CIP catalogue record for this book can be obtained from the British Library

Library of Congress Cataloging in Publication Data
Stibbe, Matthew.
  Germany, 1914–1933 : politics, society, and culture / Matthew Stibbe. – 1st ed.
    p. cm.
  Includes bibliographical references.
  ISBN 978-1-4058-0136-2 (pbk.)
  1. Germany – History – 1918–1933. 2. Germany – Politics and government – 1918–1933.
3. Germany – Social conditions – 1918–1933. 4. World War, 1914–1918 – Germany.
5. World War, 1914–1918 – Social aspects – Germany I. Title.
  DD237.S76 2010
  943.085—dc22

                                                                          2009052001

10 9 8 7 6 5 4 3 2 1
14 13 12 11 10

Set in 9/13.5pt stone serif by 35
Printed in Malaysia, CTP-PJB

For Paul and Hazel

Contents

List of Plates

List of Tables

Acknowledgements

I would like to thank Moritz Föllmer, Kevin McDermott, Ingrid Sharp, Chris Szejnmann and Benjamin Ziemann for their critical comments and suggestions on earlier drafts of this book, and Melanie Carter, Mari Shullaw and Christina Wipf-Perry at Pearson for their encouragement and forbearance over the several years it has taken for this project to come to fruition. I would also like to extend my special gratitude to the staff at the Adsetts Learning Centre, Sheffield Hallam University, who continue to deal with my endless inter-library loan requests with great speed and efficiency. Your efforts are much appreciated.

Sam, Nicholas and Hannah – as always a big thank you for everything.

I dedicate this book to my father Paul and step-mother Hazel, in recognition of their wonderful support through my school and university education and beyond.

Matthew Stibbe
Chorlton-cum-Hardy, Manchester
May 2009

Publisher's Acknowledgements

We are grateful to the following for permission to reproduce copyright material:

The Deutsches Historisches Museum (German Historical Museum) in Berlin for Plates 1.1, 2.2, 3.2, 5.1, 6.2 and 6.3; Bundesarchiv (Federal Archives) for Plates 2.1 and 4.2; Bildarchiv Preussischer Kulturbesitz for Plate 3.1; Hulton Archive/ Getty Images for Plate 4.1; the Kunst Museum, Stuttgart for Plate 5.2; Archiv der sozialen Demokratie der Friedrich-Ebert-Stiftung, Bonn, for Plate 6.1.

Yale University Press for the song lyric on p.103, from Appignanesi, L., *The Cabaret* (Yale University Press, 2004); A & C Black Publishing and Suhrkamp Verlag for the extract on p.109 from Brecht, Bertolt, *The Threepenny Opera*, trans. Manheim, R. and Willett, J. (Methuen Drama, 2005); WW Norton & Co for the extracts on pp.141 and 150 from Roth, J., *What I Saw: Reports from Berlin, 1920–1933* (WW Norton & Co, 2004); Taylor & Francis for the tables on pp.168, 178 and 186 from Kolb, E., *The Weimar Republic*, 2nd edn (Routledge, 2005); Cambridge University Press for the table on p.182 from Muhlberger, D., *The Social Bases of Nazism* (CUP, 2003).

In some instances we have been unable to obtain copyright permission, and we would appreciate any information that would enable us to do so.

Chronology

1914

28 June	Assassination of Austrian Archduke Franz Ferdinand by Serb nationalists during royal visit to Sarajevo
5 July	German 'blank cheque' to Austria encouraging latter to take firm stand against Serbia
23 July	Austrian ultimatum to Serbia
28 July	Austrian declaration of war on Serbia; 100,000-strong anti-war demonstration takes place in Berlin
30 July	Russian mobilisation in support of Serbia
31 July	Declaration of state of siege in Germany
1 August	German declaration of war on Russia
3 August	German declaration of war on France
4 August	German invasion of Belgium; unanimous vote for war credits in Reichstag; British declaration of war on Germany
23 August	Japan enters war on side of Allies
26–29 August	German victory against Russians at Battle of Tannenberg marks beginning of Hindenburg 'cult'; followed by further success at the Battle of the Masurian Lakes (10–14 September)
5–12 September	Battle of the Marne. German failure to reach Paris leads to 'race for the ports' and beginnings of trench warfare on the Western Front. Helmuth von Moltke, the German chief of general staff, suffers nervous collapse and is replaced by Erich von Falkenhayn

29 October	Turkey enters war on side of Central Powers
1 November	Hindenburg becomes commander in chief on the Eastern Front (and chief rival of Falkenhayn)
2 December	Karl Liebknecht becomes first Reichstag deputy to vote against the extension of war credits to the government, and is subsequently expelled from the SPD parliamentary group

1915

4 February	German government declares naval exclusion zone around British isles
25 April	Allied landings at Gallipoli in the Dardanelles
7 May	Sinking of the *Lusitania* leads to increased diplomatic tension between Germany and the USA
23 May	Italy enters war on side of Allies
28 May	1,500 women stage an anti-war demonstration in front of the Reichstag in Berlin
May–December	Major successes for Central Powers against Russia and Serbia
4–5 August	Entry of German troops into Warsaw
14 October	Bulgaria enters war on side of Central Powers
December	Last Allied troops evacuated from Gallipoli

1916

1 January	Formation of revolutionary Spartacist League by Karl Liebknecht and Rosa Luxemburg
21 February	German offensive launched at Verdun
15 March	Admiral von Tirpitz resigns as head of Reich Naval Office following Kaiser's refusal to approve continuation of unrestricted submarine warfare
24 March	A further 18 SPD Reichstag deputies vote against the extension of war credits, and are expelled from the SPD parliamentary group

1 May	Karl Liebknecht arrested following anti-war demonstration in Berlin
31 May	Battle of Jutland; German and British navies square up to each other with indecisive outcome
5 June	Reich Chancellor Bethmann Hollweg attacks his right-wing critics in a major speech in the Reichstag
28 June	One-day strike, supported by 55,000 workers in Berlin and elsewhere, in support of Liebknecht
1 July	Allied offensive launched on the Somme
27 August	Romania enters war on side of Allies
29 August	Falkenhayn forced to resign as chief of staff; appointment of Hindenburg and Ludendorff to third supreme command
5 November	Central Powers declare nominally independent 'Kingdom of Poland'
5 December	Auxiliary Service Law approved in Reichstag
6 December	German troops enter the Romanian capital Bucharest
12 December	German peace offer (rejected by Allies on 30 December)

1917

9 January	Decision to launch unrestricted submarine warfare (announced 31 January)
3 February	USA breaks off diplomatic relations with Germany; enters war on Allied side on 6 April
8 March	Revolution in Russia overthrows the Tsar
6–8 April	Independent Social Democratic Party (USPD) launched at Gotha conference
7 April	Kaiser's Easter Message announcing vague promise of domestic political reform after the war
8–14 April	First major strike wave in Germany: 200–300,000 workers down tools, with main centres of unrest in Berlin and Leipzig

23 April	Conference of Central Powers on war aims at Bad Kreuznach
14 July	Resignation of Bethmann Hollweg; appointment of Georg Michaelis as new Reich Chancellor
19 July	Reichstag Peace Resolution
2 September	Formation of German Fatherland Party at Königsberg in East Prussia
31 October– 1 November	Michaelis resigns as Reich Chancellor and is replaced by Georg von Hertling
7 November	Bolshevik Revolution in Russia
15 December	Armistice signed on Eastern Front

1918

28 January	Beginning of week-long strike involving up to one million workers throughout Germany's major industrial regions
3 March	Treaty of Brest-Litovsk signed between Germany and Soviet Union; Germany makes large-scale territorial gains in the East
15 March	Treaty of Brest-Litovsk approved in the Reichstag; USPD votes against while SPD abstains
21 March	German spring offensive launched on Western Front
July–August	Allied counter-offensive on Western Front
29 September	Army Supreme Command calls for immediate armistice and introduction of parliamentary government during private audience with the Kaiser
3 October	Formation of new government under Prince Max von Baden, including ministers from Reichstag parties
3–4 October	Armistice negotiations opened with President Wilson
26 October	Ludendorff replaced as First Quarter-Master General by Wilhelm Groener
28 October	Constitutional amendment makes the Reich government responsible to the Reichstag for the first time

3 November	Austria-Hungary surrenders to Allies
3–9 November	Revolution in Kiel and Wilhelmshaven, spreading to rest of Germany. Formation of Soviets in many German towns and cities
9 November	Proclamation of German republic; abdication of Kaiser Wilhelm II; formation of new government in Berlin headed by Friedrich Ebert (SPD) and led by the Council of People's Commissars (SPD-USPD)
10 November	Ebert-Groener Pact seals deal between new government and army to counter threat from the extreme left
11 November	Armistice ends the First World War on the Western Front
15 November	Stinnes-Legien Pact between industrialists and trade unions
29 December	USPD members withdraw from Council of People's Commissars
30 December– 1 January 1919	Founding congress of German Communist Party (KPD) takes place in Berlin

1919

5–12 January	Spartacist uprising in Berlin, ending in murder of Karl Liebknecht and Rosa Luxemburg (15 January)
19 January	Elections held for new National Assembly
6 February	National Assembly opened in Weimar
13 February	Dissolution of Council of People's Commissars. Formation of new SPD-led coalition government under Philipp Scheidemann; Ebert elevated to Reich President
21 February	Murder of Bavarian Minister-President Kurt Eisner (USPD)
March	Further unrest in Berlin; wildcat strikes in the Ruhr and Central Germany
7 April–2 May	Short-lived Soviet Republic in Munich

18 May	Publication of KPD programme 'Basic Principles of Peace'
21 June	Resignation of Scheidemann government; appointment of new coalition government under Gustav Bauer (SPD)
28 June	Treaty of Versailles signed
12 July	Wartime Allied economic blockade lifted
11 August	Weimar constitution formally approved

1920

13–17 March	Right-wing Kapp Putsch defeated by general strike of Berlin workers
27 March	Resignation of Bauer government; appointment of new coalition government under Heinrich Müller (SPD)
March–April	Left-wing uprisings in the Ruhr and Central Germany
April	Beginning of Polish-Soviet War
6 June	Reichstag election results in major losses for the parties of the 'Weimar coalition' (SPD, DDP, Centre Party).
21 June	Formation of new 'bourgeois' coalition government under Constantin Fehrenbach (Centre Party), without inclusion of SPD
30 June–25 August	First international Dada Fair held in Berlin. Some of the chief organisers later prosecuted for 'insulting the German army'
August	Red Army reaches gates of Warsaw but pushed back by Polish counter-offensive (the 'miracle on the Vistula')
December	Left-wing of USPD joins KPD

1921

February–March	London conference on reparations
March	KPD launches so-called 'March offensive' in Central Germany

5 May	Allied ultimatum on reparations
10 May	Formation of new coalition government with Joseph Wirth (Centre Party) as Reich Chancellor and Gustav Bauer (SPD) as his deputy
26 August	Murder of Catholic Centre politician Matthias Erzberger by right-wing extremists

1922

21 January	Walther Rathenau (DDP) becomes Foreign Minister
16 April	Treaty of Rapallo signed between Germany and the Soviet Union
24 June	Murder of Rathenau by right-wing extremists
18 July	Law for the Protection of the Republic (*Republikschutzgesetz*) passes through Reichstag
July	Beginnings of hyperinflation
24 September	Merger of the right-wing of the USPD with the SPD
22 November	Resignation of Wirth government. Formation of new 'bourgeois' coalition government under Wilhelm Cuno (non-party), without participation of the SPD

1923

11 January	Franco-Belgian occupation of Ruhr following Germany's default on reparations; German government declares policy of 'passive resistance'
13 August	Resignation of Cuno government. Formation of 'grand coalition' government under Gustav Stresemann (DVP), with SPD participation
26 September	'Passive resistance' called off in the Ruhr; hyperinflation peaks with complete collapse of value of the Mark
October	Communist uprisings in Hamburg, Saxony and Thuringia
3 November	SPD ministers resign from Stresemann government
9 November	Hitler's failed 'Beer Hall Putsch' in Munich

15 November	Introduction of new currency, the Rentenmark
30 November	Formation of new 'bourgeois' coalition under Wilhelm Marx (Centre Party) with Stresemann as foreign minister

1924

10 April	Death of industrialist Hugo Stinnes leads to collapse of his business empire
16 April	German government agrees to Dawes Plan involving rescheduling of reparations payments
4 May	Reichstag election, government parties and SPD lose seats to Communists and nationalist DNVP
November	Publication of Thomas Mann's *The Magic Mountain*
7 December	Fresh Reichstag election, modest gains for government parties and SPD, but also for DNVP

1925

15 January	Formation of new 'bourgeois' cabinet under Hans Luther (non-party) including (for the first time) ministers from the DNVP
28 February	Death of President Friedrich Ebert
26 April	Hindenburg elected President in second round of election, defeating main rival Wilhelm Marx (Centre Party)
15–16 October	Locarno Treaties signed in Switzerland; DNVP ministers resign from government in protest

1926

16 May	Resignation of Luther government; Wilhelm Marx again becomes Reich Chancellor at head of new 'bourgeois' coalition

20 June	Referendum on the dispossession of former German royal houses; SPD-KPD backers win an impressive 14.5 million votes (36.4 per cent of the electorate) but fall some way short of the 19.9 million needed to change the law
8 September	Germany enters League of Nations
3 December	'Law against Trashy and Smutty Literature' passed by Reichstag
10 December	Stresemann awarded Nobel Peace Prize (alongside French and British Foreign Ministers Aristide Briand and Sir Austen Chamberlain)

1927

29 January	DNVP agrees to join reshuffled 'bourgeois' cabinet; Marx continues as Reich Chancellor with Oskar Hergt (DNVP) as his deputy
16 July	New Law on Unemployment Insurance passed in Reichstag

1928

20 May	Reichstag election results in significant gains for the SPD and big losses for the right-wing DNVP
29 June	Formation of 'grand coalition' government under Hermann Müller (SPD), without participation of DNVP
July–August	Sixth Congress of the Comintern marks the beginning of the ultra-left 'Third Period' in communist policy, and in Germany a considerable worsening of relations between the KPD and the SPD
31 August	Opening performance of Bertolt Brecht's *Threepenny Opera* at the Theater am Schiffbauerdamm in Berlin
20 October	Alfred Hugenberg becomes new leader of DNVP, signalling party's shift to the extreme right

| October–December | Ruhr steel lock-out marks one of the biggest industrial disputes of the Weimar era. Unemployment levels also rising in winter of 1928/9 |

1929

January	Publication of Erich Maria Remarque's controversial anti-war novel *All Quiet on the Western Front*, having already been serialised in the *Vossische Zeitung* in November–December 1928
1–3 May	'Blood May' riots in Berlin between pro-communist demonstrators and the SPD-controlled Berlin police
7 June	Publication of Young Plan, representing revision of reparations schedules set out in Dawes Plan
June–December	Right-wing parties (DNVP, NSDAP, Stahlhelm) launch a major joint campaign against Germany's adoption of Young Plan
3 October	Death of Gustav Stresemann
Late October	Wall Street Crash
10 December	Thomas Mann announced as winner of the Nobel Prize for Literature
22 December	Referendum on Young Plan; Hugenberg and his right-wing allies win only 5.8 million votes (13.8 per cent of the electorate), well short of the 22 million needed to force a change in the law
End 1929	Unemployment already at 1.5 million

1930

12 March	Reichstag approves Young Plan
27 March	Resignation of Müller government after it fails to reach agreement on budget; formation of minority government under Heinrich Brüning (Centre Party) which introduces major cuts in welfare spending
30 June	Final withdrawal of all Allied troops from the Rhineland

16 July	Reichstag dissolved by Presidential decree
14 September	Reichstag election; first significant gains for the Nazis at national level
December	American film version of Remarque's *All Quiet on the Western Front* banned throughout Germany following Nazi-led protests at its first screening in Berlin
End 1930	Unemployment stands at over 3 million

1931

March	France vetoes proposed customs union between Germany and Austria
11 May	Collapse of Austrian Credit-Anstalt bank
20 June	President Hoover announces one year moratorium on reparations payments
July	Major banking crisis in Germany; Hans Luther, as President of the Reichsbank, forced to declare a series of 'bank holidays' and to introduce strict new foreign currency controls to stem further flight of capital
3 October	Resignation of Foreign Minister Julius Curtius (DVP) following criticism of his customs union plan with Austria by the International Court at The Hague
11 October	Meeting of 'nationalist opposition' parties at Bad Harzburg leads to proclamation of short-lived Harzburg Front
16 December	Formation of pro-republican 'Iron Front' by SPD, trade unions and Reichsbanner

1932

February	Unemployment peaks at over 6 million
13 March–10 April	Hindenburg re-elected in two-round presidential election, defeating main rival Adolf Hitler

13 April	The Nazi paramilitary organisation the SA is banned in most of Germany
24 April	Elections to Prussian Landtag – massive gains for Nazis, 'Weimar coalition' led by Otto Braun (SPD) loses its majority but continues as minority administration
12 May	Resignation of Wilhelm Groener as Defence Minister
30 May–1 June	Resignation of Brüning government; formation of 'government of national concentration' under Franz von Papen
4 June	Reichstag dissolved by presidential decree
16 June	Ban on SA rescinded
16 June–9 July	Lausanne Conference agrees to the complete abolition of reparations
20 July	Prussian government of Otto Braun dissolved in an army-backed coup; Papen takes over as 'Reich Commissioner for Prussia'
31 July	Reichstag election; NSDAP becomes largest party with 230 seats
13 August	Meeting between Hindenburg and Hitler; Hitler refuses President's offer of appointment as Vice Chancellor, while Hindenburg refuses Hitler's demand to be made Chancellor
12 September	Reichstag again dissolved by presidential decree following vote of no confidence in Papen government
6 November	Fresh Reichstag election: NSDAP loses 2 million votes and 34 seats but remains largest party
2 December	Resignation of Papen government; formation of new government under General Kurt von Schleicher

1933

4 January	Secret meeting between Hitler and Papen near Cologne

28 January	Schleicher resigns when it becomes clear that he no longer has the President's confidence
30 January	Hitler appointed Reich Chancellor
1 February	Reichstag dissolved by presidential decree
27/28 February	Reichstag Fire; Emergency Decree for the Protection of People and State leads to suspension of many civil liberties and a de facto ban on the KPD
5 March	Reichstag election of dubious validity gives Nazis and DNVP an overall majority of 52 per cent
23 March	Enabling Act grants new government emergency powers for four years
10 May	Mass burnings of left-wing and anti-Nazi books in Berlin and many other German university towns and cities

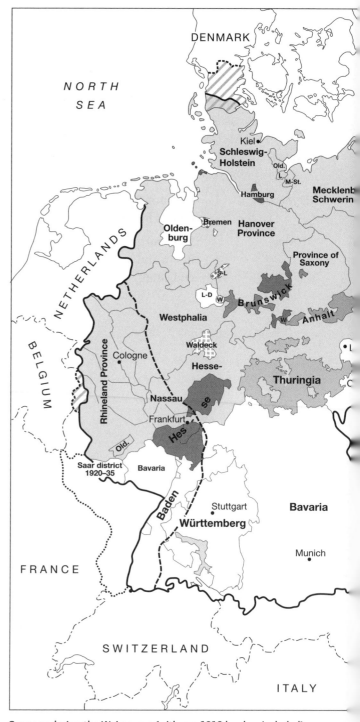

Germany during the Weimar era (with pre-1918 borders included).

LITHUANIA

BALTIC SEA

East Prussia

Free City
of Danzig

Pomerania

Posen-West Prussia

Grenzmark

POLAND

Lower
Silesia

• Breslau

Upper
Silesia

ZECHOSLOVAKIA

STRIA

L	Lübeck
L-D	Lippe-Detmold
SL	Schaumburg-Lippe
M-St	Mecklenburg-Strelitz
W	Waldeck (absorbed into Prussia in 1929)
——	Border of the German Reich from 1919/21 to 1937
··········	Border of the German Reich up to 1914
▨	Plebiscite areas, 1919–1921
----	Eastern boundary of demilitarised zone

Introduction

The division of history into periods is not a fact, but a necessary hypothesis or tool of thought, valid in so far as it is illuminating, and dependent for its validity on interpretation.

E. H. Carr[1]

The collapse of the Weimar Republic in 1933 is a landmark historical event in German and world history. It has come to symbolise not merely the passing of one historical period and the beginning of another, but also the end of the German Reich as a state based on the rule of law (*ein Rechtsstaat*) and the rise of a criminal regime whose policies wiped out entire peoples and communities and almost led to the complete destruction of European civilisation. As the late Wolfgang J. Mommsen, one of the leading experts on this period, has remarked:

The question as to why Germany, a country with an advanced culture and a highly developed economy, could fall under the rule not merely of a dictatorship, but of fascism in its worst form, must still engage us today. It is not simply a matter of preventing a repetition of the Nazi phenomenon, now and in the future. Over and beyond that, the answers we give to this question have far-reaching consequences for our personal attitudes and for the founding principles [Grundwerte] of our political life.[2]

Nazism, in other words, contains a 'warning from history', a warning which subsequent generations have, quite rightly, been anxious not to forget.[3]

A separate but related question is the place of the Weimar Republic itself in German history. In particular, what accounts for the immense colour and vitality of the republic's culture and politics? And how can the failure of this

short-lived democratic regime be explained? Leaving aside for one moment
the more immediate causes such as the Wall Street Crash and the Great
Depression, a number of different theories have been put forward. Each of
these theories in turn suggests a particular way of looking not only at the
years 1918–33, but also at the period that preceded them, namely that of
the German empire from 1871 to 1918.[4]

Thus one influential school of thought, the *Sonderweg* thesis, maintains
that Germany's political development had already begun to diverge from
that of the liberal West under the old empire, with backward, authoritarian,
'semi-feudal' attitudes becoming entrenched during the Bismarck era
(1871–1890) and continuing into the 1920s and beyond, especially in institutions such as the military, the judiciary, the universities and the civil
service. Germany, so this argument goes, had missed out on the kind of
successful 'bourgeois' revolution which had transformed countries like
Britain, France and the United States into well-established, self-confident
parliamentary democracies by the late nineteenth century, with fatal consequences for the survival of the Weimar Republic.[5] On the other hand, a
more recent narrative, based in particular on the work of the scholar Detlev
Peukert, rejects the idea of German 'backwardness' and instead focuses on
the *modernity* of the German empire from the 1890s onwards, a modernity
which reached its final, crisis stage in the 1920s and early 1930s. In this
view, the path which Germany took in the early twentieth century was not
unique; rather it was emblematic of more general, European-wide or even
global trends in the modern, post-1890 era.[6] Finally, there is also a powerful
discourse which emphasises the 'missed opportunities' or 'betrayals' of the
years 1918–19, when the German revolution, while overthrowing the Kaiser
and ending the war, failed to secure the foundations for a lasting, progressive
political system. Here in particular blame is attached to the leaders of the
German Social Democratic Party (SPD) who came to power on 9 November
1918 but then unwisely, mistakenly or perhaps even treacherously, agreed
to share some of that power with the forces of the old order.[7]

The purpose of this book is to offer an alternative to all of these perspectives by arguing that the year 1914, rather than 1890 or 1918–19, should be
seen as the starting point of a new era in German history, marked by ongoing political, socio-economic and cultural crisis and ending in the Nazi
seizure of power in 1933. In so doing, the intention is not to suggest a direct
line of continuity leading from the outbreak of the First World War to Hitler,
but rather to uncover the full range of possible outcomes which emerge when
one seeks to challenge conventional forms of periodisation. At the same time,
it is also intended to use this approach as a means of demonstrating how

recent developments in cultural history,[8] and especially in the social and cultural history of modern warfare,[9] have helped to bring a fresh understanding of key political events and processes in late Imperial and Weimar Germany. In short, the book aims to integrate some of the insights gained from the new cultural history into the more established framework of political history writing. It understands culture in the broadest sense as being made up of individual and collective efforts to interpret and represent the world by means of language, gestures and symbols. And it presents politics as being about the aspiration to, and exercise of, power, a process which took on new meanings and generated new fears and ambitions as Europe began to enter the 'age of the masses' in the late nineteenth and early twentieth centuries.[10] In order to understand this further, it will first be necessary to examine previous works which treat the years 1914 to 1933 as a distinct period in German history in their own right, particularly from the social and cultural standpoint.

Interestingly, one of the first post-war scholars to regard 1914 as a significant chronological marker pointing to trends beyond the year 1918 was the art historian John Willett, in a book published in 1978. In his view, the First World War was a landmark event in German culture not only because of the deep emotional experiences which it gave rise to, but also because of the changed political context, namely 'the breakdown in normal relations with Western Europe'.[11] Thus:

The war interrupted Germany's absorption of the newest Latin movements, to which pre-war Expressionism had owed so much; it closed theatres and imposed a censorship which held up important new plays and books, forcing some of the more critical writers and editors to move to neutral soil. It turned internationalists into nationalists, often in the most unexpected way . . . [It also] led to temporary suspension or permanent transfer of key institutions . . . [and] caused an interruption of modern building everywhere but in neutral Holland.[12]

On the other hand, in contrast to Britain and France, a powerful mass anti-war movement developed in Germany from 1917 onwards which had its nucleus in the Independent Social Democratic Party (USPD) and also 'decisively influenced a good proportion of those concerned with the arts'. The violent upheavals of war and revolution were therefore central to the development of Weimar culture, and not simply an 'interruption' to new artistic trends already in evidence before 1914.[13]

A decade later, in 1989, Modris Eksteins expanded on these themes in a book which argued that the First World War gave birth to 'the modern age' by unleashing a series of violent and revolutionary developments in the arts, the sciences, music, theatre, politics and social relations. At the centre of this storm lay Germany, the 'modernist nation *par excellence*'.[14] Its approach to war, just like its approach to art and politics, was marked by radical innovation and by a fundamental urge to break free from the restraints of the past into a brighter, more 'modern' and more 'heroic' future. By contrast, England, Germany's arch-enemy, became 'the principal representative of the old order against which she [Germany] was rebelling':

Britain felt not only her pre-eminence in the world but her entire way of life threatened by the thrusting energy and instability Germany was seen to typify. British involvement in the 1914 war was to turn it from a continental power struggle into a veritable war of cultures.[15]

Finally, while Willett and Eksteins were primarily interested in develop-ments in 'high culture', Peter Fritzsche, in his book *Germans into Nazis* (1999) came to similar conclusions when examining the experience of the masses in 1914. In his view, the spontaneous coming together of thousands of patriotic Germans in the 'August days' of 1914 represented a new form of 'popular mobilization' from below which for the first time made Nazism possible (but not inevitable):

Because the war so thoroughly revised the national imagination and recombined 60 million people in novel and often dangerous ways, 1914 is the appropriate point of departure for an account of how the Nazis came to power.[16]

More recently, several historians have chosen 1914 as their starting point, without necessarily endorsing any of the arguments outlined above. Stefan Berger, for instance, has emphasised the 'deep impact of the First World War on constructions of the nation in the Weimar Republic'.[17] As he convinc-ingly shows, rival interpretations of the war were at the centre of the various discourses of German nationhood offered by the Communists, the Social Democrats and the political right during the 1920s. I adopted a similar perspective in discussing different manifestations of German wartime anglophobia in a study published in 2001, concluding that the 'German preoccupation with "enemies all around", with competition for world power and with the search for a "place in the sun" took on a new and more brutal form after the outbreak of war in 1914'.[18] Finally, Jeffrey R. Smith has depicted the years 1913–14 as marking the rise of a new revolutionary 'nationalist-vernacular' in the German public sphere which challenged tra-ditional monarchical authority 'from below' and ultimately 'pave[d] the way for the volatile political climate of the 1920s' and early 1930s.[19]

However, to some extent the focus of research is now shifting away from the impact of war on national imaginations towards looking at its role in shaping supranational, regional and local identities too. As a variety of studies have emphasised, home fronts became as important as fighting fronts for winning the war,[20] while even those living in exile, in captivity or under enemy occupation had a part to play.[21] Military leaders responsible for directing policies at regional level were often overly concerned with issues of regulation, planning and control, and in many ways it was this mass mobilisation for war which was to have the strongest implications for society and politics under Weimar. In the words of Richard Bessel, 'the conduct of the war exacerbated conflicts between government and people, between the civil authorities and the military, between front and home front, between rich and poor, between producers and consumers, between employers and employees, between town and country'.[22] Yet there was also a certain amount of voluntary self-mobilisation and self-expression, a desire to take part, which affected the way in which individuals and communities saw themselves and others, and contributed significantly to the formation of different war cultures as the conflict progressed. Some of these war cultures were pro-war, others pacifist,[23] while others still were against the war without necessarily harnessing themselves to the rival ideologies of extreme nationalism and militant socialism.[24]

The debate about the German experience of the First World War is thus far from over, and in some ways is only just beginning.[25] The same can be said of the debate about the German experience of demobilisation after 1918.[26] Some recent accounts, for instance, have called into question the extent to which post-war Germany became a 'violent' or 'brutalised' society as a direct consequence of the front-line experience. In fact, many veterans of the trenches voiced their hostility towards violence through membership of pacifist and anti-militarist bodies like the 'No More War Movement' and the pro-republican *Reichsbanner Schwarz-Rot-Gold*.[27] Yet other studies have been impressed by the continuation of more aggressive war cultures into the post-war world, especially around themes such as masculinity and comradeship,[28] occupation and national identity[29] and militarisation and reproduction.[30] Perhaps most significantly of all, the war had led to a blurring of the traditional distinction between combatants and non-combatants, with 'ordinary' civilians and soldiers becoming targets for previously unheard of forms of collective violence, including beatings, executions, deportations, internment and starvation through economic blockade.[31] Germans appeared as both victims and perpetrators in this process, with personal memories and subjective interpretations sometimes agreeing and sometimes conflicting with official discourses on the war into the 1920s and beyond.[32]

The scope of this book

The issues raised above underline, in my view, the need for an approach to writing the history of Weimar Germany which begins in 1914, rather than 1918. Of course, such an approach does not set out to devalue other works which have chosen different periodisations. Still less does it seek to imply that 1914 inevitably led to 1933. Rather, the aim is to provoke further debate by offering a critical interpretation of the most recent research and placing it within a broader framework of competing methodologies and historical narratives, all of which attempt to 'tell the story' of the Weimar Republic.

The study itself is divided into six chapters which follow broadly in chronological sequence. Chapter 1 begins by offering a view of the war 'from above', exploring some of the major problems facing the political, military and industrial leaders of Germany as they sought to mobilise the nation's material and spiritual resources for war. Chapter 2 then goes on to consider how the war was experienced 'from below', by the millions of German soldiers who fought and died in occupied foreign lands, and by the millions of civilians who held out on the home front. Particular emphasis will be placed here both on the strong links between fighting front and home front, and also on the gradual emergence of an anti-war movement which the government and military tried, but failed, to crush. These developments in turn form the background to the revolution in late 1918 which overthrew the monarchical system and led to the armistice of 11 November.

Chapter 3 examines the political and psychological consequences of the war, paying particular attention to the difficulties in establishing a new republican consensus in the face of military defeat, administrative collapse and widespread hunger, and the challenges posed by the rise of new extremist parties on the left and right. The extent to which German society became more acclimatised to violence in the wake of the war and post-war political troubles will also be addressed. Meanwhile, Chapter 4 will look at the social history of the 1920s, focusing in particular on big business and labour, the urban poor, the 'old' and 'new' middle classes, and finally on rural society.

Chapter 5 moves on to discuss key aspects of Weimar culture: the new mood of experimentalism in the high arts and architecture, modern patterns of consumption, the rise of 'mass culture' and the 'New Woman', the 'American wave' in advertising and film, the birth of modern 'pulp fiction', and so on. It will also explore some of the darker sides of modernity, especially in relation to the emergence of new and violent forms of homophobia, misogyny, racism and anti-Semitism as the 1920s progressed. Here too the importance of Germany's experience of the First World War in shaping both democratic and anti-democratic values in the post-war era will be demonstrated.

Chapter 6, the last chapter, then moves back towards high politics, examining the impact of the Great Depression which followed the Wall Street Crash, the sudden emergence of the Nazis as a serious contender for power, the ideological divisions on the left which weakened the opposition to fascism, and the behind-the-scenes political intrigues which led to Adolf Hitler's appointment as Reich Chancellor in January 1933.

Finally, the conclusion will briefly re-examine the causes of Weimar's collapse in the light of new research and fresh historical interpretations. 1914 had begun as an era of great hope for Germany, bringing forth a war which was supposed to go down in history as 'the German war'.[33] Yet paradoxically, by 1933 the ideology of national unity which was rooted in the 'August experience' and the comradeship of the trenches had brought to power a dictatorship which would end in the final, total destruction of the German imperial (and masculine) ideal. More particularly, in the 1920s and early 1930s radical right-wing narratives of the war which portrayed the front-line fighters as heroes and Germany's defeat as a deliberate act of betrayal by Jews and socialists at home triumphed over the great wave of popular anti-war sentiment experienced during and immediately after the conflict, with catastrophic consequences for the survival of democracy. In this sense, I would agree with a number of recent historians who have suggested that the ways in which the war was presented to the public from 1914 onwards, and the myths it gave rise to, had a lasting effect in terms of legitimising the Nazi seizure of power in 1933.[34]

Notes

1 E. H. Carr, *What is History?* (London, 1961), pp. 54–5.

2 Wolfgang J. Mommsen, '1933: Die Flucht in den Führerstaat', in Carola Stern and Heinrich August Winkler (eds), *Wendepunkte deutscher Geschichte, 1848–1990*, 2nd edition (Frankfurt/M, 1994), pp. 127–58 (here p. 128).

3 Laurence Rees, *The Nazis: A Warning from History*, with a foreword by Ian Kershaw (London, 1997). Also very useful here is David Art, *The Politics of the Nazi Past in Germany and Austria* (Cambridge, 2006).

4 For an excellent overview see Matthew Jefferies, *Contesting the German Empire, 1871–1918* (Oxford, 2008).

5 A classic statement of this position is Hans-Ulrich Wehler's *The German Empire, 1871–1918* (Leamington Spa, 1985). For a trenchant critique of the *Sonderweg*

thesis see David Blackbourn and Geoff Eley, *The Peculiarities of German History. Bourgeois Society and Politics in Nineteenth-century Germany* (Oxford, 1984).

6 Detlev J. K. Peukert, *The Weimar Republic. The Crisis of Classical Modernity* (London, 1991).

7 The clearest accusation of treachery can be found in Sebastian Haffner, *Die verratene Revolution. Deutschland 1918/19* (Bern, 1969). More moderate and measured critiques of the SPD are provided in Hans Mommsen, *The Rise and Fall of Weimar Democracy* (Chapel Hill, NC and London, 1996), and Eric D. Weitz, *Weimar Germany. Promise and Tragedy* (Princeton, NJ, 2007), while Heinrich August Winkler, *Weimar, 1918–1933. Die Geschichte der ersten deutschen Demokratie* (Munich, 1993), is by and large sympathetic to the SPD's position in 1918–19. For a useful overview of all of these perspectives see Eberhard Kolb, *The Weimar Republic*, 2nd edition (London, 2005).

8 On cultural history in general see e.g. Peter Burke, *What is Cultural History?* (Cambridge, 2004); and Simon Gunn, *History and Cultural Theory* (Harlow, 2006). For an influential set of essays on recent German history written from within the cultural history paradigm see Geoff Eley (ed.), *Society, Culture and State in Germany, 1870–1930* (Ann Arbor, MI, 1996).

9 On the new social and cultural history of modern warfare and its impact on the historiography of the First World War in particular see Pierre Purseigle and Jenny Macleod, 'Introduction: Perspectives in First World War Studies', in Jenny Macleod and Pierre Purseigle (eds) *Uncovered Fields. Perspectives in First World War Studies* (Leiden, 2004), pp. 1–23; and Jay Winter and Antoine Prost, *The Great War in History. Debates and Controversies, 1914 to the Present* (Cambridge, 2005).

10 Michael Denis Biddis, *The Age of the Masses. Ideas and Society in Europe since 1870* (London, 1977). See also Geoff Eley, 'Cultural Socialism, the Public Sphere and the Mass Form: Popular Culture and the Democratic Project, 1900 to 1934', in David E. Barclay and Eric D. Weitz (eds), *Between Reform and Revolution. German Socialism and Communism from 1840 to 1990* (Oxford, 1998), pp. 315–40.

11 John Willett, *Art and Politics in the Weimar Period. The New Sobriety, 1917–1933* (New York, 1978), p. 13.

12 Ibid., p. 18.

13 Ibid., p. 13.

14 Modris Eksteins, *Rites of Spring. The Great War and the Birth of the Modern Age* (London, 1989), p. xvi.

15 Ibid., p. xv.

16 Peter Fritzsche, *Germans into Nazis* (Cambridge, MA, 1999), p. 7.

17 Stefan Berger, *Inventing the Nation: Germany* (London, 2004), p. 112.

18 Matthew Stibbe, *German Anglophobia and the Great War, 1914–1918* (Cambridge, 2001), p. 9.

19 Jeffrey R. Smith, *A People's War. Germany's Political Revolution, 1913–1918* (Lanham, Md, 2007), pp. 198 and 21.

20 See e.g. the various contributions to John Horne (ed.), *State, Society and Mobilization During the First World War* (Cambridge, 1997), and to Karen Hagemann and Stefanie Schüler-Springorum (eds), *Home/Front. The Military, War and Gender in Twentieth-Century Germany* (Oxford, 2002).

21 For further examples see Pierre Purseigle, '"A Wave on to our Shores": the Exile and Resettlement of Refugees from the Western Front, 1914–1918', *Contemporary European History*, 16/4 (2007), pp. 427–44; Rainer Pöppinghege, *Im Lager unbesiegt. Deutsche, englische und französische Kriegsgefangenen-Zeitungen im Ersten Weltkrieg* (Essen, 2006); and Annette Becker, *Oubliés de la grande guerre. Humanitaire et culture de guerre. Populations occupées, déportés civils, prisonniers de guerre* (Paris, 1998).

22 Richard Bessel, 'Germany from War to Dictatorship', in Mary Fulbrook (ed.), *Twentieth-century Germany. Politics, Culture and Society, 1918–1990* (London, 2001), pp. 11–35 (here p. 13).

23 See e.g. the different examples provided by the contributors to Alison S. Fell and Ingrid Sharp (eds), *The Women's Movement in Wartime. International Perspectives* (Basingstoke, 1997). Also, more generally, Biddiss, *The Age of the Masses*, p. 186.

24 See in particular Benjamin Ziemann's study, *War Experiences in Rural Germany, 1914–1923* (Oxford, 2007). On the notion of war cultures more generally see John Horne, 'Introduction: Mobilizing for "Total War", 1914–1918', in Horne (ed.), *State, Society and Mobilization*, pp. 1–17 (esp. pp. 6–7).

25 For an excellent introduction to the most recent historiography see Belinda Davis's review article 'Experience, Identity and Memory. The Legacy of World War I', *Journal of Modern History*, 75/1 (2003), pp. 111–31.

26 The pioneering work in this field is Richard Bessel's *Germany after the First World War* (Oxford, 1993). See also Bessel, 'Demobilmachung', in Gerhard Hirschfeld, Gerd Krumeich and Irina Renz (eds), *Enzyklopädie Erster Weltkrieg* (Paderborn, 2003), pp. 427–30.

27 Benjamin Ziemann, 'Germany after the First World War – A Violent Society? Results and Implications of Recent Research on Weimar Germany', *Journal of Modern European History*, 1 (2003), pp. 80–95 (here pp. 83–4).

28 Klaus Theweleit, *Male Fantasies*, 2 vols (Cambridge, 1987–9); Karen Hagemann, 'The Military, Violence and Gender Relations in the Age of the World Wars', in Hagemann and Schüler-Springorum (eds), *Home/Front*, pp. 1–41 (esp. pp. 13–17); John Horne, 'Masculinity in Politics and War in the Age of Nation-States and World Wars, 1850–1950', in Stefan Dudink, Karen Hagemann and John Tosh (eds), *Masculinities in Politics and War. Gendering Modern History* (Manchester, 2004), pp. 22–40 (esp. pp. 31–4).

29 Vejas Gabriel Liulevicius, *War Land on the Eastern Front. Culture, National Identity and German Occupation in World War I* (Cambridge, 2000); Robert L. Nelson,

'German Comrades – Slavic Whores: Gender Images in the German Soldier Newspapers of the First World War', in Hagemann and Schüler-Springorum (eds), *Home/Front*, pp. 69–85.

30 Elizabeth Domansky, 'Militarization and Reproduction in World War I Germany', in Eley (ed.), *Society, Culture and State*, pp. 427–63; Cornelie Usborne, '"Pregnancy is the Woman's Active Service": Pronatalism in Germany during the First World War', in Richard Wall and Jay Winter (eds), *The Upheaval of War. Family, Work and Welfare in Europe, 1914–1918* (Cambridge, 1988), pp. 389–416.

31 John Horne and Alan Kramer, 'War Between Soldiers and Enemy Civilians, 1914–1915', in Roger Chickering and Stig Förster (eds), *Great War, Total War. Combat and Mobilization on the Western Front, 1914–1918* (Cambridge, 2000), pp. 153–68; idem., *German Atrocities, 1914. A History of Denial* (New Haven and London, 2001); Alan Kramer, *Dynamic of Destruction. Culture and Mass Killing in the First World War* (Oxford, 2007).

32 Cf. Robert L. Nelson, '"Ordinary Men" in the First World War? German Soldiers as Victims and Participants', *Journal of Contemporary History*, 39/3 (2004), pp. 425–35 (here pp. 427–30). Also Bernd Ulrich and Benjamin Ziemann (eds), *Krieg im Frieden. Die umkämpfte Erinnerung an den Ersten Weltkrieg* (Frankfurt/M, 1997).

33 Paul Rohrbach, *Warum es der deutsche Krieg ist!* (Stuttgart and Bonn, 1915).

34 See in particular the important studies by Jeffrey Verhey, *The Spirit of 1914. Militarism, Myth and Mobilization in Germany* (Cambridge, 2000), and Boris Barth, *Dolchstosslegenden und politische Desintegration: das Trauma der deutschen Niederlage im Ersten Weltkrieg, 1914–1933* (Düsseldorf, 2003). Also Bernd Ulrich, *Die Augenzeugen: Deutsche Feldpostbriefe in Kriegs-und Nachkriegszeit, 1914–1933* (Essen, 1997); Wolfgang G. Natter, *Literature at War, 1914–1940. Representing the 'Time of Greatness' in Germany* (New Haven and London, 1999); and Benjamin Ziemann, 'Republikanische Kriegserinnerung in einer polarisierten Öffentlichkeit. Das Reichsbanner Schwarz-Rot-Gold als Veteranenbund der sozialistischen Arbeiterschaft', *Historische Zeitschrift*, 267 (1998), pp. 357–98.

CHAPTER 1

The War From Above

The assassination of the Austrian Archduke Franz Ferdinand by
Serbian nationalists during his visit to Sarajevo on 28 June
1914 set in train a series of events which led, within five to six weeks, to the
outbreak of the First World War. Imperial Germany's own responsibility for
this calamity is still the subject of intense historical controversy, and it is
not the intention to retrace this debate in any great detail here.[1] Suffice it to
say that in offering Austria-Hungary a blank cheque to deal with Serbia as it
saw fit, Germany's leaders at the very least took a conscious risk that the two
Central Powers might become embroiled in a war with Russia, Serbia's main
protector in Europe. On top of this, German military strategy – based on the
Schlieffen Plan of 1905 – meant that a war with Russia would very likely
have to begin with a knockout blow against France, Russia's ally, in order to
overcome the obvious disadvantages of a prolonged two-front campaign.
The violation of Belgian neutrality – another product of the Schlieffen Plan
– in turn ensured that Britain would enter the war on the side of Russia and
France. After the breakdown of diplomatic negotiations, the final unravel-
ling of this process took place between 30 July (Russian mobilisation in
support of Serbia) and 4 August (Britain's declaration of war on Germany).[2]

This chapter will examine the 'war from above', in other words, the war
as seen and experienced by the chief policy makers in Germany between
1914 and 1918. In particular it will explore the views of the generals and
admirals who directed military operations, and of the politicians, industrialists, bankers and army officers who helped to determine policy on the home
front during the war. It will also look at the bitter domestic controversy over
unrestricted submarine warfare between 1915 and 1917, and the growth
of opposition to government policy among the moderate parties in the
German parliament, the Reichstag. Firstly, though, it will be necessary to

consider the issue of political and economic mobilisation for war on a broader level.

The *Burgfrieden*

On 4 August 1914 the Reichstag or German parliament met to debate the outbreak of hostilities and the granting of war credits to the government, without which the latter would be unable to finance its military campaigns. Of the six major political parties (from right to left, Conservatives, Free Conservatives, National Liberals, Catholic Centre Party, Progressives and the Social Democrats or SPD) a question mark hung only over the response of the left-wing Social Democrats. Would they remain true to the principles of the Socialist International, and vote against war, or would they embrace the concept of a defensive war, thus proving their loyalty to the nation in its hour of need? In the event, the SPD parliamentary caucus, meeting earlier that day, voted 78 to 14 in favour of approving war credits, with the minority agreeing to abide by the decision of the majority in line with the requirements of party discipline. In one single afternoon, the party leadership had therefore abandoned the anti-war movement, which on 28 July had brought 100,000 protesters onto the streets of Berlin. It had also abandoned all opposition to the manner of prosecuting the war on the home front, including the granting of sweeping new powers to the military under the state of siege, such as the right to curb labour protest, ban strikes and intern political suspects.[3]

The SPD's decision to support the government in turn gave rise to the *Burgfrieden*, a civil truce between all political parties which was intended to last for the duration of the war. Trade unions and employers' organisations also agreed to suspend their disagreements until victory had been achieved, and in the meantime to cooperate towards the maximum mobilisation of economic resources. Similar trends were evident throughout Europe in 1914–15, when social democratic parties in all the belligerent nations, with the exception of Russia, Serbia and later Italy, agreed to support the call to arms.[4] On the other side of the political spectrum, conservative and extreme right-wing parties called a temporary halt to their anti-socialist (and anti-Semitic) propaganda; social democrats and Jews, they now apparently agreed to recognise, could be good patriots and loyal citizens. Of course, this arrangement did not last for very long, and was dead and buried by 1915 at the latest.[5] Yet given the degree of political, confessional and industrial conflict in Germany before 1914, and the long-standing alienation of the SPD from the imperial state, the surprising thing is that the *Burgfrieden* was established for any length of time at all. How can this be explained?

One argument suggests that the SPD and trade union leaders were simply following the mood and desires of their rank and file members, who had already been exposed to much nationalist propaganda in the years before the war, and were now caught up in an unstoppable wave of patriotism which swept over Germany.[6] Hundreds of thousands of young workers volunteered to join the army in the first weeks of August and thus seemed to share in the dream of achieving a glorious victory on the battlefield. Trains taking them to the front were adorned with slogans such as 'To Paris' and 'To St Petersburg', while patriotic songs and poems published in popular newspapers welcomed the war as a test of manhood and courage. Yet it is by no means certain that the rank and file of the German labour movement wanted war in 1914.[7] Not only were there mass demonstrations against Austria's ultimatum to Serbia at the end of July, but also a broader feeling of indifference and fatalism, rather than enthusiasm for the coming conflagration.[8] The crowds who thronged the streets of Berlin, Munich and other major cities, apparently to welcome the announcement of mobilisation for war, were, it is now known, made up largely of middle-class students and civil servants rather than members of the organised working class. The latter tended to stay away and were also under-represented among recruits.[9] In rural areas, too, peasants and farm labourers palpably did not greet the call to arms with joyous celebrations, although admittedly here the SPD's political influence was much less extensive, and concerns about labour shortages at harvest time were more paramount.[10]

A second theory focuses on longer-term developments within German Social Democracy, in particular the ideological split which took place at around the turn of the century between 'revolutionaries' who remained loyal to orthodox Marxism and the cause of proletarian revolution, and 'revisionists' who developed an alternative strategy based on the belief that modern capitalism would gradually evolve into socialism via parliamentary methods and participation in existing legislative processes. The move away from core Marxist beliefs, in this view, necessarily weakened the SPD's firm commitment to collective struggles for international peace and led it to pursue new strategies which linked social and political rights to the question of citizenship and positive integration into the existing nation-state.[11] Yet in fact, Eduard Bernstein, the key proponent of revisionism, and his leading critic, the 'centrist' Marxist Karl Kautsky, joined forces in March 1915 to oppose the war in an important pamphlet entitled *Das Gebot der Stunde* (*The Demand of the Hour*), co-written with former party chairman Hugo Haase. Later all three men broke with the majority SPD (MSPD) to vote against an extension of war credits in March 1916, leading to their expulsion from the parliamentary party. Whether a Social Democrat belonged to the revisionist or revolutionary wing of the party before 1914, in other words, did not necessarily dictate the position they would take in the event of war.[12]

A third explanation focuses on the activities of a small group of influential right-wing Social Democrats and labour officials who met with senior government representatives in the last days before war and who are said to have had a decisive influence on negotiations inside the party. Foremost among them were the Reichstag deputies Eduard David, Albert Südekum and Max Cohen-Reuß, and the national trade union leaders Carl Legien and Gustav Bauer, all of whom believed that tactical SPD support for the war would bring the party and the labour movement great benefits in the guise of domestic political reform, including trade union recognition and equal votes for all in Prussia, the largest of the German states.[13] This was David's intention in particular, as his diary entries for 1914 and beyond clearly show.[14] Yet he was not the only senior figure in the SPD who adopted a pro-war stance. In fact, the two leading members of the party executive who really determined the outcome of the vote on war credits in the parliamentary caucus, Friedrich Ebert and Philipp Scheidemann, were not part of David's group at all, and remained highly sceptical as to whether war would really bring domestic reform. Rather, their main concern in 1914 was defensive: to hold the party together and prevent a damaging split which could be exploited by the SPD's main enemies on the right. They also feared that the government might move to restrict the activities of the party or ban it altogether if it refused to approve war credits, thus undoing all of its achievements in terms of creating a mass political movement with increasing parliamentary representation in the years since 1890.[15]

Finally, it may be that some Social Democrats were simply swept away by a personal enthusiasm for war, helping them to complete an intellectual journey from international Marxism to 'Prussian socialism' or straightforward German nationalism. This was the case, for instance, with Conrad Haenisch and Paul Lensch, both of whom celebrated the war as a battle between a revolutionary, economically advanced Germany and a counter-revolutionary, reactionary England, and later contributed articles on this theme to *Die Glocke*, a radical periodical founded by the pro-German Russian socialist Alexander Helphand ('Parvus') in 1915. However, as both Haenisch and Lensch originally belonged to the left wing of the party and had voted against supporting war in the parliamentary caucus on 4 August 1914, their influence was not decisive.[16]

Whatever explanation one chooses, two things are clear. Firstly, the decision to support war credits on 4 August 1914 was one of the long-term causes of the split on the left which characterised much of German politics in the 1920s and early 1930s. Revolutionary socialists such as Karl Liebknecht and Rosa Luxemburg, who were both murdered during the Spartacist Uprising in January 1919, never forgave the SPD leadership for its alleged betrayal of the cause of proletarian internationalism in 1914. Nor did Liebknecht and Luxemburg's successors in the German Communist Party (KPD) after 1919.[17]

Secondly, it is also evident that with one or two significant exceptions, a majority of Social Democrat leaders were convinced in August 1914 that Germany was fighting a defensive war against Russian aggression, and not a war of conquest for territorial gains in Europe and overseas. This made it easier for them to support the government's own efforts towards economic and political mobilisation for total war, including the establishment of tight wage, price and rent controls. An important starting point here was the foundation of the War Raw Materials Department (*Kriegsrohstoffabteilung*) of the Prussian Ministry of War on 13 August 1914, under the initial leadership of the industrialist Walther Rathenau, which had extensive powers to pro-cure and distribute raw materials according to military priorities.[18] On top of this, the government set up several agencies to deal with the food ques-tion, including the Price Monitoring Authority (*Preisprüfungsstelle*), the War Food Office (*Kriegsernährungsamt*) and the State Distribution Office (*Staatsverteilungsstelle*).[19]

Significantly, Social Democrats, as well as representatives from the 'bour-geois' parties, sat on many of these committees and thus exerted a more direct impact on government policy than had been possible before the war. Indeed, under the impact of such collaboration leading parliamentary figures like the left-liberal Conrad Haußmann even began to revive earlier pre-war plans for a grand bloc of reformist parties in the Reichstag, stretch-ing from the National Liberals under Ernst Bassermann and Gustav Stresemann to the moderate wing of the SPD under Friedrich Ebert and Philipp Scheidemann, which would work together to modernise the German political system. Wolfgang Mommsen is undoubtedly correct to stress the slim prospects for the realisation of this project as things stood in 1914–15, particularly given that the different parties had radically opposed views on questions like war aims, states' rights and female suffrage, and also given that the Social Democrats continued to be regarded, and to regard themselves, as political outsiders. Nonetheless, it is still possible to see here the origins of a more concerted cross-party campaign for the liberalisation or reform of the Reich constitution in the years 1917–18, which ended, in the last weeks of the war, in the government conceding the principle of cabinet accountability to parliament. Later the former leaders of this largely loyal wartime Reichstag majority, and their supporters in the legal profession and the universities, collaborated in producing the Weimar constitution of 1919.[20]

More generally the increased state direction of labour into factories during the war, and the gradual militarisation of all social relations, went hand in hand with the growth of a rudimentary welfare state which began to take over the functions traditionally performed by private charities.[21] New technology and the rationalisation of production processes allowed for the recruitment of new types of workers, especially women and older children.[22] Smaller companies went to the wall, while larger companies competed viciously with each other for scarce raw materials and labour resources. This often meant being forced to procure housing and extra food supplies in order to attract and retain a sizeable workforce, or alternatively applying to the army for an allocation of prisoners of war (POWs) or foreign civilian workers.[23] It also meant the beginnings of new forms of cooperation between government and big business, with the now officially recognised social democrat trade unions as junior partners, willing to make concessions on conditions and pay, and to accept restrictions on the right to strike, in the 'national interest'.[24]

Yet in many ways, and perhaps not surprisingly, economic mobilisation was at first very slow in meeting the demands of total war. Only in August 1916, with the coming to power of the third supreme command (OHL) under Hindenburg and Ludendorff, did the military finally take a more central role in the coordination of the home front, and in particular the efforts of industry and labour.[25] Before then their ambitions were blocked not so much by the SPD and the left, as by old-fashioned inertia within the civilian, army and naval bureaucracies.

The war on land and at sea, 1914–1916

Contrary to the chief of the general staff Helmuth von Moltke's confident predictions in the summer of 1914, the war was not 'over by Christmas'. Indeed, in spite of initial successes in the west, Germany failed to take Paris within six weeks, and instead suffered a major defeat at the Battle of the Marne (5–12 September 1914), which was followed by a race to the Channel ports and then, by November, stalemate and trench warfare. Moltke himself suffered a nervous collapse in September and was eventually replaced by the Prussian Minister of War, Erich von Falkenhayn. On the Eastern Front, meanwhile, the Russian army was able to mobilise more quickly than the

German general staff had anticipated, and launched a successful incursion into East Prussia in the second half of August. General Paul von Hindenburg, recently recalled from retirement to command the German eighth army, counter-attacked and won two important victories at Tannenberg (26–29 August) and later at the Masurian Lakes (10–14 September). The Russians were forced to withdraw from East Prussia altogether, while Hindenburg was appointed commander-in-chief in the east in early November, and soon acquired cult-like status as the 'hero of Tannenberg' and the symbol of Germany's 'iron determination' to hold out for victory.[26]

Further south the Russians had more success, at least until the spring of 1915, advancing against the Austrians into Galicia and Bukovina, taking over key towns like Lemberg and Czernowitz, and twice laying siege to the fortress at Przemyśl. The Serbs also repulsed two attempted Austrian invasions in 1914 and had retaken control of Belgrade by the end of the year.[27] The one substantial bonus for the Central Powers was the entry of Turkey into the war in October 1914, putting pressure on Russia in the Caucasus and on Britain in Egypt, Suez and India. In 1915 the combined German-Turkish defeat of the attempted Allied assault on the Dardanelles was partly offset by Italy's declaration of hostilities against Austria-Hungary in May, opening up another front which had to be defended. Meanwhile, it was only with the support of their new ally Bulgaria that Germany and Austria together were finally able to defeat Serbia at the end of 1915, allowing them for the first time to establish a continuous supply line from Berlin through to Constantinople and beyond.[28]

The biggest success for the German army in 1915, however, was in the east, against the Russians. Here a joint German-Austrian breakthrough at Gorlice-Tarnów in Galicia in May 1915 paved the way for an advance all across the Eastern Front and the German entry into Warsaw in early August. Later that month German troops advanced as far as Brest-Litovsk and Vilnius, and now occupied most of Russian Poland and Lithuania. At the same time, they were able to hold their own against several Allied offensives on the Western Front, including at Champagne and Artois (December 1914–March 1915); Neuve Chapelle (10–12 March 1915); Aubers (9 May); Festubert (15–25 May); Artois (May–July); Loos (September–October) and again at Champagne and Artois (September–October). In December 1915 the last British and ANZAC troops were evacuated from Gallipoli in the Dardanelles.[29]

In 1916 overcoming the stalemate on the Western Front posed the biggest strategic problem for the German general staff, and for Falkenhayn in particular. In contrast to Hindenburg and his deputy, Ludendorff, who

favoured concentrating on the war in the east, Falkenhayn opted for a policy of attrition in France. He chose Verdun as the location of an attack
which began in February 1916 and was intended to draw French forces into
the trap of defending what was in effect a militarily insignificant (albeit
nationally highly symbolic) fortress.[30] Eventually abandoned in November
1916, the battle of Verdun was largely a failure, leading to massive casualties
on both sides, while allowing the British time to prepare their own mass
offensive, launched on the Somme on 1 July 1916. When Romania entered
the war on the Allied side on 27 August 1916, Falkenhayn was finally
replaced as chief of general staff by Hindenburg, and sent to command the
ninth army in Transylvania. Here, ironically, he equipped himself quite
well, taking part in a successful campaign which ended in the capture of
Bucharest on 6 December.[31]

In the meantime, in Belgium and France trench warfare had become
more violent and brutal, even if there were stretches of the front line that
experienced relatively little fighting over long periods of time.[32] The temporary ceasefires of 1914 which allowed time for the burial of the dead and the
retrieval of the wounded soon became a thing of the past, for example, and
there was a growing tendency to treat enemy corpses in depersonalised and
degrading ways.[33] On top of this, both sides were involved in the use of poisonous gas and other prohibited weapons of war.[34] There were even some
isolated, but nonetheless significant bouts of prisoner-killing, giving rise to
numerous accusations and counter-accusations.[35] British soldiers captured
during German offensives often expected to be shot, for instance, and were
clearly relieved when this did not happen, as interrogation reports suggest.[36]

Away from the battlefield itself, Germany's treatment of prisoners of war
also came in for heavy international criticism, although the Prussian
Ministry of War was determined to ensure – as far as it was in its power to
ensure – that minimum standards were maintained by the officers in charge
of individual camps. Admittedly these efforts were hampered by the chaos
and confusion which characterised the early months of the war, when many
more prisoners than expected were taken. Disease in the camps was at first
rife, although it was later brought under control. Even after this reprisals
against prisoners in response to alleged misdeeds committed against the
enemy were not uncommon, such as in the case of the long-running dispute
with France over the treatment of German prisoners in Morocco, Tunisia
and Algeria in 1915–16.[37] Some rather clumsy and unsuccessful efforts were
also made to recruit Irish and Muslim prisoners to fight for the Central
Powers' cause, and from 1915 the German army on the Western Front,
which was not answerable to the Prussian War Ministry, began to make

increasing use of special labour battalions drawn from Russian (and later British, French and Italian) POWs. The latter were forced to work building fortifications and roads within the direct line of fire – a clear breach of the rules and customs of war.[38]

A much larger number of enemy POWs were set to work on the German home front, a practice which was permitted under international law and became an increasingly important means of filling labour shortages as the war continued. Thus by August 1916, more than 750,000 of Germany's 1.6 million prisoners were employed in agriculture, and 330,000 in industry.[39] Conditions varied from region to region and employer to employer, but could be very harsh, especially for those deployed in mines and quarries. In general the Russians fared worse than their British and French counterparts, mainly because their government was unable or unwilling to send extra food parcels to supplement the meagre German rations. Moreover, after the conclusion of peace with Soviet Russia in March 1918 most of the 1.3 million Russian POWs in Germany were retained as cheap labour for the remainder of the war even though their immediate repatriation was required under the 1907 Hague convention on land warfare (Hague IV).[40]

Apart from these specific examples, Germany's policy towards military prisoners was at least partly tempered by the utilitarian principle of reciprocity – the desire to ensure good conditions for its own nationals in enemy captivity.[41] The same could not be said for its treatment of enemy civilians in occupied territory, however. Thus, Allied propaganda aside, it is now clear that the invading German troops deliberately killed around 6,500 civilians in Belgium and France between August and October 1914.[42] On top of this, tens of thousands of enemy civilians from across German-occupied territories (Belgium and northern France, and later Russian Poland, Serbia and Romania) were deported into the Reich and held in camps such as Holzminden in Lower Saxony and Havelberg near Berlin. Among them were large numbers of women, children and men over 55.[43]

British civilians in German captivity were generally treated with greater humanity than their French, Belgian and Russian counterparts,[44] but there were some notable exceptions here, including the execution of Nurse Edith Cavell in German-occupied Brussels in October 1915 following her court martial on charges of aiding escaped Allied POWs and Belgian volunteers to flee across the border to the Netherlands.[45] Finally, when the German army began deporting unemployed Belgians as forced labourers in October 1916, even the Pope – supported by the Catholic Centre Party inside Germany – raised limited and carefully worded protests.[46] In total, by the end of the war some 130,000 Belgians and 500,000 to 600,000 Russian-Polish workers had been forcibly integrated into the German war economy at one point or another, while the German army's own figures revealed 111,879 enemy civilians being held in internment camps in October 1918.[47]

German civilians themselves – with the exception of colonial Germans living in Africa, China and the Pacific islands, and those who experienced the brief Russian occupation of East Prussia in August 1914 – were not exposed to any direct contact with an invading foreign army, and were not forced to work for the enemy against their will. Even so, the war brought with it a catastrophic disruption to living standards and food supplies, made worse by the entry of Britain, and later Japan, Italy, Romania, the United States, China, Argentina, Brazil and Thailand into the conflict. Indeed, in the economic war, Britain held all the trump cards. Its mastery of the seas allowed it to impose an increasingly effective economic blockade of the Central Powers, using surface ships to stop and search neutral and enemy merchant vessels and to confiscate any contraband items they found. German propagandists protested vigorously, declaring this to be an abuse of international maritime law and the wartime rights of neutrals, but with little effect. Worse still, its own submarine blockade of Britain, which was launched at the beginning of 1915, also had the potential to backfire politically and diplomatically. This was shown in particular in the international outcry caused by the sinking of the British steam liner the *Lusitania* off the coast of Ireland on 7 May 1915, with 128 Americans listed among the 1,198 dead.[48]

Meanwhile, the Kaiser refused to allow the German High Seas Fleet to risk all on a showdown with the Royal Navy for control over the North Sea, not least because Britain enjoyed a clear numerical superiority when it came to battleships. The one major exception to this rule was the Battle of Jutland on 31 May 1916, when the British and German fleets briefly squared up to each other. The result was inconclusive, although Admiral Reinhard Scheer, the Commander of the German High Seas Fleet, subsequently warned the Kaiser against allowing further engagements of this kind as 'there can be no doubt that even the best possible outcome . . . would not force England to make peace in this war'.[49] From this point on, indeed, it was clear that the war, if it was to be won at all, would also be won on the home front and not solely on one or more of the fighting fronts.

Bethmann Hollweg and the civilian war leadership, 1914–1917

Until his downfall in July 1917, one of the chief architects of German wartime strategy was the Reich Chancellor, Theobald von Bethmann

Hollweg. Already a key figure in the July crisis of 1914, Bethmann went on to play a major role in decisions regarding war aims, domestic political reform and the question of unrestricted submarine warfare in the years 1914 to 1917. His policies and intentions lay at the heart of a bitter historical dispute in West Germany during the 1960s and 70s, which did much to dent his previous reputation as a cautious, pragmatic and conservative statesman who tried to rein in the excessive war aims of generals and admirals.[50] Nonetheless, to a considerable degree he helped to define the moderate as opposed to the extreme wing of German imperialist ambitions during this period, and his removal from power in 1917 at the behest of Hindenburg and Ludendorff was certainly symbolic of a new era in German politics.[51]

When the First World War broke out Bethmann had already been in office as Chancellor for five years. In relation to war aims, his intentions were twofold. Firstly, in expectation of a great military victory, he was determined to have a clear set of demands to present to the defeated enemy which would establish Germany's position as the dominant military and economic power on the continent with a substantial overseas empire to match. In particular, as his September programme of 1914 – published by Fritz Fischer in 1961 – indicated, he wished to see France 'so weakened as to make her revival as a great power impossible for all time', Russia 'thrust back as far as possible from Germany's eastern frontier', and Belgium 'reduced to a vassal state'.[52] These demands were repeated at various confidential meetings throughout the war, not least at the Kreuznach conference in April 1917, when the Chancellor essentially endorsed the extreme war aims of the military, subject only to the condition that Germany would have to be in the position of victor, 'able to dictate the peace' on its own terms.[53]

Yet Bethmann was also aware that he might face opposition to such a programme from two quarters: the Social Democrats at home, who in theory at least had only been willing to approve war credits in the Reichstag on 4 August 1914 on the basis that Germany was fighting to defend its borders against unprovoked 'Tsarist aggression'; and the British, whom it might not be possible to defeat by military means alone. For both of these reasons, his favoured option was to pursue indirect control over Europe rather than outright annexation of foreign territory. This is why, for instance, he took a great deal of interest in the idea of establishing a customs union between Germany and its neighbours in western and central Europe – the so-called *Mitteleuropa* project – in which German economic dominance would be guaranteed.[54] Britain could be excluded from the continent by these means, thus forcing it to come to terms with German hegemony in Europe or ensuring its defeat in a 'Second Punic War'.[55] Like the Kaiser, however, Bethmann was resolutely opposed to the use of unrestricted submarine warfare against enemy merchant shipping, not least because he believed that this would damage Germany's relations with neutral states in Europe and further afield, and in particular with the United States. Instead, he favoured a policy of retaining the High Seas Fleet in port so that it could be used as a bargaining counter to force Britain to the negotiating table after a German military victory on the continent.[56]

The problem with this approach was that it could not be articulated in public, for fear of antagonising both pacifist and anti-war elements on the left and extreme nationalists on the right. The latter in particular, goaded on by elements in the military, emerged to become the wartime Chancellor's principal domestic antagonists, accusing him of acting in a 'defeatist' manner towards Britain and of failing to represent the true will of the nation, which demanded extensive annexations and a 'peace of victory'. A group around the head of the Reich Naval Office, Admiral Alfred von Tirpitz, even organised a petition and lobbied members of the Reichstag in an attempt to alter official policy, an unheard of act of insubordination in time of war.[57] The government's response, particularly after Tirpitz's own resignation on 15 March 1916, was to make even greater use of its powers of censorship under the state of siege in order to suppress public debate on the war aims and submarine questions. For instance, on 5 June 1916 Bethmann went on the offensive, referring openly to his right-wing critics as the 'pirates of public opinion' in a speech in the Reichstag. This was followed by a series of measures against particular targets, including the dismissal of Wolfgang Kapp, one of the leading figures in the U-boat agitation, from his post as a senior civil servant in East Prussia.[58]

Censorship – along with patriotic propaganda, price controls and rationing – was also seen as a means of strengthening the unity of the home front in the face of increasing privations caused by the Allied naval blockade.[59] In particular, Bethmann was determined to protect the *Burgfrieden*, and to do this it was essential, in his view, to keep moderate elements in the SPD on side while also appeasing certain sections of the right. Yet as the war continued, and as the sacrifices of ordinary working people mounted, it became increasingly difficult to postpone the question of constitutional change, and especially reform of the unequal suffrage in Prussia and the other German states. By 1916–17 this issue was indeed at the top of the Chancellor's domestic agenda, but in reality the vague package of measures promised for the end of the war in the Kaiser's Easter message of 7 April 1917 was a great disappointment. In this sense the East German historian Willibald Gutsche is right to argue that the Chancellor was more conservative, more entrenched in the old political system, than his image as an undogmatic, reform-minded statesman would suggest. When it came down to it, he was not willing to push hard enough and soon enough for the principle of equal suffrage in Prussia, leaving it to his successors to make this concession in the far less favourable circumstances of October 1918.[60]

At the same time Bethmann also failed to stem the tide of a growing right-wing backlash against the government's own very modest reform programme, a backlash also caused by exaggerated fears that the military occupation of Russian Poland (and later the Baltic states and Ukraine) would lead to an unchecked wave of Jewish migrants and left-wing agitators entering Germany from the east. Even the Kaiser was not spared from criticism, in spite of the Chancellor's efforts to protect him from radical nationalist accusations that he was too 'soft' towards socialists and Jews, or unduly influenced by his 'liberal' English cousins. One especially shocking flysheet, which was circulated in Munich and Berlin in the summer of 1916, contained the following assertions:

The Kaiser is completely surrounded by Jews. His most powerful advisors are the Israelites Ballin, Rathenau, v. Mendelssohn, Arnold, James, Simon, v. Bleichröder, Goldschmidt-Rothschild, Carow, Kappel and others, who as members of an international plutocracy take full advantage of the fact that their relatives sit in high places in all the governments of foreign lands . . . The Kaiser is visibly in close alliance with the Jews . . . [while] [t]he exclusion of the Germanic element is apparent everywhere . . .

It was now high time, the flysheet continued, to 'form a front against the suppression of *Deutschtum* in Germany and against the delivery of the government into the hands of the Jews and the international money powers'.[61] This indeed became the programme of a new revitalised radical right after 1915, including established bodies like the Pan-German League and new organisations such as Theodor Fritsch's Reichshammerbund, founded in 1912. Although they had roots in the pre-1914 period, such groups became increasingly vicious in their anti-Semitism as the war continued, calling openly for a wholesale ban on Jewish immigration from the east, the removal of all Jews from public office, and their complete exclusion from the media. Agitation suggesting Jews were 'war-shirkers' who evaded service at the front also led the Prussian Ministry of War to instigate its notorious 'Jew count' in October 1916, a census of the number of Jews on active military duty. The results were never published, lending a spurious weight to the Pan-Germans' claims.[62]

Meanwhile, although Bethmann was over-cautious as far as domestic policy was concerned – indeed, perhaps he had to be, given the strength of opposition to liberal reform within the political and military establishments – in foreign policy terms he was arguably too optimistic and too willing to trust in the notion of ultimate victory. As he wrote to the Kaiser on 11 August 1915, shortly after the successful German advance into Russian Poland and the creation of a General Government in Warsaw:

If the course of the military operations and events in Russia itself should make it possible to push back the Muscovites to the east and remove their western territories, then we will have achieved a major victory, a liberation from the nightmare in the east, which will make all the sacrifices and extreme sufferings in this war worthwhile.[63]

Likewise, in February 1916, he turned down the offer of American mediation between Britain and Germany once it had become clear that this would mean agreeing to a German withdrawal from France, Belgium and Poland. If they were serious about wanting an end to the conflict, Bethmann argued, Britain and America would first have to meet Germany's claims since 1897, namely recognition of its dominant economic and military position in Europe and its desire for world power status.[64] Meanwhile, the army chief of staff Falkenhayn was given the go ahead to pursue his disastrous strategy of attrition on the Western Front, leading to the catastrophe of the battle of Verdun, which was followed by the even bigger catastrophe of the Allied counter-attack on the Somme on 1 July 1916.[65]

True, the Chancellor's support for the replacement of Falkenhayn with the more popular Hindenburg and Ludendorff in August 1916 could be interpreted as a move towards establishing the foundations for a 'respectable peace' based on victory on the continent and compromise with Britain.[66] However, if this was his motive, he was soon to be disappointed. Hindenburg and Ludendorff immediately came out as supporters of unrestricted submarine warfare, and also sought to undermine Bethmann's position in other ways, for instance by forcing through a significant relaxation of censorship on the discussion of war aims in November 1916. In their view, the Chancellor was still useful in so far as he was able to maintain support for the war in the Reichstag; but in the meantime, they were determined to take charge of the entire domestic economy, including areas like labour deployment and industrial production which had hitherto remained the preserve of the Prussian War Ministry and the civilian authorities.[67]

In the end, Bethmann was given one last chance. With the agreement of the Kaiser and the army supreme command he was allowed to make a half-hearted peace offer to the Allies at the end of 1916. Accordingly, on 12 December the Reichstag was informed that the government was prepared to enter into preliminary peace negotiations with the enemy, although no concrete proposals were announced and it was asserted that Germany would fight on to victory if the discussions failed. In fact, it seems doubtful whether the Chancellor seriously expected his offer to be taken up. The negative response of the Allies in turn gave Germany the excuse it needed to launch unrestricted submarine warfare, a decision reached at a Crown Council held at Schloß Pleß in Silesia on 9 January 1917 and formally announced on 31 January 1917. As the chief of the Kaiser's naval cabinet, Admiral von Müller, recorded in his diary, Bethmann's acquiescence was 'not so much approval as an acceptance of the facts', and indeed he remained deeply sceptical about the prospects for success in the war at sea. However, he still hoped that the economic blockade might induce France or Italy to surrender unilaterally, thereby putting further diplomatic pressure on Britain.[68]

By the summer of 1917 it was of course clear that the submarines had failed to starve Britain and its allies into surrender, while America's entry into the war on 6 April was slowly tipping the balance against the Central Powers and in favour of the Allies. The overthrow of the Tsar in Russia in March further complicated an already dangerous split in Germany between supporters of a negotiated peace on the one hand and advocates of an annexationist 'Hindenburg peace' on the other. Bethmann's whole diplomatic and domestic strategy now lay in tatters and even the moderate, centrist parties in the Reichstag were beginning to doubt his effectiveness as a political leader able to stand up to the military. Through various committees and private discussions they drew up a formal resolution – backed by the Centre Party, the Progressives and the SPD – calling on the government to open up negotiations for a compromise peace with all of Germany's enemies. The same group of parties also began to make more concerted calls for greater parliamentary scrutiny over all areas of government business, including foreign policy.[69]

Meanwhile, the left-wing of the SPD, led by Hugo Haase, Eduard Bernstein and Karl Kautsky, had formally broken with the parliamentary leadership and had established its own grouping, the Independent Social Democratic Party (USPD) which demanded immediate and unilateral withdrawal from the war and was behind a series of highly publicised industrial and political strikes in April 1917.[70] This evident loss of support in the Reichstag and in the country as a whole enabled Ludendorff to work behind the scenes to get rid of Bethmann, threatening to resign if the Kaiser did not sack him. On 14 July 1917, five days before the passing of the Reichstag Peace Resolution, the Chancellor was replaced by a less weighty figure, the former Prussian deputy Finance Minister and head of the Reich Food Office Georg Michaelis.

In the final analysis, the best that can be said of Bethmann Hollweg was that he was 'well-intentioned' but hardly successful, even on his own liberal-conservative terms.[71] By 1917 he was seen as a barrier to total victory by his enemies on the right, and as a barrier to a negotiated peace and domestic political reform by his formerly loyal supporters on the moderate centre ground. As much as anything else this was the product of a break-down of communication, an inability to handle public opinion and to secure the confidence of the masses in his leadership.[72] Yet perhaps his most important legacy was his failure to halt the decline in the image of the monarchy during the war and the simultaneous rise of the military under Hindenburg as the new – and ultimately flawed – symbol of wartime national unity. It is to this issue that we shall now turn.

Wilhelm II and the generals

One of the notable features of Bethmann's dismissal in July 1917 was that the Kaiser, Wilhelm II, had been forced, apparently against his will, to sacrifice a key official in whom he personally still had confidence. Indeed, according to Matthew Seligmann and Roderick McLean, this 'event repre-sented a symbolic abdication on the part of Wilhelm II, for his right to con-trol appointments had been the key to his authority since his accession in 1888'.[73] Of course, there are a number of important explanations for the col-lapse of the Kaiser's personal authority and public standing during the war, some of them beyond the control of Wilhelm and his immediate entourage. For instance, Jürgen Kocka and others have shown how the war and the material hardships it gave rise to opened up new kinds of social inequality between the 'haves' and 'have-nots' and sharpened class conflicts to an unprecedented level.[74] Likewise Benjamin Ziemann, in his analysis of sol-diers' letters, has noted that the mood amongst the troops turned decisively against the monarchy and in favour of Social Democracy in the summer of 1917, when news of events in Russia, combined with support for the Reichstag Peace Resolution, led to 'far-reaching international and domestic political changes'.[75]

Finally, Isabel Hull has pointed to the 'unconscious role that mon-archists played in undermining both the monarch and the monarchy' especially through the evolution of a virulent war culture from the 1860s onwards which ultimately instrumentalised the Kaiser as a means to higher ends. This was particularly the case for those officers like Ludendorff and Colonel Max Bauer, head of section II of the general staff and a key player in Bethmann Hollweg's dismissal in July 1917, whose loyalty was no longer to the monarch but to the more radical notions of 'military necessity' and 'military honour'. Although unable to set up a fully fledged army dictatorship in the last year of the war, these men were at least able to engineer the removal of further conservative and 'sober-thinking' members of the Kaiser's entourage, including the head of the civil cabinet, Rudolf von Valentini in January 1918 and the Foreign Secretary, Richard von Kühlmann, in June 1918. The final stage in this process lay in the irrational demand that the Kaiser undertake a suicidal 'death-ride' (*Königstodesritt*) to the front in the closing days of the war. An act of personal martyrdom, it was felt, could possibly change the tide of public opinion in favour of 'going to the last extreme', thus ensuring a final-minute victory or at least the survival of 'military honour' into the post-war years.[76]

Yet – as Hull herself fully recognises – to try and explain these developments without reference to the person of the monarch and his leadership skills, or rather lack thereof, would offer an incomplete picture of the reasons for the collapse of the monarchy in 1918. The starting point of our analysis must therefore be with Wilhelm himself.

Recent research – in particular the work of John Röhl – has established a three-stage model in the decline of monarchical authority from the time of Wilhelm's accession in 1888 to his enforced abdication in November 1918. In the first phase, Wilhelm sought to establish the foundations for 'personal rule' through exploiting his extra-parliamentary power of command over the armed forces (*Kommandogewalt*) and his claim to embody a more modern, 'energetic', forward-moving Germany. This involved, among other things, a series of changes in senior appointments to the army, navy and civil administration designed both to increase the number of command posts which reported directly to the Kaiser and to symbolise his personal enthusiasm for *Weltpolitik*, the policy of transforming Germany into a leading world power. However, this phase in Wilhelm's reign came to an abrupt end with the *Daily Telegraph* affair in November 1908, when he was formally censored in the Reichstag (and in parts of the press) for making ill-judged comments to a British journalist concerning German policy during the Boer war. Thereafter, high-profile personal interventions were kept to a minimum.[77]

The second phase lasted from 1909 to 1914 and involved various clumsy attempts to compensate for the failure of *Weltpolitik* to create a more favourable international position for Germany. This led to the disaster of

the Agadir crisis of 1911, and to the even greater calamity of the outbreak of
the First World War in 1914. During this time, nationalists and members
of the army and navy officer corps became increasingly critical of various
aspects of 'personal rule', arguing that it was holding Germany back from
achieving its true national potential. Thus, in the aftermath of the humiliat-
ing climbdown in 1911, when the German government was forced to compromise over its demands for a share of French Morocco following British
intervention, Wilhelm was referred to by senior figures in the German
military as the 'peace-Kaiser', or, borrowing the phrase used by French
newspapers of that time, as *Guillaume le timide*.[78]

The final phase began with the outbreak of war, when, in the conventional view, Wilhelm became little more than a 'shadow Kaiser', or a
'prisoner of his generals', as an Austro-Hungarian minister later put it.[79]
Increasingly isolated and despised, even by his closest advisors, he proved
wholly incapable of fulfilling the constitutional role allotted to him as
Supreme Warlord, namely to coordinate the combined efforts of the army,
navy and civilian administration in pursuit of a successful outcome to the
war. This in turn meant that he was eventually eclipsed by the most popular
and successful of his generals, Paul von Hindenburg, as the embodiment of
national unity and the will to victory. Military defeat in 1918 then led
directly to his abdication.[80]

Even so, as Holger Afflerbach has recently shown, the collapse of the
Kaiser's personal authority during the war was a gradual process which did
not simply happen overnight. In particular during the first two years of the
war he retained considerable indirect control over strategy through his continued right to make or veto appointments to senior positions in the army,
navy and civilian government. This in turn placed a great deal of power in
the hands of his extra-constitutional cabinet chiefs: Generaloberst Moriz
Freiherr von Lyncker for the army, Admiral Georg Alexander von Müller for
the navy and Rudolf von Valentini for the civil service, all of whom were in
daily attendance on the Kaiser. Significantly, Valentini tended to support
the 'moderate' course also advocated by Bethmann Hollweg, which stopped
short of placing Germany on a 'total war' footing, while Lyncker was more
belligerent in this respect, and, in private, very critical of the Kaiser's shortcomings as war leader.[81] To round the picture off, Müller took a position
which was roughly midway between the other two on issues such as submarine warfare, while always being willing – as he once put it – to 'break
a lance for the Chancellor'.[82]

In terms of military appointments, there were at least three occasions
when Wilhelm's personal influence was paramount: the removal of chief of

PLATE 1.1 The Kaiser (centre) with Field Marshal Paul von Hindenburg (left) and Quarter-Master General Erich Ludendorff (right) at General Headquarters, 1917.

Source: Deutsches Historisches Museum, Berlin

the general staff Helmuth von Moltke and his replacement with Erich von Falkenhayn after the battle of the Marne in September 1914; the decision to retain Falkenhayn in January 1915 in spite of substantial lobbying against him, especially from inside the Kaiser's immediate circle; and the final agreement to replace Falkenhayn with Hindenburg and Ludendorff in August 1916, following Romania's entry into the war. A more direct influence on the course of events can also be seen in Wilhelm's determination to keep the High Seas Fleet in port, and his initial refusal to countenance unrestricted submarine warfare, moves which were bitterly opposed by the Reich Naval Office and the pro-Tirpitz press.[83] Arguably, then, Tirpitz's increasing hostility to Wilhelm – including a bizarre attempt to have him declared insane in 1915 – arose out of the latter's actual decisions in relation to naval strategy rather than his supposed passivity during the war.[84]

Significantly, after July 1917, Wilhelm was still able to veto Tirpitz's proposed appointment as Reich Chancellor (or military dictator) to replace Bethmann Hollweg.[85] Yet there is no doubt that the rise of the Third Supreme Command under Hindenburg and Ludendorff had already seriously undermined what remained of the Kaiser's personal authority. As Hagen Schulze puts it, the appointment of the 'twin generals' was 'nothing less than a spectacular concession to public opinion' and gave the military leadership 'a legitimacy which the Reichstag, elected in 1912, no longer possessed'.[86] Thus on 15 July 1917, the day after Bethmann's departure from office, one of the Kaiser's most loyal and longest-serving courtiers, the general adjutant Hans Georg von Plessen, had noted the importance of the Kaiser being seen in public with Hindenburg:

Their Majesties went into the Cathedral [in Berlin] and invited – on my recommendation and at Ludendorff's instigation – the Field Marshal and his wife to join them in the Royal Box. After the service His Majesty walked alongside Hindenburg, Her Majesty alongside Frau von Hindenburg, through the Lustgarten towards Portal IV and into the Royal Palace. The intention was to make a film of all this but the man had not turned up. Yet the public came in large numbers and could see with their own eyes how highly H.M. regarded the Field Marshal.[87]

In September 1917 the newly-founded Fatherland Party, made up of extreme nationalists under Wolfgang Kapp and Admiral von Tirpitz who were opposed to the Reichstag Peace Resolution, very clearly propagated the myth of Hindenburg and of past Prussian military leaders more than it promoted the person of the living Kaiser. As Heinz Hagenlücke puts it, Hindenburg 'was the man who, in the view of many of his contemporaries had Bismarck's prestige at his disposal and could most easily take up his inheritance'.[88] This was seen most notably during the peace negotiations with the new Bolshevik government in Russia in early 1918, which were conducted largely through the Supreme Command's chief representative at Brest-Litovsk, General Max Hoffmann, with scant regard being given either to the Kaiser or to more 'moderate' voices in the German Foreign Office.[89]

Finally, the impending military defeat on the Western Front in the autumn of 1918 arguably struck the fatal blow. The Supreme Command were now prepared not only to sacrifice the Kaiser (a plan that failed when Wilhelm rejected the 'death-ride' idea), but also the monarchical system itself. This can be seen in Ludendorff's cynical rejection of any notion of Wilhelm's abdication in favour of his son, and his insistence on the appointment of a new reforming government under the liberal Prince Max von Baden, with ministers drawn from the main parties in the Reichstag, on 3 October 1918. The intention was, of course, to shift the blame for defeat away from the military and towards the politicians at home. The fightback would begin once the civilians had signed an armistice.[90]

Ironically, while the military were busy trying to cover their own backs, some of the members of the new civilian government still believed – unrealistically – that it might yet be possible to save Wilhelm. Matthias Erzberger, the Catholic Centre Party politician and author of the Reichstag Peace Resolution, thus urged the war cabinet on 31 October 1918 not to do anything 'in haste'.[91] On the other hand, the Majority Social Democrat members of the new government, Gustav Bauer and Philipp Scheidemann, were increasingly in favour of abdication, and, as Max von Baden noted in the same cabinet sitting, even among farmers and the middle class there were no longer any defenders of the Kaiser.[92]

The problem was that none of the alternatives were likely to appeal to an increasingly divided war cabinet who had but little time to decide what to do – whether to continue the war in a last desperate bid to preserve national honour (a different concept to military honour) or whether to enter into immediate armistice negotiations, whether to risk all on continued support for the Hohenzollern dynasty in defiance of President Wilson's various notes, or whether to struggle on without any decision on this matter.[93] Indeed, the outbreak of a revolution 'from below' on 3 November and Max von Baden's announcement of the abdication of the Kaiser on the morning of 9 November caught even the Majority Social Democrats off guard. Thus Friedrich Ebert, Prince Max's successor as Reich Chancellor, was reported to be incandescent with rage when his party colleague Philipp Scheidemann made a public declaration of a republic from the balcony of the Reichstag later that day. In Ebert's view, the question of Germany's future political form should be left for an elected National Assembly to decide.[94] Scheidemann's response was that any attempt to manage the process of political change from above was now unrealistic in view of the new threat posed by the extreme left Spartacists, who were about to declare their own rival socialist republic from the balcony of the Royal Palace, just a few streets away. As he later wrote in his memoirs:

Now I saw the situation clearly before my eyes. I knew what his (Liebknecht's) demands were: 'All power to the workers' and soldiers' councils!'. Germany a Russian province, a branch of the Soviet Union?? No! A thousand times no![95]

Whatever any of the moderate Social Democrat politicians thought, however, they were unlikely to agree with the more radical criticisms of the pacifist newspaper editor Hellmut von Gerlach who wrote on 16 December 1918: 'The *monarchy brought* the injustice of the war upon us. The *Reichstag tolerated* this injustice.'[96] By now, indeed, the argument had shifted decisively away from the question of the monarchy to the question of what kind of republic Germany was to become: left-wing socialist or parliamentary?

Notes

1 For a detailed overview see Annika Mombauer, *The Origins of the First World War. Controversies and Consensus* (London, 2002).

2 On the July crisis see also James Joll, *The Origins of the First World War*, 2nd edition (London, 1992), pp. 10–41.

3 The best and most up-to-date account is Wolfgang Kruse, *Krieg und nationale Integration. Eine Neuinterpretation des sozialdemokratischen Burgfriedensschlusses 1914/15* (Essen, 1993).

4 Cf. Dick Geary, 'Arbeiter', in Gerhard Hirschfeld, Gerd Krumeich and Irina Renz (eds), *Enzyklopädie Erster Weltkrieg* (Paderborn, 2003), pp. 142–54 and Andrej Mitrović, *Serbia's Great War, 1914–1918* (London, 2007), p. 115.

5 Hans-Ulrich Wehler, *Deutsche Gesellschaftsgeschichte, Vol. 4: Vom Beginn des Ersten Weltkriegs bis zur Gründung der beiden deutschen Staaten 1914–1949* (Munich, 2003), pp. 128–9.

6 This, controversially, was the view of the East German historian Jürgen Kuczynski, *Der Ausbruch des ersten Weltkrieges und die deutsche Sozialdemokratie. Chronik und Analyse* (East Berlin, 1957), a book which was banned in the GDR because of its unorthodox Marxist-Leninist position. See also Matthew Stibbe, 'Fighting the First World War in the Cold War: East and West German Historiography on the Origins of the First World War, 1945–1961', in Andrew Plowman, Tobias Hochscherf and Christoph Laucht (eds), *Divided but not Disconnected. German Experiences of the Cold War* (Oxford, 2010), forthcoming.

7 *August 1914: Ein Volk zieht in den Krieg*, edited by the Berliner Geschichtswerkstatt (West Berlin, 1989). See also Volker Ullrich, *Kriegsalltag. Hamburg im Ersten Weltkrieg* (Cologne, 1982), pp. 10–14.

8 Verhey, *The Spirit of 1914*, esp. pp. 12–71.

9 Christoph Nonn, 'Oh What a Lovely War? German Common People and the First World War', *German History*, 18/1 (2000), pp. 97–111; Verhey, *The Spirit of 1914*, p. 99.

10 Ziemann, *War Experiences*, esp. pp. 15–27.

11 Stefan Berger, *Social Democracy and the Working Class in Nineteenth- and Twentieth-century Germany* (London, 2000), pp. 79–88.

12 Geoff Eley, 'The SPD in War and Revolution, 1914–1919', in Roger Fletcher (ed.), *Bernstein to Brandt: A Short History of German Social Democracy* (London, 1987), pp. 65–74.

13 Fritz Fischer, *War of Illusions. German Policies from 1911 to 1914* (London, 1975), pp. 524–5.

14 Eduard David, *Das Kriegstagebuch des Reichstagsabgeordneten Eduard David 1914 bis 1918*, edited by Erich Matthias and Susanne Miller (Düsseldorf, 1966).

15 Susanne Miller, *Burgfrieden und Klassenkampf: Die deutsche Sozialdemokratie im Ersten Weltkrieg* (Düsseldorf, 1974).

16 Robert Sigel, 'Die Lensch-Cunow-Haenisch Gruppe. Ihr Einfluss auf die Ideologie der deutschen Sozialdemokratie im Ersten Weltkrieg', *Internationale wissenschaftliche Korrespondenz zur Geschichte der deutschen Arbeiterbewegung*, 11 (1975), pp. 421–36.

17 See Eric D. Weitz, *Creating German Communism, 1890–1990* (Princeton, NJ, 1997), esp. pp. 62–99.

18 In fact Rathenau resigned in March 1915 in favour of Major Koeth, citing potential conflicts of interest with his other positions in German industry and noting that he had always intended to leave early. For further details see Hartmut Pogge von Strandmann (ed.), *Walther Rathenau. Industrialist, Banker, Intellectual and Politician. Notes and Diaries, 1907–1922* (Oxford, 1985), esp. pp. 186–91 and 195–7.

19 Belinda J. Davis, 'Food, Politics and Women's Everyday Life during the First World War', in Hagemann and Schüler-Springorum (eds), *Home/Front*, pp. 115–37 (here p. 121).

20 Wolfgang J. Mommsen, *Max Weber and German Politics, 1890–1920* (Chicago and London, 1984), pp. 198 and passim.

21 Young-Sun Hong, 'World War I and the German Welfare State. Gender, Religion and the Paradoxes of Modernity', in Eley (ed.), *Society, Culture and the State in Germany*, pp. 345–69.

22 Ute Daniel, *The War From Within. German Working-Class Women in the First World War* (Oxford, 1997); idem., 'Frauen', in Hirschfeld *et al.* (eds), *Enzyklopädie Erster Weltkrieg*, pp. 116–34.

23 Ulrich Herbert, *A History of Foreign Labor in Germany, 1880–1980. Seasonal Workers/Forced Laborers/Guest Workers* (Ann Arbor, MI, 1990), pp. 87–119.

24 Hans-Joachim Bieber, 'The Socialist Trade Unions in War and Revolution', in Fletcher (ed.), *Bernstein to Brandt*, pp. 74–85 (here pp. 76–7).

25 The best study is Gerald Feldman's *Army, Industry and Labor in Germany, 1914–1918* (Princeton, NJ, 1966).

26 On the 'Hindenburg cult' see Bernd Sösemann, 'Der Verfall des Kaisergedankens im Ersten Weltkrieg', in John C. G. Röhl (ed.), *Der Ort Kaiser Wilhelms II. in der deutschen Geschichte* (Munich, 1991), pp. 145–70; and Anna Menge, 'The *Iron Hindenburg*: A Popular Icon of Weimar Germany', *German History*, 26/3 (2008), pp. 357–82.

27 Mitrović, *Serbia's Great War*, p. 72.

28 Matthew Stibbe, 'The First World War: Aims, Strategy and Diplomacy', in Gordon Martel (ed.), *A Companion to Europe 1900–1945* (Oxford, 2006), pp. 228–42.

29 See the entries 'Ostfront' (Norman Stone), 'Westfront' (John M. Bourne), and 'Gallipoli' (Robin Prior and Trevor Wilson) in Hirschfeld *et al.*, *Enzyklopädie Erster Weltkrieg*, pp. 762–4, 960–7 and 517–18.

30 On Verdun see Ian Ousby, *The Road to Verdun* (London, 2002); and on Falkenhayn see Holger Afflerbach, *Falkenhayn: Politisches Denken und Handeln im Kaiserreich* (Munich, 1994).

31 Roger Chickering, *Imperial Germany and the Great War, 1914–1918*, 2nd edition (Cambridge, 2004), p. 75.

32 Ziemann, *War Experiences*, pp. 53–6.

33 Alexander Watson, *Enduring the Great War. Combat, Morale and Collapse in the German and British Armies, 1914–1918* (Cambridge, 2008), pp. 70–1.

34 Alan Kramer, 'Kriegsrecht und Kriegsverbrechen', in Hirschfeld *et al.* (eds), *Enzyklopädie Erster Weltkrieg*, pp. 281–92 (here p. 288).

35 For a detailed discussion of this phenomenon see Niall Ferguson, 'Prisoner Taking and Prisoner Killing in the Age of Total War. Towards a Political Economy of Military Defeat', *War in History*, 11/2 (2004), pp. 148–92; and idem., *The Pity of War* (London, 1998), pp. 339–88.

36 Watson, *Enduring the Great War*, p. 72.

37 Marc Michel, 'Intoxication ou "brutalisation"? Les "represailles" de la grande guerre', *14–18 aujourd'hui today heute*, 4 (2001), pp. 175–97.

38 See here Heather Jones, 'A Missing Paradigm? Military Captivity and the Prisoner of War, 1914–18', *Immigrants and Minorities*, 28/1–2 (2008), pp. 19–48 (here p. 30).

39 Ibid., p. 28.

40 Reinhard Nachtigal, 'The Repatriation and Reception of Returning Prisoners of War, 1918–22', *Immigrants and Minorities*, 28/1–2 (2008), pp. 157–84 (here pp. 168–9).

41 See Uta Hinz, *Gefangen im Großen Krieg. Kriegsgefangenschaft in Deutschland, 1914–1921* (Essen, 2006); and Matthew Stibbe, 'Prisoners of War during the First World War', *Bulletin of the German Historical Institute London*, 28/2 (2006) pp. 47–59.

42 Horne and Kramer, *German Atrocities 1914*, p. 419.

43 Becker, *Oubliés de la grande guerre*; Matthew Stibbe, 'Civilian Internment and Civilian Internees in Europe, 1914–20', *Immigrants and Minorities*, 28/1–2 (2008), pp. 49–81.

44 Matthew Stibbe, *British Civilian Prisoners of War in Germany. The Ruhleben Camp, 1914–1918* (Manchester, 2008).

45 Martin Gilbert, *The First World War* (London, 2004), pp. 202–3.

46 Jens Thiel, *'Menschenbassin Belgien'. Anwerbung, Deportation und Zwangsarbeit im Ersten Weltkrieg* (Essen, 2007), pp. 129, 183–5 and 226–8.

47 Herbert, *A History of Foreign Labor*, p. 106; Jochen Oltmer, 'Zwangsmigration und Zwangsarbeit – Ausländische Arbeitskräfte und bäuerliche Ökonomie im Ersten

Weltkrieg', *Tel Aviver Jahrbuch für deutsche Geschichte*, 27 (1998), pp. 135–68 (here p. 143); Richard B. Speed III, *Prisoners, Diplomats and the Great War. A Study in the Diplomacy of Captivity* (New York, 1990), p. 216.

48 The *Lusitania* crisis is dealt with in detail in Ernest R. May, *The World War and American Isolation, 1914–1917* (Cambridge, MA, 1959), pp. 197–252. Figures on deaths in Gilbert, *The First World War*, p. 157.

49 Cited in Stibbe, *German Anglophobia*, p. 135.

50 Bethmann's chief critic was Fritz Fischer – see Fischer, *Germany's Aims in the First World War* (London, 1967), while his main defender was Gerhard Ritter – see the third volume of his history of German militarism, *Die Tragödie der Staatskunst. Bethmann Hollweg als Kriegskanzler (1914–1917)* (Munich, 1964). On the 'war aims' controversy see also Mombauer, *The Origins of the First World War*.

51 Apart from Ritter, the key biographies of Bethmann were written in the 1970s – see Konrad Jarausch, *The Enigmatic Chancellor. Bethmann Hollweg and the Hubris of Imperial Germany* (New Haven, CT and London, 1973), and Willibald Gutsche, *Aufstieg und Fall eines kaiserlichen Reichskanzlers. Theobald von Bethmann Hollweg 1856–1921. Ein politisches Lebensbild* (East Berlin, 1973). See also Fritz Fischer, 'Theobald von Bethmann Hollweg', in Wilhelm von Sternburg (ed.), *Die deutschen Kanzler. Von Bismarck nach Kohl*, new edition (Frankfurt/M, 1994) [1985], pp. 87–114.

52 Fischer, *Germany's Aims*, pp. 103–6.

53 Ibid., pp. 346–51.

54 Ibid., pp. 101–3.

55 Fritz Fischer, *From Kaiserreich to Third Reich. Elements of Continuity in German History, 1871–1945*, (London, 1986), p. 62.

56 On the submarine controversy see Stibbe, *German Anglophobia*, pp. 110–64.

57 Raffael Scheck, *Alfred von Tirpitz and German Right-Wing Politics, 1914–1930* (Atlantic Highlands, NJ, 1997), pp. 39–40.

58 Stibbe, *German Anglophobia*, p. 119.

59 Cf. Wolfgang J. Mommsen, 'Die deutsche öffentliche Meinung und der Zusammenbruch des Regierungssystems Bethmann Hollweg im Juli 1917' (1968), reproduced in Mommsen, *Der autoritäre Nationalstaat. Verfassung, Gesellschaft und Kultur im deutschen Kaiserreich* (Frankfurt/M, 1990), pp. 422–40 (here p. 424).

60 Gutsche, *Aufstieg und Fall*, p. 217.

61 Stibbe, *German Anglophobia*, p. 158.

62 Werner T. Angress, 'Das deutsche Militär und die Juden im Ersten Weltkrieg', *Militärgeschichtliche Mitteilungen*, 19/1 (1976), pp. 77–146. On anti-Semitism in wartime Germany more generally see Wehler, *Deutsche Gesellschaftsgeschichte*, Vol. 4, pp. 128–34; and Werner Jochmann, 'Die Ausbreitung des Antisemitismus in Deutschland 1914–1923', in idem., *Gesellschaftskrise und Judenfeindschaft in Deutschland 1870–1945* (Hamburg, 1988), pp. 99–170. Also chapter 5 below.

63 Fritz Fischer, 'Theobald von Bethmann Hollweg', p. 105.

64 Stibbe, *German Anglophobia*, pp. 133–4.

65 Stibbe, 'The First World War', pp. 235–6.

66 Fritz Stern, 'Bethmann Hollweg and the War: The Bounds of Responsibility' (1968), reproduced in Stern, *The Failure of Illiberalism. Essays on the Political Culture of Modern Germany*, new edition (New York, 1992), pp. 77–118 (here p. 107); Mommsen, 'Die deutsche öffentliche Meinung', p. 426.

67 On the Hindenburg programme see Feldman, *Army, Industry and Labor*, passim; and Chickering, *Imperial Germany*, pp. 76–82.

68 Walter Görlitz (ed.), *The Kaiser and His Court. The Diaries, Note Books and Letters of Admiral Georg Alexander von Müller, Chief of the Naval Cabinet, 1914–1918* (London, 1961), p. 230 (Müller's diary entry for 9 January 1917). See also Mommsen, 'Die deutsche öffentliche Meinung', p. 428.

69 Chickering, *Imperial Germany*, pp. 161–2.

70 On the USPD see Robert F. Wheeler, *USPD und Internationale: Sozialistischer Internationalismus in der Zeit der Revolution* (Frankfurt/M, 1975); and Hartfrid Krause, *USPD: Zur Geschichte der Unabhängigen Sozialdemokratischen Partei Deutschlands* (Frankfurt/M and Cologne, 1975).

71 Stern, 'Bethmann Hollweg and the War', p. 118.

72 Chickering, *Imperial Germany*, p. 162.

73 Matthew S. Seligmann and Roderick R. McLean, *Germany from Reich to Republic, 1871–1918* (London, 2000), p. 168.

74 Jürgen Kocka, *Facing Total War. German Society, 1914–1918* (Oxford, 1984). See also chapter 2 below.

75 Ziemann, *War Experiences*, p. 149.

76 Isabel V. Hull, 'Military Culture, Wilhelm II, and the End of the Monarchy in the First World War', in Annika Mombauer and Wilhelm Deist (eds), *The Kaiser. New Research on Wilhelm II's Role in Imperial Germany* (Cambridge, 2003), pp. 235–58. See also Bruno Thoß, 'Nationale Rechte, militärische Führung und Diktaturfrage in Deutschland 1913–1923', *Militärgeschichtliche Mitteilungen*, 42/1 (1987), pp. 27–76.

77 See Röhl's three-volume biography of the Kaiser, Vol.1: *Wilhelm II. Die Jugend des Kaisers, 1859–1888* (Munich, 1993); Vol. 2: *Wilhelm II: Der Aufbau der persönlichen Monarchie, 1888–1900* (Munich, 2001); Vol 3: *Wilhelm II. Der Weg in den Abgrund, 1900–1941* (Munich, 2008). Also Isabel V. Hull, ' "Persönliches Regiment" ', in Röhl (ed.), *Der Ort Kaiser Wilhelms II.*, pp. 3–23; Christopher Clark, *Kaiser Wilhelm II. Profiles in Power* (London, 2000).

78 Clark, *Kaiser Wilhelm II*, p. 147.

79 Ibid., p. 227.

80 Röhl, *Wilhelm II. Der Weg in den Abgrund*, esp. pp. 1203–8 and 1232–5; Wilhelm Deist, 'Kaiser Wilhelm II. als Oberster Kriegsherr', in Röhl (ed.), *Der Ort Kaiser Wilhelms II.*, pp. 25–42.

81 Holger Afflerbach, 'Wilhelm II as Supreme Warlord in the First World War', *War in History*, 5/4 (1998), pp. 427–49. See also Afflerbach, (ed.), *Kaiser Wilhelm II. als Oberster Kriegsherr im Ersten Weltkrieg. Quellen aus der militärischen Umgebung des Kaisers 1914–1918* (Munich, 2005).

82 Görlitz (ed.), *The Kaiser and His Court*, esp. pp. 228–31 (Müller's diary entries for 8–9 January 1917).

83 Röhl, *Wilhelm II. Der Weg in den Abgrund*, pp. 1209–14; Clark, *Kaiser Wilhelm II*, p. 227.

84 Cf. Matthew Stibbe, 'Germany's "last card". Wilhelm II and the Decision in Favour of Unrestricted Submarine Warfare in January 1917', in Mombauer and Deist (eds), *The Kaiser*, pp. 217–34.

85 Heinz Hagenlücke, *Deutsche Vaterlandspartei: Die nationale Rechte am Ende des Kaiserreichs* (Düsseldorf, 1997), pp. 280–1; Hull, 'Military Culture', p. 237; Röhl, *Wilhelm II. Der Weg in den Abgrund*, pp. 1222–3.

86 Hagen Schulze, *Weimar: Deutschland 1917–1933* (West Berlin, 1982), p. 145.

87 Hans Georg von Plessen, diary entry for 15 July 1917, in Afflerbach (ed.), *Kaiser Wilhelm II. als Oberster Kriegsherr*, p. 908.

88 Hagenlücke, *Deutsche Vaterlandspartei*, pp. 218–9.

89 For a detailed analysis of the peace negotiations at Brest-Litovsk see Fischer, *Germany's Aims*, pp. 475–509; and Röhl, *Wilhelm II. Der Weg in den Abgrund*, pp. 1227–32.

90 Hull, 'Military Culture', pp. 249–50.

91 Cited in Sösemann, 'Der Verfall des Kaisergedankens', p. 164, n. 78.

92 Ibid., p. 165.

93 Hull, 'Military Culture', pp. 252–3.

94 Schulze, *Weimar*, p. 162.

95 Horst Lademacher, 'Philipp Scheidemann', in von Sternburg (eds), *Die deutschen Kanzler*, pp. 161–75 (here pp. 172–3).

96 Hellmut von Gerlach, 'Fetisch Nationalversammlung', *Welt am Montag*, 50, 16 December 1918. Cited in Sösemann, 'Der Verfall des Kaisergedankens', p. 169.

CHAPTER 2

The War From Below

The statesmen, generals, admirals, civilian officials and political leaders discussed in the previous chapter all had their particular views of the war which have been passed down to us in various secret memoranda and in published speeches, memoirs, diaries, newspaper articles and pamphlets. But how was the war seen from below, by the millions of soldiers called up to fight at the front, and by the millions of women, children and older men battling for existence on the home front? As Volker Ullrich, the author of an earlier and very influential study of Hamburg during the war has written:

The war took place at a distance, but it was also very much present in the letters and stories told by soldiers, in the ever-lengthening casualty lists, in the suffering of women who had to support themselves and their children in the absence of their men, and in the inhumane tempo of work in the armaments factories. Hunger claimed its victims on the 'home front'. While battles raged in the war zones, the German interior was placed under a state of siege, and every shade of opposition was subject to the threat of repression.[1]

The view of the war from below has indeed been the main focus of research over the last ten years or so. In particular, the idea that home front and fighting front were separated by a huge gulf in understanding and experience is no longer seen as tenable. Home front and fighting front were in constant touch with each other. Soldiers were mostly civilians in uniform; women were present on the front line as nurses and army auxiliaries; at home they were also fighters in the daily battle for food, fuel and medicines as the Allied economic blockade made savage inroads into ordinary people's living standards.[2] Meanwhile, the anti-war movement emerged at a much earlier stage than previous accounts suggest. The first signs of war weariness were already apparent in the autumn of 1914; but it was only later that the opposition to war became politicised through strikes and demonstrations, culminating in the revolution which overthrew the Kaiser and ushered in a republic on 9 November 1918. The aim of this chapter is thus to consider the background to the 1918 revolution from the standpoint not of high politics but of the new social history of 'experience' (*Erfahrungsgeschichte*) and 'everyday life' (*Alltagsgeschichte*).[3]

The food question

Food shortages, as Belinda Davis has argued, were an essential part of the German war experience, particularly for those living in the major cities.[4] This is perhaps less surprising when one considers that before 1914, Germany depended on foreign imports for around one-third of its food needs, and more particularly for roughly 27 per cent of its proteins and 42 per cent of its fats.[5] After the outbreak of war, sea-borne imports of course fell as a result of the Allied blockade, while the agricultural sector suffered acute labour shortages as large numbers of farmers were called up to the front or for service in the reserves.[6] Price controls, which were imposed haphazardly in October 1914, and rationing, which began in January 1915, failed to ensure a constant and equitable flow of supplies while creating the ideal conditions for a flourishing black market.[7] In fact, as early as October 1914 newspaper and police reports were indicating a growing concern at the rising price of certain types of food, including bread, potatoes, pork, fats and butter, and the effect this was having on the public mood. As the Social Democrat newspaper *Vorwärts* noted on 27 October 1914: 'Complaints are coming from all directions about over-charging. Urgent demands are being made for the fixing of a maximum price for potatoes across the Reich.'[8] This was confirmed in police reports from the Berlin area, such as the following, written by an official responsible for the working-class district of Wedding in March 1915:

Discontent is spreading among the masses because of the growing cost of food. The potato question is the most serious and most pressing issue, because the potato plays such an important part in the diet of the poorer sections of the population. Since small retailers are often charging a whole mark for five kilos of potatoes, things have reached the point where people are saying that they cannot go on like this, and that the potato question must be resolved in the same manner as the bread question. But over-charging in respect to the most important foodstuffs must also be stopped, because members of the poorest sections of the population are convinced that the price increases are unjustified and occur only to suit the interests of unscrupulous profiteers . . . Since the beginning of the war this has been the foremost complaint of the population, including among the lower middle classes [the Mittelstand*].*[9]

Increasingly, too, anger was turning away from individual shopkeepers and retailers and towards the state itself. On 28 May 1915, for instance, 1,500 women staged a demonstration in front of the Reichstag in Berlin under the slogan: 'We want peace and our men back! We want bread for our children!'[10] And in June 1915 police in Hamburg confiscated the following anonymous letter addressed to the Senate from 'many Hamburg women and soldiers' wives':

Where is the government of Hamburg when you need it? Does it not disgust you to the soul when the poor are so exploited? Is it not high time that force is used to stop over-charging . . . ? The profiteers should have their profits confiscated and handed over to the poor. Just wait and see what happens when we write to our husbands and tell them what is happening. After all, it is our husbands who are holding back the enemy [at the front] . . . We demand urgent action to stop us from starving. The newspapers are full of stories about the English and French, who are supposedly suffering from hunger, but nothing at all is said about Hamburg. Things must change here.[11]

Finally, the increasing food shortages were also illustrated by the growing dependence of the urban poor on public soup kitchens, which seemed to exacerbate existing class tensions.[12] Some were provided by municipal authorities and some by private charities; some were open to all, while some targeted specific groups, such as soldiers' wives or women with large families. The lower middle classes shunned them, and accused municipal authorities of delivering the best food to them, while working-class clients had little choice but to use them, although they resented being patronised by the scores of middle-class do-gooders who acted as servers.[13] Meanwhile, soldiers' wives were attacked on all sides as freeloaders whose extra money allowances and other privileges 'became the symbols of undeserved benefit'.[14] Even the Berlin police chief, Traugott von Jagow, felt called upon to criticise the 'wives of combatants', who 'use the money they are provided with improperly. It is significant that the refreshment rooms of the department stores are almost always full.'[15]

Indeed, by October 1915 the police and the press were reporting – with a surprising degree of sympathy – on the first of what became a wave of urban food riots in Germany. Often these were led by 'women of lesser means', who marched on town halls in several of the big cities to protest against cuts in the bread, flour, milk, potato or meat ration. Too much food, it was claimed, was going into the hands of 'corrupt' officials and war profiteers, while 'patriotic' consumers – many of whom had sons or husbands fighting at the front – were forced to queue for hours for over-priced and substandard products.[16] In this way, new ideas about citizenship and democracy, including the importance of female as well as male participation in the public sphere, and the role of relations of consumption as well as production within the economic system, came to the fore. This in turn was to have a lasting impact into the 1920s and beyond.[17]

Apart from censoring newspaper reports and using police and troops against demonstrators, the Reich government responded in two ways. Firstly, it created a range of new agencies which actively intervened in the production, distribution and pricing of food, thereby lending legitimacy to some of the protestors' demands without actually solving the food crisis itself.[18] Secondly, it sought to shift the blame for the shortages onto Britain and its 'perfidious' attempts to encircle Germany and strangle its economy. Yet this strategy was only partly successful. True, there is some evidence for the wider popularity of Anglophobia in wartime Germany. For instance, according to various reports and testimonies, British prisoners captured on the battlefield and paraded through German towns and villages were treated with greater hostility by ordinary members of the public than their French and Russian counterparts.[19] 'Gott strafe England!' ('May God Punish England!'), and the reply 'Er strafe es!' (He will!) became a popular greeting, used both by soldiers at the front and civilians at home, and could also be found on postcards, mugs, pocket knives, ashtrays and other items of mass-produced wartime kitsch.[20] When Admiral von Tirpitz resigned as head of the Reich Naval Office in March 1916, the American diplomat James W. Grew reported to the US presidential advisor Colonel House that:

there are many [in Berlin] who see Germany's salvation only in starving out England by means of unrestricted submarine warfare and who want to get Tirpitz back into power. Disquieting resolutions are being introduced into the Reichstag and on Tirpitz's birthday [19 March] mounted police were on guard at certain points in the city to prevent demonstrations.[21]

But very quickly ordinary people began to shift the focus of their anger towards the state authorities who were allegedly responsible for the continued mishandling of food distribution and food pricing, and by extension, for the mismanagement of the war itself.

PLATE 2.1 Women and children queuing outside a Berlin food store, summer 1917.
Source: Bundesarchiv (Federal Archives) (Bild 183-N0703-343)

Princess (then Countess) Blücher, the English-born wife of a German aristocrat asked in her diary in November 1915

How must a mother feel whose only son is in daily danger when, going into some hotel like the 'Esplanade', she sees people feasting in splendour, smartly dressed and laughing and in every way in the lap of luxury? Will she feel anything but hatred for these thoughtless, indifferent creatures? Will she not say: Is this what we are sacrificing everything for? Is this the great country, the culture to redeem the world?[22]

The shift in mood was also noted by police officials who came from the same working- or lower middle-class backgrounds as many of the people they were paid to watch, namely those forced to queue for food.[23] By the time of the 'turnip winter' of 1916–17 ordinary civilian rations had fallen below 1,000 calories a day, or less than 50 per cent of the recommended minimum intake of 1,985 calories.[24] The resulting tension was to turn urban consumers against rural producers, and 'women of lesser means' against government bureaucrats, helping to forge new and volatile alliances which cut across traditional class and political allegiances and ultimately led to a catastrophic breakdown of trust between government and people.[25] Thus, in April 1917, on the eve of the first major strike wave in Berlin and other industrial centres, a report circulated by the deputy general commands noted:

In the realm of nutrition the situation has deteriorated so far that even otherwise trustworthy parts of the population, who have long sought to obey the conspicuous rationing regulations, are now providing for themselves as best they can without regard to the laws. They call it self-help and even consider it legally justifiable because, in their minds, the authorities are negligent in their duty to equally and adequately care for the population.[26]

In July 1918 a group of shipyard workers in Hamburg who had been recalled from military duty were reported to have told the authorities that they would rather return to the front than 'slowly starve to death' on the rations allotted to them at home.[27]

How far the economic blockade 'caused' Germany's eventual defeat is a matter of debate in itself. After 1918 feelings on this subject ran high, not least because the Allies decided to continue their blockade until 12 July 1919. Official German estimates immediately after the war suggested that 763,000 civilians had succumbed to hunger,[28] and while this figure has been challenged in some quarters, the latest research indicates that the number of 'excess civilian war-related deaths in Germany' was at least close to 500,000.[29] Both nationalists and pacifists blamed the British 'hunger blockade' directly. In April 1919, for instance, the *Berliner Lokalanzeiger* carried an article by Julius Schwalbe, Professor of Medicine at the University of Berlin, who argued that the English were aiming at the 'racial destruction' of the Germans by means of a systematic policy of starvation:

I am convinced that not only tens of thousands of as yet unborn Germans are destined for a life of physical inferiority, but that further thousands, who have not even been conceived yet, will also fall victim to the same fate. The 'English disease' ['englische Krankheit'] will be the affliction which one most often meets in unfit Germans in the time after the war.[30]

In May 1919 the ecumenical priest, anti-war activist and Berlin youth worker Pastor Friedrich Siegmund-Schultze argued in a pamphlet:

The infanticide in Bethlehem was child's play compared with the starvation of German children as a result of the three years of economic blockade to which our poor country has been subjected. But even the other atrocities committed against children during the war, such as those in Belgium and France, East Prussia and Poland, Serbia and Macedonia, cannot be compared in terms of scale or brutality with this, the greatest infanticide in the whole of history. Only the deportation of the Armenians, in terms of its impact on children, can be regarded as something of a match for the English hunger blockade.[31]

Yet these claims are worth challenging, at least in the period down to November 1918. Certainly the blockade prevented sea-borne imports from reaching Germany when they were needed to replace falling food production at home, and also had an indirect impact on domestic output by denying German farmers access to fertilisers.[32] However, the real problem was the war, not the blockade, in that it took away soldiers and horses from the countryside, impeded normal transport and distribution networks, forced the government to invest in heavy industry rather than agriculture, and consumed large amounts of food for the army.[33] Rationing and forced requisitioning of food from farmers in turn bred huge resentment in the countryside, particularly in Bavaria and other parts of the Catholic south and west, where it added to a host of other grievances against Prussian 'state socialism' and central direction from Berlin.[34]

During the war an increasing number of Germany's agricultural and population experts began looking towards expansion in the east as the best means of securing Germany's long-term food needs.[35] Yet the German occupation of Romania at the end of 1916 and of large parts of the Ukraine and the Baltic states in early 1918 did little to help. On the contrary, the huge population displacements in eastern Europe destroyed agriculture in what had previously been a food-rich area, while essentially encouraging a negative view of the 'disorderly, filthy lands and peoples' of the occupied east among ordinary German soldiers.[36] Whatever food could be found was nonetheless confiscated for use by the army or by civilians on the home front. Enemy civilians in occupied territories were at the bottom of the ration chain, and received fewer calories per day than any other category of civilian worker.[37] Military POWs could in turn be deported or retained in occupied territories as a special punishment or in reprisal for alleged misdeeds of the enemy, as in the case of 30,000 French prisoners sent to work in Courland in present day Latvia in April 1916.[38]

By contrast, the authorities on the home front could not starve enemy POWs, or block their access to Red Cross food parcels, as the Nazi regime did in the case of Soviet prisoners after 1941. Over and above any humanitarian considerations, the officials who ran the POW department (*Unterkunfts-departement*) of the Prussian Ministry of War had their hands tied by the Geneva and Hague conventions, by regular Red Cross inspections, by the need to use POWs as labour, and by the fact that large numbers of German soldiers were in enemy hands. Vast sums of money therefore had to be spent on housing and feeding up to 2.4 million POWs, many but not all of whom could be forced to work in order to offset the costs of keeping them.[39] German newspapers also continued to insist that Germany treated its POWs much better than the Allies, who were the real 'barbarians'. Or as one official report released by the War Press Office in 1916 put it:

Taking revenge on defenceless prisoners, an act which has no place in the German understanding of war, has been put into practice by our enemies to a degree which threatens culture and civilisation. In particular the French have turned the mistreatment of German POWs into a planned and organised system, and one which deliberately violates the rights and personal protection granted to prisoners under international law.[40]

Propaganda aside, such claims bound the German authorities to treat their prisoners in strict accordance with international conventions, even when feeding, clothing and housing them became increasingly expensive in the last two years of the war.

Home front and fighting front

Historical writing on the First World War has traditionally worked on the assumption that an unbridgeable gulf existed between the experiences of the home front and the fighting front.[41] For one thing, the fighting front was supposedly where all the action took place. Trench warfare in particular became associated with attitudes of reckless indifference to life and death (as exemplified in Ernst Jünger's graphic post-war memoir *Storm of Steel*, first published in 1920) and extreme stress (as shown by the numerous cases of shellshock).[42] For another thing, combat-hardened soldiers did not share the hurrah-patriotism and pathetic hatred of the enemy prevalent among arm-chair strategists and newspaper columnists at home. Instead a crude 'live and let live' system operated, especially on the Western Front, where soldiers from the opposing sides developed a bizarre culture of mutual respect and consideration, albeit punctuated by sudden waves of mass depersonalised killing and acts of vengeance against enemy prisoners and corpses.[43]

Finally, the 'brutalising' experiences of trench war were also crucial in supporting certain cherished literary tropes in the post-war years, such as the idea of the 'lost generation' associated with writers like Erich Maria Remarque in Germany and Siegfried Sassoon and Robert Graves in Britain. Thus in one of the final passages of his famous anti-war novel *Im Westen Nichts Neues (All Quiet on the Western Front)* (1929) Remarque gave voice to the bitter sense of alienation and rejection felt by many veterans in the late 1920s:

Had we returned home in 1916, out of the suffering and the strength of our experiences we might have unleashed a storm. Now if we go back we will be weary, broken, burnt out, rootless, and without hope. We will not be able to find our way any more.[44]

However, more recently, studies based on private communications and personal recollections rather than official or literary sources, have forced historians to revise this view of home front and fighting front being two distinct, mutually incomprehensible experiences. For instance, letters between soldiers and their relatives at home, as well as periods of leave, allowed the civilian population to learn something of the mood in the trenches. Alternatively, soldiers became accustomed to seeing the war through the eyes of their families, and were often aware of the key political issues of the day, such as rising food prices, forced requisitioning of grain and cattle, or strikes in munitions factories. Not all conscripts, moreover, had extensive or prolonged experience of battle. Some were classed as only suitable for service in the replacement army on the home front, while others were posted for long periods to regiments in the rear areas of the fighting zones. Conditions on the Eastern Front, or in the war at sea, were also entirely different to those prevailing in France and Belgium. There was no single type of conscript, in other words, and no single 'front experience'.[45]

Wherever they were posted, soldiers and sailors missed their wives, lovers and families, and often longed for the war to be over. They were also devastated by the death in action of friends and comrades, whether from the same regiment or the same community back at home. Belief in God or the nation or both was an important motivation for some. Yet significantly, military chaplains from the Protestant and Catholic churches generally avoided references to war aims and nationalism in their field sermons, and instead spoke of human sin and the spiritual power of redemption through sacrifice. This offered a more comforting explanation for wartime grief and suffering than the 'ideological rationales' or hate propaganda delivered in the official news bulletins.[46]

Mourning was of course a shared experience, bringing people closer together, and uniting grieving soldiers with their families and communities back at home.[47] Yet even this could not disguise the fact that war also intensified existing age, regional, class and gender inequalities. To put it crudely, younger working-class conscripts from the big cities were more likely to be killed in action than their rural or older counterparts. Their wives and older children were also more likely to have to work because separation allowances for urban soldiers' families were inadequate to cover increasing food, heating and rent costs.[48] True, large numbers of young middle-class officers were also killed, including many students and high school volunteers in 1914, providing the military with opportunities for the construction of new legends based around the idea of 'patriotic youth' and 'sacrificial death'.[49] Skilled workers and farmers, on the other hand, could expect to be recalled from the front for prolonged periods, especially before 1917, and rural conscripts, because of their expert knowledge of horses, were more frequently deployed in artillery regiments in the rear area than were city dwellers.[50] Over time, such inequalities in sacrifice became a cause of demoralisation and anger, especially for families coping with the long-term absence, or even death, of the main breadwinner.

Another source of resentment, especially in the big cities, was the army's heavy-handed use of censorship, with a variety of popular entertainments, from cinemas to cabaret and vaudeville performances, subject to bans or tighter controls on the grounds that they were 'not in keeping with the seriousness of the present times'. In 1916, for instance, the Berlin police reported that it had carried out 1,700 visits to local theatres, cafés and music halls, and had discovered over 900 breaches of wartime regulations. Several popular establishments had had their licences withdrawn for a month due to 'indecent and burlesque incidents', and a decision had been made to change the standard closing time from 11 to 10 p.m. In the same year the magistrate of the village of Erdmannsdorf in rural Saxony noted in a report sent to district officials in Flöha that 'young people under 18 years old, *especially girls from better circles*, have been roaming the streets after 9:00 at night without chaperones. It would be appreciated if you could repeat the announcement of the ordinance forbidding such behavio[u]r.'[51] The conflicting priorities of the military authorities, who wished for a 'disciplined' approach to the war and remained convinced that victory depended on upholding the 'moral integrity' of the home front, and those of ordinary soldiers and civilians, who simply hoped to get through in one piece and in the meantime sought distraction in simple pleasures and amusements, were increasingly laid bare through such practices.

For most rank and file soldiers, the notion of *Durchhalten* ('holding out') commanded broad, if grudging acceptance in 1915 and 1916, particularly as it was buttressed by strict military discipline in the fighting zones.[52] However, things began to change after the Reichstag Peace Resolution of July 1917, when left-liberals and Catholic politicians moved closer to the programme advocated by the Majority Social Democrats (MSPD) – a negotiated peace 'without annexations or indemnities' – while right-wing liberals and conservatives joined forces with the extreme nationalist Fatherland Party to demand a 'Hindenburg Peace', including large-scale territorial annexations in east and west. Although many officers supported the

Fatherland Party, there is little doubt which side the soldiers were on. As one
farmer's son wrote from the field to the Bavarian Centre Party politician and
peasant leader Georg Heim in April 1918:

The biggest traitors of the Fatherland are the members of the Fatherland Party.
The leaders of these rascals belong in prison. By opening their big mouths and
making their demands, they are ruining the courage of the soldiers at the front.
All the soldiers believe that no part of our Fatherland should be lost. But the
gentlemen with the big money have the governments in their pocket in every
country, and these then make demands which are impossible to achieve through
negotiation. They want to expand the national territory, compensation and all
sorts of other things. If only these people had to get by on 70 pfennigs a day and
could see shell splinters flying past, a lot of things would be different.[53]

Meanwhile, on the home front the entire population were affected by the
shortages of food, clothing, housing, light and fuel, but the greatest hardships were experienced by the poor, and in particular by women, children
and the elderly.[54] Working-class women employed in munitions factories
often had to work for long hours at lower rates than their male colleagues,
while breaks – essential for performing domestic chores such as cooking and
shopping – were cut down to fifteen or twenty minutes for every eight hours
in some cases. In 1917 one firm in Göttingen even noted in a letter to the
local military authorities that breaks during the night shift 'must be shorter
than those during day-light hours, because otherwise there is a danger that
the workers will fall asleep'.[55] Perhaps not surprisingly, some women and
adolescent boys were tempted into vice or crime to feed and support their
families, and indeed the conviction rate for minor acts of theft and other
offences against property or 'public decency' grew noticeably towards the
end of the war.[56]

   Single women and those whose husbands were absent were also con-
fronted with a double standard of sexual morality, whereby they were
expected to remain chaste, while soldiers were provided with an outlet for
their urges through a regulated system of army brothels.[57] Women suspected
of having relationships with enemy POWs were pilloried in their local press
and community, and, if convicted, were sometimes even handed short
prison sentences, while unlicensed prostitutes, rather than their male
patrons, were held responsible for the increased prevalence of sexually
transmitted infections (STIs).[58] Given widespread male anxieties about
'uncontrolled female sexuality', and the growing material burdens placed
on women in everyday life, it is highly questionable whether the war really
advanced the cause of gender equality, and of women's suffrage in particular.

The USPD nonetheless demanded the immediate introduction of equal votes for men and women at its founding congress in Gotha in April 1917, thereby implicitly challenging the MSPD's failure to promote this issue in line with the principles enshrined in the SPD Erfurt programme of 1891.[59]

Prostitution and juvenile delinquency were just two of the many problems aggravated by wartime conditions. For instance, Germany's 1,700 criminal prisons had reached crisis point by 1918, with overcrowding, disease and malnutrition leading to a death rate of over 10 per cent in some of the worst jails.[60] Cases of drunken soldiers going on the rampage also became more common towards the end of the war, especially in garrison towns or towns close to the front line, such as Freiburg im Breisgau.[61] The military authorities were continually complaining about the negative impact of leave on the morale of both fighting front and home front, and were particularly concerned when soldiers began telling their families not to subscribe to war loans.[62] More generally, periods of leave could lead to marital strife or breakdown, especially in cases where infidelity was mutually suspected or proven. Some wives even faced rape or other forms of domestic violence at the hands of returning soldier-husbands.[63] More vulnerable still were women in occupied territories, who were often the victims of economic and sexual exploitation. Thousands were held as hostages or deported as forced labourers from urban to rural areas, especially in the last two years of the war.[64] Evidence from British interrogations of captured German troops on the Western Front also indicates that many were eager to 'boast . . . of ravishing French women' in the towns and villages that had temporarily fallen to them during the spring offensive of 1918.[65]

For most soldiers, however, simple determination to survive the war unscathed and in one piece became the predominant mode of thinking in 1918. This was especially evident after the successful Allied counter-offensive in mid-July, when discipline in the German army began to disintegrate, not because of any process of collective radicalisation, but rather as a result of individual acts of disobedience and desertion 'on a massive scale'.[66] As Niall Ferguson has shown, Allied military propaganda also became more subtle and effective in 1918, with German soldiers being enticed to give themselves up through offers of food and humane treatment in an effort to undermine enemy morale.[67] In other cases officers retained their authority by leading their men towards what Alexander Watson describes as an 'ordered surrender', although it is not always clear whether a desire to uphold the cohesion of their unit or simple exhaustion among officers themselves was the key ingredient here.[68] Finally, when news of the poor harvest reached the cities in August 1918, women began writing to their sons and husbands openly calling on them to abandon their posts and return home.[69] The war was now effectively over, and in the Rhineland provinces fears grew as to what would happen should 'the huge German army settle down to winter quarters in their land, as they say there is no discipline left'.[70]

Of course none of this appeared in the German newspapers or later in official regimental histories. Indeed, only in the final weeks of the war did censorship on the home front begin to break down, so that even the most rabid right-wingers ceased to believe official bulletins. Before then, the official view was that Germany was winning the war, and any expression to the contrary was condemned as 'defeatism'. In the name of national unity, pacifist organisations like the Bund Neues Vaterland (New Fatherland League or BNV) had their offices raided and shut down in 1916, while the leaders of the extreme left Spartacist League, Karl Liebknecht and Rosa Luxemburg, spent most of the war in prison and were released only in October 1918.[71] Even so, the anti-war movement, broadly defined, was able to build on the suffering of ordinary people and the desire for peace among rank and file soldiers and sailors to become a significant force in German domestic politics by 1917. Here too, as Belinda Davis has shown, 'the links between the homefront and the battlefront were tight and critical'.[72]

Strikes and political demonstrations

Alongside censorship, the army also had wide powers to intervene in labour relations during the war, as we have seen. This included fixing rations and wages so that skilled armaments workers received as much as 3,270 calories a day,[73] and creating a new Office for the Recruitment of Female Labour (*Frauenarbeitszentrale*) within the Prussian Ministry of War in order to recruit women munitions workers who had previously stayed out of the wartime labour force.[74] Part of the Auxiliary Service Law of 5 December 1916 also required further employer recognition of social democrat trade unions, although this was again accompanied by the brutal suppression of unofficial strikes – often with the tacit approval of trade union leaders.[75] Finally, in the late spring of 1917 the military authorities inauguarated a new system of 'patriotic instruction' on the home front, with the express aim of bringing together 'all classes of the population, all parties and confessions, employers and employees, men and women . . . in a united endeavour'.[76]

Yet the same system which allowed Germany to continue the war also contained the seeds of incipient destruction. As living conditions and the real value of wages declined substantially in the second half of the war, while prices and working hours grew, organised labour increasingly turned against its masters – the state, the employers, and the Social Democratic Party.[77] Indeed, with the formation of the anti-war USPD in April 1917 the Majority SPD and official trade unions increasingly lost their claim to represent the true voice of the workers. One important factor here was the impact of the Russian revolution and the appeal of the Petrograd Soviet for a peace without annexations and indemnities. Another was the disappointment over the Kaiser's Easter message of 7 April 1917, and the paltry concessions it offered in the field of domestic political reform. As the founding manifesto of the USPD put it on 8 April 1917:

The demand for equal suffrage in Prussia was met by Reich Chancellor Bethmann Hollweg's refusal to make any concessions towards the democratisation of the Reich, and in particular of Prussia, before the end of the war. This is the reward for the unprecedented submissiveness which the [SPD] party executive and the general commission [of German trade unions] have shown. The proletariat, however, cannot wait. The war has brought with it the most rapid accumulation of capital, the sudden disappearance of the Mittelstand *[and] a massive increase in the proletariat, which after the war will wage a gigantic struggle against price increases and unemployment, against the over-powerful bosses and the overbearing weight of government taxes. This struggle has already begun today.*[78]

Meanwhile, on the shop floor the composition of the workforce was also changing, with many skilled workers in reserved occupations seeing a chance to make substantial wage claims and those at the bottom of the hierarchy, such as women, young workers, ex-farmers and enforced foreign labourers, feeling that they had little left to lose.[79] Thus it was only with some difficulty that the SPD leaders managed to limit and bring to an end the two major strike waves of April 1917 and January 1918, both of which had been called in support of political as well as industrial demands – universal suffrage in Prussia, the end of martial law and an immediate peace. Even then, they were unable to prevent retributions against individual strike leaders, further damaging their reputations as tribunes of the people.[80]

The strikes themselves, and the motives of those who took part, are also worth analysing in greater detail. At local level, the number of recorded stoppages rose from 137 in 1915 to 561 in 1917.[81] These were often led by militant workers, such as the Revolutionary Shop Stewards in Berlin, the USPD in Leipzig or the left radicals in Bremen and Hamburg. The first action of national significance was a one-day strike on 28 June 1916, supported by 55,000 workers in Berlin and several thousand others in Stuttgart, Bremen, Braunschweig and Essen. It was called in protest at the arrest and ongoing detention of the Spartacist leader Karl Liebknecht for his role in organising an illegal anti-war demonstration on 1 May.[82] This was followed by the much larger action in April 1917, sparked off by further cuts in the bread ration and a hostile reaction to the Kaiser's Easter message. In Berlin, many of the estimated 200,000–300,000 strikers were women, although the strike leaders were usually skilled male workers in the metal and munitions industries.[83] Other centres of unrest included Braunschweig, Dresden, Halle, Hanover and Magdeburg.[84] Now the issue was not just the treatment of Liebknecht, but the war itself. In Leipzig, for instance, striking workers issued a list of seven demands on 16 April, including:

1. *Adequate provision of affordable food and heating for the people.*

2. *A declaration on the part of the government that it is willing to conclude an immediate peace on the basis of a renunciation of all annexations, direct or indirect.*

3. *Immediate lifting of the state of siege and of all censorship.*

4. *Immediate lifting of all restrictions on the right of assembly and association.*

5. *Immediate lifting of the shameful law providing for forced labour [the auxiliary service law].*

6. *Immediate freeing of all political detainees [and] cessation of all political trials.*

7. *Granting of full civil liberties [and] universal, equal, secret and direct suffrage for elections to all public bodies in the Reich, the federal states and communes.*[85]

In Lichtenberg, a suburb of Berlin, a meeting on 19 April at the AG Knorr-Bremse factory, attended by 1,050 of the 1,700-strong workforce likewise demanded:

1. *The release of Liebknecht.*

2. *The release of all persons in protective custody.*

3. *The lifting of restrictions on freedom of association.*

4. *Complete freedom for political activity.*

5. *Adequate provision of food and the securing of supplies.*

6. *The lifting of the state of siege.*

7. *Peace without reparations or annexations.*[86]

Although the strike clearly took the official trade unions by surprise, they quickly regained the initiative and brought the stoppages to a halt within a matter of days.[87]

The week-long strike which began on 28 January 1918 was on a bigger scale still, and followed a series of similar actions in Austria-Hungary. Up to one million workers downed tools, including 500,000 in Berlin and tens of thousands of others in Cologne, Mannheim, Braunschweig, Bremen, Hamburg, Kiel, Danzig, Leipzig, Nuremberg and Munich.[88] The political aims were the same as in April 1917, except this time there were specific demands for workers to be given a role in the ongoing peace negotiations with Bolshevik Russia at Brest-Litovsk, and expressions of solidarity with striking workers in Vienna, Prague and Budapest.[89] Furthermore, the leaders of the MSPD, including Ebert and Scheidemann, were unable to oppose the strike for fear of losing even more support to the USPD and the radical left, and instead were forced to put themselves up for election to the Berlin Action Committee alongside representatives of the Revolutionary Shop Stewards and the Berlin Independents.[90] Once again, women played an important role in the industrial unrest and accompanying political demonstrations, and in some munitions plants they made up more than half of the strikers.[91] The military struck back, imposing martial law in the factories and banning the Social Democrat newspaper *Vorwärts* for three days. This was in spite of frantic efforts on the part of the MSPD leaders to demonstrate their continued loyalty to the government and support for the war effort.

On 3 to 4 February the strike was finally brought to an end, but only after large numbers of strike leaders had been arrested and others sent to the front.[92] Rather menacingly, on 31 January the Berlin police chief also drew up a list of thirty-one prominent bourgeois pacifists he intended to target should the unrest get out of hand. Among them were the leaders of the BNV, Count Arco, Lilli Jannasch and Kurt von Tepper-Laski, the radical feminists Minna Cauer and Helene Stöcker, the USPD Reichstag deputy Eduard Bernstein, the anti-war professors Albert Einstein and Georg Nicolai, the sexologist Magnus Hirschfeld and the Christian activist Pastor Friedrich Siegmund-Schultze.[93] Within the lower ranks of the police, however, there was increasing support for anti-war protesters. Princess Blücher thus noted in her diary in January 1918 that when leaflets were discovered in the back streets of Berlin bearing the slogan 'Down with the Kaiser, down with the Government', the police 'refuse[d] to act and are more than suspected of being behind the movement themselves'.[94]

Meanwhile the USPD group in the Reichstag had grown to some twenty-four deputies, and they were able to use parliamentary privilege to circumvent censorship regulations and criticise the war in increasingly virulent terms. For instance, while the MSPD abstained in the debate on the Treaty of Brest-Litovsk on 22 March 1918, the 'annexationist' peace settlement signed with Bolshevik Russia, the USPD group voted against it.[95] By this time, the new party had grown to around 100,000 members, with particular strongholds in Berlin, Leipzig, Halle, Hamburg, Bremen, Stuttgart, Braunschweig and parts of the Ruhr and Lower Rhine.[96] Its most radical wing, the Spartacists, openly championed the cause of violent revolution as a means of bringing the war to an end, although even they were not entirely uncritical of Lenin and the Bolshevik model as practised in the new Russia.[97] The labour movement was now clearly and irrevocably split, and few on the radical left celebrated when the new government of Max von Baden announced the appointment of the Majority Social Democrats Philipp Scheidemann and Gustav Bauer as ministers on 4 October 1918.[98]

The revolution of November 1918

While Max von Baden and his new ministers prevaricated over the question of how to end the war without admitting defeat, events on the ground soon took a very different turn. At the beginning of November 1918, a general desire for peace led to spontaneous revolution in which both soldiers and civilians took part. Overthrowing the monarchy – and not simply installing a new government – was now widely understood to be the precondition for securing an armistice. This was particularly the case given the external pressures coming from America, which suggested – via President Wilson's second and third peace notes of 14 and 22 October – that Wilhelm II was the chief obstacle to ending the war.[99] Authority was also rapidly slipping away from the military authorities on both home and fighting fronts, and even loyal monarchists accepted that the war was lost. As the *Regierungspräsident* (governor) of Hildesheim in Lower Saxony put it on 24 October, there was now a 'shocking apathy in the face of the seriousness of our external position and an astonishing ignorance regarding the consequences of a peace foisted on us by the enemy'.[100] Ordinary Germans, in other words, were making it clear that they were not prepared to continue the war for another winter.

The trouble began in the naval ports of Kiel and Wilhelmshaven in north-western Germany, where an order was issued on 28 October to prepare for a major engagement with the Royal Navy in the North Sea and English Channel. The Naval High Command were determined that the war should not end without a last-minute trial of strength with the British, so

that at least they could rescue the battle fleet's honour and prestige following the ignomony of four years of almost total inaction. However, the ordinary sailors who made up the crews of the battleships knew full well that
this was tantamount to a suicide mission or *Todeskampf*, and refused to obey
orders to set sail. Instead, they arrested their commanding officers and took
over the ships themselves. After several days of noisy demonstrations, the
forces of law and order withdrew from both ports, and on 3 November
authority passed into the hands of newly elected councils (or soviets) of
soldiers' and sailors' deputies.[101]

From Kiel and Wilhelmshaven, the councils' movement spread to other
towns and cities in the north-west of Germany, and even as far afield as
Hanover, Braunschweig and Frankfurt am Main. The principal fear seemed
to be that the actions of the Naval High Command were intended to scup-
per negotiations for an armistice and thus delay the onset of peace; yet in
very few cases did the councils or representatives of organised labour themselves lead the revolution. This was left to ordinary soldiers and civilians
who rose up spontaneously against the prospect of a continuation of the
war. Only after military authority had collapsed did the councils emerge to
take charge of events.[102]

In most cases, the old Imperial authorities seemed to surrender authority
with hardly a shot being fired. In Munich, the capital of Bavaria, for
instance, the monarchical system collapsed in the night of 7–8 November
1918 when the aged king, Ludwig III, fled from his palace, never to return.
The following morning it was announced that Kurt Eisner, a pacifist intellectual and USPD member, who had only recently been released from a
prison sentence imposed for 'incitement to mutiny' in January 1918, had
become the first Prime Minister of the newly created Bavarian Republic.[103]
On 9 November, as we have seen, the revolution reached Berlin and Philipp
Scheidemann, for the Majority Social Democrats, declared the existence of a
German republic from the balcony of the Reichstag. Two days later, on the
same day that the armistice was signed ending the war, the Habsburg
Emperor Charles withdrew from Vienna, leaving Austria to become a republic too. The old order was gone, and with it the princely houses which had
ruled in German-speaking central Europe over many centuries.[104]

On the surface, the revolution had spread remarkably quickly and with
the same result throughout Germany. Yet every town and city had its own
experience of revolution, and no two experiences were exactly the same.
In Hamburg, for example, the revolution came quickly and unexpectedly
on 6 November, and was led primarily by militant workers against the
opposition of the MSPD and union leaders 'who did not want this revolution

and set themselves against it until the last minute'.[105] Political authority here moved from the Senate to the Council of Workers' and Soldiers' Deputies, which in turn elected to exclude MSPD members and instead promoted left-wing radicals, many of whom, like Eisner in Munich, had only recently been let out of jail.[106]

In Freiburg, on the other hand, which from 1917 had been headquarters of the army staging area for the south-west front, soldiers played the key role in overthrowing the old order, and none of the left-wing parties was initially involved.[107] In other small towns like Göttingen in Lower Saxony, where reformism had dominated locally within the pre-war SPD, the MSPD were able to challenge the USPD for control over the local councils, and lead the latter towards active cooperation with local representatives of the bourgeois parties and the old order.[108]

In Berlin the key event was the formation of the Council of People's Commissars (*Rat der Volksbeauftragten*) as the new revolutionary government on 9 November 1918, made up of three representatives of the MSPD and three members of the USPD. In practice, though, the council's chairman, Friedrich Ebert (MSPD), quickly established himself as the dominant figure, particularly as he was able to use his additional, albeit uncertain authority as Reich Chancellor (and therefore legal successor to Max von Baden) to limit the influence of the left. From day one, Ebert's aim, which he intended to achieve with or without the USPD, was to work towards a coalition with the moderate bourgeois parties. This had less to do with appeasing the Allies than with maintaining adequate food supplies and ensuring the smooth reintegration of soldiers into civilian life. An additional consideration was lack of preparedness for office. Or, as Princess Blücher put it:

The revolution . . . [had come] too suddenly, even for the Socialists themselves, and what ought to have evolved from a natural course of events was prematurely hurled at us by the unexpected insurrection of the sailors in Kiel and Hamburg. Therefore the Socialists ha[d] not had time to develop a really strong Government, or to test the practical working of theories in a country which is still at heart for the greater part monarchist in its sympathies.[109]

For all of these reasons, Ebert was determined that the Council of People's Commissars should govern 'on a strictly caretaker basis' until elections to a new constituent National Assembly could be held. All other decisions, including the future constitution of the republic, would have to be put on hold until then. In this aim he was supported by Wilhelm Groener, Ludendorff's successor as Army Quarter-Master General, who telephoned the Reich

Der Rat der Volksbeauftragten

PLATE 2.2 The Council of People's Commissars, founded in Berlin on 9 November 1918.
Source: Deutsches Historisches Museum, Berlin

Chancellery on the evening of 10 November 1918 to offer a conditional pledge of loyalty to the new government. In return, he called for Ebert's cooperation in preserving military discipline and preventing a threatened disintegration of the armed forces.[110]

In the USPD strongholds of Braunschweig, Magedeburg, Mannheim, Halle, Leipzig and Stuttgart, the Spartacists and the more militant elements within the shop stewards movement posed something of a threat to the new government's authority. In their view, the councils were not simply temporary instruments for the maintenance of law and order, but tools for the promotion of public ownership of industry, or even for the establishment of a proletarian dictatorship along Russian lines. Within such circles, opposition to any deal with the bourgeois parties was fierce; socialism should be introduced before the staging of any elections. This was the view, for instance, of the new Police President in Berlin, Emil Eichhorn, a leading figure on the left-wing of the USPD, who remained in his new post until 4 January 1919, in spite of the resignation of the USPD members from the Council of People's Commissars on 28 December.[111]

Yet none of these groups – the left-wing of the USPD, the Revolutionary Shop Stewards or the Spartacists – had a clear-cut programme to rival that of the moderate socialists. The Spartacist League in particular – which had a few thousand members at the most and whose leaders, Liebknecht and

Luxemburg, had just been released from prison – was hardly in a position to win a mass following in the last weeks of 1918. And even within the extreme left, there were plenty of people who disagreed profoundly with Liebknecht and Luxemburg on questions of tactics, and poured scorn on their notion of revolutionary spontaneity.[112] The foundation of the KPD – German Communist Party – on 30 December 1918, with support from the Spartacists and the Revolutionary Shop Stewards, did not therefore mark a decisive shift in the direction of mass proletarian revolution, as even East German historians in the 1950s and 60s were willing to concede.[113]

Radical leftists also played only a tiny role in the new soldiers' and workers' councils which had been elected in nearly every municipality and workplace between 3 and 9 November 1918; here the usual pattern, particularly in the first phase of the revolution, down to January 1919, was for an alliance between the MSPD and moderate elements within the USPD.[114] In most cases the MSPD became the dominant partner. There were some important exceptions, though. For instance, in 'Red' Saxony, the heartland of pre-war left-wing Social Democracy, the USPD was able to claim the leading positions within the new revolutionary government (the foreign, interior, defence and finance portfolios) leaving the MSPD with the less powerful posts (justice, labour and education).[115] The same applied, as we have seen, in Hamburg, Stuttgart and Munich, and also in some of the cities in the Ruhr,[116] although not in Berlin, where, according to Reinhard Rürup, 'Ebert's central position . . . [was] indisputable'.[117]

What accounts for these differences? The relative strength of the MSPD and USPD in particular areas was important. So too was the attitude of the local military authorities, who in some cases, and especially in Berlin and Hamburg, directly worked with the MSPD against the left, a strategy which claimed some successes but usually only provoked bitterness and alienation between the two socialist parties.[118] However, over and above these party political factors, food continued to play a large role. Thus in smaller towns like Göttingen or Freiburg, the fact that workers could more easily feed themselves through cultivation of small urban plots or through bartering with local farmers strengthened the tendency towards reformist ideologies, whereas lack of opportunity for the same – as in the case of Hamburg, Leipzig or Munich – strengthened the hand of the left.[119]

The food question also helped to reinforce existing tensions between town and countryside, and between the Catholic south and west and the Protestant north. Thus in southern Bavaria farmers formed paramilitary groups (*Einwohnerwehren*) to protect their property and communities against 'urban looters' and deliberately withheld foodstuffs from the new revolutionary government. Demobbed soldiers from rural areas were simply pleased to have survived the war, and were keen to benefit as much as they could from the new economic opportunities resulting from the dismantling of wartime price controls. They were willing to fight against communism if it came near their homes, but were otherwise uninterested in politics or in the plight of their urban compatriots. As one Swabian farmer commented in 1923, hungry workers from Munich who complained about rising food prices should 'spread cow dung on their bread instead of butter'.[120]

In fact, the end of the first phase of the revolution was already evident in Bavaria on 12 January 1919, when Eisner's Independent Social Democrats were roundly beaten by the MSPD and the centre right Bavarian People's Party (BVP) in elections to the new provincial parliament or Landtag.[121] Three days later in Berlin, the left-wing Spartacist Uprising, caused partly by the dismissal of Police President Eichhorn on 4 January, was brutally crushed by pro-government troops and right-wing irregulars, the *Freikorps*. The KPD leaders Liebknecht and Luxemburg were murdered on their way to prison, an event which is said to have horrified Ebert on a personal level.[122] Thereafter, in spite of further proto-communist revolts, including a short-lived Soviet republic in Munich in April–May 1919, the radical left suffered defeat after defeat. In fact, it seems likely that the threat of communism was more imagined than real, becoming a convenient means by which the Ebert and Scheidemann governments sought to win concessions from the victorious Allies, and in particular a lifting of the economic blockade.[123] Fear of Bolshevism also became an excuse for not reforming the old Imperial army, with catastrophic results for the future of the republic, as we shall see in the following chapter.[124]

Notes

1 Ullrich, *Kriegsalltag*, p. 7.

2 See in particular the various contributions to Hagemann and Schüler-Springorum (eds), *Home/Front*, *passim*. Also Daniel, *The War From Within*, *passim*.

3 On *Erfahrungsgeschichte* see Ziemann, *War Experiences*, esp. pp. 9–11.

4 Belinda J. Davis, *Home Fires Burning. Food, Politics and Everyday Life in World War I Berlin* (Chapel Hill, NC and London, 2000).

5 Ibid., p. 22.

6 Ziemann, *War Experiences*, esp. pp. 21–41.

7 Chickering, *Imperial Germany*, pp. 42–6.

8 'Kartoffelpreise', *Vorwärts*, 27 October 1914. Copy in Landesarchiv Berlin, Rep. 30, Tit. 95, Bl. 205.

9 Police report, Kriminalwachtmeister Starost, 5 March 1915, reproduced in Ingo Materna and Hans-Joachim Schreckenbach (eds), *Dokumente aus geheimen Archiven, Vol. 4: Berichte des Berliner Polizeipräsidenten zur Stimmung und Lage der Bevölkerung in Berlin, 1914–1918* (Weimar, 1987), p. 48.

10 Ursula Herrmann, 'Sozialdemokratische Frauen in Deutschland im Kampf um den Frieden vor und während des Ersten Weltkriegs', *Zeitschrift für Geschichtswissenschaft*, 33/3 (1985), pp. 213–30 (here p. 222).

11 Cited in Ullrich, *Kriegsalltag*, p. 40.

12 Ibid., p. 41.

13 Davis, *Home Fires Burning*, pp. 138–46.

14 Roger Chickering, *The Great War and Urban Life in Germany. Freiburg, 1914–1918* (Cambridge, 2007), p. 479.

15 Police report, Traugott von Jagow, 23 January 1915, in Materna and Schreckenbach (eds), *Berichte des Berliner Polizeipräsidenten*, pp. 38–9. English translation in Daniel, *The War From Within*, pp. 182–3.

16 On 'food riots' see ibid., esp. pp. 246–50; and Davis, *Home Fires Burning*, esp. pp. 76–88. Also Herrmann, 'Sozialdemokratische Frauen', p. 223.

17 Cf. Davis, 'Homefront', p. 115; and Davis, 'Reconsidering Habermas, Gender and the Public Sphere: The Case of Wilhelmine Germany', in Eley (ed.), *Society, Culture and the State in Germany*, pp. 397–426.

18 Davis, *Home Fires Burning*, pp. 114–21. The agencies in question included the Price Monitoring Authority (*Preisprüfungsstelle*), the War Food Office (*Kriegsernährungsamt*) and the State Distribution Office (*Staatsverteilungsstelle*). See also Chapter 1 above.

19 Heather Jones, 'Encountering the "Enemy": Prisoner of War Transport and the Development of War Cultures in 1914', in Pierre Purseigle (ed.), *Warfare and Belligerence. Perspectives in First World War Studies* (Leiden, 2005), pp. 133–62.

20 Stibbe, *German Anglophobia*, p. 18.

21 Grew to House, 23 March 1916, in Houghton Library, Cambridge, MA, Grew Papers, MS Am 1687, Vol. 8.

22 Evelyn, Princess Blücher, *An English Wife in Berlin* (London, 1920), p. 95.

23 Davis, *Home Fires Burning*, pp. 148–9.

24 Ibid., p. 180.

25 Ibid., esp. pp. 159–60 and 237–8.

26 *Monatsberichte*, 3 April 1917. Cited in Daniel, *The War From Within*, p. 197.

27 Ullrich, *Kriegsalltag*, p. 81. Also cited in Kramer, *Dynamic of Destruction*, p. 153.

28 The figure comes from the calculations of Geheimrat Dr. Hamel, a medical expert in the Reich Office of Interior, and is cited – uncritically – by the anti-war activist Friedrich Siegmund-Schultze in his pamphlet *Die Wirkungen der englischen Hungerblockade auf die deutschen Kinder* (= Sonderheft der 'Eiche'), Berlin, May 1919, pp. 11–12.

29 Kramer, *Dynamic of Destruction*, p. 154, citing Jay Winter, 'Surviving the War: Life Expectation, Illness and Mortality Rates in Paris, London and Berlin, 1914–1919', in Winter and Jean-Louis Robert (eds), *Capital Cities at War. Paris, London, Berlin, 1914–1919* (Cambridge, 1997), pp. 487–523.

30 Julius Schwalbe, 'Die englische Krankheit', *Berliner Lokalanzeiger*, 19 April 1919.

31 Siegmund-Schultze, *Die Wirkungen der englischen Hungerblockade*, p. 4. On Siegmund-Schultze see also Stefan Grotefeld, *Friedrich Siegmund-Schultze. Ein deutscher Ökumeniker und christlicher Pazifist* (Gütersloh, 1995).

32 Cf. C. Paul Vincent, *The Politics of Hunger. The Allied Blockade of Germany, 1915–1919* (Athens, OH and London, 1985); Avner Offer, 'The Blockade of Germany and the Strategy of Starvation, 1914–1918', in Roger Chickering and Stig Förster (eds), *Great War, Total War. Combat and Mobilization on the Western Front, 1914–1918* (Cambridge, 2000), pp. 169–88.

33 Kramer, *Dynamic of Destruction*, p. 154.

34 Ziemann, *War Experiences*, esp. pp. 142–4 and 168–81.

35 See e.g. Max von Gruber, 'Völkische Außenpolitik', *Deutschlands Erneuerung*, 1/1 (April 1917), pp. 74–87.

36 Liulevicius, *War Land on the Eastern Front*, p. 159.

37 Kramer, *Dynamic of Destruction*, p. 153.

38 Jones, 'A Missing Paradigm?', p. 27.

39 Hinz, *Gefangen im Großen Krieg*, *passim*; Stibbe, 'Prisoners of War During the First World War', *passim*. Officer POWs could not be forced to work.

40 Uta Hinz, 'Die deutschen "Barbaren" sind doch die besseren Menschen. Kriegsgefangenschaft und gefangene "Feinde" in der Darstellung der deutschen Publizistik, 1914–1918', in Rüdiger Overmans (ed.), *In der Hand des Feindes. Kriegsgefangenschaft von der Antike bis zum Zweiten Weltkrieg* (Cologne, 1999), pp. 339–61 (here p. 351).

41 The classic study in this genre is Paul Fussell, *The Great War and Modern Memory* (London, 1975).

42 See e.g. Tim Travers, 'The War in the Trenches', in Martel (ed.), *A Companion to Europe*, pp. 213–27.

43 Tony Ashworth, *Trench Warfare, 1914–1918. The Live and Let Live System* (London, 1980). See also Watson, *Enduring the Great War*, pp. 69–72.

44 Erich Maria Remarque, *All Quiet on the Western Front*, translated by A. W. Wheen (London, 1929), p. 190. On Remarque see also Chapter 5 below.

45 Ziemann, *War Experiences*, pp. 30–41.

46 Ibid, pp. 120–1, 138 and 271. See also Patrick Porter, 'New Jerusalems: Sacrifice and Redemption in the War Experiences of English and German Military Chaplains', in Purseigle (ed.), *Warfare and Belligerence*, pp. 101–32.

47 For a pan-European view, see Jay Winter, *Sites of Memory, Sites of Mourning. The Great War in European Cultural History* (Cambridge, 1995).

48 Adelheid von Saldern, *Auf dem Wege zum Arbeiter-Reformismus. Parteialltag in sozialdemokratischer Provinz Göttingen (1870–1920)* (Frankfurt/M, 1984), p. 203.

49 See e.g. the popular collection of student essays edited by Philipp Witkop, *Kriegsbriefe deutscher Studenten* (Gotha, 1916) which had gone through seven editions by 1928. The 1929 English language edition has recently been republished as *German Students' War Letters*, with a foreword by Jay Winter (Philadelphia, PA, 2002). More generally see George L. Mosse, 'The Cult of the Fallen Soldier' in Mosse, *Fallen Soldiers. Reshaping the Memory of the World Wars* (Oxford, 1990), pp. 70–106, and Chapter 3 below.

50 Ziemann, *War Experiences*, pp. 39–40.

51 Gary D. Stark, 'All Quiet on the Home Front: Popular Entertainments, Censorship and Civilian Morale in Germany, 1914–1918', in Frans Coetzee and Marilyn Shevin-Coetzee (eds), *Authority, Identity and the Social History of the Great War* (Oxford, 1995), pp. 57–80 (quotations on p. 63); Elizabeth B. Jones, *Gender and Rural Modernity. Farm Women and the Politics of Labor in Germany, 1871–1933* (Farnham, 2009), pp. 106–7.

52 Ziemann, *War Experiences*, pp. 57–64.

53 Cited in ibid., p. 141.

54 See Daniel, *The War From Within*, *passim*; Davis, *Home Fires Burning*, *passim*; Chickering, *The Great War and Urban Life in Germany*, *passim*.

55 Von Saldern, *Auf dem Wege zum Arbeiter-Reformismus*, p. 203.

56 Ibid., pp. 208–9; Daniel, *The War From Within*, pp. 200–3, 250 and 283.

57 This theme is also addressed by Nelson, 'German Comrades – Slavic Whores', *passim*.

58 Chickering, *The Great War and Urban Life in Germany*, pp. 357–63. See also Hinz, *Gefangen im Großen Krieg*, pp. 191–201.

59 Werner Thönnessen, *The Emancipation of Women. The Rise and Decline of the Women's Movement in German Social Democracy, 1863–1933* (London, 1973), p. 108.

60 Nikolaus Wachsmann, 'Between Reform and Repression: Imprisonment in Weimar Germany', *Historical Journal*, 45/2 (2002), pp. 411–32 (here p. 413).

61 Chickering, *The Great War and Urban Life in Germany*, p. 352.

62 Ziemann, *War Experiences*, pp. 65 and 67.

63 This theme is hardly touched upon in any of the existing literature, with the exception of Klaus Theweleit's *Male Fantasies*, *passim*. See also Benjamin

Ziemann's useful comments in 'Germany after the First World War – A Violent Society?', pp. 93–4.

64 On French and Belgium women deportees see Becker, *Oubliés de la grande guerre*, pp. 68–77 and 84–6; Helen McPhail, *The Long Silence. Civilian Life under the German Occupation of Northern France, 1914–1918* (London, 1999), pp. 166–70; and Matthew Stibbe, 'Elisabeth Rotten and the "Auskunfts- und Hilfsstelle für Deutsche im Ausland und Ausländer in Deutschland", 1914–1919', in Alison S. Fell and Ingrid Sharp (eds), *The Women's Movement in Wartime. International Perspectives, 1914–19* (Basingstoke, 2007), pp. 194–210.

65 Watson, *Enduring the Great War*, p. 182.

66 Ziemann, *War Experiences*, p. 108.

67 Niall Ferguson, 'Prisoner Taking and Prisoner Killing', *passim.*; idem., *The Pity of War*, pp. 339–88.

68 Watson, *Enduring the Great War*, pp. 215–31 and 235.

69 Davis, *Home Fires Burning*, p. 231.

70 Blücher, *An English Wife*, p. 252.

71 On the BNV see Stibbe, 'Elisabeth Rotten', pp. 199–200, and Herrmann, 'Sozialdemokratische Frauen', pp. 222–3; and on Liebknecht and Luxemburg see Weitz, *Creating German Communism*, pp. 78–83.

72 Davis, *Home Fires Burning*, p. 231.

73 Kramer, *Dynamic of Destruction*, p. 153.

74 Matthew Stibbe, 'Anti-Feminism, Nationalism and the German Right, 1914–1920: A Reappraisal', *German History*, 20/2 (2002), pp. 185–210 (here pp. 195–6). See also Daniel, *The War From Within*, pp. 65–89.

75 Feldman, *Army, Industry and Labor, passim*; Chickering, *Imperial Germany*, p. 151. For examples of cooperation between official trade unions and the police and military authorities in Hamburg in 1917/18 see also Ullrich, *Kriegsalltag*, pp. 107–8.

76 Stibbe, 'Anti-Feminism', p. 197. On 'patriotic instruction' see also Wilhlem Deist, 'Censorship and Propaganda in Germany During the First World War', in Jean-Jacques Becker and Stéphane Audoin-Rouzeau (eds), *Les sociétés européenes et la guerre de 1914–1918* (Paris, 1990), pp. 199–210 (here pp. 205–7).

77 Geary, 'Arbeiter', pp. 148–52.

78 Manifest des Gründungsparteitages der USPD vom 6. bis 8. April 1917, reproduced in *Dokumente und Materialien zur Geschichte der deutschen Arbeiterbewegung, Vol. 1: Juli 1914 – Oktober 1917*, edited by the SED-Institut für Marxismus-Leninismus (East Berlin, 1958), pp. 594–7 (here p. 595).

79 Berger, *Social Democracy and the Working Class*, pp. 92–3.

80 Stephen Bailey, 'The Berlin Strike of January 1918', *Central European History*, 13/2 (1980), pp. 158–74.

81 Mark Baker, 'The War and Revolution', in Martel (ed.), *A Companion to Europe*, pp. 243–58 (here p. 252).

82 Francis L. Carsten, *Revolution in Central Europe, 1918–1919* (London, 1972), p. 14; Chickering, *Imperial Germany*, p. 153; Herrmann, 'Sozialdemokratische Frauen', p. 224.

83 Davis, *Home Fires Burning*, pp. 200–03; Herrmann, 'Sozialdemokratische Frauen', pp. 224–5.

84 Herrmann, 'Sozialdemokratische Frauen', p. 225; Chickering, *Imperial Germany*, p. 155.

85 Forderungen der streikenden Leipziger Arbeiter, 16 April 1917, reproduced in SED-Institut für Marxismus-Leninismus *Dokumente und Materialien zur Geschichte der deutschen Arbeiterbewegung*, vol. 1, p. 612.

86 Police Report, Berlin-Lichtenberg, 19 April 1917, reproduced in ibid., p. 613.

87 Bieber, 'The Socialist Trade Unions in War and Revolution', p. 79.

88 Bailey, 'The Berlin Strike', p. 159; Bieber, 'The Socialist Trade Unions', p. 81.

89 Fritz Klein *et al.*, *Deutschland im Ersten Weltkrieg*, 3 vols (East Berlin, 1968–9), vol. 3, pp. 150–1.

90 Carsten, *Revolution in Central Europe*, p. 15.

91 Herrmann, 'Sozialdemokratische Frauen', pp. 228–9.

92 Bailey, 'The Berlin Strike', p. 163.

93 Liste der im Landespolizeibezirk Berlin und Umgebung wohnhaften namhaften Pazifisten, 31 January 1918. Reproduced in Materna and Schreckenbach (eds), *Berichte des Berliner Polizeipräsidenten*, pp. 243–4.

94 Blücher, *An English Wife*, p. 190.

95 Klein *et al.*, *Deutschland im Ersten Weltkrieg*, Vol. 3, p. 199.

96 Chickering, *Imperial Germany*, p. 157.

97 Weitz, *Creating German Communism*, p. 83.

98 Berger, *Social Democracy*, p. 93.

99 Klaus Schwabe, *Woodrow Wilson, Revolutionary Germany and Peacemaking, 1918–1919: Missionary Diplomacy and the Realities of Power* (Chapel Hill, NC and London, 1985).

100 Von Saldern, *Auf dem Wege zum Arbeiter-Reformismus*, p. 209.

101 The classic account of the November revolution in English is Richard M. Watt, *The Kings Depart: The German Revolution and the Treaty of Versailles, 1918–1919*, Penguin ed. (London, 1973). For an even better account in German see Heinrich August Winkler, *Die Sozialdemokratie und die Revolution von 1918/19. Ein Rückblick nach sechzig Jahren* (Bonn, 1979); and idem., *Von der Revolution zur Stabilisierung: Arbeiter und Arbeiterbewegung in der Weimarer Republik, 1918 bis 1924* (Bonn, 1984).

102 Mommsen, *The Rise and Fall of Weimar Democracy*, p. 25.

103 David Clay Large, *Where Ghosts Walked. Munich's Road to the Third Reich* (London, 1997), pp. 77–81.

104 Carsten, *Revolution in Central Europe*, pp. 36–8 and *passim*.

105 Ullrich, *Kriegsalltag* p. 160.

106 Ibid., p. 159.

107 Chickering, *The Great War and Urban Life in Germany*, pp. 567–8.

108 Von Saldern, *Auf dem Wege zum Arbeiter-Reformismus*, pp. 209–13; idem., 'Latent Reformism and Socialist Utopia: The SPD in Göttingen, 1890 to 1920', in David E. Barclay and Eric D. Weitz (eds), *Between Reform and Revolution. German Socialism and Communism from 1840 to 1990* (Oxford, 1998), pp. 195–221 (here pp. 214–15).

109 Princess Blücher, *An English Wife*, p. 302.

110 Kolb, *The Weimar Republic*, p. 13.

111 Mommsen, *The Rise and Fall of Weimar Democracy*, p. 35.

112 Weitz, *Creating German Communism*, pp. 78–83.

113 Klein *et al.*, *Deutschland im Ersten Weltkrieg*, Vol. 3, pp. 590–1. On East German views of the November revolution see also Andreas Dorpalen, *German History in Marxist Perspective. The East German Approach* (London, 1985), pp. 313–24; and Jürgen John, 'Das Bild der Novemberrevolution 1918 in Geschichtspolitik und Geschichtswissenschaft der DDR', in Heinrich August Winkler (ed.), *Weimar im Widerstreit. Deutungen der ersten deutschen Republik im geteilten Deutschland* (Munich, 2002), pp. 43–84.

114 Cf. Eberhard Kolb, *Die Arbeiterräte in der deutschen Innenpolitik* (Düsseldorf, 1962).

115 Claus-Christian W. Szejnmann, *Vom Traum zum Alptraum. Sachsen in der Weimarer Republik* (Leipzig, 2000), p. 19.

116 According to Francis Carsten, the workers' and soldiers' council in Essen was based on equal representation between the SPD and USPD, while the council at Düsseldorf 'was dominated by the Independents and had two Spartacist members' – see Carsten, *Revolution in Central Europe*, p. 153.

117 Reinhard Rürup, 'Friedrich Ebert und das Problem der Handlungsspielräume in der deutschen Revolution 1918/19', in Rudolf König, Hartmut Soell and Hermann Weber (eds), *Friedrich Ebert und seine Zeit. Bilanz und Perspektiven der Forschung* (Munich, 1991), pp. 69–87 (here p. 72).

118 Bailey, 'The Berlin Strike of 1918', pp. 169–70; Ullrich, *Kriegsalltag*, pp. 107–8.

119 Von Saldern, *Auf dem Wege zum Arbeiter-Reformismus*, p. 205; Chickering, *The Great War and Urban Life in Germany*, pp. 184–6 and 243–4.

120 Ziemann, *War Experiences*, p. 198.

121 Ibid., p. 221. The results were 35 per cent for the BVP and 33 per cent for the MSPD, compared to just 2.5 per cent for the USPD.

122 Mommsen, *The Rise and Fall of Weimar Democracy*, p. 37.

123 Fritz Klein, 'Between Compiègne and Versailles: The Germans on the Way from a Misunderstood Defeat to an Unwanted Peace', in Manfred F. Boemeke, Gerald D. Feldman and Elisabeth Glaser (eds), *The Treaty of Versailles. A Reassessment After 75 Years* (Cambridge, 1998), pp. 203–20 (here p. 211).

124 Francis L. Carsten, *The Reichswehr and Politics, 1918–1933* (London, 1968). The central importance of this 'failure . . . to replace the old Prussian-German army with a republican defense force' after 1918 has also recently been re-emphasised by the late Henry Ashby Turner Jr – see his scholarly note 'The Myth of Chancellor von Schleicher's *Querfront* Strategy', *Central European History*, 41/4 (2008), pp. 673–81 (here p. 681).

CHAPTER 3

Political and Psychological Consequences of the War

On 19 January 1919, four days after the suppression of the Spartacist uprising, voting took place across Germany for the election of a new constituent National Assembly. A total of 76.1 per cent of German voters opted to support the pro-republican parties (MSPD 37.9 per cent, Catholic Centre Party 19.7 per cent and the left-liberal DDP 18.5 per cent). The outcome was a defeat for the right-wing, anti-republican DNVP (10.3 per cent) but also for the socialist USPD (7.6 per cent), and for socialism more generally. The victors, and in particular the leaders of the MSPD, were moderates who were more interested in building bridges with representatives of the old order than in changing the course of world history. Certainly they were no admirers of Lenin and balked at any radical break with the past. Yet on the surface at least, the revolution had achieved some important progressive goals, for instance the granting of female suffrage, the abolition of the unfair three-class franchise in Prussia and other federal states, legal recognition of the right to strike, and above all an end to the war. Law and order had meanwhile been upheld, and famine averted. The work of government-backed demobilisation committees at state, regional and local level also allowed for a relatively smooth reintegration of veterans into the post-war economy. Male unemployment at first remained at surprisingly low levels, not least because large numbers of women (and ex-POWs and foreign civilian labourers) were forced out of temporary wartime jobs to make way for the returning soldiers.[1]

Even so, the war clearly had a deep impact on the psychology of the German nation after 1918, and this was bound to be reflected in post-war political life too. Ordinary Germans had been told by the government that they were winning the war up until October 1918; then suddenly everything collapsed around them. The old order was gone and the new political

PLATE 3.1 'Ebert and Noske in der Sommerfrische', front cover of the *Berliner Illustrierte Zeitung*, 24 August 1919.

Source: Bildarchiv Preussischer Kulturbesitz

system was based on very shaky foundations. Communists and extreme right-wing groups both tried to overthrow the new republic on several occasions during the first years of its existence. Right-wingers also carried out a wave of targeted assassinations against republican politicians, including the USPD leader Hugo Haase (October 1919), the Catholic Centre party spokesman Matthias Erzberger (August 1921) and the Jewish Foreign Minister Walther Rathenau (June 1922). Even Ebert, who was elevated from Reich Chancellor to Reich President in February 1919, was not spared the ridicule and contempt of those seeking to undermine the new regime. When an unauthorised photograph of the *Reichspräsident* on holiday by the sea with Defence Minister Gustav Noske, clad only in swimming trunks and looking small and inept, was published on the front cover of the *Berliner*

Illustrierte Zeitung in August 1919, his reputation as a Biedermeier – a middle-class philistine who lacked the dignity of a true statesman in the Prussian tradition – was firmly sealed in the public eye. More seriously, conservative enemies of the republic repeatedly castigated him as one of the 'November criminals' who had supposedly 'betrayed' Germany by instigating the revolution at the end of 1918, and he was never seen to possess the legitimacy of a Bismarck or a Hindenburg.[2]

This chapter will explore the political and psychological consequences of the war, paying particular attention to the challenges posed by extremist political movements. It will also examine more broadly the argument put forward by George Mosse that the First World War led to a 'brutalisation' of German politics.[3] First, though, it will be necessary to address the more positive achievements of the revolution and the attempts by moderates to create a new consensus built around the Stinnes-Legien agreement of 15 November 1918 and the Weimar constitution of August 1919.

A fragile post-war consensus

The political shape of post-war Germany was arguably established in two different ways. The first of these lay in the realm of industrial relations and the planned deregulation of the German economy in line with the interests of private enterprise and trade union rights. The starting point was the Stinnes-Legien agreement, brought about when a group of business leaders, led by the Ruhr steel and shipping magnate Hugo Stinnes, came together with representatives of the Free (i.e. Social Democrat) Trade Unions, led by Carl Legien, to establish certain principles for the management of the transition from war to peace. In essence, the unions agreed to drop their demands for widespread nationalisation in return for certain concessions from the employers, notably the introduction of the eight-hour day and collective labour contracts in larger workplaces. Industrialists also agreed not to hire 'yellow labour' (strike breakers) while union leaders achieved reaffirmation of their status as representatives of the workforce, which had already partly been conceded under the wartime Auxiliary Service Law of 1916. Finally, both sides agreed to the establishment of a consultative body, the *Zentralarbeitsgemeinschaft* (central working association or ZAG), which brought workers and bosses together in a common forum.[4]

The agreement was concluded on 15 November, although in fact its origins lie in discussions held before the revolution, in October 1918.[5] On the left it is often seen as part of the 'betrayal' of the revolution in Germany in 1918–19, particularly as it became a way of restoring the traditional authority of the old trade unions and industrialists vis-à-vis the workers' councils and the independent strike movement.[6] Indeed, disappointment at low wages and the failure to nationalise the mines in particular led to a wave of unofficial wildcat strikes throughout Germany in March 1919, centred on Berlin, the Ruhr, Saxony and the Halle-Merseburg region.[7] The strikes were brutally put down by regular government troops and *Freikorps* units acting at the behest of Defence Minister Noske, who rapidly earned the nickname of 'blood-hound of the revolution'.[8] When a Soviet Republic was declared in Munich in April–May 1919, this too was smashed by the German army and the extreme right-wing Ehrhardt brigade acting under orders from Berlin.[9]

More recently, however, the negative view of the Stinnes-Legien agreement as a 'betrayal' has been partially modified by scholars like Heinrich August Winkler and Peter-Christian Witt, who stress the narrow room for manouevre that Legien and the official trade unions had in 1918–19.[10] Thus Winkler notes that large-scale nationalisation, as demanded by the USPD, was incompatible with the economic interests of ordinary trade union members and the rather limited goals of their leaders, which centred on wages, working hours and the right to strike. The only realistic option was an agreement with the owners of industry, particularly after the MSPD – the principal political ally of the official trade unions – failed to win an outright majority of seats in the National Assembly.[11]

Conan Fischer, meanwhile, has advanced an even bolder defence of the labour accords negotiated between the employers and the official trade unions in 1918–19. In his view, the leaders of the 'revolution from below', namely the USPD and the councils movement, 'lacked any comprehensive strategic vision upon which a domestic political settlement and an international settlement and reparations regime acceptable to the Allies could have been built'. By contrast the MSPD leaders and their labour and trade union colleagues who managed the revolution 'from above' showed a practical grasp of realities and a willingness to negotiate with (rather than bow down to) representatives of the old order. The result, by 1920, was a 'triumph of moderation over utopian extremism in all its forms'.[12]

In reality, the truth probably lies somewhere between these two views. Thus it is doubtful whether the councils movement really had the potential to develop into a more democratic system of industrial relations and worker representation than that offered by the MSPD and the Stinnes-Legien agreement, even though most of the councils were initially controlled by moderate socialists rather than Spartacist-style revolutionaries. Furthermore, in the countryside, as Richard Bessel and Benjamin Ziemann have both shown, any attempt to impose socialism or land redistribution would have met with fierce resistance, and possibly even civil war.[13] Given this, there was no option but to suspend decisions about nationalisation and instead follow the path of early elections, even if this meant surrendering the MSPD's alliance with the USPD and negotiating a return to coalition with the centre-right middle-class parties. The outcome of the January 1919 poll indeed indicated that there was no popular mandate for a socialist type of economy; rather the voters had indicated their preference for a partnership between the moderate, pro-republican parties. Yet it is still the case that more could have been done to meet some of the demands of the unofficial strike movement that swept the country in 1919 and 1920, such as democratic reform of the army and greater worker participation in the management of private enterprises. Or, as Wolfgang Mommsen puts it, a more accommodating response might have averted the extreme polarisation in the labour movement which proved so 'damaging to the social foundations of the new state during the battles that lay ahead'.[14]

The second foundation stone of the new republic lay in the realm of formal party politics rather than industrial relations. Thus, in the aftermath of the dissolution of the Council of People's Commissars on 13 February 1919, the new SPD-led coalition governments of Philipp Scheidemann (February–June 1919) and Gustav Bauer (June 1919–March 1920) worked towards the establishment of a written document which would provide the basis for a functioning democratic parliamentary system, albeit with certain powers reserved for a directly elected president. The final draft of the constitution, which was approved by the National Assembly on 31 July 1919, and signed into law on 11 August 1919, was actually first and foremost the work of Hugo Preuß, a leading left-liberal and professor of public law at the University of Berlin. Other important figures involved included the Heidelberg sociologist Max Weber and the liberal politician Friedrich Naumann.[15] The final document was a compromise between rival visions, including parliamentary versus presidential powers, individual liberties versus welfare rights, and the unitary versus the federal principle. Even its title – 'Verfassung des Deutschen Reiches' or 'Constitution of the German Reich' – represented a significant symbolic concession on the part of those on the centre-left who had initially wanted the inclusion of the word 're-public' towards those on the centre-right who wished to stress continuities with the German empire created by Bismarck in 1871.[16] It was approved by a vote of 262 for and 75 against, with the SPD, DDP and Centre Party voting for, and the USPD, DNVP and DVP against.[17]

As in the case of the trade unions' pact with Stinnes and other industrialists, the SPD in particular have been criticised for not taking more of a lead in preparing the constitution, and for allowing the bourgeois parties to seize every opportunity to insert checks against 'unfettered' democratic rule. The latter undoubtedly feared that in future, a socialist majority in the Reichstag might enact legislation which would do permanent damage to middle-class interests or undermine 'national unity' or the role of religion in public life.[18] These concerns were increased with the narrow left-wing victories in state elections in Thuringia (1921), Saxony (1920 and 1922) and Braunschweig (1920 and 1922). To counter this, the Reich President was given extra-ordinary powers under Article 48 to suspend the constitution, dissolve or set aside state governments or the Reichstag, and rule by emergency decree in situations where public order and security were 'seriously endangered', a mechanism exploited on several occasions by Presidents Ebert (1919–25) and Hindenburg (1925–34). Proportional representation, which was already in use in Reichstag elections under the old empire, was also retained in a slightly different form, a factor which, in the new democratic parliamentary system, usually worked to the disadvantage of the left. This is because it allowed negative majorities of bourgeois parties or special interest groups to block the formation of progressive administrations led by the largest party, the SPD (Saxony and Thuringia in the early 1920s were exceptions here, as were the Prussian government headed by the Social Democrat Otto Braun between 1920 and 1932). Admittedly, proportional representation also probably prevented the establishment of a majority National Socialist government in 1932.[19]

Article 48 was itself hugely controversial, not least because at Reich level, it reinforced the inherent dualism between the directly elected Reich President and the indirectly elected Reich Chancellor. Under the new constitution the President (in the eyes of some a substitute monarch) was directly chosen by the people in a ballot which took place every seven years. The Chancellor, on the other hand, was obliged to cultivate the goodwill of the President *and* at least in theory have a working majority in the Reichstag, a challenge not to be underestimated given the levels of mutual hostility between the political parties during the 1920s. Indeed there were no fewer than fifteen chancellors between 1918 and 1933, and the last three before Hitler, Heinrich Brüning, Franz von Papen and Kurt von Schleicher, were entirely dependent on Hindenburg's favour for their continued stay in office, as they lacked sufficient support in the Reichstag. More generally, as George Mosse points out, Article 48 and the emergency law and order decrees issued under it, were about defending the authority of 'the state itself rather than . . . parliamentary democracy', allowing in effect long periods of extra-parliamentary rule should the President be so inclined.[20]

Perhaps the most serious failure of the new constitution, however, was its reluctance to tackle the power of the Reichswehr, the German army, which continued to act as a state within a state, pursuing its own indepen- dent line in foreign and domestic policy without having to account for itself to parliament or to the Chancellor of the day – and without having formally to recognise the new republican regime. One early indication of this was the Reichswehr's support for the Soviet Union during the Polish-Soviet war of 1920–1, which laid the basis for secret German rearmament in alliance with the Red Army in later years. Indeed, while the civilian governments of the day officially took a neutral stance, at least until the signing of the Treaty of Rapallo in April 1922, the reorganised general staff (now known as the *Truppenamt* or troop office) saw a revival of Russian power as in Germany's best interests. Or, as General Hans von Seeckt, the head of the *Truppenamt*, put it in a memorandum in February 1920, on the eve of the Polish-Soviet war:

Only in firm cooperation with a Great Russia will Germany have the chance of regaining her position as a great power . . . Britain and France fear the combination of the two land powers and try to prevent it with all their means – hence we have to seek it with all our strength . . . Whether we like or dislike the new Russia and her internal structure is quite immaterial.[21]

At home, however, the Reichswehr's political interventions were almost entirely against the left. Thus over 1,000 working-class demonstrators were killed in skirmishes with government security forces and right-wing militia groups in Berlin in March 1919, and in the spring of 1919 and again in January 1920 military action was used to compel striking workers in the Ruhr and central Germany to return to work.[22] Ebert's policy, as Reich President, was to back the army and the representatives of law and order in every instance, even when their use of force was clearly excessive. His main motive appears to have been an exaggerated fear of Bolshevism, combined with a concern that the Reich as a whole might fall apart or descend into civil war if the strike wave continued. Following the Kapp Putsch in March 1920, however (see below) even he could no longer hold onto Defence Minister Noske, who was dismissed for counter-revolutionary activities and replaced by the DDP politician Otto Gessler.[23] The crushing of the subse- quent left-wing rebellion in the Ruhr in late March and early April 1920 again cost in excess of 1,000 workers' lives, many of whom were shot after surrendering: 208 Reichswehr members and 41 policemen were also killed, and 123 Reichswehr soldiers were reported missing.[24] Other serious injuries and deaths occurred in related prison riots where 'highly politicized inmates were pitched against reactionary governors and warders', including a mass break-out of jailed radicals at Brandenburg penitentiary on 28 March 1920.[25]

Meanwhile Ebert's harsh clampdown on strikes and workers' councils was arguably a key factor in the dramatic fall in the SPD's share of the national vote in the June 1920 Reichstag election, from 37.9 to 21.7 per cent, and the simultaneous rise in support for the USPD, from 7.6 to 17.9 per cent.[26] The propaganda of the extreme left, and its skilful exploitation of the resentments felt by many workers towards the new regime, nonetheless also played a part.

The extreme left

On 18 May 1919, a few days after the publication of the Allied peace terms at Versailles and subsequent protests in the German National Assembly at Weimar, the German Communist Party (KPD) presented a new revolutionary programme under the title 'Basic Principles of Peace'. The programme is interesting not because it had any basis in reality, but because of what it tells us about the mentality of the extreme left at this time. In it, the party advocated neither acceptance nor rejection of the Allied peace terms, as both options would bring 'endless misery' to the German proletariat. Acceptance would mean that the socio-economic foundations of German militarism and imperialism would be spared so that the west could use the Reich in its battle against the Soviet Union, leading sooner or later to war. Rejection would mean foreign occupation and economic subjugation to 'Entente capitalists'. Thus:

The only possible and unavoidable solution is the overthrow of this government and of bourgeois rule altogether, and the establishment of a proletarian dictatorship . . . and so participation in the world revolution.[27]

In the violent atmosphere of the immediate post-war era, Leninist-style world revolution certainly appeared, to some at least, as a distinct possibility. Budapest, for instance, also experienced a short-lived Soviet republic in the period March to August 1919. In Italy large-scale strikes and factory occupations broke out in 1919 and again in 1920, involving hundreds of thousands of workers. In the Soviet Union itself civil war raged between Reds and Whites from 1918 to 1920 while in Germany, the USPD – at its March 1919 congress in Berlin – devised a new left-wing programme which essentially endorsed public ownership of industry and the idea of the 'dictatorship of the proletariat'.[28]

Even so, as Hans Mommsen argues, most militant workers in Germany in 1919–20 were more interested in food, working conditions and wages than in utopian politics. In spite of the antipathy towards the MSPD which state repression caused, there were frequent calls for the reunification of the two main social democratic parties (SPD and USPD) and a recognition that 'socialization had less to do with restructuring property rights than with . . . eliminat[ing] arbitrary rules in the factories' and enforcing the eight-hour day.[29] It is therefore a misnomer to depict the Weimar Republic as a 'democracy between Lenin and Hitler', as Ernst Nolte has done.[30] In fact, in spite of their revolutionary rhetoric, neither USPD nor KPD succeeded in gaining control of the strike movement or steering it in a particular political direction. Furthermore, the KPD remained tiny, with only 106,656 members in the autumn of 1919, and a mere 66,323 by the autumn of 1920.[31] At this stage it was even being threatened by the emergence of a new, more radical splinter party, the KAPD or Communist Workers' Party, which was founded in April 1920 and was even admitted to the Comintern – the Moscow-based Third International – in November of that year.[32]

Meanwhile, the actions of Noske and his allies in the Reichswehr pushed more and more alienated workers towards the left, while the actions of Lenin and Trotsky in Russia pushed most of the moderate USPD leaders, including Bernstein and Kautsky, back towards the idea of coalition or fusion with the MSPD. Thus according to the 'centrist' Kautsky, writing in late 1919, the Bolshevik regime had created a 'new class' of bureaucratic functionaries which 'gradually appropriated to itself all actual and virtual control, and transformed the freedom of the workers into a mere illusory freedom'.[33] A victory for Lenin in the civil war would, he predicted, come only at the expense of the freedom and material well-being of ordinary workers:

The Bolsheviks of necessity were responsible for civil war and, as a result also of necessity, for the abolition of the Soldiers' Councils. The Bolshevik dictatorship has reduced these Workmen's Councils to mere shadows, by taking away . . . all their most important functions, and even their right of election of their own officers. As in former days these latter are now appointed by the Government; and since the volunteers are not sufficient, they have had recourse to compulsory recruiting, as in the times before Bolshevism existed. This forms another object of conflict between the population and the Government. Numerous peasant revolts have their origin in this, and it also makes imperative an increase in the army. Desertions in whole numbers belong to the order of the day, and they are punished by mass executions.[34]

The unexpected success of the Soviet Union in driving back the Poles and reaching the gates of Warsaw in early August 1920 sent alarm bells ringing across Europe, not least in Berlin, where even socialists and trade unionists feared that 'Moscow intended the Red Army to proceed from conquered Poland into Germany and there help its sympathizers [to] seize power'.[35] Nor were these fears without justification. Indeed, on 10 August the Soviet authorities ordered German communists living in Russia to be sent to the front in Poland, and on 14 August Trotsky instructed the Comintern to draw up leaflets in German to distribute to the local population in anticipation of a Red Army advance into Reich territory.[36] The danger only passed with the Polish counter-attack on 16–17 August, leading to the 'miracle of the Vistula' and eventual Soviet withdrawal from the whole of Polish territory.

The German government had of course been in no position to aid Poland, militarily or politically, even if it had wanted to. Neutrality was its only option. Moreover, as we have seen, there were even some in the new Reichswehr – and on the nationalist and counter-revolutionary right – who had secretly hoped for a Soviet victory as a means of weakening Poland and the Entente more generally.[37] The threat of communism was nonetheless still being exaggerated, largely for domestic purposes. Only in 'Red' Saxony did the different left-wing parties come together in a united front against the threat of right-wing reaction. The result was the formation of a minority socialist coalition of SPD and USPD after the state election of November 1920, a coalition which was also 'tolerated' by the KPD – but not by its radical offshoot, the ultra-left KAPD – until September 1922.[38]

The one area of real strength for the KPD, in fact, was the Halle-Merseburg region in Central Germany, although here too it had to compete with the KAPD.[39] In March 1921 the two parties joined forces to launch an ill-fated armed revolt (known as the 'March Action') which began in Merseburg and the nearby Mansfeld mining district, with support from 10,000 dock workers in Hamburg.[40] However, unlike the fighting in the Ruhr in March 1920, this was no mass proletarian uprising but an ill-disguised coup attempt planned by the Comintern in Moscow and the KPD *Zentrale* in Berlin, against the advice of former party leader Paul Levi.[41] When the joint KPD-KAPD call for a general strike across Germany on 24 March failed to attract significant support, the local armed rebellions in Mansfeld and at the Leuna chemical works near Merseburg were quickly crushed by forces loyal to the SPD-led Prussian government, leading to 145 civilian and 35 police deaths, as well as 6,000 arrests.[42]

Meanwhile, at Reich level the USPD finally split in October 1920 over the question of joining the Comintern, with a majority, including future East German leaders like Walter Ulbricht and Franz Dahlem, voting to merge with the KPD at a special unity conference in December.[43] A much smaller USPD, with a power base in Saxony, continued in existence until September 1922, when it in turn voted to reunite with the MSPD.[44] Only after this did the KPD become a mass-based party of protest against the SPD and the moderate left. By September 1923 it had acquired 294,230 new members, largely due to its prominent role in organising workers' resistance to the French occupation of the Ruhr, and had become the largest communist party outside the Soviet Union.[45]

However, the party's success was short-lived. Its nadir came in the aftermath of a series of failed uprisings in Saxony, Thuringia and Hamburg in the autumn of 1923, causing membership to fall to 121,394 by April 1924, a position from which it failed to recover until the early 1930s.[46] In May 1924 it won only 12 per cent of the vote and 62 seats in the Reichstag election, falling back to 45 seats in the December 1924 election with 9 per cent of the vote. This could be compared with the 17.9 per cent won by the USPD in 1920.[47] From 1925, under a new leader, Ernst Thälmann, the KPD increasingly followed the Soviet model of democratic centralism, adopting a hard-line, Stalinist viewpoint and expelling dissident members, including the leftists Werner Scholem, Arthur Rosenberg and Karl Korsch in 1926/7, and the rightists Heinrich Brandler and August Thalheimer in 1928.[48]

In spite of these purges and schisms, the KPD continued to develop as the main voice of the extreme left, with a significant presence in the factories, in workers' sports and gymnastics associations and within the left-wing arts scene.[49] Party newspapers like *Arbeiter Illustrierte Zeitung* and *Rote Fahne* had a mass readership, and promoted popular youth cultures, workers' theatre and the profile of artists like John Heartfield.[50] In other ways, too, the party developed a leading role in the public spheres of Weimar Germany, for instance through its backing for the referendum to dispossess the former royal houses without compensation in June 1926,[51] or through its support for the campaign to legalise abortion in the late 1920s and early 1930s.[52] Yet all this was combined with a continued commitment to revolutionary activity on the streets, including violent confrontations with the police, fascist parties and even representatives of the SPD and Free Trade Unions.[53] Indeed, as Eric Weitz puts it, in spite of developing a myriad of other activities, the KPD always pushed 'harsh physical engagement' to the top of its agenda, helping to forge a 'party culture that venerated male physical prowess as the ultimate revolutionary quality'.[54]

Violent clashes with the state, for instance during the famous 'Blutmai' encounters with the police in Berlin on 1–3 May 1929, as well as memories of the murders of Liebknecht and Luxemburg in 1919, were also clearly crucial in reinforcing divisions on the left.[55] However, another important factor was that communists continued to blame the SPD leadership for supporting the war in 1914, and for undermining the strikes of 1917 and 1918. In many ways, indeed, the vote for war credits in the Reichstag on 4 August 1914 was seen as the original act of 'betrayal', and explains why – in spite of their cooperation on other issues, such as the 1926 referendum on dispossession of former royal houses – the SPD and KPD were unable to mount a joint campaign against the tide of 'revisionist' or 'heroic' war memory which hit Germany in the latter half of the 1920s and into the early 1930s. In short, the KPD accused the SPD of abandoning its revolutionary traditions in 1914, while the SPD denounced the KPD as 'unpatriotic' or as a tool of Moscow. These bitter accusations also continued to divide the German left in the very different atmosphere of the Cold War era after 1945.[56]

The anti-republican right

One of the most striking facts about the revolution of November 1918 is that even the most convinced monarchists appeared to accept the inevitability of political change and the need to move forward in new directions.[57] Nobody, it seemed, not even out and out reactionaries, wanted the Kaiser himself back. The mood in military and naval circles was best summed up by Admiral Albert Hopman, a close confidante of Admiral von Tirpitz, who wrote in his diary on 6 October 1918:

Everything which I predicted, not just in the last few weeks, but for much, much longer, has come true. What Germany has sinned in the last three decades it must pay for. It was politically paralysed through its blind faith in [and] its slavish submission to the will of a puffed-up, vainglorious and self-overestimating fool.[58]

Many traditional conservatives also blamed Wilhelm personally for the paralysis in Germany's wartime leadership, and in particular for the failure to devise a fair and equitable system of rationing.[59] His actions in fleeing to the Netherlands, rather than engaging in a heroic *Königstodesritt* ('death–ride') destroyed his reputation forever. As the *Kreuzzeitung*, the chief organ of Prussian conservatism, wrote on 9 November 1918: 'The dream of a German Kaiser is over [*ausgeträumt*], the splendour and world position of the German empire destroyed.'[60] For the next twenty-two-and-a-half years, until his death in August 1941, Wilhelm lived the life of an exile, first at Amerongen, then at Huis Doorn, unable to come to terms with his own responsibility for the fatal decisions which led to war in 1914 and defeat in 1918.[61] None of the various schemes for the restoration of the Prussian monarchy had the slightest chance of success, even if the links between monarchist and fascist circles are revealing in other ways.[62]

Even more surprising than the almost complete abandonment of traditional monarchical feeling by the conservative right and the military in November 1918 is the fact that the middle classes at first seemed to accept the end of the *Kaiserreich* with hardly a murmur.[63] The most depressing aspect of the November revolution, according to one of its critics, the military historian Hans Delbrück, was the sudden loss of the 'courage and feeling of duty that once created Prussia and the German empire'.[64] Catholics of course continued to back the Catholic Centre Party or its Bavarian equivalent, the BVP, which was anti-Prussian and socially very conservative. Among the Protestant middle classes, however, the size of the vote for the left-leaning, pro-Weimar DDP in January 1919, at 18.5 per cent, is remarkable in view of its collapse just eighteen months later.[65] The people, it seemed, really did want a new beginning and not just a change at the top. Thus it is noteworthy that the middle-class *Bürgerräte* (citizens councils) elected in some German towns and cities at the end of 1918 voiced anti-monarchical sentiments, even while calling for a citizens' alliance against the left.[66] In Nördlingen in Bavaria a local justice official and National Liberal summed up the mood within non-socialist circles at the end of 1918 when he wrote that 'a truly free referendum' would 'decisively reject the monarchy and endorse a people's state'.[67]

Even so, the old right soon re-emerged in a new guise, and gained increased support from those sections of the middle class who were frightened by the working-class militancy evident in the strike waves of 1919–20, or angered by the harsh terms imposed on Germany under the Treaty of Versailles. One major indication of this was the gradual rise in support for the right-wing parties, the DNVP and DVP, from modest showings in the January 1919 election to more solid results in the Reichstag poll of June 1920 and in various state elections.[68] Another, more worrying indication was the Kapp Putsch of March 1920, the first concerted effort by the forces of reaction to overthrow the new republic by force. Among the more disturbing features of this event was the neutral position adopted by the Reichswehr, which failed to support the republic against an illegal coup attempt, and the widespread sympathy which Kapp evoked within the DNVP, the successor to the old German Conservative Party.[69]

The coup itself was led by Wolfgang Kapp, an ex-civil servant from East Prussia and co-chairman of the Fatherland Party in 1917, and General Walther von Lüttwitz, Reichswehr commander in the Berlin region. It was sparked off when the Weimar coalition government ordered the disbanding of a local *Freikorps* unit, the Ehrhardt marine brigade, a move resisted by Lüttwitz on the grounds that this would leave the Reich capital 'defenceless' against the left. On 13 March 1920, acting under Lüttwitz's orders, a 6,000-strong division of the Ehrhardt brigade marched on Berlin, occupied government buildings and proclaimed a military dictatorship with Kapp as Reich Chancellor and Traugott von Jagow, the wartime chief of police in Berlin, as Interior Minister. The government responded by ordering the regular army to suppress the rebellion, an order which was refused by the head of the *Truppenamt*, Hans von Seeckt, on the grounds that 'a split within the Reichswehr had to be avoided at all costs'.[70]

As the government fled, first to Dresden and then to Stuttgart, the SPD executive issued an appeal endorsed by President Ebert which called upon its supporters to bring down the coup leaders by means of a general strike. With Berlin paralysed by a mass walk-out of ordinary workers and employees, the coup collapsed within five days, and Kapp and Lüttwitz, fearing arrest on charges of high treason, fled to Sweden.[71] Only von Jagow was captured and later sentenced to five years in jail, a rather lenient punishment when compared to those handed down to left-wingers convicted of treason or other politically motivated acts of violence – some of whom even faced the death penalty.[72] Meanwhile, Hans von Seeckt and other senior Reichswehr commanders were left in post by the new SPD-led administration under Hermann Müller, seemingly untouchable in the face of left-wing demands for their resignation. Seeckt was even promoted to the new position of head of Army Command (*Chef der Heeresleitung*) on 25 March 1920, in spite of his failure to protect the republic in its hour of need.[73]

One individual who arrived in Berlin too late to witness the end of the Kapp Putsch in 1920 was Adolf Hitler, then a part-time soldier and leader of a new radical right-wing party in Munich, the National Socialist German Workers' Party (NSDAP). Significantly, Hitler was sent to Berlin, together with his party colleague Dietrich Eckart, by his former boss in the intelligence branch of the Bavarian army, Captain Mayr, to inform Kapp of the developing situation in Bavaria.[74] Here, under the cover of the Kapp Putsch, a new authoritarian government had also been installed under Gustav Ritter von Kahr, who was something of an old-fashioned Bavarian separatist with strong anti-republican and anti-socialist leanings. Henceforth Bavaria was to become a stronghold of right-wing reaction in Germany, and a haven for extremists on the run from the police in social democratic Prussia in the north.[75]

Hitler himself left the army at the end of March 1920 to embark on a full-time career as a political agitator. His chief asset was his gifts as a speaker, which enabled the party to attract hundreds of new recruits in the beer halls of Munich in the early 1920s.[76] But even then, the National Socialists were just one of many far-right groupings and individuals in Bavaria at this time. Other influential organisations included the rabidly anti-Semitic *Germanenorden*, the occultist Thule Society and the *Aufbau* circle, made up of White Russian and Baltic German emigrés who had fled their homes in the aftermath of the Bolshevik revolution.[77] What distinguished these groups from other nationalist parties, and from the Reichswehr, was their belief in a 'Judeo-Bolshevik' world conspiracy, and their desire to destroy not only the 'Versailles system' and the 'Marxist' Weimar Republic, but also the Soviet Union, whose lands and territories would become new 'living space' for future generations of 'Aryan' Germans.[78] Calling themselves the *Deutscher Kampfbund* ('German combat league') these different bodies and individuals came together in November 1923 to take part in a violent attempt to overthrow the government of Bavaria, for which Hitler, as one of the putsch's leaders, received a short jail sentence. Ludendorff, the other key conspirator, was acquitted.[79]

In north Germany, meanwhile, a number of other racist and extreme right-wing groups were beginning to emerge. Among them was the *Deutschvölkischer Schutz- und Trutzbund* (German Völkisch Defence and Defiance League) (DVSTB), established in September 1918 and with its main base in Hamburg, albeit with a significant presence in all major German towns and cities. By the time of its dissolution in June/July 1922, indeed, it claimed to have between 160,000 and 180,000 members, organised in up to 600 different local branches.[80] Another example would be the *Deutsch-Völkische Freiheitspartei* (German Völkisch Freedom Party) (DVFP), founded in Berlin in 1922 as an anti-Semitic breakaway from the DNVP by the Pan-German Albrecht von Graefe and the extreme nationalist and Anglophobe Count Ernst zu Reventlow.[81] In 1920 Reventlow had been among those on the German right who supported the idea of a Soviet victory over Poland, and in 1923 he briefly flirted with ideas of 'national bolshevism', writing carefully worded articles for the communist *Rote Fahne* in which he praised German workers' resistance to the French occupation of the Ruhr. In 1927 he went over to the NSDAP, and served as one of its Reichstag deputies until 1943, although at first he was associated with the Strasserite 'north German' faction of the party.[82]

While all of these groupings – the NSDAP, the DVFP, the DVSTB and so on – drew most of their support from among the lower middle-classes, the universities also became hotbeds of anti-Semitism and right-wing radicalism in the 1920s, albeit of a more upper-middle class, elitist variety. Nationalist students who rejected the Weimar Republic thus took their ideas from 'conservative revolutionaries' like Oswald Spengler, Ernst Jünger and Arthur Moeller van den Bruck and from pre-war racist ideologues like Houston Stewart Chamberlain and Paul de Lagarde.[83] Inflated notions of masculinity and physical strength also formed part of their imagined war experience, an experience imbued with an idealised image of the link between soldiering, modern technology and the student volunteers of 1914.[84] The most notorious of their actions was the hounding of the Jewish professor Theodor Lessing from his chair at the Technical University of Hanover in 1925, a move which the university administration and the Prussian state authorities failed adequately to oppose.[85]

Finally, in spite of their previous and ongoing hostility towards women's emancipation and female suffrage, both the conservative and the *völkisch* right became increasingly adept during the 1920s at mobilising women for its causes.[86] An early foretaste of this had already been seen in the German Fatherland Party in 1917, which opened its doors to female membership and indeed reached the point in May 1918 when one third of its recruits were women.[87] After the dissolution of the Fatherland Party in late 1918, some right-wing women went into the middle-class DNVP or DVP parties and associated charities or housewives organisations,[88] while others joined looser nationalist associations such as the *Deutscher Frauenausschuss zur Bekämpfung der Schuldlüge* (German Women's Committee for the Struggle Against the War-Guilt Lie) or the *Frauenbund der Deutschen Kolonialgesellschaft* (Women's League of the German Colonial Society).[89] Women were also prominent in the many 'pilgrimages' undertaken by right-wing organisations to visit ethnic Germans forced to live under 'foreign' (i.e. Polish) rule under the Versailles peace settlement.[90]

In fact, Hitler's National Socialists, in refusing to allow women to stand as parliamentary candidates, formed something of an exception in right-wing circles. Yet even this party recruited women as ordinary members, including Elsbeth Zander, who founded the militantly pro-Nazi *Deutscher Frauenorden* (German Women's Order) in Berlin in 1923.[91] Other prominent right-wing women who developed strong Nazi sympathies included Käthe Schirmacher, a former progressive and suffrage campaigner turned virulent anti-Polish nationalist, and Guida Diehl, leader of the ultra-conservative *Neulandbewegung* (New Land Movement).[92]

Meanwhile, the more respectable conservative right was hardly damaged at all by its association with the Kapp Putsch, or by accusations from the left that its extreme nationalist propaganda had encouraged the murders of Erzberger and Rathenau in 1921–22. On the contrary, the DNVP increased its share of the national vote from 10.3 per cent in January 1919 to 15.1 per cent in June 1920, 19.5 per cent in May 1924 and 20.5 per cent in December 1924.[93] This was in spite – or maybe because of – its overt hostility to the republic and its espousal of heroic narratives of the war at odds with the reality of military defeat in 1918.[94] As with the Catholic Centre Party, a larger than average proportion of its votes came from middle-class women, doubtless due to its association with the Protestant Church.[95] In some states, such as Mecklenburg-Schwerin and Mecklenburg-Strelitz, it became the dominant political force, and in others, such as Braunschweig and Thuringia after 1923, it joined forces with the DVP and other groups to form an anti-socialist 'bourgeois bloc' (*Bürgerblock*) which prevented the left from retaining power. Yet it was only in the very different atmosphere of the years 1925–6 and 1927–8 that the party entered coalition governments at Reich level, in this sense responding, somewhat uncomfortably and uneasily, to the broader move towards 'bourgeois unity' which had also enabled Hindenburg's election as Reich president against the republican candidate Wilhelm Marx in April 1925.[96]

Germany in the early 1920s: a violent society?

As historical writing on the early Weimar Republic moves away from a focus on parties and personalities, on missed opportunities and failed revolutions, towards questions of experience, identity and memory, a key question has become whether the war experience itself helped to create a more violent, conflict-ridden or racist society.[97] Here opinions have differed. In the 1970s and 1980s George Mosse led the way in showing how the First World War was a key moment in what he termed the 'nationalisation of the masses', foreshadowing the emergence of fascism and the Third Reich after 1933. Important symbols – in particular the 'cult of the fallen soldier' – were used to generate new emotions and hatreds, particularly in defeated nations like Germany, where such ideas were monopolised by the conservative and radical right rather than by supporters of the republican system.[98]

An example here would be the famous Langemarck myth, based on the exploits of a group of German student volunteers at Langemarck, Belgium, in November 1914, who – according to the legend – 'stormed the enemy trenches and took them, singing "Deutschland, Deutschland über alles"'.[99] These patriotic students were then 'remobilised' in the 1920s as a powerful symbol of the wartime spirit of self-sacrifice and youthful heroism which was allegedly betrayed during the November revolution. Or, as one right-winger put it: 'Before the Reich covered its face in shame and defeat, those at

Langemarck sang . . . and through the song with which they died, they are resurrected.'[100] Indeed, the bitterness that dealing with symbols of the war aroused in Germany was such that, in contrast to Britain and France, there could be no agreement on the construction of a national memorial to honour the unknown war dead until the early 1930s. *Volkstrauertag*, the day of mourning for fallen soldiers established in 1925, was also marked by separate commemorations organised by rival veterans associations, in spite of regular appeals for unity.[101]

Mosse's ideas have been backed by more recent studies looking, for instance, at the legacy of violence in occupied territories or at intolerance towards former POWs, civilian deportees and refugees held within Germany itself.[102] After the Soviet government renounced the Treaty of Brest-Litovsk on 13 November 1918, for instance, distrust of former Russian POWs, who were viewed as either communist agitators or simply as unworthy competitors for food, housing and jobs, became widespread; some 900,000 were repatriated in the space of two months, before the western Allies intervened to put a halt to this practice.[103] Galician and Ukrainian Jews who fled to Germany during the First World War or the Russian civil war were also regarded with hostility and suspicion, largely for the same reasons. Berlin in November 1923 even experienced two days of violent anti-Semitic riots directed mainly at the so-called 'Ostjuden' (Eastern Jews) who lived in the narrow streets of the impoverished Scheunenviertel, close to Alexanderplatz.[104]

Meanwhile, hatred of the former enemy again became very important following the shock of the strict terms imposed by the Allies at Versailles, particularly in relation to disarmament and reparations. For instance right-wing propagandists, together with extreme nationalist veterans' leagues such as the *Stahlhelm, Bund der Frontsoldaten*, made much of the 'black horror' on the Rhine, a reference to the use of African soldiers in the French occupation army in western Germany, which was deemed to be a particular affront to European cultural values.[105] Yet even communists used anti-Western and especially anti-French nationalism as a powerful symbol of masculinised proletarian resistance during the Franco-Belgian occupation of the Ruhr in 1923.[106] Anti-Semitism also reared its head, with communist hardliners like Ruth Fischer seeking to outbid extreme right-wingers like Count Reventlow in denouncing 'Jewish capital' as the lackey of French imperialism and the enemy of German workers.[107]

On a deeper level, the Ruhr invasion really brought home to all Germans that they had been defeated in the war. Yet at the same time, it also highlighted the role of the French occupation, and other border struggles such as

PLATE 3.2 Theo Matejko, 'Hände weg vom Ruhrgebiet!' (Hands off the Ruhr!), poster produced in 1923.

Source: Deutsches Historisches Museum, Berlin

those with Poland over Upper Silesia and Danzig, as sites of permanent cultural and political remobilisation for the imagined wars of the future.[108] Across the political spectrum, the situation of German people living on the border areas was presented as being 'unbearable', a constant reminder of the injustices of the peace settlement.[109] For right-wing women activists like Käthe Schirmacher, the loss of parts of Upper Silesia to Poland in 1921 was even akin to the loss felt by a mother when one of her children dies:

Pride and motherliness rise up against the handover of German territory wherever it may be. We are Germania, who cannot bear the loss of any of her children. We suffer with Upper Silesia, our hearts our burning . . . Burning land needs burning hearts! To the Upper Silesian front, oh burning hearts of German women![110]

More generally, there was an internalisation of violence in all European societies as a result of the war and post-war conflicts. As Michael Biddiss writes, 'the toll of lives [lost in the war] was literally incalculable' so that people became used to estimating deaths in terms of 'the odd million'.[111] In the German case, the cultural historian Bernd Widdig also draws an interesting parallel between wartime violence and the hyperinflation of the years 1922–3, when the currency – like life itself – could be debased simply by adding zeros to the end of figures. Both the war and the hyperinflation, he argues, led to 'an enormous redistribution of wealth' which was 'not directly linked to specific classes or milieus but proceed[ed] rather arbitrarily'.[112] Both events also replaced pre-war values – thrift, sobriety, business acumen – with the notion of the gambler's luck, and brought into sharp relief the 'centrality of money' in the construction of modern cultural identity.[113] In particular, inflation represented a 'modernity out of bounds':

Things lose their uniqueness and become part of the mass, everything has its monetary value, all culture is levelled so that it too can join the hectic and ceaseless circulation of goods and services which characterises the modern world.[114]

Finally, inflation, like war, defeat and military occupation, was linked to the degradation of women, whose bodies – at least in the artistic and cultural representations of the day – became mere commodities, to be bought and sold, used and abused, in accordance with male desires and fantasies.[115] Indeed, women were often demonised in popular and high culture after the war. They were accused of either starting or prolonging the conflict, out of a perverse 'feminine' blood-lust, or of having stabbed the army in the back through strikes and demonstrations on the home front.[116] Rosa Luxemburg in particular was held up by the German right as an example of 'female', as well as 'Jewish' treachery, and as the ultimate symbol of the Red Woman Fighter, a 'monstrosity' that had to be 'annihilated'.[117] Her brutal killing by members of the *Freikorps* in January 1919 represented a significant breach in previous thresholds of political violence. During the inflation years, too, women were depicted as symbols of the rampant consumerism and sexual excess which was allegedly undermining the fabric of the nation (or, on the left, the ideological purity of the party).[118] The theme of 'Lustmord' (sexually motivated murder/violation of female corpses) appeared frequently in the work of left-wing male artists like George Grosz and Otto Dix, as will be discussed in more detail in Chapter 5.[119]

So was Germany overall a violent society in the early 1920s?

Undoubtedly in defeated nations like Germany (and even in victorious ones like Italy) there were problems with what John Horne refers to as an 'ultra-militarised masculinity', especially among groups of young men who refused to accept that the war was over.[120] Those members of the Ehrhardt brigade who fought against the Bavarian Soviet Republic in 1919 and who later took part in the Kapp Putsch in 1920 stand out in particular as a destructive and untamable element.[121] However, there is still a question mark over how representative their views were of war veterans in general. More recently, a number of historians have questioned the extent of brutal-isation in Germany in the 1920s, and of the failure to demobilise from wartime mindsets. In the big cities, for instance, the largest veterans' organisation was the social democratic *Reichsbund der Kriegsbeschädigten, Kriegsteilnehmer und Kriegshinterbliebenen* (Reich Association of War Dis-abled, War Veterans and War Dependants), and its ideology was decidedly pacifist, or at least anti-war. Membership of this body peaked at 830,000 in 1922, over twice the number who joined the *Freikorps*.[122] The re-publican *Reichsbanner Schwarz-Rot-Gold* organisation, founded in 1924, also contained between one and two million war veterans who viewed right-wing nationalism with the greatest suspicion. The Langemarck myth certainly did not represent their version of the war experience.[123]

The two main lobby groups for ex-POWs, the *Reichsvereinigung ehemaliger Kriegsgefangener* (ReK), and its sister organisation, the *Volksbund zum Schutze der deutschen Kriegs- und Zivilgefangenen*, were likewise largely non-partisan, if rather conservative, in approach. Over one million German soldiers had spent time in enemy captivity, and the process of repatriation, especially from France and Russia, was long, drawn-out and painful. Even so, the ReK, unlike the Stahlhelm and other veterans' leagues, studiously avoided polit-ical point scoring or recourse to extreme nationalist politics, and instead sought to reintegrate ex-prisoners into the nation through a moderate pro-gramme based on ideas of a common *Volksgemeinschaft* linking Germans of all classes and political creeds.[124] In the meantime, the Swedish Red Cross nurse Elsa Brändström, known to ex-prisoners as the 'Angel of Siberia' because of her wartime work among German and Austrian POWs in Russia and her post-war efforts on behalf of POW orphans, also served as an import-ant symbol of national unity and reconciliation. As the diarist Count Harry Kessler put it, she became in the 1920s the paragon of a 'secular saint': 'What is so profoundly moving about her is not that she saved thousands of lives, but the faith of these thousands in humanity.'[125]

Finally, in the countryside, as Benjamin Ziemann has shown in his study of southern Bavaria, the desire for post-war normalisation was even more apparent, and there was little evidence of any desire for further radical changes in line with left- or right-wing ideologies. Demobbed soldiers were simply pleased to have survived the war, and were keen to benefit as much as they could from the new economic opportunities resulting from the dismantling of wartime price controls. They were willing to fight the communists in Munich and elsewhere, but not if it meant sacrificing their lives or livelihoods. They were also willing to tolerate the SPD-led government and the republic, but only for as long as its policies did not overtly favour urban consumers over rural producers. True, 'some elements of the peasant mentality, such as monarchism, were thrown overboard in the wake of the war', but on the whole, 'continuity outweighed change'.[126]

So was post-war German society really brutalised by the war? The answer to this question in part depends on whether one views German soldiers as victims or as perpetrators, or as both, as Robert Nelson has recently argued.[127] Of course, the dominant discourses of the post-war era depicted German soldiers as both victims (of international and domestic treachery) and as heroes who had made great sacrifices for the nation in its hour of need. The idea of the stab in the back became hegemonic in post-war culture – partly because even Social Democrats sometimes connived at the suppression of alternative anti-war discourses. Or, as Richard Bessel puts it:

Whatever had actually taken place in the trenches or on the way back home in 1918 and 1919, it is clear that the image of the heroic soldier – who had experienced 'that pure and noble comradeship which is generated only in war' – and then was allegedly stabbed in the back by an ungrateful home-front – remained intact for millions. This image was reflected in political discussion throughout the Weimar period, from the ill-judged but politically necessary welcome given by Friedrich Ebert to returning soldiers in Berlin in early December 1918, when he declared that they had been undefeated on the battlefield, to the propaganda of the Nazi party.[128]

On top of this, the sheer number of veterans among the electorate discouraged all political parties, including even the communists, from denying the heroic status of the ordinary front-line soldier. The Communists' paramilitary organisation actually called itself the *Roter Frontkämpferbund* (RFB) or Red Front Fighters' League, a deliberate allusion to the experience of the First World War.[129] Yet the existence of such discourses should not blind us to the fact that ordinary soldiers could be participants too, not only in war crimes, but also in post-war myth-making. Thus in the 1920s the denial of German war guilt came from the bottom as well as from the top, from rank and file ex-servicemen and local veterans' organisations as well as from the former commander-in-chief, President Hindenburg.[130] The same applies to the denial of rising levels of domestic violence towards women noted in

Chapter 2, although the evidence for this is, by the very nature of the crimes it deals with, necessarily incomplete. Soldiers' letters, for instance, reveal husbands and wives missed each other and longed to be reunited. However, divorce and illegitimacy rates also rose in the post-war era with wartime marriages particularly vulnerable to breakdown.[131] All in all, the idea of a harmonious return to family life after 1918 is difficult to sustain.[132]

Even so, if one scratches the surface, to get at the attitudes of ordinary men and women, rather than the minority involved in extremist politics, it does seem that anti-war attitudes were still very prevalent in the early 1920s. On 31 July 1921, for instance, more than 500,000 demonstrators, including 200,000 in Berlin, joined the anti-militarist protests which marked the seventh anniversary of the outbreak of the war.[133] The popularity of women artists such as Käthe Kollwitz, and the universality of bereavement which she depicted through the figure of the mourning mother and the grieving parents, would be a further illustration of the sombre mood during this time.[134] Only in the very different atmosphere of the late 1920s and early 1930s did *political* views of the war become more polarised, as paramilitary groups like the Reichsbanner, the Stahlhelm, the SA and the Red Front fought each other, often murderously, for primacy in the streets. This is also a theme we shall return to in Chapters 5 and 6.

Notes

1   Bessel, *Germany After the First World War*, pp. 114 and *passim*.

2   Cf. Richard Evans, *The Coming of the Third Reich* (London, 2003), p. 81.

3   George L. Mosse, 'The Brutalization of German Politics', in idem., *Fallen Soldiers*, pp. 159–81.

4   Bessel, *Germany After the First World War*, pp. 56 and 107–8.

5   Cf. Gerald D. Feldman, 'The Origins of the Stinnes-Legien Agreement: A Documentation', *Internationale wissenschaftliche Korrespondenz zur Geschichte der deutschen Arbeiterbewegung*, 19/20 (1972), pp. 45–102.

6   See esp. Haffner, *Die verratene Revolution, passim*.

7   Carsten, *Revolution in Central Europe*, esp. pp. 150, 153–3, 165.

8   Ibid., pp. 107, 252; Mommsen, *The Rise and Fall of Weimar Democracy*, p. 46.

9   Richard Grunberger, *Red Rising in Bavaria* (London, 1973), esp. pp. 128–9.

10 Winkler, *Die Sozialdemokratie und die Revolution von 1918/19, passim*.; idem., *Von der Revolution zur Stabilisierung, passim*.; Peter-Christian Witt, *Friedrich Ebert: Parteiführer, Reichskanzler, Volksbeauftragter, Reichspräsident* (Bonn, 1987).

11 Winkler, *Weimar*, p. 46.

12 Conan Fischer, 'A Very German Revolution? The Post-1918 Settlement Re-Evaluated', *Bulletin of the German Historical Institute London*, XXVIII/2 (2006), pp. 6–32 (here p. 32).

13 Bessel, *Germany After the First World War*, pp. 195–219; Ziemann, *War Experiences*, pp. 191–209.

14 Wolfgang J. Mommsen, 'The German Revolution, 1918–1920: Political Revolution and Social Protest', in W. J. Mommsen, *Imperial Germany 1867–1918. Politics, Culture and Society in an Authoritarian State* (London, 1995), pp. 233–54 (here p. 254).

15 Mommsen, *Max Weber and German Politics*, esp. pp. 332–89.

16 Sebastian Ullrich, 'Mehr als Schall und Rauch: Der Streit um den Namen der ersten deutschen Demokratie 1918–1949', in Moritz Föllmer and Rüdiger Graf (eds), *Die 'Krise' der Weimarer Republik: Zur Kritik eines Deutungsmusters* (Frankfurt/M, 2005), pp. 187–207 (here pp. 189–95).

17 Winkler, *Weimar*, p. 105.

18 Mommsen, *The Rise and Fall of Weimar Democracy*, pp. 58–60.

19 A. J. Nicholls, *Weimar and the Rise of Hitler*, 4th edition (New York, 2000), pp. 39–40.

20 Mosse, 'The Brutalization of German Politics', p. 172.

21 Carsten, *The Reichswehr and Politics*, p. 68.

22 Winkler, *Weimar*, p. 76; Weitz, *Creating German Communism*, p. 96.

23 Nicholls, *Weimar and the Rise of Hitler*, p. 71.

24 Winkler, *Weimar*, pp. 134–5.

25 Wachsmann, 'Between Reform and Repression', pp. 413–14.

26 Mommsen, 'The German Revolution', p. 253.

27 Fritz Klein, 'Versailles und die deutsche Linke', in Gerd Krumeich with Silke Fehlemann (eds), *Versailles 1919. Ziele – Wirkung – Wahrnehmung* (Essen, 2001), pp. 314–22 (here p. 318).

28 Julius Braunthal, *History of the International, vol. 2: 1914–1943* (London, 1967), p. 176.

29 Mommsen, *The Rise and Fall of Weimar Democracy*, p. 49.

30 Ernst Nolte, *Die Weimarer Republik. Demokratie zwischen Lenin und Hitler* (Munich, 2006).

31 Weitz, *Creating German Communism*, p. 97.

32 Ibid., p. 95; Winkler, *Weimar*, p. 152; Ben Fowkes, *Communism in Germany under the Weimar Republic* (London, 1984), p. 54.

33 Karl Kautsky, *Terrorism and Communism*, translated by W. H. Kerridge (London, 1919). Available online at http://www.marxists.org/archive/kautsky/1919/terrcomm/index.htm

34 Ibid.

35 Richard Pipes, *Communism. A Brief History* (London, 2001), p. 93.

36 Adam Zamoyski, *Warsaw 1920. Lenin's Failed Conquest of Europe* (London, 2008), p. 102.

37 Mommsen, *The Rise and Fall of Weimar Democracy*, pp. 103–4; Braunthal, *History of the International*, vol. 2, pp. 185–6, n. 3.

38 Szejnmann, *Vom Traum zum Alptraum*, pp. 33–9; William Carl Matthews, 'The Rise and Fall of Red Saxony', in Barclay and Weitz (eds), *Between Reform and Revolution*, pp. 293–313 (here pp. 296–9).

39 Weitz, *Creating German Communism*, p. 103.

40 Fowkes, *Communism in Germany*, pp. 63–8.

41 Ibid., p. 64; Winkler, *Weimar*, p. 153; Braunthal, *History of the International*, vol. 2, p. 226. Levi was later expelled from the party after publicly describing the *Zentrale's* decision to launch the 'March Action' as an 'anarchist adventure' in a pamphlet published in April 1921 – see Fowkes, *Communism in Germany*, pp. 69–70.

42 Winkler, *Weimar*, pp. 153–4.

43 Weitz, *Creating German Communism*, p. 98; Mario Frank, *Walter Ulbricht. Eine deutsche Biografie* (Berlin, 2001), pp. 60–1. The enlarged KPD was for a time known as the United Communist Party or VKPD.

44 Szejnmann, *Vom Traum zum Alptraum*, p. 34.

45 Fowkes, *Communism in Germany*, p. 205; Berger, *Germany*, p. 125.

46 On the 'failed October' of 1923 see Szejnmann, *Vom Traum zum Alptraum*, pp. 39–46; Matthews, 'The Rise and Fall of Red Saxony', pp. 300–2; Fowkes, *Communism in Germany*, pp. 91–109; and Harald Jentsch, *Die KPD und der 'Deutsche Oktober' 1923* (Rostock, 2005). For membership figures see Fowkes, *German Communism*, p. 205.

47 Kolb, *The Weimar Republic*, p. 224.

48 For a useful overview of developments in the KPD after 1925 see Kevin McDermott, 'Hermann Webers Konzept der "Stalinisierung" der KPD und der Komintern. Eine kritische Bewertung', *Jahrbuch der Historischen Kommunismusforschung* (2008), pp. 197–206.

49 Eric D. Weitz, 'Communism and the Public Spheres of Weimar Germany', in Barclay and Weitz (eds), *Between Reform and Revolution*, pp. 275–91.

50 On Heartfield and the *AIZ* see Willett, *Art and Politics in the Weimar Period*, pp. 179 and *passim*.

51 Fowkes, *Communism in Germany*, p. 137.

52 On the campaign to overturn Paragraph 218 of the Reich Penal Code, which outlawed abortion, see Cornelie Usborne, *The Politics of the Body in Weimar Germany* (London, 1992), pp. 156–201, and Chapter 4 below.

53 Eve Rosenhaft, *Beating the Fascists? The German Communist Party and Political Violence, 1929–1933* (Cambridge, 1983).

54 Weitz, *Creating German Communism*, p. 7.

55 On the 'Blutmai' see Chris Bowlby, 'Blutmai 1929. Police, Parties and Proletarians in a Berlin Confrontation', *Historical Journal*, 29/1 (1986), pp. 137–58. Also Chapter 5 below.

56 See Stibbe, 'Fighting the First World War in the Cold War', *passim*. On the revitalisation of 'heroic' views of the war in the late 1920s and early 1930s see also Chapters 5 and 6 below.

57 Peter Fritzsche, 'Breakdown or Breakthrough? Conservatives and the November Revolution', in Larry Eugene Jones and James Retallack (eds), *Between Reform, Reaction and Resistance. Studies in the History of German Conservatism from 1789 to 1945* (Providence, RI, 1993), pp. 299–328.

58 Cited in John C. G. Röhl, *The Kaiser and his Court: Wilhelm II and the Government of Germany* (Cambridge 1996), p. 27.

59 Fritzsche, *Germans into Nazis*, p. 110.

60 Cited in Axel Schildt, *Konservatismus in Deutschland. Von den Anfängen im 18. Jahrhundert bis zur Gegenwart* (Munich, 1998), p. 131.

61 Röhl, *Wilhlem II. Der Weg in den Abgrund*, pp. 1247–1326; Willibald Gutsche, *Ein Kaiser im Exil. Der letzte deutsche Kaiser Wilhelm II. in Holland* (Berlin, 1991).

62 See the two items in note 61 above and Willibald Gutsche, 'Monarchistische Restaurationsstrategie und Faschismus. Zur Rolle Wilhelms II. im Kampf der nationalistischen und revanchistischen Kräfte um die Beseitigung der Weimarer Republik', in Röhl (ed.), *Der Ort Kaiser Wilhelms II.*, pp. 287–96.

63 Smith, *A People's War*, esp. pp. 194–5.

64 Hans Delbrück's testimony to the Reichstag's committee investigating the causes of the German collapse, cited in Schivelbusch, *The Culture of Defeat*, p. 360, n. 36.

65 Kolb, *The Weimar Republic*, pp. 224–5. The DDP's vote was already down to 8.3 per cent in June 1920, and slid even further in subsequent elections, to just 1 per cent in the July and November 1932 polls.

66 Smith, *A People's War*, p. 195.

67 Fritzsche, *Germans into Nazis*, pp. 109–10.

68 Kolb, *The Weimar Republic*, pp. 224–5.

69 Carsten, *The Reichswehr and Politics*, pp. 71–99.

70 Mommsen, *The Rise and Fall of Weimar Democracy*, p. 82.

71 The most detailed study is Johannes Erger, *Der Kapp-Lüttwitz Putsch. Ein Beitrag zur deutschen Innenpolitik, 1919/20* (Düsseldorf, 1967).

72 Richard J. Evans, *Rituals of Retribution. Capital Punishment in Germany, 1600–1987* (London, 1996), p. 489.

73 Gordon A. Craig, *The Politics of the Prussian Army, 1640–1945* (Oxford, 1955), pp. 382–3; Carsten, *The Reichswehr and Politics*, p. 92.

74 Ian Kershaw, *Hitler, 1889–1936: Hubris* (London, 2000), p. 153.

75 On Bavaria, and especially Munich, in the 1920s see Large, *Where Ghosts Walked, passim.*

76 Membership of the NSDAP grew from 55 in 1919 to 3,000 in 1921 and 55,000 in 1923. See Michael H. Kater, *The Nazi Party. A Social Profile of Members and Leaders, 1919–1945* (Oxford, 1983), p. 254.

77 Reginald Phelps, 'Before Hitler Came. Thule Society and *Germanenorden*', *Journal of Modern History*, 25/3 (1963), pp. 245–61; Michael Kellogg, *The Russian Roots of Nazism. White Emigrés and the Making of National Socialism, 1917–1945* (Cambridge, 2005).

78 See Barbara Miller Lane and Leila J. Rupp (eds), *Nazi Ideology Before 1933. A Documentation* (London, 1978).

79 On the failed Beer Hall Putsch see Large, *Where Ghosts Walked*, pp. 157–94, and Kershaw, *Hitler*, pp. 169–219.

80 Uwe Lohalm, *Völkischer Radikalismus. Die Geschichte des Deutschvölkischen Schutz- und Trutzbundes 1918–1923* (Hamburg, 1970), pp. 90 and 93.

81 Ibid., pp. 269–70; Schildt, *Konservatismus in Deutschland*, p. 151.

82 On Reventlow see Kershaw, *Hitler, 1889–1936*, p. 297, and Conan Fischer, *The German Communists and the Rise of Nazism* (London, 1991), pp. 63, 72 and 78–9.

83 On the influence of these thinkers see Fritz Stern, *The Politics of Cultural Despair. A Study in the Rise of the Germanic Ideology* (Berkeley, CA, 1961); Jeffrey Herf, *Reactionary Modernism. Technology, Culture and Politics in Weimar and the Third Reich* (Cambridge, 1984); and Rolf Peter Sieferle, *Die konservative Revolution. Fünf biographische Skizzen* (Frankfurt/M, 1995).

84 Ulrich Herbert, 'Generation der Sachlichkeit. Die völkische Studentenbewegung der frühen zwanziger Jahre' (1991), reproduced in Herbert, *Arbeit, Volkstum, Weltanschauung. Über Fremde und Deutsche im 20. Jahrhundert* (Frankfurt/M, 1995), pp. 31–58.

85 Anette Schröder, *Vom Nationalismus zum Nationalsozialismus. Die Studenten der Technischen Hochschule Hannover von 1925 bis 1938* (Hanover, 2003), esp. pp. 38–43.

86 The most comprehensive study is Christiane Streubel, *Radikale Nationalistinnen. Agitation und Programmatik rechter Frauen in der Weimarer Republik* (Frankfurt/M, 2006). See also Kirsten Heinsohn, 'Im Dienste der deutschen

Volksgemeinschaft: Die "Frauenfrage" und konservative Parteien vor und
nach dem Ersten Weltkrieg', in Ute Planert (ed.), *Nation, Politik und Geschlecht.
Frauenbewegungen und Nationalismus in der Moderne* (Frankfurt/M, 2000),
pp. 215–33; and Christiane Streubel, 'Raps Across the Knuckles: How Right-
Wing Women Showed "True National Behaviour" in German Newspapers', in
Ingrid Sharp and Matthew Stibbe (eds), *Aftermaths of War. Women's Movements
and Individual Activists, 1918–1923* (forthcoming).

87 Stibbe, 'Anti-Feminism', pp. 199–203; Hagenlücke, *Deutsche Vaterlandspartei*,
pp. 184–5.

88 See Raffael Scheck, 'German Conservatism and Female Political Activism in the
Early Weimar Republic', *German History*, 15/1 (1997), pp. 34–55; and idem.,
Mothers of the Nation. Right Wing Women in Weimar Germany (Oxford, 2004).
Also Nancy R. Reagin, *Sweeping the Nation. Domesticity and National Identity in
Germany, 1870–1945* (Cambridge, 2007); idem., *A German Women's Movement.
Class and Gender in Hanover, 1880–1933* (Chapel Hill, NC and London, 1995);
Renate Bridenthal, ' "Professional" Housewives. Stepsisters of the Women's
Movement', in Renate Bridenthal, Atina Grossmann and Marion Kaplan (eds),
When Biology Became Destiny. Women in Weimar and Nazi Germany (New York,
1984), pp. 153–73; and Bridenthal, 'Organized Rural Women and the
Conservative Mobilization of the German Countryside in the Weimar
Republic', in Jones and Retallack (eds), *Between Reform, Reaction and Resistance*,
pp. 375–405.

89 Andrea Süchting-Hänger, 'Die Anti-Versailles-Propaganda konservativer Frauen
in der Weimarer Republik – Eine weibliche Dankesschuld?', in Krumeich with
Fehlemann (eds), *Versailles 1919*, pp. 302–13; Raffael Scheck, 'Women against
Versailles. Maternalism and Nationalism of Female Bourgeois Politicians in the
Early Weimar Republic', *German Studies Review*, 22/1 (1999), pp. 21–42; Raffael
Scheck., *Mothers of the Nation*, pp. 117–30; Lora Wildenthal, 'Mass-Marketing
Colonialism and Nationalism: The Career of Else Frobenius in the "Weimarer
Republik" and Nazi Germany' in Planert (ed.), *Nation, Politik und Geschlecht*,
pp. 328–45.

90 Elizabeth Harvey, 'Pilgrimages to the "Bleeding Border". Gender and Rituals
of Nationalist Protest in Germany, 1919–1939', *Women's History Review*, 9/2
(2000), pp. 201–28.

91 For the Nazi attitude to the 'woman question' in the 1920s see Matthew Stibbe,
Women in the Third Reich (London, 2003), pp. 16–21 and *passim*.

92 On Schirmacher see Anke Walzer, *Käthe Schirmacher. Eine deutsche
Frauenrechtlerin auf dem Wege vom Liberalismus zum konservativen Nationalismus*
(Pfaffenweiler, 1991); and on Diehl, Silvia Lange, *Protestantische Frauen auf dem
Weg in den Nationalsozialismus: Guida Diehls Neulandbewegung 1916–1935*
(Stuttgart, 1998).

93 Kolb, *The Weimar Republic*, pp. 224–5.

94 Annelise Thimme, *Flucht in den Mythos. Die Deutschnationale Volkspartei und die Niederlage von 1918* (Göttingen, 1969).

95 For a detailed investigation of the impact of female suffrage on Weimar elections see Julia Sneeringer, *Winning Women's Votes. Propaganda and Politics in Weimar Germany* (Chapel Hill, NC and London, 2002) Some interesting figures on female voting patterns are also provided in Gabriele Bremme, *Die politische Rolle der Frau in Deutschland. Eine Untersuchung über den Einfluß der Frauen bei Wahlen und ihre Teilnahme in Partei und Parlament* (Göttingen, 1956), Table IV, pp. 243–52.

96 Peter Fritzsche, *Rehearsals for Fascism. Populism and Political Mobilization in Weimar Germany* (Oxford, 1990), pp. 10 and 151–65.

97 Cf. Belinda Davis's review article 'Experience, Identity and Memory', *passim*.

98 George L. Mosse, *The Nationalisation of the Masses. Political Symbolism and Mass Movements in Germany from the Napoleonic Wars through to the Third Reich* (New York, 1975).

99 Mosse, 'The Cult of the Fallen Soldier', p. 70.

100 Ibid., pp. 72–3.

101 Ibid., pp. 97–8; Berger, *Germany*, pp. 118 and 128; Bernd Ulrich and Benjamin Ziemann (eds), *Krieg im Frieden. Die umkämpfte Erinnerung an den Ersten Weltkrieg* (Frankfurt/M, 1997), pp. 138–9.

102 Becker, *Oubliés de la grande guerre*, *passim*; Liulevicius, *War Land on the Eastern Front*, *passim*; Nelson, 'German Comrades – Slavic Whores', *passim*.

103 Nachtigal, 'The Repatriation and Reception of Returning Prisoners of War', p. 169.

104 David Clay Large, ' "Out with the Ostjuden": The Scheunenviertel Riots in Berlin, November 1923', in Christhard Hoffmann, Werner Bergmann and Helmut Walser Smith (eds), *Exclusionary Violence. Antisemitic Riots in Modern German History* (Ann Arbor, MI, 2002), pp. 123–40. For a further discussion of these riots see also Chapter 5 below.

105 Keith L. Nelson, 'The "Black Horror on the Rhine". Race as a Factor in Post-World War I Diplomacy', *Journal of Modern History*, 42 (1970), pp. 606–27; Volker Berghahn, *Der Stahlhelm. Bund der Frontsoldaten 1918–1935* (Düsseldorf, 1966).

106 Berger, *Germany*, p. 125; Conan Fischer, *The Ruhr Crisis, 1923–1924* (Oxford, 2003), esp. pp. 168–9 and 198–9; Fischer, *The German Communists*, pp. 41–69.

107 Peter Pulzer, *The Rise of Political Anti-Semitism in Germany and Austria*, 2nd edition (London, 1988), p. 294; Fischer, *The German Communists*, pp. 59–60.

108 John Horne, 'Kulturelle Demobilmachung 1919–1933. Ein sinnvoller historischer Begriff?', in Wolfgang Hardtwig (ed.), *Politische Kulturgeschichte der Zwischenkriegszeit 1918–1939* (Göttingen, 2005), pp. 129–50 (here p. 150).

109 Cf. Streubel, 'Raps Across the Knuckles', *passim*.

110 Harvey, 'Pilgrimages to the "Bleeding Border"', p. 212.

111 Biddiss, *The Age of the Masses*, p. 184.

112 Bernd Widdig, *Culture and Inflation in Weimar Germany* (London, 2001), p. 14.

113 Ibid., pp. 24, 54 and 128–9.

114 Ibid., p. 213.

115 Theweleit, *Male Fantasies*, *passim*; Nelson, 'German Comrades – Slavic Whores', *passim*.

116 Ingrid Sharp, 'Blaming the Women: Women's "Responsibility" for the First World War' in Fell and Sharp (eds), *The Women's Movement in Wartime*, pp. 67–87.

117 Cf. Elizabeth Harvey, 'National Icons and Visions of Modernity. Asserting and Debating Gender Identities in New National Contexts', in Johanna Gehmacher, Elizabeth Harvey and Sophia Kemlein (eds), *Zwischen Kriegen. Nationen, Nationalismen und Geschlechterverhältnisse in Mittel- und Osteuropa, 1918–1939* (Osnabrück, 2004), pp. 305–15 (here p. 308). Also Theweleit, *Male Fantasies*, esp. vol. 1: *Women, Floods, Bodies, History*.

118 Widdig, *Culture and Inflation*, pp. 196–220.

119 Maria Tatar, *Lustmord. Sexual Murder in Weimar Germany* (Princeton, NJ, 1995).

120 Horne, 'Masculinity in Politics and War', p. 33.

121 Theweleit, *Male Fantasies*, *passim*; Liulevicius, *War Land on the Eastern Front*, *passim*; Kellogg, *The Russian Roots of Nazism*, pp. 78–108; Barth, *Dolchstoßlegenden und politische Desintegration*, pp. 229–54; Bernhard Sauer, 'Vom "Mythos eines ewigen Soldatentums". Der Feldzug deutscher Freikorps im Baltikum im Jahre 1919', *Zeitschrift für Geschichtswissenschaft*, 43/10 (1995), pp. 869–902.

122 Bessel, *Germany After the First World War*, p. 258; Ulrich and Ziemann (eds), *Krieg im Frieden*, p. 110.

123 Cf. Ziemann, 'Republikanische Kriegserinnerung', esp. pp. 389–98. Also Ziemann, 'Germany after the First World War – A Violent Society?', pp. 83–4; Ulrich and Ziemann (eds), *Krieg im Frieden*, esp. pp. 94–5, 112–18 and 171–2; Berger, *Germany*, p. 128.

124 On the ReK see Rainer Pöppinghege, ' "Kriegsteilnehmer zweiter Klasse"? Die Reichsvereinigung ehemaliger Kriegsgefangener 1919–1933', *Militärgeschichtliche Zeitschrift*, 64/2 (2005), pp. 391–423; and Heather Jones, 'The Enemy Disarmed. Prisoners of War and the Violence of Wartime. Britain, France and Germany, 1914–1920', Ph.D dissertation, Trinity College, Dublin, 2005, Chapter 7.

125 Count Harry Kessler, *The Diaries of a Cosmopolitan, 1918–1937*, translated and edited by Charles Kessler (London, 1971), pp. 282–3 (diary entry for 22 February 1926).

126 Ziemann, *War Experiences*, p. 273.

127 Nelson, ' "Ordinary Men" in the First World War?', *passim*.

128 Bessel, *Germany After the First World War*, p. 263.

129 Rosenhaft, *Beating the Fascists?*, *passim*.

130 Horne and Kramer, *German Atrocities*, pp. 375–400 and esp. pp. 385–6.

131 Benjamin Ziemann, 'Geschlechterbeziehungen in deutschen Feltpostbriefen des Ersten Weltkrieges' in Christine Hämmerle and Edith Saurer (eds) *Briefkulturen und ihr Geschlecht. Zur Geschichte der privaten Korrespondenz vom 16. Jahrhundert bis heute* (Vienna, 2003), pp. 261–8; Ziemann, *War Experiences*, pp. 155–66; Bessel, *Germany After the First World War*, pp. 231–2.

132 Cf. Ute Frevert, *Women in German History. From Bourgeois Emancipation to Sexual Liberation* (Oxford, 1998), p. 186.

133 Verhey, *The Spirit of 1914*, p. 210.

134 Claudia Siebrecht, 'The *Mater Dolorosa* on the Battlefield – Mourning Mothers in German Women's Art of the First World War', in Heather Jones, Jennifer O'Brien and Christoph Schmidt-Supprian (eds), *Untold War. New Perspectives in First World War Studies* (Leiden, 2008), pp. 259–91.

CHAPTER 4

Economy and Society in the 1920s

Hyperinflation, as we saw in the previous chapter, is inextricably linked with the popular image of Germany in the early 1920s. Legends abound of people using worthless banknotes as wallpaper to decorate their houses, or of the man who fell victim to thieves after leaving a wheelbarrow full of money outside a shop; when he returned he found his money was still there but the wheelbarrow was gone. Yet by the time such tales were in popular circulation, Germans had already experienced almost ten years of constant price rises. Some historians therefore prefer to speak of the 'inflation decade', 1914–1923/4, as marking a distinct era in its own right.[1] The figures indeed speak for themselves. In July 1914 one US dollar was worth 4.2 Marks, in January 1919 8.9 Marks, in January 1920 64.8 Marks, and eighteen months later, in July 1921, 76.7 Marks. After this things grew even worse. In January 1922 one dollar bought 191.8 Marks, in July 1922 493.2 Marks, in January 1923 17,972 Marks, in July 1923 353,412 Marks and in September 1923 almost 99 million Marks. On 15 November 1923 things hit rock bottom when the dollar stood at 4,200 billion old Marks.

Of course, inflation and hyperinflation are not quite the same thing. Inflation can be defined as 'the state of an economy in which prices are steadily rising, resulting in a steady fall in the value of money',[2] a process which had already begun during the war and continued thereafter. In the early post-war period there was even something of a consensus between big business, the unions and the state that high levels of inflation might be a good thing, at least for jobs, exports and debt reduction.[3] Hyperinflation, on the other hand, which arrived in Germany from July 1922, is

inflation that is so rapid as to move uncontrollably towards a radical breakdown in the monetary system and the complete collapse of all long-term expectations

TABLE 4.1 US dollar quotations for the Mark; selected dates for 1914 and 1919–23

July 1914	4.2
January 1919	8.9
July 1919	14.0
January 1920	64.8
July 1920	39.5
January 1921	64.9
July 1921	76.7
January 1922	191.8
July 1922	493.2
January 1923	17,972.0
July 1923	353,412.0
August 1923	4,620,455.0
September 1923	98,860,000.0
October 1923	25,260,208,000.0
November 1923	4,200,000,000,000.0

Source: Paul Bookbinder, *Weimar Germany. The Republic of the Reasonable* (Manchester: Manchester University Press, 1996), p. 255.

concerning price, so that in a very short time money is no longer effective as a medium of exchange.[4]

The latter situation had serious consequences, not only for Germany's relations with other countries, but also for industrial production, which fell by 34 per cent in 1923,[5] and for the lives of ordinary citizens. Regarding external relations, the suspicion remained that German financiers and government ministers had deliberately allowed the situation to get out of hand in order to prove the impossibility of meeting the Allies' demands for reparations. Defaults on payments led, eventually, to the Franco-Belgium occupation of the Ruhr in January 1923 and to an international crisis which came to an end only with the introduction of a new German currency, the *Rentenmark*, in November 1923, and to a revision of reparations under the Dawes Plan in 1924.[6]

In this chapter, however, our primary concern will be with the impact of the era of hyperinflation and subsequent currency restabilisation on the German domestic economy, and also on German society more generally, starting with the implications for big business, labour and the state.

Big business, labour and the state

Marxist historians in East Germany often claimed that the Weimar Republic was a tool of big business, which had an automatic power of veto over government policy.[7] Certainly there is some evidence of this. The onset of war had seen a growing identification of interests between capital and the state, for instance through the formation of the *Kriegsausschuß der Deutschen Industrie* and other industrial cartels, and this trend continued into the post-war, and especially the post-inflation era.[8] As Richard Overy, a non-Marxist British historian, puts it, in the 1920s

amalgamation was most marked in the iron and steel, chemicals and electrical industry. The consolidation of the country's three largest chemical firms in IG Farben-Industrie AG in 1925, the formation of Vereinigte Stahlwerke AG (United Steel) in 1926, and the pre-war development of the electrical giant Siemens & Halske, produced three of the four largest concerns in the world.[9]

Yet it is also important to differentiate quite clearly between the various branches of industry, and not to treat the entire sector as an undifferentiated whole. Big business was far from united in terms of its goals, and this necessarily put limits on its ability to influence events in both the economic and the political arenas.

Thus some export-oriented industries and representatives of high finance were quite pro-Western in outlook and were interested principally in restoring overseas trade with Britain and America after the conclusion of peace.[10] If a parliamentary republic was the only means of achieving this, then the Kaiser and the old Imperial order had to go. Examples here would include the former colonial secretary Bernhard Dernburg, who briefly served as Finance Minister in the Scheidemann cabinet from April to June 1919, and the Hamburg banker Max Warburg, who acted as an advisor to the German delegation at Versailles during the same period.[11] During the war they had opposed unrestricted submarine warfare and had donated funds to humanitarian organisations like the *Auskunfts– und Hilfsstelle für Deutsche im Ausland und Ausländer in Deutschland*.[12] After 1918 they tended to orientate themselves towards the DDP, the German Democratic Party, which was largely internationalist in foreign policy terms (although it strongly opposed the Treaty of Versailles and had withdrawn from the government coalition in June 1919 in protest against it).[13] Admittedly the DDP's electoral support fell quite dramatically after 1919, and as it became less popular, it also became more open to populist and anti-democratic/anti-Western ideas, eventually joining forces with the 'Young German Order' in 1930 to create the proto-fascist State Party (*Staatspartei*).[14] Only the DDP's 'extreme left', as Hans Mommsen puts it, remained loyal to the values of internationalism.[15]

Heavy industry – which was represented through the right-wing DVP and DNVP parties – was much more authoritarian and nationalistic in attitude from the outset, although it too could be flexible and pragmatic when

PLATE 4.1 Hugo Stinnes, c.1920   Source: Hulton Archive/Getty Images

it wanted to be.[16] The classic example would be Hugo Stinnes, the Ruhr iron and steel magnate, co-author of the Stinnes-Legien agreement in November 1918, and DVP Reichstag deputy from 1920 to 1924, who was widely reckoned to be the richest, and therefore the most powerful man in Germany in the early 1920s.[17] In particular, the inflation, and then hyperinflation, of the post-war period allowed him to pile up hitherto unimaginable levels of wealth by borrowing to invest in new factories, newspapers or shipping businesses and then paying his creditors back in worthless currency at a later date. By the time of his death in April 1924 he was said to own shares in around 1,650 companies, and was described by the London *Times* as 'one of the greatest financial geniuses of his age'.[18]

After 1919 Western observers often identified Stinnes as the leading proponent of German 'revanchism' and as a threat to the stability of the Versailles peace settlement as a whole. Thus as a member of the team of experts sent to Spa in July 1920 to negotiate with the Allies over the question of coal deliveries to France, he advocated a hard-line, non-compliant stance which won him plaudits in the nationalist press and strong criticism abroad.[19] In May 1921 he also called for a repudiation of the London ultimatum, which set a final figure on reparations and a heavy schedule of payments, backed by Allied threats to occupy the whole of the Ruhr should Germany refuse.[20] Left-wing historians, on the other hand, have more often seen him as a cynic rather than an idealist or patriot, a man who 'judged that it was initially best to compromise and to collaborate with the SPD' and the Allies – and to distance himself from the Kapp Putsch – while secretly funding shadowy right-wing groups like the Anti-Bolshevik League.[21]

In fact, Stinnes' primary concern was to save Ruhr industry from the threat of high taxation, state regulation, Allied confiscation, or – worse still – nationalisation in the post-war period. This meant pursuing a policy of timely concessions to the moderate trade unions in order to sideline the more radical factory councils. It also meant adopting a pragmatic approach to the question of increased wage demands, which anyway could easily be met by borrowing money and speculating against the Mark. However, Stinnes was less keen on the eight-hour day, something that he was only willing to concede under the pressure of circumstances and on the understanding that other capitalist nations were also likely to follow suit in the near future. When the latter failed to happen, he and other Ruhr industrialists like Reusch, Thyssen, Springorum, Vögler and Kirdorf, began actively campaigning for more flexible, i.e. longer, working hours.[22] Often they linked this to the reparations issue on the grounds that Germany's current international disadvantage made it an 'economic and national priority' to increase production and export levels as the only realistic means of liberating the country from the heavy burdens imposed under the peace settlement.[23] In this way, too, the Allies, rather than German business or the German right, could also be blamed for bringing to an end the 'socialist experiment' of 1918–20, including factory councils and the eight-hour day.[24]

Beyond this, Stinnes' rise to prominence seemed to symbolise the ascent of the new industrialist class during the war and their entry into the corridors of power, where they were now able to rub shoulders with army and naval officers, diplomats, university professors and senior civil servants on more or less equal terms.[25] Stinnes, along with Krupp, Thyssen, Hugenberg and Rathenau, became household names, almost ersatz royalty. They were also a favourite target for left-wing writers and satirists. Stinnes, for instance, appeared in a number of popular cabaret songs, such as the following written by Walter Mehring, Heinrich Mann and Siegfried Vegesack for a political revue in Munich:

Hugo, wo hast du wieder deine Finger drin?	Hugo, what pie is your finger in now?
Hugo, wo hast du wieder deine Finger drin?	Hugo, what pie is your finger in now?
Hugo, wo schaust du Wieder mal so giering hin?	Hugo, where are you looking so greedily now?
Alle deine Taschen sind voll bis an den Rand und du streckst nach überall die gierige Hand.	All your pockets are full to the top And still you stretch your paw without stop.
Kohle! Stahl! Papier! Alles ist schon dein,	Coal! Steel! Paper! All already in your ken.
Und du steckst dir immer neue Sachen ein!	And you constantly stuff new things in!
Ich tu's ja nicht nur wegen des Gewinnes!	I don't do it only for profit!
Ich tu's ja nur als grosser Patriot!	Patriotism's my real motive!
Ich bin ja nur der Hugo Stinnes,	I'm only Hugo Stinnes,
Nur Stinnes, nur Stinnes!	Only Stinnes, only Stinnes!
Friss (oder Stirb!) mein Brot!	Eat my bread, or die![26]

The Weimar constitution of course guaranteed freedom of speech and opinion under Article 118, thus allowing such criticisms of public figures to be made in the name of art or political agitation. Even so, newspapers – in the 1920s still the dominant means of communicating political ideas and opinions – fell increasingly under the direct or indirect control of big business, which in turn often placed restrictions on their editorial independence. This applied in particular to the local and provincial press, which had a wider circulation than the national newspapers, and, being almost wholly reliant on advertising for its income, was much more vulnerable to fluctuations in the economy. During the hyperinflation of 1922–3, 300 newspapers disappeared altogether, but many more 'slipped . . . into financial dependence on big business and heavy industry', as Modris Eksteins puts it. In the process they often had to abandon their previous party political affiliation for a superficially non-partisan, but usually right-wing stance, particularly on matters of 'national interest' such as reparations and revision of the Treaty of Versailles.[27]

One of the most sophisticated political operators here was Alfred Hugenberg, a director of the Krupp armaments firm in Essen and controller of the Scherl publishing house, who from 1917 created a number of investment-loan companies to rescue – and in practice control – provincial newspapers facing financial difficulties due to the war and the post-war inflation crisis. In theory such newspapers would remain independent. However, in practice it was automatically understood that editors support- ing pro-republican or left-wing political views would have to go. The same applied to newspapers directly owned by Scherl, such as the *Berliner Lokal- anzeiger, Der Tag* and *Die Woche*. After 1928, in his new role as chairman of the DNVP, Hugenberg helped to organise the referendum against the Young Plan in 1929 (see Chapter 6 this volume), and increasingly promoted a sympathetic attitude towards the Nazis in the right-wing provincial press. Already in 1927 he had acquired a majority stake in the Universum Film Company (UFA), the largest film-making enterprise in Germany. In 1933, finally, he brought the DNVP into a direct alliance with the NSDAP and briefly served in the first Hitler cabinet as Minister for Economics, Agriculture and Food, before being forced to resign in June 1933.[28]

Hugenberg and Stinnes apart, however, the direct power and political influence of big business is less easy to pinpoint. Of course, the three most important foreign ministers of the Weimar era, Walther Rathenau (1921–2), Gustav Stresemann (1923–9) and Julius Curtius (1929–31), all came from business backgrounds, and all three aligned themselves with the 'national' liberal parties, Rathenau with the DDP and Stresemann and Curtius with the DVP. Stresemann in particular had a keen sense of the potential role of German economic might in overcoming the military barriers to the Reich's recovery as a European great power. In 1926 he organised the secret acquisi- tion of a substantial holding for the Reich in the influential pro-business newspaper the *Deutsche Allgemeine Zeitung* (DAZ), and used this as a means of propagating the official Foreign Office line against the more overtly nationalist Hugenberg-controlled press.[29] Ideas of a German-dominated Central Europe (*Mitteleuropa*), incorporating Austria, Czechoslovakia, Poland and even the Baltic States 'through the force of "economic neces- sity"' were also very much alive in the pages of the DAZ, paving the way for the abortive attempt at a customs union with Austria in March 1931.[30]

Organisations like the RdI (*Reichsverband deutscher Industrie*, founded in 1919) continued to have considerable leverage in domestic affairs too.[31] Even the SPD had its own economic experts, like Rudolf Hilferding, who served twice as Reich Finance Minister (1923 and 1928–9) and was remark- ably orthodox and pro-business in terms of his policies. In particular he promoted the formation of industrial cartels as a means of accelerating the development of a more 'organised', productive, union-friendly form of capitalism which would gradually evolve into socialism.[32] But after 1923 politics triumphed over economic rationalism. This can be seen, for instance, in the proliferation of right-wing splinter parties claiming to represent particular economic interest groups or simply an anti-tax, anti-union and pro-business agenda.[33] Between them, these parties won 13.9 per cent of the vote in the May 1928 Reichstag election, nearly double what they had achieved in December 1924, while the DDP, DVP and DNVP all saw a decline in support.[34] It can also be seen in the growing division of the RdI into 'moderate', export-oriented and 'extreme' heavy industrial wings, the former favouring a pro-republican stance and 'responsible collaboration' with the SPD, and the latter advocating a hard-nosed authoritarian approach which would reverse some of the social concessions of the early years of the republic.[35] Business was split politically, and as the split widened, so its direct influence on government policy gradually declined.[36]

Meanwhile, in the sphere of industrial relations, the cynical and self-interested pact with the unions, which as late as May 1922 led Stinnes to name one of his ships the 'Carl Legien',[37] did not survive the end of inflation and the relatively high levels of unemployment which continued throughout the late 1920s. True, there was some progress towards greater protection for factory workers through the establishment of a new state-backed system of unemployment insurance and unpaid maternity leave in July 1927, although – as with the eight-hour day – the beneficiaries did not include agricultural labourers, domestic servants, and the long-term unemployed.[38] Rationalisation, defined as the 'application of scientific methods to the production process' in order to achieve more effective control and management of the workforce, also promised much, particularly where it was linked to paternalistic company welfare policies, such as the provision of modern, low-cost housing and other social benefits for employees and their families. An important example here would be the above-mentioned electronics giant Siemens & Halske, which employed over 66,000 workers in Berlin alone in 1925 from its base in Siemensstadt, a desirable and 'high-tech' suburb to the north-west of the city.[39]

Yet at the same time as the rationalisation boom set in, the old, privately arranged ZAG disappeared, and with it the era of consensus in industrial relations. Fear of renewed inflation now dominated government economic policy, to the extent that cooperation with the unions became increasingly difficult. Instead, successive bourgeois coalition governments, anxious to stabilise the new currency, the *Rentenmark*, intervened much more heavily in wage disputes through a new system of compulsory arbitration. The result was to undermine the legitimacy of republican institutions in the eyes of both workers and employers, and to increase the number and the intensity of industrial disputes, as seen in the Ruhr steel lock-out of November

1928. Industrial accidents also rose as workers were expected to produce more in the same period of time and employers sought to cut costs as part of the rationalisation drive.[40] By the end of the 1920s, indeed, a number of industrial leaders, including the chairman of the RdI, IG Farben boss Carl Duisberg, were looking for a more right-wing form of government, one that would do away with union power for good and restore the older employer– employee relationships of the pre-1914 era.[41] The idea of an equal partner- ship between big business, labour and the state, which some democratic politicians had envisaged, albeit rather unrealistically, during the war and in the early years of the Weimar Republic, was now well and truly in abeyance.

The urban poor

It is often thought that the middle classes, and in particular the self- employed, were the main economic victims of the post-war years,[42] but in fact the real losers were the urban poor. During the war and its immediate aftermath, and again at the time of the hyperinflation of 1922–3, infant and maternal mortality rates rose considerably, infectious diseases like tubercu- losis claimed increasing numbers of victims, and the inhabitants of the big- ger cities faced chronic shortages of affordable food, fuel and housing.[43] In 1919 the Quakers opened food kitchens all over Germany, and, according to one account, were responsible for feeding over one million undernourished children whose parents could not afford to support them.[44] War widows, war orphans and disabled ex-servicemen were particularly badly affected by cuts in the state support they received and by the ongoing erosion of the value of their pensions; unlike the fallen soldiers on the battlefield, no monuments were ever built to commemorate their wartime sacrifices or heroism.[45] As the contemporary social investigator Günther Dehm wrote, unemployment was also a 'spectre constantly haunting' the working-class communities of Berlin and other large cities in the post-war years:

If a downturn lasts for a long time it causes severe economic hardship. Relief support is just barely sufficient to pay the rent and procure the essential foodstuffs. If the father has work, then the family more or less gets through it. Things are better if there are grown children who earn money. They usually pay only a very little for board, but mutual support is the rule in emergencies. In other aspects of life, the most important thing is having good clothes.[46]

Dehm's final statement here is particularly relevant to understanding the plight of the tens of thousands of impoverished Germans (and their depen- dants) who were sentenced to prison for minor acts of theft and other crimes of poverty during this period. Thus of the 100 male convicts who were sent to Plötzensee jail in Berlin in 1921, 50 had no shirt, 60 no shoes and 80 no socks.[47] By 1923 the German prison population had itself climbed to an estimated daily average of 100,000, a figure far above the pre-war and even the wartime rates. This, however, proved to be a turning point; by 1929 the number of state prisoners had been halved to around 50,000, partly due to more lenient sentencing policies and partly due to the moderately better economic conditions.[48]

After the currency restabilisation in 1924, real wages rose gradually for those in work, but so too did housing costs and prices for basic goods, especially food and other staples. A study conducted for the trade union journal *Gewerkschaftsarchiv* in 1929 concluded that in comparison to the situation before the war, consumption of milk, butter, cheese, meat, bread, pastries, vegetables, fruit, coffee, tea and chocolate had all fallen in the average urban proletarian household: 'The worker of today has a significantly worse life than in 1907. But his life is not only worse, it is also more expensive.'[49] Meanwhile, those with skilled jobs guarded them jealously against the unskilled. The eight-hour day did not benefit all and caused as much ill-feeling as the benefits it accrued. Employment levels were erratic, even after the stablisation of the Mark. Thus the jobless rate stood at only 7 per cent in 1925, but climbed to 18 per cent in 1926. It fell to 8–9 per cent in 1927 but rose again in the second half of 1928 and throughout the year 1929.[50] Significantly women, and especially young single women, were more likely to be on welfare and unemployment benefits than men, at least in the period before the Great Depression of the early 1930s.[51]

The status of women workers also remained extremely low throughout the Weimar Republic, and during downturns they were often the first to be fired, a policy supported by the state and by the official, male-dominated trade unions.[52] Paid employment after marriage in particular was frowned upon, although many married women were forced to work from economic necessity. Indeed, in the 1925 census one third of all adult women were categorised as wage earners, of whom over half (2.2 million out of 4.2 million) were in poorly paid manual jobs.[53] White-collar work offered some younger working-class women the opportunity for social mobility, and such positions were highly prized by families who could no longer afford to support unmarried and non-wage-earning daughters. However, they were still often seen as a means to an end – marriage – as opposed to an end in themselves: economic independence and job satisfaction.[54] On the other hand, working-class girls who left school early (the vast majority) were more likely to find themselves doing long shifts in dead-end factory jobs for less pay than their male counterparts.[55]

For older married women, washing, cleaning, mending, cooking and childcare took up most of the hours of the day not given over to paid employment. The double burden of housework and factory work took its toll in the form of physical and mental exhaustion, especially as men rarely helped out in the domestic sphere.[56] Admittedly, working-class women, like their middle-class counterparts, were also choosing to have fewer children, a trend which had begun in the late nineteenth century and had even given rise to talk of a 'pregnancy strike' in the immediate pre-war years.[57] Partly to combat this tendency, midwifery was reformed and increasingly profession-alised under a new law in Prussia in 1922, but the state was still far from being in a position to offer adequate standards of care to all pregnant women, and childbirth in the big city tenements was both an agonising experience, and at times a life-threatening one.[58] Family breakdown and the abandonment of wives by their husbands were also commonplace. To cite the contemporary investigator Günther Dehm again:

It is characteristic of the proletarian district that the normal family (father, mother and children from a single marriage) is often not the rule. There are very many premarital and extramarital children in the families. One also finds many foster children, or children being raised by their grandparents. Our poor district also has a lot of widows who have children and are obliged to work.[59]

Contraception, when available, was often expensive, although it was at least accepted by the law. Abortion, by contrast, was illegal, but widespread. Left-wing parties, especially the KPD, campaigned for the removal of Paragraph 218 of the Reich Penal Code of 1871, which made abortion a criminal offence. In their view, the question of women's reproductive rights was a class issue, as the rich could always find a 'sympathetic' doctor to perform a medical abortion, provided they were willing to pay, while the poor were forced into unsafe and illegal back-street terminations, or, indeed, into carrying unwanted pregnancies to term, as Dehm's observations above also suggest. The campaign was supported by some academics and health profes-sionals, and by a number of progressive writers like the medical practitioner Friedrich Wolf, whose drama about a back-street abortion, *Cyankali. § 218*, was first performed in Berlin in 1929 and was made into a film in 1930. However, it was strongly opposed by the churches and the bourgeois parties, who saw abortion as a moral issue or an issue of national importance in view of the declining birthrate more generally.[60] The BDF, the mainstream bour-geois women's movement, for instance, firmly distanced itself from demands for the abolition of Paragraph 218,[61] while Bertha Hindenberg-Delbrück, leader of the Hanover branch of the German Housewives

Association, went even further, holding young women responsible 'for the destruction of unborn life' and for a population loss which 'now exceed[s] all deaths in the Great War'.[62] Meanwhile, only radical sex reform groups, like the *Bund für Mutterschutz*, sought a more 'modern' vision of motherhood through supporting a married woman's right to choose the number of children she had.[63]

Did the poor have a voice of their own? Here the problem is that our image of urban life in 1920s Germany is very much connected with particular cultural representations of the era which tend to glamorise or exploit human suffering for particular political or artistic ends. Otto Dix's paintings of war-wounded beggars and scrawny-looking prostitutes, for instance, or Christopher Isherwood's depiction in his memoir *Goodbye to Berlin* (1939) of the urban slums around Hallesches Tor, where he briefly lodged with the Nowak family, would both be good examples of this. So too would be the famous photograph of a Berlin tenement block (Köpenicker Straße 34/35) during the rent strike of September 1932, which was deliberately manipulated by different newspapers to make it look as if all the tenants were Communists, or Nazis, or a mixture of both. Here, indeed, the poor were reduced to pawns in the coming 'racial' or 'class' struggle; it was the party that claimed the right to determine how they should think, act and feel.[64]

Alternatively the poor were the object of intrusive social workers, midwives and welfare reformers who, for all their enlightened, 'scientific' attitudes and claims to 'expert knowledge', were increasingly inclined to see their clients in negative terms. In Hamburg, for instance, frequent complaints were made by social workers that welfare-dependant mothers were abusing the various maternity benefits they were entitled to, spending the money on themselves or their partners rather than on their children. By contrast 'wealthy and middle-class mothers . . . were often exempted from surveillance and control altogether'.[65] This was a phenomenon that Bertolt Brecht poked fun at in his play *The Threepenny Opera* (1928):

Ihr, die ihr euren Wanst und unsre Bravheit liebt	You lot, who preach restraint and watch your waist as well
Das eine wisset ein für allemal:	Should learn for all time how the world is run:
Wie ihr es immer dreht und wie ihr's immer schiebt	However much you twist, whatever lies you tell
Erst kommt das Fressen, dann kommt die Moral.	Food is the first thing. Morals follow on.[66]

PLATE 4.2 Berlin, Köpenicker Straße 34/35 during the rent strike of September 1932.
Source: Bundesarchiv (Federal Archives) (Bild 146-1970-050-13)

Yet the poor did have a voice of their own – if not over government policies, then at least over the politics and culture of the street, the neighbourhood and the welfare office. Thus David Crew notes that 'Welfare clients often spoke of themselves as victims – of the war, inflation, and the Depression – who were competing with each other for scarce and shrinking welfare benefits.'[67] Frequently their opposition to state welfare policies was expressed by way of individual acts of defiance [*Eigensinn*] – ranging from quite subtle refusal to conform to particular dress codes to acts of violence against welfare officials.[68] In many urban districts, for instance, 'wild cliques' made up of young boys, and less often girls, roamed the streets in search of fun and excitement, provoking fears that the war – by taking away the fathers – had led to an irreversible breakdown in parental authority and control. The activities of these street gangs indeed ranged from symbolic acts of disobedience towards the police and other state authorities to theft and other forms of outright criminality.[69]

Likewise Cornelie Usborne found in her study of criminal abortion trials in Weimar Germany that working-class women who were prosecuted for illegally terminating their own pregnancies often contested the legitimacy of male-dominated court proceedings. They did this either by adopting a 'matter-of-fact', rational approach to abortion as an everyday, 'normal' occurrence, or by refusing to accept 'modern' medico-legal definitions which insisted that menstruation and abortion were mutually distinct and distinguishable events. Instead, as defendants and as women they often claimed to know better than male 'experts' (doctors, policemen, jurists) what the difference was between a 'real' pregnancy and a late period which had had to be induced:

[H]ere is evidence of an alternative language of somatic perception on the part of women which may well originally have been used by more women in their statement[s] but which had subsequently become obscured or entirely obliterated in the course of the police or court interrogations, in which carefully leading questions were asked and women's own accounts were turned into an official abortion narrative. Just occasionally it seems some women's traditional notions and images seeped through to reveal different perceptions.[70]

Implicitly, of course, these women were questioning not only the court proceedings themselves, but also the right of the state to determine what happened to women's bodies more generally. Also being challenged here was the 'ideology of motherhood in religious and conservative circles, according to which pregnancy signified "good hope" . . . and children were always to be celebrated as a blessing . . .'.[71]

However, in spite of these demonstrative acts of *Eigensinn* and individual self-assertion against the dominant discourses of the day, it was equally clear that the urban poor could not fit into the conventional party landscape or form a coherent political narrative of their own, particularly when generational conflicts led to a growing alienation between young and old. In her study of female youth culture in Wedding, a working-class district in Berlin, for instance, Dagmar Reese notes that political campaigns among the young, if they were to have any effect, had 'to correspond to and resonate with a social milieu that was susceptible'.[72] Yet politicians from all parties, including those on the left, frequently dismissed young proletarian women as 'frivolous' and 'flighty', or as too easily distracted by the 'pleasures of consumption' to make them worthy supporters of the cause. Certainly there was no attempt to speak to them on their own terms.[73]

More generally, the SPD had long burned its bridges with the poorest members of society, not least because of its association with Weimar housing and welfare policies, especially at local level, and with the policing of adolescents, political radicals, street-beggars and back-street abortionists in working-class areas.[74] Support for the Communists, on the other hand, was patchy and often veered off towards the Nazis or other extremists, especially in the years 1930–33.[75] Communists in turn tended to have a rather scornful view of the urban poor or what Marx described as the *Lumpenproletariat*. Instead it was left to writers like Brecht, Wolf and Alfred Döblin (*Berlin Alexanderplatz*, 1929) to bring such characters to life through literature aimed at provoking the establishment and criticising bourgeois manners and hypocrisy. The Austrian journalist and writer Joseph Roth likewise championed the cause of the down and out in some of his reports from Berlin, criticising reactionary anti-vagrancy laws which criminalised the homeless with the retort: 'Isn't it rather the case that *finding* accommodation within five days in Berlin these days should be taken as proof of criminality?'[76] Apart from these few examples, however, it was the poor, and not poverty, who were increasingly presented as 'the problem'; and greater discipline or class solidarity as the answer.

The middle classes

While the poor have often been ignored in historiography, the lower middle classes (or Mittelstand) and upper middle classes (academics and independent professionals) are of principal interest to historians of modern Germany because their alienation from the conventional liberal parties (i.e. the DDP and the DVP) as a result of the inflation and other economic pressures is conventionally held to be one of the main long-term causes of the collapse of the Weimar Republic.[77] As Eric Weitz puts it:

To find a skilled worker, perhaps, or a speculator living better than oneself, to discover one's liquid assets reduced to nothing, to be repaid in worthless currency for loans granted to friends, relatives or business associates, to be placed in the demeaning position of waiting in line for hours on end to purchase a loaf of bread – all that was very difficult to accept and became seared into the memory of these people, shaping their behavior for decades to come.[78]

In other words, those of middle-class origin, having initially backed the republic (as seen in the high vote of 18.5 per cent for the DDP in January 1919) turned first to the DNVP, then to anti-republican splinter parties, and eventually to the Nazis, as a protest against the perceived threat of proletarianisation or of being reduced to the ranks of mere wage-earners. Of course they blamed the corporate rich for their misfortune, but they blamed republican politicians, and especially the left and the unions, more.[79] Taxes were allegedly being misspent on social welfare and insurance for 'lazy' unemployed workers, while the middle classes suffered. However, the biggest cause of resentment was the manner in which the *Rentenmark* was created, with little compensation for small savers, investors and retailers who had lost everything during the hyperinflation and the subsequent currency restablisation. By contrast, workers and welfare recipients had supposedly been able to bargain for higher wages and other benefits through mechanisms such as the Labour Courts which replaced the older guild courts. This upset middle-class notions of thrift, 'fairness' and 'hard work'.[80]

Two German social scientists with left-wing sympathies perhaps best caught the anxiety of the times: Theodor Geiger and Hans Speier. In their view, the emergence of fascism was the result of a 'panic in the Mittelstand' arising from what was primarily an imagined as opposed to real decline in their economic position.[81] According to Geiger in particular, the chief material cause for middle-class anxieties lay in the 'rapid increase in the number of lower-level civil servants which was already evident from the turn of the century' and simultaneous fears about the emergence of an 'intellectual proletariat' as the number of people with university degrees also rose.[82] Some 5.3 million white-collar workers faced only 4 million members of the self-employed middle class and professions in the 1925 occupational census.[83] On top of this, the revolution and inflation seemed to have wiped out traditional respect for education and cultivation (*Bildung*) and laid bare the reality of middle-class economic dependency which had previously been concealed by the old-fashioned ideology of the former Imperial regime. For Geiger in particular:

The times have passed when public opinion was shaped by and among the upper middle-class educated elite; this stratum is no longer representative of the national culture. If there is any one element of society which can claim to have declined in terms of significance and social prestige since the previous century, then that fate belongs to the educated classes much more than to the propertied classes.[84]

However, as Geiger also went on to argue, leaving the educated elite aside, the middle class were far from being an undifferentiated whole in 1920s. Instead, he divided them into two distinct groups: the old and the new Mittelstand.

The old Mittelstand, made up of independent craftsmen, tradesmen and shopkeepers, had firmly established values which were rooted in an ideal-ised vision of a pre-industrial past. In spite of suffering to some extent under the effects of increasing state intervention and price controls during the war, in many ways they were beneficiaries of post-war deregulation and the return to a market economy in 1919–20.[85] Yet their prospects were dam-aged in the short-term by the hyperinflation of 1922–3, and in the long-term by increased price competition in the form of mass-produced factory goods sold cheaply through large-scale urban retailers.[86] A key characteristic of the old middle class, indeed, was their self-employed status and their subsequent dependence on the family as the main unit of production:

This trait, which has become even stronger in recent times, has had an extremely important impact on the mentality of this particular group, especially those involved in the handicrafts and in the retail trade. Indeed, between 1907 and 1925 the number of persons listed as economically active in the family business has risen from 3.77 million to 5.44 million.[87]

This in turn gave the old Mittelstand a very strong sense of social identity, based on their rejection of the values of modernity. To cite Geiger again, they were a 'relic of a bygone age whose powers of resistance and moral force should nonetheless not be underestimated'.[88] Indeed, the Nazis too had some problems in penetrating this part of society in the mid- to late-1930s, even though the old Mittelstand were among the most enthusiastic supporters of the party during its rise to power from 1930 to 1933. The result was more passive compliance than active enthusiasm for National Socialist values.[89]

The new Mittelstand, on the other hand, made up of salaried employees, shop workers, lower-level professionals and civil servants, were less rooted in the past and more focused on the present. By 1925, as we have seen, there were 5.3 million of them, compared to only around 1.3 million at the time of the 1907 census.[90] Their sudden rise has been seen as a stark illustration of the pathologies of rapid social mobility in a society ravaged by war, re-volution and constant economic and political uncertainty. Or, as Detlev Peukert puts it, they became an 'ominous symbol of the rationalistic, empty, consumption-dominated world of industrial modernity'.[91] Indeed, in 1930 only 20 per cent of white-collar workers in Germany had fathers who had been employed in the same sector of the economy.[92] Yet paradoxically increased social mobility went hand in hand with a significant loss of job security, even for those employed by the state. Thus many white-collar workers were dismissed between October 1923 and March 1924, when the government slashed civil service posts by up to 25 per cent in an effort to stabilise public finances in the wake of the currency reform.[93] The banking, insurance and financial sectors were also notoriously unstable, dependent as they were on the ups and downs of world trade and the international money markets.

On top of this, increased female competition in the workplace was perceived to have a downward effect on wages: women in white-collar jobs received on average 33 per cent less pay than their male counterparts.[94] Here, indeed, gender inequalities seemed to cut across inequalities of class, so that women from proletarian families often found that it was their sex, rather than their father's occupational background, that was the biggest barrier to career advancement.[95] Those with education often ended up in the expanded, but insecure and badly paid public sector – in jobs like social work, nursing, public administration and teaching – which they were expected to leave upon marriage. On the other hand, women who adopted a male 'work ethic' and sought to rise within their chosen profession were branded as aggressive and 'unfeminine' or, if they were married, as *Doppelverdiener* (dual income-earners) who selfishly kept unemployed men (or single women) out of a job.[96]

More generally, white-collar and public sector work no longer held the status it once did, particularly as it was so interchangeable.[97] Academics likewise found their previously exalted position as the purveyors of *Bildung* or cultural values under threat: 'Many had to sell their libraries, often to foreigners, and professors and students alike took manual jobs on the side in order to maintain their families.'[98] Fears of the creation of an academic proletariat also led many students and university graduates into supporting the Nazis, the DNVP or other racist parties; here the hope was that the introduction of a *numerus clausus* restricting the number of Jews (and women) entering into university system would help to reduce the competition for jobs in certain professions, such as medicine, dentistry and law.[99]

To some extent, Geiger's theories concerning middle-class anxieties have stood the test of time. Yet today historians have also built their own, more complex models for understanding sociopolitical cleavages and milieus in Weimar Germany. In particular, over and above class and occupational divisions, the 'confessional cleavage' is seen as one of the defining social characteristics of the German electorate in the 1920s and beyond.[100] Thus, many Catholics, even those from the new rather than the old Mittelstand, continued to vote for the Catholic Centre Party, or in Bavaria for the BVP (Bavarian People's Party).[101] Academics from Protestant backgrounds generally supported the DVP or DNVP. Those who drifted into the Nazi camp in the early 1930s did so for a variety of complex reasons, but anti-Marxism and for some, anti-Semitism, were important factors.[102]

Moving down the social scale, by the late 1920s the lower middle-class German-National Commercial Employees' Union (*Deutschnationaler Handlungsgehilfenverband* or DHV), which had no formal political allegiance but generally backed the parties of the conservative and moderate right, claimed over 400,000 members, a significant number in political terms.[103] Its message was strongly anti-socialist and anti-feminist, and the majority of its members probably went over to supporting the NSDAP in the early 1930s. Even so, in Protestant cities significant numbers of white-collar workers from proletarian backgrounds continued to back the SPD, which remained the largest party in all the Reichstag elections until 1932, or even the KPD. Indeed, perhaps an equally important phenomenon in the 1920s is that the working class, hitherto tenacious in its loyalties and values, also began to subdivide.[104] Those with aspirations, especially towards the consumer culture and the eight-hour day, might vote for the SPD or even for one of the bourgeois parties, while those outside the system went to the Communists, who cast themselves as the inheritor of the values of the pre-war SPD (or at least of its revolutionary, anti-revisionist wing). Even so, both the SPD and KPD, as well as the DVP and the DNVP on the right, remained 'clearly rooted in Protestant regions'.[105] Workers in Catholic cities, like their rural counterparts, tended to remain loyal to the Centre Party, a phenomenon which was already apparent in Wilhelmine Germany and continued into the Weimar Republic.[106]

The increasing heterogeneity, and to a lesser degree, the partial embourgeoisement of the skilled working class is therefore something which cannot be left out of the equation here. It accounts for a certain de-politicisation of those on the left who had previously championed the cause of socialism and labour rights. Those who had achieved the eight-hour day, for example, seemed less interested in obtaining it for others. Artisans, retailers and self-employed craftsmen from working-class backgrounds opposed it altogether.[107] However, no other class was as divided as the new Mittelstand, which ranged, as Hans Speier argued in the early 1930s, 'from the Lumpenproletariat in one direction to the strata of small businessmen and directors of medium and large companies in the other'.[108] The inflation crisis had given them a jolt, and they were now more prone to forming their own trade unions, pressure groups and professional associations, or joining existing ones. But it had also left them without any values other than naked material self-interest, and without any inclination to develop bonds with manual workers, or, for that matter, with members of the old Mittelstand.[109] To that extent they had become 'value parasites', lacking 'the reassuring support of a moral tradition that they could truly call their own'.[110] This, together with a unifying anti-Marxism, probably made them more vulnerable to the Nazi appeal for a movement of national renewal 'above classes' in the wake of the global economic crisis after 1929.[111]

The countryside

Given the very diverse nature of the rural economy in Germany, it is difficult to make statements about conditions in the countryside in the 1920s which would be valid for all farming and agricultural communities. How any one area experienced the inflation period and its aftermath indeed depended on a variety of local as well as national factors.[112] Thus patterns of landowning tended to be small-scale and peasant-based in western and southern Germany, with farmers producing for local markets and relying on the unpaid labour of family members, especially wives and daughters, to keep their costs down. By contrast, in the grain-producing east, agricultural holdings were larger and more dependent on seasonal workers, and there-fore more vulnerable to developments in international markets and/or to competition from industrial employers offering higher wages.[113] This in turn effected peasant politics: traditionally the dairy and livestock farmers of western Germany favoured (or at least did not virulently oppose) liberalism and free trade, while large landowners in the Prussian east (the *Junker*) sup-ported protectionism and the old German Conservative Party, which merged with other right-wing groups to form the DNVP in December 1918.[114]

On the other hand, economic conditions in the 1920s, and the loss of key agricultural territories to Denmark and Poland under the Treaty of Versailles, tended to undermine previous political differences between farm-ers, with the DDP in particularly suffering in northern and eastern rural areas due to its close association with the Weimar Republic and the hated post-war settlement (see Table 4.2). Or, as Jeremy Noakes puts it, there was now a 'growing belief that the front was no longer *Junker* versus small farmer, but agriculture and rural society as a whole versus industry and the urban interest'.[115] Labour shortages also continued into the early 1920s as former Russian POWs and former rural conscripts were repatriated and female farm hands (*Mägde*) showed a marked reluctance to return to the agricultural sector after being demobilised. Some deliberately chose to re-locate to the cities, where the unemployment benefits on offer made them reluctant to 'accept work on the land', as the Silesian Agricultural Chamber protested in a report in 1919.[116]

TABLE 4.2 Decline in the electoral fortunes of the DDP in the Reichstag elections of 1919, 1920, May 1924 and December 1924 in selected parts of north-western and north-eastern Germany

State or province	Reichstag election January 1919 (%)	Reichstag election June 1920 (%)	Reichstag election May 1924 (%)	Reichstag election December 1924 (%)
Oldenburg	30.94	15.49	11.75	12.36
Mecklenburg-Schwerin	29.49	8.29	4.12	5.46
Mecklenburg-Strelitz	35.58	15.75	5.79	6.29
Schleswig-Holstein	27.23	9.38	8.01	8.68
Hanover Province	14.65	6.10	4.20	4.75
Pomerania	21.66	4.46	2.60	3.76
East Prussia	18.80	5.58	3.54	3.99
National vote overall	18.56	8.28	5.65	6.34

Source: *Wahlen in der Weimarer Republik*, at http://www.gonschior.de/weimar.

Even so, recent research has shown that the transition from war to peace in the countryside, while hardly harmonious or pain-free, was also much less catastrophic in socio-economic terms than previously believed.[117] Thus, in spite of fears that the continuation of wartime price controls into the post-war period would force many small farmers out of business, in practice there was relatively little buying and selling of rural property during this period. Instead rural producers were able to use hyperinflation to wipe out debts or purchase new machinery and household items on cheap credit (or in exchange for food).[118] Others developed survival strategies which indicate a growing assertiveness on the part of previously downtrodden people. In rural Hesse, for instance, as Cornelie Usborne discovered in her study of a criminal abortion trial in 1924, poorer married couples were increasingly inclined to limit family size in line with the rising cost of food and housing and the uncertain economic outlook more generally. Their 'matter-of-fact' attitudes towards abortion and contraception were indeed quite similar to those to be found in urban working-class areas during the same period.[119] In southern Bavaria, on the other hand, the younger sons and daughters of wealthier farmers who had done well from the war sometimes found that they no longer needed to go out and toil for others, but could stay in the parental home, thus benefitting from the family's growing prosperity. There were even cases of ostentatious spending and lavish parties, particularly when sons returned from the war or daughters got married.[120]

More generally, farmers had a built-in advantage during the immediate post-war period, as food was scarce and therefore a valuable commodity which could be sold for high prices on the black market. Indeed, as Robert Moeller found in his study of the Rhineland and Westphalia, the growing numbers of ordinary householders opting to purchase or rear livestock in the early 1920s 'suggests that many sought to supplement their food supply' or perhaps to make a little money on the side 'by becoming part-time farmers'.[121] The sector, in other words, managed to survive the period of demobilisation without suffering the complete collapse that some doom-mongers in 1918–19 had predicted.[122]

However, rural producers often did not see things this way. For them, the war and the coming of the Weimar Republic meant socialism, increased state control of agricultural prices, and the victory of the urban consumer as the dominant voice in parliamentary politics – a process which had actually begun in 1914 and did not end in 1923.[123] Some complained about the apparent new militancy of agricultural workers, who staged a series of largely unsuccessful strikes in 1919–20. Others feared the large numbers of unemployed and hungry urbanites who descended on the countryside in search of food, and allegedly stole everything in sight.[124] Farmers' ongoing loss of patriarchal status, and the 'overburdening' of farmers' wives due to loss of domestic staff, was a further issue, as many younger rural women continued to leave the countryside in the 1920s, attracted by the higher wages and shorter working hours apparently on offer in the big cities.[125] In the east, some landowners even went back to hiring foreign Polish workers, as they had done before and during the war, but the Poles too – it was now complained – wanted more pay, especially the men.[126]

Meanwhile, those farmers who had got rid of debts in the inflation years soon piled them back on during what was supposed to be the 'golden years' of the Weimar Republic between 1924 and 1929. The feeling grew that the established Weimar parties were ignoring farmers and rural housewives, who claimed to represent the true interests of the nation against the 'selfishness' and 'greed' of the urban consumer.[127] Low food prices, increased competition from foreign imports, and a credit squeeze leading to higher interest rates meant that by 1927 many farmers and big landowners were struggling to keep their heads above water, in spite of various government schemes to provide financial assistance to those in greatest need.[128] Bankruptcies and foreclosures inevitably followed.[129]

The initial beneficiaries of rural discontent were the anti-Weimar DNVP and the closely related *Reichslandbund* (RLB), the post-war successor to the old Agrarian League. The DNVP vote had risen from 15.1 per cent in June 1920 to 20.5 per cent by the time of the December 1924 Reichstag election,

TABLE 4.3 Rise in the electoral fortunes of the DNVP in the Reichstag elections of 1919, 1920, May 1924 and December 1924 in selected parts of north-western and north-eastern Germany

State or province	Reichstag election January 1919 (%)	Reichstag election June 1920 (%)	Reichstag election May 1924 (%)	Reichstag election December 1924 (%)
Oldenburg*	2.23	4.97	17.29	18.40
Mecklenburg-Schwerin	13.49	21.71	28.07	27.73
Mecklenburg-Strelitz	14.23	25.42	26.95	32.65
Schleswig-Holstein	7.29	20.48	31.02	33.10
Hanover Province*	3.54	6.67	14.47	17.84
Pomerania	23.96	35.47	49.48	49.13
East Prussia	11.87	31.10	38.91	39.22
National vote overall	10.27	15.07	19.45	20.49

*Unlike the other areas listed here, Oldenburg and Hanover provinces also had a sizeable vote for the Catholic Centre Party, reflecting their more mixed Catholic/Protestant populations.
Source: *Wahlen in der Weimarer Republik*, at http://www.gonschior.de/weimar.

and much of its support came from Protestant farming areas across the northern and eastern parts of Germany.[130]

Farmers and aristocratic landowners in Catholic areas of western Germany, by contrast, tended to stick with the Catholic Centre Party, or, in Bavaria, with the BVP, without, however, being any less hostile towards the Weimar Republic.[131] Even so, all three of these established political parties lost at least some of their supporters to the various rural protest movements which emerged in the late 1920s. The DNVP was especially vulnerable in this respect, particularly given the intense disappointment at the failings (or perceived betrayals) of *Reichslandbund* leader Martin Schiele, who served as Reich Minister for Food and Agriculture in the bourgeois coalition government between 1927 and 1928 and introduced what was seen as a poorly funded programme of relief for struggling farmers and landowners.[132] Rural militancy also increased following the establishment of the new SPD-led grand coalition government in June 1928, from which the DNVP/RLB, clear losers in the May Reichstag election, were excluded (see Table 4.4). Thus whereas the new Social Democrat Reich Chancellor Hermann Müller described the election results as a 'triumph for the constitutional idea [*Sieg der Verfassungsidee*]', rural protestors spoke of a 'victory for the Marxists' and even of an imminent 'Sovietisation of Germany'.[133]

TABLE 4.4 Results of the Reichstag election of May 1928 in selected parts of north-western and north-eastern Germany

State or province	SPD (%)	DNVP (%)	NSDAP (%)	Rural protest parties (%)
Oldenburg*	28.38	8.68	8.24	10.70
Mecklenburg-Schwerin	40.93	16.20	2.28	15.92
Mecklenburg-Strelitz	39.66	23.05	0.81	9.87
Schleswig-Holstein	35.13	22.87	4.09	5.73
Hanover Province*	36.16	9.68	3.57	7.42
Pomerania	30.22	41.55	1.51	5.24
East Prussia	26.83	31.35	0.81	2.05
National vote overall	29.76	14.25	2.63	7.99

*The Catholic Centre Party won 17.13% in Oldenburg and 8.15% in Hanover province. The Guelph separatist party also won 11.66% in Hanover.
Source: *Wahlen in der Weimarer Republik*, at http://www.gonschior.de/weimar.

Such hysteria led to a marked intensification of anti-republican activity in the countryside as the decade ended. For instance, a new *Landvolkbewegung* (Rural People's Movement or LVB) emerged in Schleswig-Holstein in northern Germany in January 1928 and spread from there to neighbouring Oldenburg, Hanover/Lower Saxony and Westphalia. Under its leaders Klaus Heim and Wilhelm Hamkens, it engaged in demonstrations and violent attacks on tax inspectors and government offices, even resorting to bombings on some occasions.[134] Worse still, the supposedly more respectable *Reichslandbund* openly supported such actions, particularly as now it was no longer bound by the responsibilities of government. Thus in April 1929 the leader of the Pomeranian branch of the RLB, Hans-Joachim von Rohr Demmin, backed a proposed food producers' strike as a 'service to the fatherland'. This was because it would raise unemployment levels and allow 'the political crisis [to] reach full maturity', ending in the collapse of the democratic system 'which has to die if Germany wants to live'.[135]

Finally, Protestant rural areas of northern Germany were among the first to witness what was a modest 'breakthrough' in terms of support for the Nazis in 1928–9. Although the party did very badly in the May 1928 Reichstag election, scoring a mere 2.6 per cent of the vote nationally, it achieved its best results not in its traditional Bavarian heartland, but in a few select farming districts in Schleswig-Holstein, Hanover province and northern Oldenburg.[136] (See Table 4.4 above). This in turn reflected a positive decision, made around the end of the year 1927 and announced by Hitler in an important speech in Hamburg, to direct party propaganda more clearly towards farmers and small businessmen as opposed to competing with the left for the industrial working-class vote. In the Lower Saxon constituency of South Hanover-Brunswick, for instance, the party even dumped its original candidate, a railway employee, in favour of a farmer and landowner, Werner Willikens, who had been a leading figure in the *Reichslandbund* in Goslar.[137] Meanwhile, the party programme itself was reinterpreted in April 1928 in order to 'clarify' what was meant by Article 17, which originally had called for land nationalisation. The only land which would now be confiscated by a Nazi government, it appeared, was land acquired by 'Jewish speculators'. Otherwise, private property would be respected, and steps would be taken to protect the German farmer from the burdens of 'interest slavery'.[138]

After May 1928 the party continued to make gains in rural parts of northern Germany. In state elections in Mecklenburg-Schwerin, for instance, it increased its vote from 5,575 (1.8 per cent) in May 1927 to 12,721 (4.05 per cent) in June 1929. Although the SPD remained the strongest party in Mecklenburg-Schwerin, a right-wing unity coalition led by the DNVP and DVP was able to exclude it from power, thus foreshadowing the break-up of the grand coalition at Reich level some nine months later.[139] In Schleswig-Holstein, membership of the NSDAP grew by 300 per cent over the course of the year 1928, while the number of local branches (*Ortsgruppen*) rose from 37 in March 1928 to 113 by the autumn and 140 by January 1929.[140] Politics in this part of Germany were henceforth characterised by a 'hard struggle' [*harter Konkurrenzkampf*] between the NSDAP and the DNVP for the right-wing vote; indeed, support for the DNVP had already fallen by over 10 percentage points in Schleswig-Holstein between the Reichstag elections of December 1924 and those of May 1928, from 33.1 to 22.87 per cent, and by roughly similar amounts in Mecklenburg-Schwerin and Mecklenburg-Strelitz (see Tables 4.3 and 4.4 above).

Even so, it was not until the early 1930s that the NSDAP's share of the vote was clearly greater than that of the DNVP in rural parts of the north and east.[141] Before then, it was still one of many protest parties competing for the farmers' vote. In May 1928 the SPD had even made some limited electoral gains among rural workers in Protestant areas, perhaps benefiting here from its new agricultural programme drawn up in 1927 and from the fact that it was not associated with the 'betrayals' of previous bourgeois coalition governments.[142] Yet this disguised the extent of the rural–urban divide which had grown bigger since the currency stabilisation of 1923–4 and which rested on the demand of farmers for high subsidies for themselves and lower wages and benefits for the urban poor. The bigger threat to the stability of the Weimar Republic, in other words, at least from the vantage point of 1928/9 rather than 1930, was not the NSDAP, but the alienation of large sections of the Mittelstand and peasantry from the democratic system, and the willingness of some of their representatives to condone acts of violence and criminality against representatives of the democratically elected government, even before the onset of the Great Depression. Only in the wake of the Wall Street Crash of October 1929 were the Nazis able to exploit this situation more fully to their own political advantage.

Notes

1 See e.g. Gerald D. Feldman's *The Great Disorder. Politics, Economics and Society in the German Inflation, 1914–1924* (Oxford, 1993); Carl-Ludwig Holtfrerich, *The German Inflation 1914–1923. Causes and Effects in International Perspective* (West Berlin and New York, 1986); Robert G. Moeller, *German Peasants and Agrarian Politics, 1914–1924. The Rhineland and Westphalia* (Chapel Hill, NC and London, 1986); Martin H. Geyer, *Verkehrte Welt. Revolution, Inflation und Moderne. München, 1914–1924* (Göttingen, 1998). Benjamin Ziemann, in his study of rural southern Bavaria, also speaks of the 'inflation decade from 1914 to 1923', and Detlev Peukert likewise uses the term 'the decade of inflation' in his very different view of crisis-racked, modern Germany – see Ziemann, *War Experiences*, p. 8; and Peukert, *The Weimar Republic*, p. 50.

2 Roger Scruton, *A Dictionary of Political Thought* (London, 1982), p. 223.

3 Weitz, *Weimar Germany*, p. 130.

4 Scruton, *A Dictionary*, p. 211. Widdig, *Culture and Inflation*, p. 43, notes that 'After July 1922 the inflation turned into a hyperinflation of hitherto unknown dimensions.'

5 Widdig, *Culture and Inflation*, p. 43.

6 For a detailed account see Fischer, *The Ruhr Crisis, passim*.

7 See e.g. Wolfgang Ruge, *Weimar – Republik auf Zeit* (East Berlin, 1969).

8 Feldman, *Army, Industry and Labor*; Feldman, *Iron and Steel in the German Inflation, 1916–1923* (Princeton, NJ, 1977).

9 Richard Overy, 'The German Economy, 1919–1945', in Panikos Panayi (ed.), *Weimar and Nazi Germany. Continuities and Discontinuities* (London, 2001), pp. 33–73 (here p. 55).

10 Hans Jaeger, *Unternehmer in der deutschen Politik (1890–1918)* (Bonn, 1967), pp. 214–56.

11 On Dernburg see Werner Schiefel, *Bernhard Dernburg, 1865–1937. Kolonialpolitiker und Bankier im wilhelminischen Deutschland* (Zurich, 1974); and on Warburg see Niall Ferguson, 'Max Warburg and German Politics. The Limits

of Financial Power in Wilhelmine Germany', in Geoff Eley and James Retallack (eds), *Wilhelminism and Its Legacies. German Modernities, Imperialism, and the Meanings of Reform, 1890–1933. Essays for Hartmut Pogge von Strandmann* (Oxford, 2003), pp. 185–201.

12 Stibbe, 'Elisabeth Rotten', pp. 201–4.

13 Warburg, for instance, described the final version of the treaty as 'the worst act of world piracy ever perpetrated under the flag of hypocrisy' – cited in Margaret MacMillan, *Paris 1919. Six Months that Changed the World* (New York, 2003), p. 465.

14 On the DDP more generally see Dieter Langewiesche, *Liberalism in Germany* (London, 2000), esp. chapter 5.

15 Hans Mommsen, 'The Decline of the Bürgertum in Late Nineteenth and Early Twentieth-Century Germany', in Mommsen, *From Weimar to Auschwitz. Essays in German History* (Cambridge, 1991), pp. 11–27 (here pp. 22–3).

16 Bernd Weisbrod, *Die Schwerindustrie in der Weimarer Republik* (Wuppertal, 1978).

17 The best study of Stinnes is Gerald D. Feldman's *Hugo Stinnes: Biographie eines Industriellen 1870–1924* (Munich, 1998). Also good is Peter Wulf, *Hugo Stinnes: Wirtschaft und Politik, 1918–1924* (Stuttgart, 1976).

18 Widdig, *Culture and Inflation*, p. 137. See also *The Times*, 11 April 1924, as cited in Thomas Wittek, *Auf ewig Feind? Das Deutschlandbild in den britischen Massenmedien nach dem Ersten Weltkrieg* (Munich, 2005), p. 367.

19 See Jonathan Wright, *Gustav Stresemann. Weimar's Greatest Statesman* (Oxford, 2002), p. 169; and Pogge von Strandmann, *Walther Rathenau*, pp. 243–4.

20 Wright, *Stresemann*, p. 180; Feldman, *Stinnes*, pp. 706–7.

21 Donny Gluckstein, *The Nazis, Capitalism and the Working Class* (London, 1999), pp. 18 and 14.

22 Wulf, *Hugo Stinnes*, pp. 87–107; Fischer, *From Kaiserreich to Third Reich*, pp. 76–7; Feldman, *Iron and Steel*, pp. 285, 332, 338–40; Weisbrod, *Schwerindustrie in der Weimarer Republik*, pp. 301–13.

23 See also the arguments put forward in *Die Arbeitszeitfrage in Deutschland. Eine Denkschrift verfaßt von der Vereinigung der Deutschen Arbeitgeberverbände* (Berlin, 1924), p. 64; reproduced in Peter Longerich (ed.), *Die Erste Republik. Dokumente zur Geschichte des Weimarer Staates* (Munich, 1992), pp. 277–8.

24 Harold James, *A German Identity, 1770–1990*, revised edition (London, 1990), p. 126.

25 Pogge von Strandmann, *Walther Rathenau*, p. 11.

26 Cited in Lisa Appignanesi, *Cabaret. The First Hundred Years* (London, 1975), p. 121.

27 Modris Eksteins, *The Limits of Reason. The German Democratic Press and the Collapse of Weimar Democracy* (Oxford, 1975), p. 75.

28 Ibid., pp. 78–81; J. A. Leopold, *Alfred Hugenberg. The Radical Nationalist Campaign Against the Weimar Republic* (New Haven, CT and London, 1977).

29 Eksteins, *The Limits of Reason*, p. 72; Wright, *Stresemann*, pp. 369–70, n. 167. In 1927, when the public found out about this purchase, the DAZ was sold to a consortium of Ruhr industrialists, but it continued to receive government subsidies and to reject the extreme nationalist propaganda of Hugenberg.

30 Fischer, *From Kaiserreich to Third Reich*, pp. 84–5. See also Iago Gil Aguado, 'The Creditanstalt Crisis of 1931 and the Failure of the Austro-German Customs Union Project', *Historical Journal*, 44/1 (2001), pp. 199–221 (here pp. 207–8).

31 Wehler, *Deutsche Gesellschaftsgeschichte*, vol. 4, pp. 373–6.

32 Peukert, *The Weimar Republic*, p. 112; Berger, *Social Democracy*, pp. 124–5.

33 Peter Fritzsche, 'Weimar Populism and National Socialism in Local Perspective', in Larry Eugene Jones and James Retallack (eds), *Elections, Mass Politics and Social Change in Modern Germany. New Perspectives* (Cambridge, 1992), pp. 287–306 (here pp. 292–3).

34 Jürgen Falter, *Hitlers Wähler* (Munich, 1991), pp. 25 and 30.

35 Mommsen, *The Rise and Fall of Weimar Democracy*, p. 220; Berger, *Germany*, p. 129.

36 On political fragmentation among different bourgeois economic interest groups more generally during the mid- to late-1920s, including the world of business and commerce, see also Fritzsche, *Rehearsals for Fascism*, pp. 105–50.

37 Wulf, *Hugo Stinnes*, p. 107.

38 Weitz, *Weimar Germany*, pp. 108–9.

39 Ibid., pp. 73–5 and 151–2. See also Carola Sachse, *Siemens, der Nationalsozialismus und die moderne Familie. Eine Untersuchung zur sozialen Rationalisierung in Deutschland im 20 Jahrhundert* (Hamburg, 1990); idem., *Industrial Housewives. Women's Social Work in the Factories of Nazi Germany*, introduced and edited by Jane Caplan (London, 1987).

40 Weitz, *Weimar Germany*, p. 153.

41 Fischer, *From Kaiserreich to Third Reich*, pp. 77–9; Wehler, *Deutsche Gesellschaftsgeschichte*, Vol. 4, p. 374; Mommsen, *The Rise and Fall of Weimar Democracy*, p. 220; Winkler, *Weimar*, pp. 361–2.

42 See e.g. Jürgen Kocka, 'The First World War and the "Mittelstand": German Artisans and White-Collar Workers', *Journal of Contemporary History*, 8/1 (1973), pp. 101–23 (here p. 122).

43 See Bessel, *Germany after the First World War*, esp. pp. 166–94.

44 Elizabeth F. Howard, *Across Barriers* (London, 1941), p. 13.

45 Karin Hausen, 'The German Nation's Obligations to the Heroes' Widows of World War I', in Margaret Randolph Higonnet, Jane Jenson, Sonya Michel and

Margaret Collins Weitz (eds), *Behind the Lines. Gender and the Two World Wars* (New Haven, CT and London, 1987), pp. 126–40; Bessel, *Germany after the First World War*, pp. 225–8; Sabine Kienitz, *Beschädigte Helden. Kriegsinvalidität und Körperbildung 1914–1923* (Paderborn, 2008).

46 Günther D. Dehm, *Proletarische Jugend. Lebensgestaltung und Gedankwelt der großstädtischen Proletarierjugend* (Berlin, n.d.), pp. 16–19. Reproduced in Anton Kaes, Martin Jay and Edward Dimendberg (eds), *The Weimar Republic Sourcebook* (London, 1994), pp. 245–7.

47 Wachsmann, 'Between Reform and Repression', p. 414.

48 Ibid., p. 417.

49 'Die Ernährungslage der Arbeiternehmerschaft', *Gewerkschaftsarchiv*, 11 (1929), pp. 24–7. Reproduced in Longerich (ed.), *Die Erste Republik*, pp. 239–41.

50 Patricia Clavin, *The Great Depression in Europe, 1929–1939* (London, 2000), p. 91.

51 David F. Crew, *Germans on Welfare. From Weimar to Hitler* (Oxford, 1998), pp. 116 and ff.

52 Tim Mason, 'Women in Germany, 1925–1940: Family, Welfare and Work', *History Workshop Journal* (1976), Part I, pp. 74–113; Renate Bridenthal and Claudia Koonz, 'Beyond *Kinder, Kirche, Kuche*: Weimar Women in Politics and Work', in Renate Bridenthal, Atina Grossmann and Marion Kaplan (eds), *When Biology Became Destiny. Women in Weimar and Nazi Germany* (New York, 1984), pp. 33–65; Helen Boak, 'The State as an Employer of Women in the Weimar Republic', in W. R. Lee and Eve Rosenhaft (eds), *State, Social Policy and Social Change in Germany, 1880–1994*, revised edition (Oxford, 1997), pp. 64–101.

53 Mason, 'Women in Germany', pp. 78–80.

54 Ibid., pp. 80–1; Frevert, *Women in German History*, pp. 180–1.

55 Dagmar Reese, *Growing up Female in Nazi Germany* (Ann Arbor, MI, 2006), p. 48.

56 Weitz, *Weimar Germany*, pp. 153–5.

57 Reese, *Growing up Female*, p. 176.

58 Usborne, *The Politics of the Body*, pp. 51–3.

59 Dehm, *Proletarische Jugend* (as note 46 above).

60 On this campaign see Usborne, *The Politics of the Body*, esp. pp. 156–201; Paul Weindling, *Health, Race and German Politics between National Unification and Nazism, 1870–1945* (Cambridge, 1989), pp. 457–62; and Atina Grossmann, *Reforming Sex: The German Movement for Birth Control and Abortion Reform, 1920–1950* (Oxford, 1995), pp. 78–106.

61 Usborne, *The Politics of the Body*, p. 172; Atina Grossmann, 'Abortion and Economic Crisis: The 1931 Campaign Against Paragraph 218', in Bridenthal *et al.* (eds), *When Biology Became Destiny*, pp. 66–86 (here p. 75).

62 Reagin, *A German Women's Movement*, p. 227.

63 Usborne, *The Politics of the Body*, pp. 7–8 and 118–23. On the *Bund für Mutterschutz* see also Amy Hackett, 'Helene Stöcker: Left-Wing Intellectual and Sex Reformer' in Bridenthal *et al.* (eds), *When Biology Became Destiny*, pp. 109–30; and Peter Davies, 'Transforming Utopia: The "League for the Protection of Mothers and Sexual Reform" in the First World War', in Fell and Sharp (eds), *The Women's Movement in Wartime*, pp. 211–26.

64 Henrick Stahr, '"Erst Essen – dann Miete!" Mieterkrawalle, Mieterstreiks und ihre bildliche Repräsentation', in Diethart Kerbs and Henrick Stahr (eds), *Berlin 1932. Das letzte Jahr der Weimarer Republik* (Berlin, 1992), pp. 90–114 (here pp. 108–9).

65 Crew, *Germans on Welfare*, pp. 120–1.

66 Bertolt Brecht, *The Threepenny Opera*, translated and introduced by Ralph Manheim and John Willett (London, 1979), p. 55.

67 Crew, *Germans on Welfare*, p. 205.

68 See ibid., p. 157–65, and Kienitz, *Beschädigte Helden*, pp. 133.

69 See the extracts from Otto Voß and Herbert Schön, 'Die Cliquen jugendlicher Verwahrloster als sozial-pädagogisches Problem' (1930), reproduced in Longerich (ed.), *Die Erste Republik*, pp. 205–11. Also Bessel, *Germany After the First World War*, pp. 240–1; and Elizabeth Harvey, *Youth and the Welfare State in Weimar Germany* (Oxford, 1993), pp. 186–203.

70 Cornelie Usborne, *Cultures of Abortion in Weimar Germany* (Oxford, 2007), p. 148.

71 Ibid., p. 157.

72 Reese, *Growing Up Female*, p. 235.

73 Ibid., pp. 48 and 192.

74 See Harvey, *Youth and the Welfare State*, esp. pp. 203–17 and 256; and David F. Crew, 'A Social Republic? Social Democrats, Communists and the Weimar Welfare State, 1919 to 1933', in Barclay and Weitz (eds), *Between Reform and Revolution*, pp. 223–49. Also Kienitz, *Beschädigte Helden*, p. 146.

75 Crew, *Germans on Welfare*, pp. 85 and 205.

76 Joseph Roth, 'With the Homeless' (article in the *Neue Berliner Zeitung – 12-Uhr-Blatt*, 23 September 1920), reproduced in Roth, *What I Saw. Reports from Berlin, 1920–33*, translated and introduced by Michael Hofmann (London, 2003), pp. 63–8 (here p. 64).

77 This view is put forward most forcefully by Larry Eugene Jones, 'The "Dying Middle": Weimar Germany and the Fragmentation of Bourgeois Politics', *Central European History*, 5/1 (1972), pp. 23–54. See also Langewiesche, *Liberalism in Germany*, p. 264; and Horst Möller, *Die Weimarer Republik. Eine unvollendete Demokratie*, 8th edition (Munich, 2004), pp. 166–7.

78 Weitz, *Weimar Germany*, p. 137.

79 Peukert, *The Weimar Republic*, pp. 156, 230–1; Kocka, 'The First World War and the "Mittelstand"', p. 123.

80 Jeremy Noakes, *The Nazi Party in Lower Saxony, 1921–1933* (Oxford, 1971), p. 111.

81 The phrase comes from Theodor Geiger's famous essay 'Panik im Mittelstand', *Die Arbeit*, 7 (October 1931), pp. 638–53. See also Geiger's longer work, *Die soziale Schichtung des deutschen Volkes. Soziographischer Versuch auf statistischer Grundlage* (Stuttgart, 1932).

82 Geiger, *Die soziale Schichtung*, p. 101.

83 Weitz, *Weimar Germany*, p. 156.

84 Geiger, *Die soziale Schichtung*, p. 100.

85 Peukert, *The Weimar Republic*, p. 156.

86 Kocka, 'The First World War and the "Mittelstand"', p. 122; Weitz, *Weimar Germany*, p. 156.

87 Geiger, *Die soziale Schichtung*, p. 85.

88 Ibid., p. 84.

89 Ian Kershaw, *Popular Opinion and Political Dissent in the Third Reich. Bavaria 1933–1945* (Oxford, 1983), pp. 111–55.

90 For the results of the 1907 census see Gerd Hohorst, Jürgen Kocka and Gerhard A. Ritter (eds), *Sozialgeschichtliches Arbeitsbuch: Materialien zur Statistik des Kaiserreiches, 1871–1914* (Munich, 1975), p. 67. The figure of 1.3 million includes 406,385 sales assistants who in 1907 were still counted as 'workers' but by 1925 had been reclassified as 'salaried employees' (ibid., p. 68, n. 8). Cf. http://www.germanhistorydocs.ghi-dc.org/pdf/eng/210_Census%20Figures_23.pdf.

91 Peukert, *The Weimar Republic*, p. 157.

92 Weitz, *Weimar Germany*, p. 156.

93 Boak, 'The State as an Employer of Women', p. 81.

94 Weitz, *Weimar Germany*, p. 157.

95 Frevert, *Women in German History*, pp. 177–8.

96 Ibid., p. 197; Bridenthal and Koonz, 'Beyond *Kinder, Kirche, Kuche*', pp. 52–3.

97 Peukert, *The Weimar Republic*, p. 158.

98 Weitz, *Weimar Germany*, p. 138.

99 Pulzer, *The Rise of Political Anti-Semitism*, p. 299.

100 Jürgen Falter, 'The Social Bases of Political Cleavages in the Weimar Republic, 1919–1933', in Jones and Retallack (eds), *Elections, Mass Politics and Social Change*, pp. 371–97 (here p. 387).

101 Idem., *Hitlers Wähler*, esp. pp. 169–93.

102 Marijke Smid, 'Protestantismus und Antisemitismus 1930–1933', in Jochen-Christoph Kaiser and Martin Greschat (eds), *Der Holocaust und die Protestanten. Analysen einer Verstrickung* (Frankfurt/M, 1988), pp. 38–72 (esp. pp. 50–5); Karen Schönwälder, 'Akademischer Antisemitismus. Die deutschen Historiker in der NS-Zeit', *Jahrbuch für Antisemitismusforschung*, 2 (1993), pp. 200–29.

103 Pulzer, *The Rise of Political Anti-Semitism*, p. 298. On the DHV see also Larry Eugene Jones, '"Between the Fronts": The German National Union of Commercial Employees from 1928 to 1933', *Journal of Modern History*, 48/3 (1976), pp. 462–82.

104 Erich Fromm, *The Fear of Freedom*, new edition (London, 1991) [1942], p. 181.

105 Falter, 'The Social Bases', p. 387.

106 In a recent essay, Jonathan Sperber calculates that 85 per cent of those who voted SPD in 1912 were Protestant and 15 per cent Catholic. This tallies with similar figures produced by Jürgen Falter for the 1920s and early 1930s, when between 87 per cent and 91 per cent of SPD voters were non-Catholic. See Sperber, 'The Social Democratic Electorate in Imperial Germany', in Barclay and Weitz (eds), *Between Reform and Revolution*, pp. 167–94 (here p. 190); and Falter, 'The Social Bases', p. 392.

107 Berger, *Social Democracy*, p. 118.

108 Hans Speier, *German White-Collar Workers and the Rise of Hitler*, new edition (New Haven and London, 1986) [1932], p. 8.

109 Weitz, *Weimar Germany*, p. 159. Siegfried Kracauer, another social commentator, also noted in 1930 that the 'mass of white-collar employees . . . are living at present without a doctrine to which they can look up, without a goal to guide them'. See Kracauer, 'Asyl für Obdachlose', in *Die Angestellten* (Frankfurt/M, 1930), pp. 91–101; reproduced in Kaes *et al.*, *The Weimar Republic Sourcebook*, pp. 189–91.

110 Speier, *White-Collar Workers*, pp. 8–9.

111 Cf. Wehler, *Deutsche Gesellschaftsgeschichte*, Vol. 4, p. 301. Also Chapter 6 below.

112 Weitz, *Weimar Germany*, p. 159.

113 Moeller, *German Peasants and Agrarian Politics*, pp. 13–14; Mason, 'Women in Germany', pp. 78–9; Jones, *Gender and Rural Modernity*, passim.

114 J. E. Farquharson, *The Plough and the Swastika. The NSDAP and Agriculture in Germany, 1928–45* (London, 1976), p. 4; F. L. Carsten, *A History of the Prussian Junkers* (London, 1989), p. 160; Shelly Baranowski, *The Sanctity of Rural Life. Nobility, Protestantism and Nazism in Weimar Prussia* (New York, 1995), p. 8.

115 Noakes, *The Nazi Party in Lower Saxony*, pp. 115–6.

116 Bessel, *Germany After the First World War*, p. 206; Jones, *Gender and Rural Modernity*, p. 115.

117 Bessel, *Germany After the First World War*, pp. 217–19.

118   Moeller, *German Peasants and Agrarian Politics*, pp. 139–40.

119   Usborne, *Cultures of Abortion*, pp. 163–200.

120   Ziemann, *War Experiences*, pp. 199–200.

121   Moeller, *German Peasants and Agrarian Politics*, p. 140.

122   Bessel, *Germany After the First World War*, p. 218.

123   Moeller, *German Peasants and Agrarian Politics*, p. 157; Ziemann, *War Experiences*, pp. 196–7.

124   Bessel, *Germany After the First World War*, pp. 205 and 215; Ziemann, *War Experiences*, pp. 227–8; Moeller, *German Peasants and Agrarian Politics*, p. 113.

125   Elizabeth Bright Jones, 'A New Stage of Life? Young Farm Women's Changing Expectations and Aspirations about Work in Weimar Saxony', *German History*, 19/4 (2001), pp. 549–70.

126   Bessel, *Germany After the First World War*, p. 210.

127   On the rural housewives movement see Bridenthal, 'Organized Rural Women', passim; and Reagin, *Sweeping the Nation*, pp. 78–83; and Jones, *Gender and Rural Modernity*, pp. 161–97.

128   Baranowski, *The Sanctity of Rural Life*, pp. 118–26; Noakes, *The Nazi Party in Lower Saxony*, pp. 109–11.

129   Carsten, *A History of the Prussian Junkers*, p. 164; Evans, *The Coming of the Third Reich*, p. 208.

130   Lewis Hertzman, *DNVP. Right-Wing Opposition in the Weimar Republic, 1918–1924* (Lincoln, Nebr., 1963); Noakes, *The Nazi Party in Lower Saxony*, pp. 115–16; Baranowski, *The Sanctity of Rural Life*, pp. 43–4 and 127–8.

131   Moeller, *German Peasants and Agrarian Politics*, esp. pp. 116–38; Dietrich Orlow, *Weimar Prussia, 1918–1925. The Unlikely Rock of Democracy* (Pittsburgh, 1986), p. 173; Larry Eugene Jones, 'Catholic Conservatives in the Weimar Republic: The Politics of the Rhenish-Westphalian Aristocracy, 1918–1933', *German History*, 18/1 (2000), pp. 60–85; Ziemann, *War Experiences*, pp. 220–2.

132   Carsten, *A History of the Prussian Junkers*, p. 165; Baranowski, *The Sanctity of Rural Life*, pp. 129 and 153; Fritzsche, 'Weimar Populism and National Socialism', pp. 292–3.

133   Rudolf Rietzler, *'Kampf in der Nordmark'. Das Aufkommen des Nationalsozialismus in Schleswig-Holstein* (Neumünster, 1982), p. 424.

134   Farquharson, *The Plough and the Swastika*, p. 5; Fritzsche, *Rehearsals for Fascism*, pp. 114–18; Baranowski, *The Sanctity of Rural Life*, pp. 129–35.

135   Carsten, *A History of the Prussian Junkers*, p. 165.

136   Rietzler, *'Kampf in der Nordmark'*, pp. 419–24; Noakes, *The Nazi Party in Lower Saxony*, p. 121; Fritzsche, *Rehearsals for Fascism*, p. 201; Kershaw, *Hitler, 1889–1936*, p. 303; Evans, *The Coming of the Third Reich*, p. 209.

137 Noakes, *The Nazi Party in Lower Saxony*, pp. 105–6.

138 Ibid., p. 107; Farquharson, *The Plough and the Swastika*, p. 3; Kershaw, *Hitler, 1889–1936*, p. 301; Evans, *The Coming of the Third Reich*, p. 209.

139 Kerstin Urbschat, 'Mecklenburg-Schwerin in den letzten Jahren der Weimarer Republik', in Frank Bajohr (ed.), *Norddeutschland im Nationalsozialismus* (Hamburg, 1993), pp. 83–98 (here pp. 85–6).

140 Rietzler, *'Kampf in der Nordmark'*, p. 425.

141 Falter, 'The Social Bases', p. 387; Baranowski, *The Sanctity of Rural Life*, p. 8.

142 Noakes, *The Nazi Party in Lower Saxony*, p. 119; Berger, *Social Democracy*, p. 117; Baranowski, *The Sanctity of Rural Life*, pp. 127–8; Donna Harsch, *German Social Democracy and the Rise of Nazism* (Chapel Hill, NC and London, 1993), pp. 41–2.

CHAPTER 5

Weimar Culture

In the introduction to this book, culture was defined broadly as being made up of individual and collective efforts to interpret and represent the world by means of language, gestures and symbols. Following the work of the British theorist Raymond Williams, culture here will also be considered in relation to technological innovation and societal change, and not in purely artistic or aesthetic terms. Thus, according to Williams, modern understandings of the word 'culture' are intimately linked to evolving usages of other key words like 'industry', 'democracy', 'nation', 'family' and 'class'. Together these developments in meaning:

bear witness to a general change in our characteristic ways of thinking about our common life: about our social, political and economic institutions; about the purposes which these institutions are designed to embody; and about the relations to these institutions and purposes of our activities in learning, education and the arts.[1]

Applying this specifically to the Weimar Republic, we can note that few epochs in modern German history have given rise to such rapid social movement – seen, for instance, in loosening class and political allegiances, decreasing religious observance and conflicts between the generations – and at the same time to such richness and diversity in the world of art, literature and intellectual ideas. Some historians, most notably Detlev Peukert, even speak of a 'crisis of classical modernity' in the 1920s because it was then that 'modern ideas and movements . . . achieved their breakthrough', creating a set of contradictory expectations in the field of social policy, education and technological progress which, because of Germany's parlous post-war economic state and declining birth rate, could not be met. The result was a 'popular mood oscillating between enthusiasm and anxiety, hopes of national reawakening and fears of national extinction'.[2]

Other scholars have depicted a society which was far less prone to radical experimentation and much more inclined towards sobriety, a society, in other words, which followed the paradigmatic shift from Expressionism to *Neue Sachlichkeit* (new objectivity) in the arts in the period after 1923.[3] More recently, it has even been suggested that the whole notion of 'Weimar Culture' should be revised in order to rid it of its 'nostalgic' associations with avant-garde art forms which were simply 'not emblematic of interwar German cultural praxis'.[4] However, in my view this is an argument which goes too far in blurring the boundaries between the pre- and post-1933 periods. A better way of formulating this, in fact, would be to recognise the 'cultural diversity' of the 1920s and the 'coexistence of science and superstition', or of competing visions of modernity and tradition, in Weimar film, architecture and art, as in various facets of everyday life under the republic.[5] Socialism, democratic reformism and cultural modernism were a key part of this dynamic, and all owed a great deal to the German experience of war as well as to longer traditions dating back to the nineteenth century. However, an equally important cultural legacy of the years 1914–18 was the rise of new racist, militarist, anti-welfare and homophobic world views which, for some on the right, offered a fresh, cutting edge vision of a collectivistic or individualistic future shorn of Jewish 'egotism' and Western 'materialism'.[6]

A separate but related part of Weimar culture consisted of a more straightforward conservative or illiberal reaction against modernity. However, the importance of this particular strand has been called into question by scholars like Peter Fritzsche, who instead stress the 'common assumptions' of both left and right in 1920s Germany, and the 'open-endedness' or 'ambiguity' of the 'Weimar' narrative more generally. In his view, terms like 'crisis', 'reaction' and 'failure' do not do justice to the 'eclectic experimentalism' and sheer 'malleability' of the period, which had the potential to produce both 'landscapes of danger' in the form of irrationalism, intolerance and violence, and 'landscapes of design', leading to social and/or environmental improvement.[7]

In what follows, we will explore some of the problems thrown up by these different interpretations of Weimar culture for the vexed issues of art and politics, leisure and mass consumption, sex and sexuality and finally the position of German Jews in the 1920s and early 1930s.

Art and politics in the Weimar Republic

For many cultural historians the years 1920–1930 were the 'golden twenties', a time when Germany, and especially Berlin, became the centre of cutting-edge developments in philosophy, literature, art, music and industrial design. This was the decade, for instance, in which Thomas Mann won the Nobel Prize for literature for his novel *The Magic Mountain* (1924); when the left-wing intellectuals Georg Lucáks, Ernst Bloch and Walter Benjamin established fresh approaches to Marxist philosophy and cultural/literary criticism; when the expressionist film director Fritz Lang made some of the classics of the silent era like *Dr Mabuse, der Spieler* (1922) and *Metropolis* (1927); and when the architect Erich Mendelsohn built his world-famous *Einsteinturm* (1920–4), a modern astrophysical observatory located in a science park in Potsdam, near Berlin, and designed as a monument to Einstein's theory of relativity. Above all, as Eric Weitz has emphasised, it was a time when German artists and intellectuals 'search[ed] for new forms of expression suitable to the cacophony of modern life', and demonstrated a 'belief in the possibilities of the future'.[8]

Interest in the cultural heritage of Weimar indeed experienced something of a revival throughout the Western world in the late 1960s and early 1970s, providing a spur for some of the student protest movements of those years. Yet until the 1990s most historians in Germany, whether they worked in the capitalist Federal Republic or in the Communist-ruled German Democratic Republic in the east, appeared unwilling to engage in debates about Weimar art, preferring instead to focus on 'bigger' structural or sociopolitical explanations for the failure of republican democracy.[9] It was therefore left to two outsiders, Walter Laqueur (born in Breslau in 1921) and Peter Gay (born in Berlin in 1923), to write what have become the standard accounts of the relationship between art and politics in Weimar Germany. Interestingly, both of them were German Jews who emigrated as teenagers in the 1930s and later made academic careers for themselves in the English-speaking world. Their own personal stories are thus part of the broader tale of exile in 1933 and non-return after 1945.[10]

Gay's 1968 book *Weimar Culture* stands out in particular as a classic in the genre of interpretive essays. In it he depicts Weimar as a golden age in which avant-garde artists for a brief period became 'insiders', winning unparalled access to state patronage and critical acclaim. This was an era of 'exuberance', 'creativity' and 'expectation', particularly in the fields of theatre, publishing and journalism which were now liberated from the stuffy conventions and censorship practices of the old regime.[11] The greatest triumph for republican values, in his view, was the emergence of the Bauhaus school of painting and architecture, a movement which created functional art and housing for a new age and argued that democracy and passion, creativity and utility, must be reconciled for the benefit of humanity.[12] Equally important was the development of world-famous centres for scientific research and scholarship including the Warburg Institute for Art History in Hamburg, the Institute for Psychoanalysis in Berlin and the Institute for Social Research in Frankfurt-am-Main (whose members were later known as the Frankfurt school).[13] Yet Gay is also critical of 1920s art for encouraging irrationalism and excessive idealism, noting that what was good for culture was not always good for politics, and vice versa. 'If Weimar needed anything', he writes, 'it needed rational politics . . . But the possibility was not realized, the need not filled.'[14]

Laqueur's 1974 study *Weimar: A Cultural History*, is more wide-ranging and extensive, but also a little more downbeat. In his view, the influence of left-wing artists and intellectuals on mainstream republican culture may have been over-estimated, particularly as 'fame is frequently a matter of accident'.[15] For instance, the 'esoteric language' favoured by the Frankfurt school and other German neo-Marxists 'made their whole endeavour intelligible only to a small circle of like-minded people',[16] while the revival of their ideas in the late 1960s tells us 'more about the mood of [that era] than about the realities of the 1920s'.[17] Even so, Laqueur agrees with Gay that Weimar culture was the 'first truly modern culture' on German soil and that Nazism 'was the antithesis to everything Weimar stood for'.[18] Hitler, and not the left, was ultimately responsible for the destruction of democracy and the burial of those values and institutions which made artistic experimentation and intellectual creativity possible.

Both authors also note some of the profound paradoxes within Weimar culture, in particular its lack of a coherent direction and message and its uneven development across Germany. This can be seen on a number of different levels.

In the first instance, while the Republic did indeed create an environment more conducive to avant-garde art, it was not entirely a haven of tolerance and free speech. Thus, while Article 118 of the Weimar constitution guaranteed 'every German' the right 'to express his opinion freely in word, writing, print, picture or in any other manner', in practice this guarantee was qualified by the equal duty incumbent on all citizens to 'remain within the bounds of the general laws' as set down in the Reich Penal Code of 1871, and to protect young people against the dangers of moral corruption in popular fiction and public entertainments in particular.[19] Since the interpretation of these laws was often left in the hands of conservative judges whose loyalty to the republic was at best in doubt, considerable scope remained for restricting the right to free expression.[20] Furthermore, the Reich President could invoke the powers granted to him under Article 48 of the constitution to suspend the provisions of Article 118, and, in certain circumstances, so too could local police ordinances, particularly where there was a perceived threat to 'public order' or 'national security'.[21]

The two examples most often given of this are firstly, the decision of the Berlin Board of Film Censors to ban further showings of Lewis Milestone's adaptation of Erich Maria Remarque's novel *All Quiet on the Western Front* (1929) after violent protests organised by the NSDAP on the night of its first screening in December 1930;[22] and secondly, the successful prosecution of the anti-militarist campaigner and editor of *Die Weltbühne*, Carl von Ossietzky, who was given an eighteen-month prison term for 'high treason' in November 1931 after exposing details of Germany's secret rearmament programme in an article published in March 1929.[23] Both incidents bear testimony to the growing power and confidence of the nationalist right in the end phase of the Weimar Republic. So too do the frequent court actions launched in the late 1920s against the peace activist and founder of the Berlin Anti-War Museum Ernst Friedrich, who was prosecuted, among other things, for displaying on the door of his museum the words: 'Admission Price: Humans 20 Pfennigs, Soldiers Free'.[24]

Yet there are also cases which occurred much earlier on in the Republic's history. In 1921, for instance, the artists George Grosz and Wieland Herzfelde were fined 300 Marks and 600 Marks respectively by a German court for 'insulting the German army' after exhibiting a set of anti-militarist paintings, including the work *Deutschland, ein Wintermärchen* (*Germany, a Winter's Tale*) and a model of a pig in Prussian uniform, at the first International Dada Fair in Berlin in the summer of 1920.[25] This is significant, for it demonstrated that the Reichswehr was already the only institution which could not be criticised in Germany (in contrast to President Ebert or the industrialist Hugo Stinnes, who were seen as legitimate targets).[26] Meanwhile in 1924 the highly conservative government of the state of Thuringia (successor to the deposed 'red' SPD-KPD government of 1923) denounced the Weimar-based Bauhaus as a 'threat to the middle classes', thereby providing a rationale for cutting its funding and eventually forcing it out of the city in 1925.[27] Finally, in December 1926 the Reichstag passed a new 'Law against Trashy and Smutty Literature', backed by the bourgeois parties but opposed by the SPD and the KPD. This 'anti-smut' Law, as it was known, built on a series of ad hoc regulations introduced during the war (but cancelled during the revolution of 1918–19) to tighten censorship of films, publications and artistic productions with a 'sexual' content in the interests of 'youth protection'.[28] Freedom of expression was thus far from guaranteed under the Republic, even if it was formally written into the 1919 constitution.

Secondly, the work of Gay and Laqueur encouraged other scholars to explore the complex issue of the popular reception of Weimar art and literature in the 1920s and its relationship to the politics of the time. To take one obvious example, Bertolt Brecht's play *The Threepenny Opera* (1928), mentioned in the previous chapter, was intended as a political and artistic challenge, both to modern theatrical culture and to modern aesthetics more generally. Yet it is extremely difficult to assess its impact on contemporary audiences. Certainly the German Communist daily *Die Rote Fahne* disliked it, seeing it as typical expression of bourgeois vanity 'with not a vestige of modern social or political satire', even though Brecht at the time was building up his reputation as Germany's foremost left-wing playwright.[29] Its success in commercial terms was much more self-evident and it was an obvious hit with the 'fashionable Berlin public'. However, as John Willett and Ralph Manheim, two latter day critics, put it:

[I]f [the play] gave the [middle classes] an increasingly cynical view of their own institutions it does not seem to have promoted either them or any other section of society to try and change things for the better. The fact was simply that 'one has to have seen it', as the elegant and cosmopolitan Count Kessler noted in his diary after doing so with a party that included an ambassador and the director of the Dresdner Bank.[30]

The same problems apply when we seek to explore the reception of Weimar culture in the provinces. True, there were a number of important avant-garde centres outside Berlin, most notably Dessau, home to the Bauhaus school after its eviction from Weimar in 1925, and Saxony, where Expressionist painting continued under the guise of the 'Gruppe 1919' led by Conrad Felixmüller and where an Expressionist dance school was opened by Mary Wigman in 1920.[31] Meanwhile in the late 1920s and early 1930s professorships were awarded to Paul Klee in Düsseldorf, Max Beckmann and Willi Baumeister in Frankfurt-am-Main, Oskar Schlemmer and Otto Mueller in Breslau, and Otto Dix and Oskar Kokoschka in Dresden.[32] Yet in general older class distinctions and political allegiances still ruled in the provinces, with social democrat and communist cultural organisations tending to be as wary of 'commercialism' and avant-garde 'adventurism' as their bourgeois counterparts, and most opting for a safety first approach.[33] On the other hand, as Elizabeth Harvey points out, nearly every provincial town and city had at least some 'progressive' officials and artistic directors who were willing to promote more risky projects.[34]

Finally, the cuts in state funding introduced after 1923 (and not after just 1929) also had a negative impact on the avant-garde, particularly as they

often forced publicly owned galleries and theatres to adjust their programmes to cater for more mainstream (and therefore more commercially
viable) audiences.[35] In addition, as Gary Stark has shown, the anti-republican
right increasingly eclipsed the pro-republican left in terms of readership
and audience-share, not least because of the financially more secure position
of right-wing publishing houses like Eugen Diederichs and J. F. Lehmanns,
and the growing power and influence of Hugenberg's media empire.[36]
Indeed, at times it seemed that all the right had to do was to make references
to the number of Jews or Marxists involved in politics or the arts in order to
increase its profile and popularity. More ominously, from 1929 the so-called
'national circles' were joined by a Nazi front organisation, the *Kampfbund für
deutsche Kultur* (Fighting League for German Culture), which launched a
series of campaigns against feminism, jazz music, modern architecture, and
other manifestations of the 'Jew-nigger' republic.[37] The 'conservative revolution' or 'revolution from the right' called for by authoritarian-minded
thinkers like Arthur Moeller van den Bruck, Oswald Spengler, Edgar Jung
and Ernst Jünger, was now well on the way to becoming a reality, even if
none of the latter three were avid supporters of Hitler and National
Socialism.[38]

Class, leisure and mass consumption

Culture, as we saw at the beginning of this chapter, has to be understood
not just in relation to aesthetic concerns and developments in the 'high'
arts, but also in relation to changes in lifestyle habits, political systems,
reproductive patterns and standards of living made possible by technological
innovation.[39] Indeed, throughout the post-war period people from across
Europe were exposed to global cultural trends which threatened older
national identities, including the rival forces of 'modern' consumer capitalism
and Soviet-style socialism. Nowhere was this more apparent than in
Germany, a society which found its chief source of identity not so much in
national or republican symbolism but in 'its struggle against the international order', as Harold James puts it.[40]

Leaving class and political differences aside for the time being, for most
'ordinary' Germans in the 1920s it was the American wave which offered
the clearest – and for some, the brightest – vision of the future. The
'American wave' here meant things like new fashions and new entertainments, modern advertising and department stores, Hollywood and cinema,
Chicago gangsters and Californian beauty pageants, and above all night
clubs and jazz music, or 'industrialized merriment', as Joseph Roth called

it.[41] In the workplace it also meant the increased adaptation of 'scientific management' techniques according to the Taylorist or Fordist models of industrial production. Such things became part of the urban landscape in Germany in the 1920s to the extent that some commentators described Berlin as being 'more American than America'.[42] On the other hand, 'people in small provincial towns came to loathe Berlin as a center of corruption' or a 'Babel of sin'.[43]

Another icon of Weimar modernity, closely related to popular images of Berlin and the American wave, was the 'New Woman', the 'cigarette-smoking, motorbike-riding, silk-stockinged or tennis-skirted young woman out on the streets, in the bars, or on the sports field', as Elizabeth Harvey puts it.[44] Typically she worked as a sales assistant or office girl by day, and partied at night. At the weekend she played sports or went to the cinema. Above all, she was characterised by her slim body and androgynous appearance, which gave the impression of economic independence and liberation from older conventions.

More specifically, whereas in 1900 'women were visibly different from men in their clothing, manners and recreational interests' in the 1920s some of these behavourial codes were challenged, leading to anxieties about women who dressed like men, wore their hair short like men, and 'went out to work and earned their own money' like men.[45] Or, as a more positive take on the New Woman phenomenon put it:

The woman of yesterday was intent on the future; the woman of the day before yesterday was focused on the past. For the latter, in other words, there was no higher goal than honouring the achievements of the 'good old days' . . . In stark contrast, the woman of today is oriented exclusively towards the present. That which is is decisive for her, not that which should be or should have been according to tradition.[46]

The New Woman in turn became a symbol for a variety of other cultural phenomena that shaped everyday life in Weimar Germany, such as illustrated magazines and billboards, department stores and consumerism, keep fit and spectator sports and romance and 'trash fiction'.[47] In many ways, indeed, the New Woman was the creation of the advertising industry, a marketing tool aimed at selling certain products and 'elegant' lifestyles to young, affluent females. The (only slightly) higher salaries, brighter offices and smarter dress of women white-collar workers were indeed supposed to put them above manual labourers, and/or offer them a chance to attract a suitable husband.[48] Deportment and good looks were thus often presented in the media as the best way for a young woman to improve her prospects in

PLATE 5.1 Advertisement for 'Regatta Light' cigarettes, Berlin, c.1930.
Source: Deutsches Historisches Museum, Berlin

both the employment and marriage markets, with school career advisors often finding themselves alone in promoting a more sober or humdrum view of the world.[49] Reality was of course very different from the image put forward in magazines. Thus most young single women worked out of economic necessity rather than career interest; opportunities for promotion were few and far between; offices, like factories, became sites of automation and de-personalised, exploitative working relationships; and pay was often lower than that paid to a man doing a similar job.[50] Above all 'only a minority [of young women] could afford to rent a flat or furnished room of their own'.[51] Yet still, the image offered something to aspire to, something to dream about.

Indeed, whatever the material reality of the New Woman phenomenon, there is no doubt that young people adapted more easily to the 'new world of sport and commercialized leisure', and of 'pulp fiction and dance halls', leading to cultural conflicts between different generations.[52] In particular tensions arose between young women and older feminists of the pre-1914 era, with the latter accusing the former of taking for granted many of the liberties that their forebears had fought so hard to achieve. Or as Emmy Beckmann, a leading figure in the German Women's Teaching Association, complained in a pamphlet published in 1932:

These young women now see the tasks and lifestyles which await them as an unwanted burden and responsibility, a cold and empty substitute for the fulfillment to be gained from a peaceful home and the close family ties of husband, wife and child . . . for [them] the ideal of liberation . . . which the previous generation followed with such conviction, has faded away.[53]

Many commentators also expressed concern at the levelling effects of mass consumption and the new culture of leisure. As in America, class (as well as gender) differences seemed – at least on the surface – to be disappearing. Thus, as Joseph Roth put it in a journalistic report on the 'pleasure industry' in 1930:

In a city like Berlin there are stock companies that are capable of satisfying the entertainment needs of several social classes at once, catering to the 'cosmopolite' in the West End, providing 'solid bourgeois' pleasures in other parts of the city, and in a third supplying that part of the lower middle class that wants to have an inkling of the 'grande monde' . . . And just as in a department store there are clothes and food for every social class and even for the myriad delicate nuances in between, carefully graded by price and 'quality', so the great names of the pleasure industry supply every class with the appropriate entertainment and the appropriate – and affordable – drink, from champagne and cocktails to cognac and kirsch to sweet liqueurs down to Patzenhofer beer . . . As I went [from the West End to less expensive parts of town] I noticed the schnapps getting stronger, the beers lighter and brighter, the wines more acidic, the music cheaper, and the women older and stouter. Yes, I had the sensation that somewhere there was some merciless force or organization – a commercial undertaking of course – that implacably forced the whole population to nocturnal pleasures . . .[54]

It is even possible to see a link between anxieties about the erosion of class distinctions and Fritz Lang's famous silent film *Metropolis* (1927), in which the 'cool', 'calculating' industrialist Joh Fredersen rules over a vast, vertically organised and soulless business emporium, while the workers toil away in day and night shifts deep under the ground in order to provide light and power to the city above. Here there could be no room for individual initiative, community identity or cultural creativity, but simply a cold worship of money and power. In this sense, *Metropolis* became a metaphor for the broader cultural unease felt by many educated middle-class Germans in the face of modernity and its arrival in the workplace in the form of Lang's pathological vision of a rationalised, profit-driven, machine-age economy taken to the extreme.[55] Or as the liberal humanist writer Stefan Zweig put it in an article for the *Berliner Börsen-Courier* in February 1925:

Whoever demands only a minimum of intellectual, physical and moral exertion is bound to triumph among the masses, for the majority is passionately in favour of such . . . Autonomy in the conduct of one's life and even in the enjoyment of life has become a goal for so few people that most no longer feel how they are becoming particles, atoms in the wash of a gigantic power. So they bathe in the warm stream that is carrying them off to the trivial. As Caesar said: ruere in servitum, *to rush into servitude – this passion for self-dissolution has destroyed every nation. Now it is Europe's turn: the world war was the first phase, Americanization is the second.*[56]

Metropolis was of course far from typical of the films produced in the 1920s. More profitable were the Hollywood melodramas and romances in which the cops catch the bad guys or the girl gets her man, or the *Heimat* and mountain films with their emphasis on the timelessness and tranquillity of rural life.[57] Documentaries or rather 'docudramas' depicting the heroic experience of the war, such as the 1929 non-fictional film *Der Eiserne Hindenburg in Krieg und Frieden* (The Iron Hindenburg in War and Peace), and the 1932 feature production *Tannenberg* were also extremely popular, and did much to promote a 'mythical narrative' of the years 1914–18 at odds with the pacifist message projected by Remarque's *All Quiet on the Western Front*.[58] On the technological front, an important breakthrough came with the increasing adaptation of sound in movie recordings from the late 1920s onwards, in time, for instance, for cinema audiences to hear the seductive voice of Marlene Dietrich singing what became her signature song *Falling in Love Again* in Josef von Sternberg's *The Blue Angel* (1930).[59] Yet if film was seen as the 'most celebrated example of the mass entertainment phenomenon', with 3,878 movie houses in Germany by 1925 and 5,000 by 1930,[60] its supposed ability to transcend class differences should not be taken completely at face value, at least until the arrival of the *Großkinos*, the big cinemas with seating for 1,000 or more, which came into existence at around the same time as the introduction of sound in 1929–30. Before then, as Karl Christian Führer points out, proletarian and middle-class audiences did not attend the same movie houses, and nor did they watch the same films. In particular workers favoured the 'street corner cinemas' (*Stammkinos*) located in residential areas, because they were cheap and easy to get to, while those with more money to spend on transport and leisure could visit the luxurious 'movie palaces' (*Paläste*) based in urban city centres.[61]

Class also continued to be a factor when it came to more traditional areas of culture, such as literature and reading. Here young working-class and petit-bourgeois audiences were offered a diet of mass-produced pulp fiction, for which cinema became a 'dynamic accompaniment',[62] while themes of cultural decay and death were more in vogue with the educated middle classes, even among those who rejected the extreme *Kulturpessimismus* (cultural pessimism) of right-wing writers like Oswald Spengler or the bleak futuristic visions of Fritz Lang.

The classic example of the 1920s 'bourgeois' novel would be Thomas Mann's masterpiece *The Magic Mountain* (1924), a story which takes place in an exclusive pre-war sanatorium in Davos, high up in the Swiss mountains. In it, Hans Castorp, a young engineer from an upper middle-class family of Hamburg merchants, is forced to extend his three-week stay to seven years, and thereby comes into contact with a collection of people who together represent the different branches of the pre-1914 European social and intellectual elite. Only his cousin, Joachim Ziemssen, longs to escape the aloof charm of his fellow tuberculosis sufferers for a life of military action and adventure, but whereas Ziemssen is forced to return to the sanatorium to die, tragically it is Hans who is conscripted and sent to meet his inevitable end somewhere on the battlefields of Europe in 1914.[63]

One reading of this novel would be the conservative one that the individual creative spirit is in danger of being overwhelmed by commercialised mass society, with all its 'moral shilly-shallying' and 'flabby humanitarianism', themes already explored by Mann in his short story *Death in Venice* (1912).[64] Yet in fact *The Magic Mountain* appears to make exactly the opposite case, namely that all human and artistic values are socially constructed and therefore 'not "natural", but "artificial"'.[65] This in turn fits with Mann's decision, reached in response to the assassination of Walther Rathenau in 1922, to declare himself in favour of the republic as the most reasonable form of political system for the new, modern, democratic Germany.[66] What was needed, he wrote, was a 'spiritual metamorphosis', so that German youth might be 'won over . . . to the side of the republic; to the side of what is called democracy, and what I call humanity.'[67]

Moving in the opposite direction were the left-wing writers and artists associated with the German Communist Party and the agitprop of the proletarian theatre and cinema. Already in 1924 Stalin had denounced the SPD (and by extension the Weimar Republic) as 'the moderate wing of fascism'; and in 1928 this theory was reiterated at the Sixth Congress of the Comintern, which launched the so-called 'Third Period' of the international.[68] In Germany, this meant that the party's energies were henceforth to be focused on attacking the SPD as 'social fascists' and severing ties with SPD-led cultural organisations. As part of this process, in 1927 the KPD called at its Eleventh Conference for the formation of a 'Red cultural front', to be led by the poet Johannes R. Becher, which would concentrate all 'proletarian-revolutionary' elements in the sphere of artistic production, while countering the values of a capitalist consumer culture.[69] As Becher went on to explain in an article in *Die Linkskurve*, the main organ of the League of Proletarian-Revolutionary German Writers, in 1928:

It goes without saying that our front must take up the struggle against all forms of bourgeois literature and even against a certain type of so-called working-class writing . . . We have recognized the essence of bourgeois freedom, which is a freedom of the individual and at the cost of bestial unfreedom for the majority of the people. We embrace the freedom of socialism, which is a freedom of people not against one another, but a freedom of people together. We embrace the struggle for this freedom, the revolutionary class struggle.[70]

The cultural split on the left was further deepened by the events of 1–3 May 1929, when serious fighting erupted in the central working-class districts of Berlin between communist demonstrators and the police acting under the orders of the SPD Police President Karl Zörgiebel. Thirty-three communists lost their lives, and almost two hundred were injured, with the police suffering fifty casualties but no deaths.[71] Henceforth the KPD continued its 'class against class' policy, declaring at its Twelfth Congress that 'Social Democracy is preparing, as an active and organizing force, the establishment of the fascist dictatorship'.[72] What this meant for communist attitudes towards popular culture was spelt out by Otto Biha in an article for *Die Rote Fahne* in 1930 in which he attacked the modern 'trash novel' as having a 'devastating influence on the consciousness of the masses':

Gigantic editions, millions of books, and a tower of printed paper issue daily from the world's printing presses . . . On their assembly lines of the mind, Scherl and Ullstein produce ideology for the world, extremely dangerous poisonous gas deployed on the cultural front . . . In its struggle for the masses, the party must repel this literature. The red mass novel will help it to do so. The novel that, instead of depicting personal conflicts and private passions, gives shape to the conflicts of our time and the struggle of the masses . . . [and carries] the ideology of revolutionary consciousness to oppressed people of all sorts.[73]

Whether the 'red mass novel' was really capable of transforming social attitudes or out-producing modern trash fiction would appear doubtful, however. Indeed, in the short term all that communist cultural policy appeared to achieve was to reinforce divisions on the left, while leaving the field open to right-wing and radical nationalist critics of American-isation and modern mass entertainment more generally. This was a trend which became even more marked as the late 1920s gave way to the early 1930s.

Sex and sexuality

While the arrival of mass culture in the 1920s produced a diverse and at times highly polarised set of responses in Germany, historians have also placed emphasis on the many tensions lying at the heart of German atti-tudes towards sex and sexuality during this period. On the one hand, as we have seen, there was an obsession on the conservative right with 'moral decadence' and the supposed evils of contraception and abortion, which often went hand in hand with a 'fear of the cities' and, for many of those living in the countryside, a determination to preserve the 'sanctity of rural life'.[74] Urban women, it was alleged, were in danger of placing individual pleasure before family and nation, causing them to neglect their 'natural' duties in the sphere of motherhood and child-rearing. In May 1922 the state of Bavaria even called for a nationwide prohibition on birth control clinics,[75] while in Catholic areas more generally the police were known for strictly enforcing those parts of the Reich Penal Code that banned the advertising (although not the sale) of contraceptives.[76]

On the other hand, running parallel to these trends, there was also grow-ing evidence of a more rational, secular approach towards human relation-ships and marriage, at least in the sphere of everyday life.[77] This could be seen, for instance, in the greater awareness of sexual hygiene issues, includ-ing the launching of public information campaigns about the dangers of venereal disease and the development of a more tolerant stance towards unwed and single mothers, especially in terms of the new health and wel-fare policies arising during the war.[78] More generally, according to Cornelie Usborne, the growing use and commercial success of artificial forms of con-traception, taken together with sharply falling birth rates and the increased prevalence of abortion, showed quite clearly that 'attitudes to reproduction had changed' among all sections of the population.[79] Indeed, the number of live births per 1,000 women of childbearing age dropped from 128.0 in 1910–11 to 90.0 by 1922 and to 67.3 by 1930.[80]

One political response to this cultural shift was the development of positive policies to encourage married couples to have more children, including
a particular emphasis on the promotion of motherhood as a 'national good'.
Thus Article 119 of the Weimar constitution, which passed into law in
August 1919, read as follows:

*(1) Marriage, as the foundation of the family and the maintenance and
reproduction of the nation, enjoys the special protection of the constitution. It
is based on equality between the sexes. (2) It is the task of both the state and
society to promote the purity, health and social welfare of the family. Families
with large numbers of children have a right to compensatory financial support.
(3) Motherhood is placed under state protection and welfare.*[81]

Nor was this simply a matter of legal niceties. Especially during the war and
in the early 1920s governments at Reich, state and municipal level were
prepared to put money into welfare and public health projects aimed
specifically at mothers and infants. In 1920, for instance, a female Catholic
Centre Party city councillor in Düsseldorf argued: 'Everywhere that private
welfare activities are insufficient, the municipality must step in to help, in
order to prevent developments for the life of our people that would be
unhealthy.'[82] In Hamburg, the number of health visitors employed by the
welfare department grew from 10 in 1917 to 108 in 1927, and the percentage of newborn babies who were seen by doctors rose from 55 per cent in
1919 to 67 per cent in 1925 and 89 per cent in 1933.[83]

Another response to the change in traditional values and attitudes
brought about by the war was a partial acceptance of homosexuality and
transvestitism, at least in some of the big cities in the early 1920s.[84] A key
role here was played by Magnus Hirschfeld, a prominent physician and
author who had already petitioned the Reichstag in 1898 to introduce legislation overturning the Reich's anti-homosexual laws (i.e. Paragraph 175 of
the Reich Penal Code, which criminalised all sexual acts between consent-
ing adult males). In 1919 Hirschfeld founded the world-famous *Institut für
Sexualwissenschaft* (Institute for Sexual Research) in Berlin, which included a
library and a museum and became the focal point for several international
congresses and the establishment of the World League for Sexual Reform.[85]
Among the many books he produced was the two-volume *Sittengeschichte
des Weltkrieges* (A History of Sexual Morals in the World War) (1930), and a
follow-up study, *Sittengeschichte der Nachkriegszeit* (A History of Sexual
Morals after the War) (1932) which combined scientific evidence with a rea-
soned plea for a more rational and tolerant approach to male and female
sexual relations.[86] At the same time he was also a strong supporter of Helene

Stöcker's *Bund für Mütterschutz*, and campaigned for free access to contraception and birth control information for young women.[87]

Yet there were also darker, more insidious aspects to this greater openness on sexual matters. Thus, in the wake of the war, as Ann Taylor Allen puts it, 'governments reconfigured even the most intimate areas of life, such as sexuality, reproduction and childbearing, as public concerns over which the state exercised [or should exercise] control'.[88] The policing of abortion throughout the Weimar era would be a good example of this 'dialectic of emancipation and social discipline', with the state moving to reduce the penalties for women convicted of terminating their own pregnancies in 1926, but at the same time taking measures to improve its systems for monitoring and detection, especially of those involved in 'commercial abortion or abortion without consent'.[89] In this, it had the full backing of the medical profession which was anxious to assert its own power by ending competition from so-called 'wise women' or lay, back-street abortionists.[90]

Another example would be the 'tremendous public concern about venereal disease', and the ever tighter health regulations imposed on those known to be carrying sexually transmitted infections (STIs).[91] Racism of various kinds also grew out of the fear that falling fertility and rising STI rates would lead to the 'death' of the German nation, or, worse still, to the proliferation of inferiors at the expense of the biologically healthy and fit. The connection between war, militarisation and reproduction – already apparent during the years 1914 to 1918 – became even more pronounced in the mid- to late 1920s, as scientific 'experts', and even some 'progressive' sex reformers, advocated sterilisation programmes and other eugenic measures to improve the future 'genetic stock' and virility of the nation.[92] Taken to their extreme, such views reduced women's bodies to mere receptacles for the soldiers and workers of the future, with pregnancy stripped of all its traditional values and meanings. Yet even the SPD-sponsored reform of midwifery in Prussia in the early 1920s could be seen as a measure more of state control than of benevolent welfarism: 'It made midwives far more dependent on doctors' orders and shifted responsibility for all but the most straightforward deliveries to the practitioner.'[93]

Meanwhile, women's apparent reluctance to have more children, and thus to return to the stable norms of the pre-1914 world, was identified as a particular problem by a variety of social commentators. Single women under 30 were thus dubbed the 'surplus two million', a section of society which had supposedly enjoyed the protections of the home front during the war and now threatened to become a destabilising element, particularly as they often had no father or husband to control them.[94] As early as December 1918, for instance, the Reich Office for Economic Demobilisation gave voice to its concerns that when the soldiers came home 'a large proportion of these women will come on to the streets, and that the danger of infection and of moral decay will thereby be heightened'.[95] Meanwhile, Germany itself was increasingly imagined in medicalised terms as a 'Volkskörper' [*people's body*] in need of urgent moral and physical regeneration, or greater discipline and control.[96] What the churches branded as 'ungodly' or 'sinful', right-wing parties (and some pro-natalist groups like the *Reichsbund der Kinderreichen* or National League for Large Families) increasingly labelled as 'unpatriotic' – namely women's postponement of marriage and mother-hood until later in life.[97] Yet even progressive sex reform movements largely confined themselves to addressing married women and working mothers; sex for women outside marriage was often a taboo subject for them too. For instance, *Die Weltbühne*, one of the most radical leftist journals in the Weimar era, carried an article in April 1926 by Margot Klages-Stange which accepted uncritically the popular image of sales girls and typists as sexual predators and quasi-prostitutes:

Their professional life takes them out of their parents' home. Moreover, due to the economic competition between the sexes, the woman often develops the view 'what the man wants is fine with me' and sees extramarital relations as her natural right. That is the case far beyond the bounds of actual prostitution. Virginity maintained until marriage has ceased to exist in the big cities. This development has advanced rapidly since the war, since the number of girls who find a husband has sharply declined . . . [There] are nearly 2.5 million women condemned to remain single and therefore to seek extramarital relations. The great danger in this is the increase in venereal diseases, determined by the growing number of women who occasionally engage in prostitution.[98]

Young single women, in other words, were expected to be chaste and were condemned if they were not.[99] On the other hand, unmarried women who were convicted of procuring an illegal abortion were sometimes treated more sympathetically by the courts than were married women, especially those who were shown to have had illicit affairs which they were attempting to conceal from their husbands.[100]

While abortion and STIs were often attributed to women's 'loose morals', many male artists also blamed 'the other sex' for having started the war through their supposed ability to arouse impulses and desires in men that could not be controlled or were impervious to reason.[101] Otto Dix, for instance, wrote in his diary that 'in the final analysis, all wars are waged over

PLATE 5.2 Otto Dix, *Metropolis* (1927–8).

Source: Kunst Museum, Stuttgart

and because of the vulva'.[102] This proposition also appeared in a number of his paintings. In his famous triptych *Metropolis* (1927–8), for instance, big-city nightlife is on display with all its garishness and trash, including the overlap between the 'respectable' worlds of commerce and money and the 'underworld' of criminality and prostitution. Here Germany's inability to move on from the devastation caused by the war – seen here in the guise of marginalised and demasculinised war cripples as well as the symbolic presence of the vulva, the supposed cause of all their suffering, in the right-hand panel – is depicted with devastating clarity.[103]

The theme of 'Lustmord' (sexually motivated murder/violation of female corpses) also frequently appeared in the work of artists like Otto Dix and George Grosz, whereby the 'violent assault on the male body' that was war was transformed into a symbolic assault on the female body as a site of passion and pleasure.[104] This fed into a broader public obsession with actual serial killers and murderers during the Weimar era. In Berlin in the early 1920s, for instance, newspapers regularly reported the discovery of the dead bodies of prostitutes in the seedy area around the *Schlesische Bahnhof*. Some of them were probably victims of Karl Friedrich Grossmann, a repeat sexual offender who committed suicide in his prison cell in July 1922 before the end of his trial for the murder of twenty women, and went on to achieve retrospective fame as the first in a long line of Weimar-era serial killers.[105] Criminologists, and in particular proponents of the abolition of the death penalty, condemned the tabloid press (and film-makers) for stirring up public panic 'in the most grotesque manner' through their irresponsible reporting of the lurid details of each 'ripper' case.[106] Yet even works of high art, such as Alfred Döblin's modernist masterpiece *Berlin Alexanderplatz*

(1929), were quite literally 'littered with the bodies of raped and murdered women'.[107]

Finally, the image that Weimar Germany had (and still has) as an era of toleration towards homosexuality must be offset by the steady rise in the number of prosecutions of men under Paragraph 175 of the Reich Penal Code for various 'acts of lewdness' (*Unzucht*) as the decade progressed. One of the causes of this was the prominent media attention given to the trial and execution of another serial killer, Fritz Haarmann, a psychopath and one-time police informer from Hanover who was convicted in late 1924 of sexually assaulting and murdering twenty-four young men between 1918 and 1923.[108] Indeed, such was the notoriety of the Haarmann case that Fritz Lang was able to make a deliberate allusion to it in the opening sequence of his film *M* (1931), about the fictitious child-killer Franz Beckert, when a little girl is heard to sing the gruesome nursery rhyme:

Just you wait 'til it's your time,
Blackman [Haarmann] will come after you,
With his chopper, oh so fine,
He'll make mincemeat out of you.[109]

Lang, perhaps a little disingenuously, later claimed that the film was intended as a critique of the modern *Angstpsychose* (public hysteria) which accompanied serial murder cases and not as a statement in favour of capital punishment. But much of this was lost on a public still reeling from the aftermath of the real child murderer Peter Kürten, the so-called 'Vampire of Düsseldorf', who at the time when the screenplay for *M* was written had yet to be caught.[110]

With life imitating art in this way, it was small wonder that more rational approaches to sexuality and penal reform were increasingly marginalised in Weimar political discourse. Also forgotten were the real-life murder victims themselves, the anonymous prostitutes, alcoholics, and vagrants who made up the 'unnamed dead', as Joseph Roth called them in a report on a gruesome display of up to one hundred photographs of unclaimed bodies exhibited at the Alexanderplatz police headquarters in Berlin in 1923:

They were found on the street, in the Tiergarten, in the river Spree or the canals. In some cases the place where they were found is not given or is unknown. The drowned bodies are puffed up and . . . the slime crusts on their faces are cracked and split like a poor-quality plaster cast. The women's breasts are grotesquely swollen, their features contorted, their hair like a pile of sweepings on their swollen heads. [111]

Yet in would be a mistake to see the debates of the late 1920s about criminality, sexuality and the role of the press simply in terms of a crisis of
modernity caused by the supposed pathologies and degeneracy of modern
urban life. Rather, as we have already seen in the case of the anti-smut law of
December 1926, a more straightforward battle was also taking place between
the advocates of censorship, harsher punishments for criminals and
vagrants, and traditional family values on the one hand, and the supporters
of freedom of expression, abolition of the death penalty and penal reform
on the other. That the former eventually won out over the latter was in no
way inevitable, at least until the early 1930s.[112]

A similar battle can also be seen over the question of homosexual emancipation, which in general had the support of the left (the KPD, SPD and
DDP) but not of the conservative and nationalist right.[113] Indeed, Magnus
Hirschfeld, who was a Jew and a Social Democrat as well as an advocate of
sexual reform, fell victim to numerous verbal and physical attacks from old
and new political enemies during this period. Thus he was badly beaten up
twice in Munich, in 1920 and again in 1921, and in 1923 a gunman fired at
him during a lecture in Vienna, injuring several members of the audience
in the process.[114] Later on in 1929, when the Communists and Social
Democrats together successfully tabled a motion in the Reichstag Criminal
Law reform committee calling for a new bill to abolish Paragraph 175, the
Nazi newspaper *Völkischer Beobachter* declared:

We congratulate you, Mr. Hirschfeld, on your victory in committee. But
don't think that we Germans will allow these laws to stand for a single day
after we have come to power . . . Among the many evil instincts that characterise
the Jewish race, one that is especially pernicious has to do with sexual
relationships. The Jews are forever trying to propagandise sexual relations
between siblings, men and animals, and men and men. We National Socialists
will soon unmask and condemn them by law. These efforts are nothing
but vulgar, perverted crimes, and we will punish them by banishment or
hanging.[115]

The bill itself failed when it was placed before the full Reichstag after
the September 1930 election, and Hirschfeld's Institute was indeed one
of the first targets of the Nazis when they came to power, being ransacked
and looted during a raid organised by the National Socialist Students'
League on 6 May 1933. When, four days later, some of the books taken from
the Institute were burned by the students in a huge fire on the *Opernplatz*
(Opera Square) opposite Berlin's main university, a bust of Hirschfeld

himself was also thrown into the flames. So too, were the works of many other Jewish and left-wing witers.[116]

Jewish and Gentile Germans

Hirschfeld was targeted by the Nazis because he was Jewish as well as because of his political campaigns for homosexual rights and sex reform. His case therefore highlights broader issues connected with the 'Jewish question' in the 1920s and early 1930s, and with the rise of anti-Semitic cultures on the right-wing of the German political spectrum more generally.

According to the 1925 census, there were 564,379 Jews living in Germany, representing 0.9 per cent of the population, a figure which had fallen to 499,682, or 0.77 per cent of the population, by 1933. They were mainly urban, concentrated in particular professions – especially in banking and publishing, where the houses of Mosse and Ullstein dominated the national, but not local markets – and largely middle-class in terms of income, education and cultural tastes. Around one-sixth (15.2 per cent in 1925 and 17.7 per cent in 1933) were so-called *Ostjuden*, i.e. recently arrived and usually impoverished immigrants from the east, but the vast majority were German-born, and saw themselves as German first, Jewish second.[117] In particular they retained a sense of gratitude towards Bismarck, the Prussian statesman and first Chancellor of the German Reich who had removed many of the legal disabilities against Jews in a series of emancipation edicts between 1869 and 1871.[118]

Although the officer corps of the army had largely been barred to Jews (and Catholics) before 1914,[119] some 100,000 German Jews served in uniform during the war, 35,000 of whom were decorated and 12,000 of whom were killed. This was a comparable with the death rate for non-Jewish German soldiers.[120] In October 1916, however, great offence had been caused when the Prussian Ministry of War – reacting to pressure from extreme nationalist groups – ordered an investigation into the number of Jews who had signed up for military duty. The official reason given for this so-called 'Jew count' (*Judenzählung*) was to counter criticism that Jews were seeking to avoid front-line service in the field. When the Ministry decided, for its own reasons, not to publish the results, right-wingers alleged a cover-up and used this as an excuse to continue with their anti-Semitic propaganda.[121]

More generally, Germany's involvement – and eventual defeat – in the First World War brought with it contradictory results for the position of the Jews in German society. On the one hand, the 1920s were a time when the process of emancipation and assimilation, which had begun back in the early nineteenth century, and was accelerated by Bismarck's legislation in 1869–71, was finally completed. Now in theory there were no more barriers, legal or otherwise, to the full entry of Jews into German society. In the highest echelons of government, for instance, the appointment of the Jewish businessman Walther Rathenau as Foreign Minister in January 1922 would have been unthinkable before 1914, as would the choice of the Austrian-born Jewish socialist Rudolf Hilferding as Finance Minister in 1923 (and again in 1928–9).[122] Jews were also active in public life as theatre directors, university professors, medical experts, journalists, writers, artists and politicians. In the field of music important contributions were made by the composers Hanns Eisler, Arnold Schönberg and Kurt Weill, and by the conductors Otto Klemperer and Bruno Walter; and from his new base in Berlin, the scientist Albert Einstein consolidated his position as the world's leading expert on theoretical physics.[123] Two of the largest national newspapers in Weimar Germany also had Jewish editors: Theodor Wolff for the *Berliner Tageblatt* and Georg Bernhard for the *Vossische Zeitung*. Both of the latter supported the DDP, the main left-liberal party in Weimar Germany, which as a result had a greater share of newspaper publicity than its overall support in the country may have warranted. Many other Jews backed the SPD, the party which did more than any other to promote the cause of emancipation in Germany. After 1918, around 10 per cent of the SPD's Reichstag deputies came from Jewish backgrounds.[124]

In terms of economic position, the Jews did no worse out of the war than other sections of German society, and no better either. Those already established in big business and the professions usually prospered in the 1920s, while those looking to get a foothold in the market usually found that there were fewer opportunities than there had been before 1914. Like their gentile counterparts, middle-class Jews engaged in the independent trade and retail sectors also often faced the prospect of financial ruin as a result of hyperinflation and worldwide pressures towards economic concentration. In others ways, too, the Jews were affected by an overall decline in expectations and living standards. For instance, as Donald Niewyk discovered, Jewish charities in 1920s Berlin were increasingly obliged to provide relief for unemployed German-Jewish families, whereas before 1914 almost all of their philanthropic activities had been directed towards helping newly arrived immigrants from the east. Furthermore, 'fewer Jews could afford to send their sons and daughters to university' so that, for instance, whereas the number of students registered at Prussian centres of higher education rose slightly during the period 1911 to 1925, the number of Jewish students actually fell from 2,212 to 1,675.[125]

In spite of this, the war bred a vicious new streak of anti-Semitism, seen in allegations of Jewish 'war-profiteering' and 'shirking', and calls from the extreme right for the full-scale eradication of Jewish influence in German life. The original programme of the NSDAP, the twenty-five points of 1920, was unequivocal on this subject:

Only he who is an ethnic comrade may be a citizen. Only he who is of German blood, regardless of religious denomination, can be an ethnic comrade. No Jew, therefore, can be an ethnic comrade.[126]

So too was the main organ of the Pan-German League, the *Alldeutsche Blätter*, which greeted the appointment of Walther Rathenau as Foreign Minister on 31 January 1922 with the words:

Now we have it. Germany has a Jewish Foreign Minister . . . His appointment is an absolutely unheard-of provocation of the people, an even more unheard-of provocation of the völkisch-thinking part of the people.[127]

How seriously ordinary Germans took the extreme racism of groups like the Pan-German League and the DVSTB is difficult to say. Certainly it seems to have influenced the men who gunned down Rathenau near his home in Berlin-Grunewald on 24 June 1922 and their co-conspirators who went on to plan the murder of other prominent Jews, including Maximilian Harden, Oskar Cohn, Max Warburg and Theodor Wolff.[128] Indeed, such was the level of anti-Semitic hatred in the extreme right-wing press in 1922, even after Rathenau's killing, that the Weimar government of Joseph Wirth was forced to pass an emergency law for the protection of the republic (*Republikschutzgesetz*) restricting freedom of expression, association and assembly for enemies of the republic. Among other things, this led to a ban on the DVSTB in all states except Bavaria and Württemberg, a move also upheld by the German Supreme Court in October 1922.[129]

Just as dangerous, perhaps, as the DVSTB was the rise of a more 'respectable' form of racial anti-Semitism adopted by the DNVP and other conservative groups who regarded the Jews as a barrier to the recovery of German greatness in the post-war period, or as a symbol of the 'uprooted-ness' and 'hybrid' nature of the modern era.[130] Here too it is possible to see the negative effects of the notorious 'Jew count' of 1916, which did little to dispel the belief that Jews had shirked from front-line duties during the war. In November 1919, for instance, the former Reich Finance Minister turned DNVP spokesman Karl Helfferich won plaudits in the nationalist press when he repeatedly refused to answer questions put to him by the Jewish USPD representative Oskar Cohn during a stormy session of the National Assembly's Committee of Investigation into the Causes of the War and of Germany's Defeat.[131] Helfferich and his colleagues in the DNVP also lent their support to phrases such as 'stab-in-the-back', 'November traitors' and 'Jew republic', so that these insults entered mainstream political discourse and poisoned public debate. When, after 1933, the Nazis created a new monument to Rathenau's assassins, 'crowned with reproductions of the steel helmets which had been worn by soldiers during the First World War', they were indeed building on a long-established series of myths and symbols which associated the war with 'manly' heroism and the Jews with a 'corrupt peace'.[132]

Finally, there was also the growth of more popular manifestations of anti-Semitic hatred, with hostility directed against *Ostjuden* in particular. This can be seen above all during the so-called Scheunenviertel riots in Berlin in November 1923, already mentioned in Chapter 3. In two days of violence between 5 and 6 November, groups of young men smashed up shops and private dwellings, and beat up passers-by in Berlin's main Jewish district; the principal victims were immigrants from Polish Galicia. Three hundred people were arrested, most of them unemployed German workers who had committed acts of violence against Jews. Members of the Reich Federation of Jewish War Veterans (*Reichsbund jüdischer Frontsoldaten* or RjF) also came into the area to defend Jewish shops against the anti-Semitic thugs. The immediate cause of the riot was later identified as being a malicious rumour that Jews had been buying up food vouchers issued to unemployed workers at below their nominal value, and then selling them on at a profit. However, the underlying motivation was a deep-seated hatred of eastern Jews, who were accused of being 'foreign' and 'unclean'.[133]

Historians are still in disagreement over the exact significance of this event, although there is now a broad consensus that the riot was a spontaneous affair, and not the work of radical right-wing groups. In other words, it had no direct connection to the events in Munich on 9 November 1923, when Hitler launched his failed putsch against the Bavarian government. This leaves two possible avenues of interpretation. Firstly, some scholars have seen the riots as being led by a traditional 'pogrom-like' mob which was upset by rising food prices and unemployment and was looking for scapegoats.[134] In contrast to this, both Trude Maurer and David Clay Large see a more ominous sign precisely in the fact that the riots were not organised, but spontaneous. In Large's words:

It showed how easily and quickly socioeconomic frustrations could boil over into anti-Jewish violence and how broad the antisemitic currents ran in postwar German society . . . [including among the urban poor] . . . the traditional constituency of the left.[135]

Worse still, the riots coincided with more minor anti-Semitic disturbances in towns like Erfurt, Nuremberg, Coburg, Bremen, Oldenburg and Breslau,[136] and with a concerted move made by the reactionary regime of state commissioner Gustav von Kahr in Bavaria to expel more than one hundred immigrant Jewish families from Bavarian territory between October 1923 and February 1924, most of them long-term residents from Polish backgrounds. In Kahr's own words, the Jews were 'responsible for much of the German misfortune and economic distress since the war'.[137] The nearly two million Germans (6.5 per cent of all voters) who supported the *Völkischer Block*, an alliance of various racist parties, in the May 1924 Reichstag election clearly agreed with him.[138]

On the other hand, it is important not to draw a direct parallel between these events and later developments during the Nazi era. For one thing, in 1923 the police intervened to stop the Scheunenviertel riots, whereas in 1933 and 1938 the police, SA and security services deliberately orchestrated anti-Jewish violence.[139] For another thing, the targets in 1923 were the recently-arrived *Ostjuden*, and not the 'abstract demonized image of "the Jew"' portrayed in later Nazi propaganda.[140] With currency restablisation and economic recovery (of sorts) under the new 'bourgeois' coalition governments of Wilhelm Marx and Hans Luther, support for extreme racist parties fell to 3.0 per cent (0.9 million votes) in the December 1924 Reichstag election and to 2.6 per cent (0.8 million votes) in the May 1928 election.[141] Anti-Semitism, it seemed, was not a real vote-winner, at least not on its own.

As for official attitudes, it is true that state governments in the 1920s did frequently use their powers under the Reich Citizenship law of 1913 to hinder or prevent the naturalisation of non-ethnic German immigrants, with Bavaria having a particularly poor record here. Prussia was less restrictive in terms of its naturalisation policies, especially in the late 1920s, although on occasion it too took fairly drastic and illiberal action to deport immigrants without papers, including Jews and non-Jews.[142] Indeed, in 1920–1 special internment camps were even set up at places like Stargard in Pomerania and Cottbus-Sielow in Brandenburg to hold those awaiting expulsion to Poland.[143] But at no point did any Weimar government, at Reich or state level, ever seriously contemplate reversing the Jewish emancipation of 1869–71, as the Nazi regime did in 1935. In short, the Jews, more than any other ethnic group in Germany, depended on the survival of the republic for their future well-being and prosperity.

Notes

1 Raymond Williams, *Culture and Society, 1780–1950*, Penguin edition (London, 1963), p. 13.

2 Peukert, *The Weimar Republic*, pp. 276–7.

3 Willett, *Art and Politics, passim*; Jost Hermand and Frank Trommler, *Die Kultur der Weimarer Republik* (Munich, 1978); Ben Lieberman, 'Testing Peukert's Paradigm: The "Crisis of Classical Modernity" in the "New Frankfurt", 1925–1930', *German Studies Review*, 17/2 (1994), pp. 287–303.

4 Menge, 'The *Iron Hindenburg*', p. 361. See also the recent works cited by Menge in ibid., p. 360, n. 16.

5 Usborne, *Cultures of Abortion*, p. 22.

6 On collectivistic visions see e.g. Thomas Mergel, 'Führer, Volksgemeinschaft und Maschine. Politische Erwartungsstrukturen in der Weimarer Republik und dem Nationalsozialismus 1918–1936', in Hardtwig (ed.), *Politische Kulturgeschichte der Zwischenkriegszeit*, pp. 91–127; Schröder, *Vom Nationalismus zum Nationalsozialismus, passim*; David F. Crew, 'The Ambiguities of Modernity: Welfare and the German State from Wilhelm to Hitler', in Eley (ed.), *Society, Culture and the State in Germany, 1870–1930*, pp. 319–44; Geoff Eley, 'Conservatives and Radical Nationalists in Germany: The Production of Fascist Potentials, 1912–1928', in Martin Blinkhorn (ed.), *Fascists and Conservatives: The Radical Right and the Establishment in Twentieth-Century Europe* (London, 1990), pp. 50–70; and Fritzsche, *Rehearsals for Fascism*, esp. pp. 210–29. On individualistic-racist discourses see above all Moritz Föllmer's new essay 'Was Nazism Collectivistic? Redefining the Individual in Berlin, 1930–1945', forthcoming in *Journal of Modern History*, 82 (2010). I would like to thank him for allowing me to see an advance copy of this essay.

7 Peter Fritzsche, 'Did Weimar Fail?', *Journal of Modern History*, 68/3 (1996), pp. 629–56; idem., 'Landscape of Danger, Landscape of Design: Crisis and Modernism in Weimar Germany', in Thomas W. Kniesche and Stephen Brockmann (eds), *Dancing on the Volcano. Essays on the Culture of the Weimar Republic* (London, 1994), pp. 29–46. The recent set of essays edited by Anthony McElligott *Weimar Germany* (Oxford, 2009) also emphasises the 'ambiguities' rather than the 'crisis' of 'classical modernity' (p. 8). Unfortunately this excellent volume came out too late for detailed consideration here; it is nonetheless to be highly recommended.

8 Weitz, *Weimar Germany*, p. 253.

9 For a useful overview see Georg Iggers, 'Introduction', in G. Iggers (ed.), *The Social History of Politics. Critical Perspectives in West German Historical Writing since 1945* (Leamington Spa, 1985); and Winkler (ed.), *Weimar im Widerstreit, passim*.

10 See e.g. Peter Gay, *My German Question. Growing up in Nazi Berlin* (New Haven and London, 1998); Walter Laqueur, *Generation Exodus. The Fate of Young Jewish Refugees from Nazi Germany* (Hanover and London, 2001). Another German-born American-Jewish scholar who contributed hugely to the theme of German social and cultural history was George L. Mosse (1918–1999), grandson of the German publisher and newspaper proprietor Rudolf Mosse. In this context see in particular his essay 'Left-Wing Intellectuals in the Weimar Republic', in George L. Mosse, *Germans and Jews. The Right, the Left and the Search for a 'Third Force' in Pre-Nazi Germany* (London, 1971), pp. 171–225.

11 Peter Gay, *Weimar Culture. The Outsider as Insider*, Penguin edition (London, 1974), p. xii.

12 Ibid., pp. 105–6.

13 Ibid., p. 32.

14 Ibid., p. 77.

15 Walter Laqueur, *Weimar: A Cultural History 1918–1933* (London, 1974), p. 65.

16 Ibid., p. 63.

17 Ibid., p. 275.

18 Ibid., pp. ix and 270.

19 Die Verfassung des Deutschen Reiches ('Weimarer Verfassung'), 11 August 1919, available at http://www.documentarchiv.de/wr.html. See also Stark, 'All Quiet on the Home Front', p. 76.

20 For some useful observations on the judiciary in Weimar-era Prussia in particular see Christopher Clark, *Iron Kingdom. The Rise and Downfall of Prussia, 1600–1987* (London, 2006), pp. 631–2.

21 Eksteins, *The Limits of Reason*, p. 70; Lynn Abrams, 'From Control to Commercialization: The Triumph of Mass Entertainment in Germany, 1900–1925?', *German History*, 8/3 (1990), pp. 278–93 (here p. 285).

22 Bessel, *Germany after the First World War*, p. 267; Modris Eksteins, 'War, Memory and Politics: The Fate of the Film *All Quiet on the Western Front*', *Central European History*, 13/1 (1980), pp. 60–82.

23 Laqueur, *Weimar*, pp. 258–9.

24 Eva Zwach, *Deutsche und englische Militärmuseen im 20. Jahrhundert. Eine kulturgeschichtliche Analyse des gesellschaftlichen Umgangs mit dem Krieg* (Münster, 1999), pp. 115–16.

25 Willett, *Art and Politics*, pp. 53–4; Ivo Kranzfelder, *George Grosz, 1893–1959* (Cologne, 1999), pp. 36–7.

26 In 1924 a criminal court imposed the symbolically low fine of 10 Marks on a man for calling Ebert 'a traitor to his country', with the judge suggesting that he agreed with the views of the defendant 'as Ebert had indeed shown himself to be a traitor by maintaining contacts with striking munitions workers in

Berlin in the last year of the war'. See Evans, *The Coming of the Third Reich*, p. 81. For other examples of targeted insults directed at Ebert and Stinnes, see Chapters 3 and 4 above.

27 Willett, *Art and Politics*, p. 82.

28 Stark, 'All Quiet on the Home Front', p. 66. Cf. Margaret F. Stieg, 'The 1926 German Law to Protect Youth against Trash and Dirt: Moral Protectionism in a Democracy', *Central European History*, 23/1 (1990), pp. 22–56; and Patrick Major, '"Smut and Trash". Germany's Culture Wars Against Pulp Fiction', in Karl Christian Führer and Corey Ross (eds), *Mass Media, Culture and Society in Twentieth-Century Germany* (Basingstoke, 2006), pp. 234–50 (here pp. 241–2).

29 Brecht, *The Threepenny Opera*, p. xv.

30 Ibid.

31 Szejnmann, *Vom Traum zum Alptraum*, p. 82.

32 Laqueur, *Weimar*, p. 165.

33 Abrams, 'From Control to Commercialization', pp. 290–1.

34 Elizabeth Harvey, 'Culture and Society in Weimar Germany: The Impact of Modernism and Mass Culture', in Fulbrook (ed.), *Twentieth-Century Germany*, pp. 58–76 (here p. 66).

35 Ibid., p. 73; Willett, *Art and Politics*, p. 74.

36 Gary D. Stark, *Entrepreneurs of Ideology: Neo-Conservative Publishers in Weimar Germany* (Chapel Hill, NC and London, 1981), pp. 15–57; Berger, *Germany*, p. 133.

37 Alan Steinweis, 'Weimar Political Culture and the Rise of National Socialism: The *Kampfbund für deutsche Kultur*', in *Central European History*, 24/4 (1991), pp. 402–23.

38 Cf. George L. Mosse, 'The Corporate State and the Conservative Revolution in Weimar Germany', in idem., *Germans and Jews*, pp. 116–43. Also Herf, *Reactionary Modernism*; and Sieferle, *Die Konservative Revolution*.

39 Cf. Peukert, *The Weimar Republic*, pp. 174–5; Abrams, 'From Control to Commercialization', pp. 280–1.

40 James, *A German Identity*, p. 125.

41 Joseph Roth, 'The Berlin Pleasure Industry', *Münchner Neueste Nachrichten*, 1 May 1930. Reproduced in Roth, *What I Saw*, pp. 171–5 (here p. 171).

42 Harvey, 'Culture and Society in Weimar Germany', p. 63.

43 Richard Plant, *The Pink Triangle. The Nazi War Against Homosexuals* (New York, 1986), p. 45; Berger, *Germany*, p. 134.

44 Harvey, 'Culture and Society in Weimar Germany', p. 61.

45 Ann Taylor Allen, *Women in Twentieth-Century Europe* (London, 2008), p. 2; Frevert, *Women in German History*, p. 176.

46 Elsa Herrmann, *So ist die neue Frau* (Hellerau, 1929), pp. 32–43. Reproduced in Kaes *et al.* (eds), *The Weimar Republic Source Book*, pp. 206–8 (here p. 207).

47 See here Bernhard Fulda, 'Industries of Sensationalism: German Tabloids in Weimar Berlin'; Gideon Reuveni, 'Reading, Advertising and Consumer Culture in the Weimar Period', and Habbo Knoch, 'Living Pictures: Photojournalism in Germany, 1900 to the 1930s' all in Führer and Ross (eds), *Mass Media, Culture and Society*, pp. 183–203, 204–16 and 217–33.

48 Frevert, *Women in German History*, p. 181.

49 Elizabeth Harvey, 'Private Fantasy and Public Intervention. Girls' Reading in Weimar Germany', in Jennifer Birkett and Elizabeth Harvey (eds), *Determined Women. Studies in the Construction of the Female Subject* (London, 1991), pp. 38–67.

50 Weitz, *Weimar Germany*, p. 157.

51 Frevert, *Women in German History*, p. 183.

52 Peukert, *The Weimar Republic*, p. 176; Abrams, 'From Control to Commercialization', pp. 283 and 289.

53 Elizabeth Harvey, 'The Failure of Feminism? Young Women and the Bourgeois Feminist Movement in Weimar Germany, 1918–1933', *Central European History*, 28/1 (1995), pp. 1–28 (here p. 1).

54 Roth, 'The Berlin Pleasure Industry' (as note 41 above), pp. 173–4.

55 Widdig, *Culture and Inflation*, pp. 159–65.

56 Stefan Zweig, 'Die Monotisierung der Welt', *Berliner Börsen-Courier*, 1 February 1925. Reproduced in Kaes *et al.* (eds), *The Weimar Republic Source Book*, pp. 397–400 (here p. 400).

57 Berger, *Germany*, p. 134.

58 Menge, 'The *Iron Hindenburg*', esp. pp. 361–66.

59 Kolb, *The Weimar Republic*, p. 97.

60 Abrams, 'From Control to Commercialization', pp. 279 and 282; Menge, 'The *Iron Hindenburg*', p. 362.

61 See Karl Christian Führer, 'Auf dem Weg zur Massenkultur? Kino und Rundfunk in der Weimarer Republik', *Historische Zeitschrift*, 262 (1996), pp. 739–81 (here pp. 755–6).

62 Abrams, 'From Control to Commercialization', p. 281.

63 On *The Magic Mountain* see also Weitz, *Weimar Germany*, pp. 253–62.

64 Thomas Mann, *Death in Venice*, Penguin edition (London, 1955), p. 17.

65 Williams, *Culture and Society*, p. 28.

66 Martin Sabrow, *Der Rathenau-Mord. Rekonstruktion einer Verschwörung gegen die Republik von Weimar* (Munich, 1994), p. 157. On Mann's conversion to republicanism and his new-found role as an 'ambassador of Weimar' after 1922 see also Nigel Hamilton, *The Brothers Mann. The Lives of Heinrich and Thomas Mann, 1871–1950 and 1875–1955* (London, 1978), pp. 203 and ff.

67 Thomas Mann, 'Von deutscher Republik: Aus einem Vortrag', *Berliner Tageblatt*, 17 October 1922. Reproduced in Kaes *et al.* (eds), *The Weimar Republic Source Book*, pp. 105–9 (here pp. 109 and 106).

68 David Beetham, *Marxists in Face of Fascism* (Manchester, 1983), pp. 153–4; Kevin McDermott and Jeremy Agnew, *The Comintern. A History of International Communism from Lenin to Stalin* (Basingstoke, 1996), pp. 81–119.

69 Willett, *Art and Politics*, p. 173.

70 Johannes R. Becher, 'Unsere Front', *Die Linkskurve*, 1/1 (August 1928). Reproduced in Kaes *et al.* (eds), *The Weimar Republic Source Book*, pp. 234–7 (here pp. 236–7).

71 Heinrich August Winkler, 'Choosing the Lesser Evil: The German Social Democrats and the Fall of the Weimar Republic', *Journal of Contemporary History*, 25/2 (1990), pp. 205–27 (here p. 215).

72 McDermott and Agnew, *The Comintern*, p. 101.

73 Otto Biha, 'Der proletarische Massenroman. Eine neue Eine-Mark-Serie des "Internationalen Arbeiterverlages", *Die Rote Fahne*, 2 August 1930. Reproduced in Kaes *et al.* (eds), *The Weimar Republic Source Book*, pp. 239–40.

74 Baranowski, *The Sanctity of Rural Life*, p. 9.

75 Weindling, *Health, Race and German Politics*, p. 371.

76 Usborne, *The Politics of the Body*, p. 80.

77 Usborne, *Cultures of Abortion*, pp. 144–5.

78 Weindling, *Health, Race and German Politics*, pp. 284–6 and 288.

79 Usborne, *The Politics of the Body*, p. 81; idem., *Cultures of Abortion*, p. 136.

80 Figures from Jill Stephenson, *Women in Nazi Germany* (London, 2001), p. 24.

81 Die Verfassung des Deutschen Reiches ('Weimarer Verfassung'), 11 August 1919, available at http://www.documentarchiv.de/wr.html.

82 Crew, *Germans on Welfare*, p. 117.

83 Ibid., p. 118.

84 James D. Steakley, *The Homosexual Emancipation Movement in Germany* (New York, 1975), pp. 78–81.

85 Ibid., pp. 91–2 and *passim*.

86 Magnus Hirschfeld (ed.), *Sittengeschichte des Weltkrieges*, 2 Vols (Leipzig and Vienna, 1930); idem., *Sittengeschichte der Nachkriegszeit*, 2 Vols. (Leipzig and Vienna, 1932).

87 Usborne, *The Politics of the Body*, pp. 118–23; Grossmann, *Reforming Sex*, pp. 16–17; Weindling, *Health, Race and German Politics*, p. 371.

88 Allen, *Women in Twentieth-Century Europe*, p. 3.

89 Anthony McElligott, 'Introduction', in McElligott (ed.), *Wiemar Germany*, pp. 1–25 (here p. 12); Usborne, *Cultures of Abortion*, p. 5.

90 Cf. Cornelie Usborne, 'Wise Women, Wise Men and Abortion in the Weimar Republic: Gender, Class and Medicine', in Lynn Abrams and Elizabeth Harvey (eds), *Gender Relations in German History* (London, 1996), pp. 143–76.

91 Bessel, *Germany After the First World War*, p. 233; Weindling, *Health, Race and German Politics*, pp. 357–9.

92 Domansky, 'Militarization and Reproduction', *passim*; Peukert, *The Weimar Republic*, p. 139; Weindling, *Health, Race and German Politics*, pp. 450–7; Grossmann, *Reforming Sex*, pp. 70–5.

93 Usborne, *The Politics of the Body*, pp. 52–3.

94 See Ingrid Sharp, 'The Debate on "Surplus Women" in Post-First World War Germany', forthcoming in Ingrid Sharp and Matthew Stibbe (eds), *Aftermaths of War. Women's Movements and Individual Activists, 1918–1923* (Leiden, 2010). Also Usborne, *The Politics of the Body*, pp. 81–2.

95 Bessel, *Germany After the First World War*, pp. 234–5.

96 Moritz Föllmer, 'Der "kranke Volkskörper": Industrielle, hohe Beamte und der Diskurs der nationalen Regeneration in der Weimarer Republik', *Geschichte und Gesellschaft*, 27 (2001), pp. 41–67; Fritzsche, 'Did Weimar Fail?', p. 632.

97 On the *Reichsbund der Kinderreichen*, which was founded in 1919, see Karin Hausen, 'Mothers Day in the Weimar Republic', in Bridenthal *et al.* (eds), *When Biology Became Destiny*, pp. 131–52 (here p. 142).

98 Margot Klages-Stange, 'Prostitution', *Die Weltbühne*, 13 April 1926, pp. 579–80. Reproduced in Kaes *et al.* (eds), *The Weimar Republic Source Book*, pp. 728–9.

99 Cf. Cornelie Usborne, 'The New Woman and Generational Conflict. Perceptions of Young Women's Sexual Mores in the Weimar Republic', in Mark Roseman (ed.), *Generations in Conflict. Youth Revolt and Generation Formation in Germany, 1770–1968* (Cambridge, 1995), pp. 137–63.

100 Usborne, *Cultures of Abortion*, pp. 135, 165 and 196–7.

101 Sharp, 'Blaming the Women', p. 80.

102 Ibid., p. 69; Tatar, *Lustmord*, p. 74.

103 Tatar, *Lustmord*, p. 75.

104 Ibid., p. 12.

105 See Horst Bosetzky, *Die Bestie vom Schlesischen Bahnhof. Dokumentarischer Roman aus den 20er Jahren* (Berlin, 2004).

106 Evans, *Rituals of Retribution*, p. 536; Abrams, 'From Control to Commercialization', p. 284; Tatar, *Lustmord*, pp. 47–8.

107 Tatar, *Lustmord*, p. 141.

108 Plant, *The Pink Triangle*, pp. 45–8.

109 Tatar, *Lustmord*, p. 3.

110 Ibid., p. 154; Evans, *Rituals of Retribution*, pp. 596–7.

111 Joseph Roth, 'The Unnamed Dead' (article in the *Neue Berliner Zeitung – 12-Uhr-Blatt*, 17 January 1923), reproduced in Roth, *What I Saw*, pp. 79–82 (here p. 81).

112 Evans, *Rituals of Retribution*, p. 536. See also Wachsmann, 'Between Reform and Repression', esp. pp. 430–1.

113 Steakley, *The Homosexual Emancipation Movement*, pp. 84–5.

114 Ibid., p. 88.

115 Plant, *The Pink Triangle*, p. 49.

116 Steakley, *The Homosexual Emancipation Movement*, pp. 103–5; Plant, *The Pink Triangle*, p. 51; Evans, *The Coming of the Third Reich*, pp. 375–6; Gerhard Sauder (ed.), *Die Bücherverbrennung: Zum 10. Mai 1933* (Munich, 1983), pp. 162–6.

117 Figures taken from Wehler, *Deutsche Gesellschaftsgeschichte*, vol. 4, p. 499, and Trude Maurer, *Ostjuden in Deutschland 1918–1933* (Hamburg, 1986), p. 72.

118 On Bismarck's relationship with the Jews see Pulzer, *The Rise of Political Anti-Semitism*, esp. pp. 17–18 and 91–2; and Fritz Stern, *Gold and Iron. Bismarck, Bleichröder and the Building of the German Empire* (London, 1977).

119 See Martin Kitchen, *The German Officer Corps, 1890–1914* (Oxford, 1968), esp. pp. 37–48.

120 Ray Rosdale, 'Enttäuschte Unterordnung. Jüdische Erfahrungen im Ersten Weltkrieg', in Berliner Geschichtswerkstatt (ed.), *August 1914*, pp. 276–84 (here pp. 277–9). Cf. Chickering, *Imperial Germany*, p. 128.

121 Angress, 'Das deutsche Militär', *passim*; Clemens Picht, 'Zwischen Vaterland und Volk. Das deutsche Judentum im Ersten Weltkrieg', in Wolfgang Michalka (ed.), *Der Erste Weltkrieg. Wirkung, Wahrnehmung, Analyse* (Munich, 1994), pp. 736–55.

122 Donald L. Niewyk, *The Jews in Weimar Germany* (Manchester, 1980), pp. 31–2.

123 Cf. Hubert Goenner, *Einstein in Berlin 1914–1933* (Munich, 2005).

124 Niewyk, *The Jews in Weimar Germany*, p. 26.

125 Ibid., p. 19.

126 Point 4 of the Nazi Party Programme, the Twenty-Five Points, reproduced in Conan Fischer, *The Rise of the Nazis*, 2nd edition (Manchester, 2002), p. 158.

127 Pulzer, *The Rise of Political Anti-Semitism*, p. 298.

128 Sabrow, *Der Rathenau-Mord*, pp. 150–1 and 169–83.

129 Ibid., p. 161; Lohalm, *Völkischer Radikalismus*, pp. 246 ff.

130 Niewyk, *The Jews in Weimar Germany*, pp. 49–51; McElligott, 'Introduction',
p. 18. Cf. Hertzman, *DNVP*, pp. 124–64; Jan Striesow, *Die Deutschnationale
Volkspartei und die Völkisch-Radikalen 1918–1922*, 2 vols (Frankfurt/M, 1981);
Scheck, *Mothers of the Nation*, pp. 27 and *passim*; Jones, 'Catholic Conservatives',
pp. 66 and *passim*.

131 Heid, *Oskar Cohn*, pp. 281–308.

132 Mosse, 'The Brutalization of German Politics', pp. 169–70.

133 Details in Large, '"Out with the Ostjuden"', *passim*; and Maurer, *Ostjuden in
Deutschland*, pp. 329–44.

134 See e.g. Peukert, *The Weimar Republic*, p. 160; Niewyk, *The Jews in Weimar
Germany*, p. 51; Dirk Walter, 'Scheunenviertel Pogrom', in Richard S. Levy (ed.),
Antisemitism. A Historical Encyclopaedia of Prejudice and Persecution (Santa
Barbara, CA, 2005), p. 641.

135 Large, '"Out with the Ostjuden"', p. 125.

136 Maurer, *Ostjuden in Deutschland*, p. 334.

137 Large, '"Out with the Ostjuden"', pp. 138–9. Cf. Maurer, *Ostjuden in
Deutschland*, pp. 403–16; Jochen Oltmer, *Migration und Politik in der Weimarer
Republik* (Göttingen, 2005), pp. 253–5; and Reiner Pommerin, 'Die Ausweisung
von "Ostjuden" aus Bayern 1923. Ein Beitrag zum Krisenjahr der Weimarer
Republik', *Vierteljahrshefte für Zeitgeschichte*, 34/3 (1986), pp. 311–40.

138 Kolb, *The Weimar Republic*, p. 224.

139 Cf. Christoph Jahr, 'Policing Anti-Semitic Crime in Weimar Germany', in
Gerard Oram (ed.), *Conflict and Legality. Policing Mid-Twentieth Century Europe*
(London, 2003), pp. 64–77 (here p. 70).

140 Peukert, *The Weimar Republic*, p. 160.

141 Kolb, *The Weimar Republic*, pp. 224–5.

142 Oltmer, *Migration und Politik*, pp. 251–61. See also Eli Nathans, *The Politics of
Citizenship in Germany. Ethnicity, Citizenship and Nationalism* (Oxford, 2004),
pp. 204–9.

143 Maurer, *Ostjuden in Deutschland*, pp. 416–35; Large, '"Out with the Ostjuden"',
p. 127.

CHAPTER 6

The Final Years of the Republic

Although German society was far from being united in the late 1920s, the republic did experience a short interlude of apparent political consensus, at least in the sphere of foreign policy. This was symbolised above all by the presence in high office of the DVP politician and statesman Gustav Stresemann, who served briefly as Reich Chancellor during the crisis months of August to November 1923, and subsequently as Foreign Minister through six different 'bourgeois' cabinets (1923–8) and into the grand coalition government which was formed under SPD leader Hermann Müller in June 1928. He died, still in post, on 3 October 1929.

Stresemann's two greatest achievements were the Locarno Treaties of 1925 and Germany's entry into the League of Nations in 1926. The former was a precondition for the latter, and involved German recognition of the Versailles settlement in Western Europe, including renunciation of any future claims on Alsace and the French ore fields. In return, Germany could expect a phased evacuation of Allied troops from the Rhineland (completed between 1925 and 1930) and growing acceptance of its claims for a revision of other aspects of the peace settlement, for instance in relation to reparations, colonies and the treatment of German minorities in Eastern Europe. Meanwhile, Stresemann also succeeded, by and large, in persuading German public opinion, officials in the Auswärtiges Amt and most of the parties in the Reichstag (Communists, Nationalists and Nazis excepted) to approve his policy of rapprochement with the west. This was no mean feat, given that a large part of the press, and in particular the papers owned by the right-wing industrialist and DNVP leader Alfred Hugenberg, were against him.[1]

However, the issue of foreign policy became divisive again in the second half of 1929, when Hugenberg joined forces with Hitler and the monarchist

Stahlhelm to demand a referendum against German acceptance of the Young Plan, the revised schedule for reparations payments drawn up by the American economist Owen D. Young earlier that year. Although Hugenberg and his allies were able to collect the necessary signatures of 10 per cent of the electorate to actually force the staging of a referendum on 22 December 1929, only 5.8 million people voted for the proposal that Germany should refuse to pay any more reparations, not the required 22 million. The government had therefore won. Even so, the campaign brought benefits for the extreme right, and for the Nazis in particular, especially in terms of gaining new publicity and access to new sources of funding and patronage. The party was no longer in the wilderness, and it had proved itself capable of establishing an important profile beyond the rural north-east and north-west.[2]

Whether this by itself would have been enough to propel Hitler to the centre stage of German politics in the early 1930s seems doubtful, however. A much more important factor was the collapse of the New York stock exchange in October 1929, and the rising levels of unemployment which it brought in its wake. In short, it was the global economic Depression, as well as the inability of German politicians to devise sensible policies for tackling it, which, in the end, spelt doom for the cause of democracy in Germany.

In what follows we will explore the final years of the Weimar Republic in terms of the emergence of National Socialism and its opposite number, German anti-fascism, as powerful social movements which attracted millions of followers from 1930 onwards. We will also consider the behind-the-scenes political intrigues which eventually brought the Nazis to power in January 1933. Firstly, though, it will be necessary to examine the political crisis brought on by the fall of the grand coalition government in March 1930.

The crisis of democracy

As we have seen, Germany's over-dependence on short-term American loans in the late 1920s made it particularly vulnerable to the sudden collapse in world markets which followed the Wall Street Crash in late October 1929.[3] Almost immediately, German companies began to go out of business, throwing hundreds of thousands out of work. Yet it was not simply the depth of the Depression, but also its longevity, which took politicians and ordinary people by surprise. By 1932 43.7 per cent of the industrial workforce was officially unemployed, and production had fallen to only 58 per cent of what it had been in 1928.[4] In the meantime, successive cuts in unemployment benefits meant that millions of households were left facing acute poverty and distress. In Berlin, for instance, more than half of the registered unemployed had used up all their insurance claims by the beginning of 1933, and were therefore forced to rely on means-tested benefits paid for out of local government funds.[5] Even those lucky enough to find themselves in work often faced wage cuts or had to make do with reduced hours and therefore reduced pay.[6] This was also reflected in declining patterns of consumption so that sales of groceries dropped by 30 per cent, of clothing and furniture by 40 per cent, of tobacco by 15 per cent and of beer by nearly 45 per cent.[7]

While the industrial working class bore the brunt of the Depression, other social strata were also affected. For instance, people who made their living in banking, shipping and insurance had their prospects threatened by the slump in world trade. This was a particular problem in port cities like Bremen, where 'salaried staff ma[d]e up over 30 per cent of the economically active population'.[8] As tax receipts fell, and access to loans dried up, local authorities and Reich and *Land* governments also laid off ever-larger numbers of civil servants. In a clear breach of the Weimar constitution, it was decided that married women could be fired from public sector jobs if their financial circumstances 'seemed constantly secure'. When a bill to this end was put before the Reichstag on 12 May 1932, only the Communists voted against it.[9] Meanwhile, deflation and falling food prices aggravated the existing crisis in agriculture, so that increasing numbers of farmers found themselves facing bankruptcy and foreclosures. This in turn created new tensions between the cities and the countryside, and added pressure on successive governments to organise a rescue package for the vastly indebted rural sector as a whole.[10]

In other ways, too, the Wall Street Crash undermined the Weimar Republic and the viability of parliamentary democracy. In the first instance, it led to the collapse of the SPD-led grand coalition on 27 March 1930, when the different parties failed to agree on a compromise formula for bailing out the bankrupt state-backed unemployment insurance fund. Essentially, the SPD demanded higher contributions from employers, while the bourgeois parties, and especially the DVP, instead advocated a cut in the overall rate of benefit. The President, Paul von Hindenburg, subsequently refused to grant the SPD Reich Chancellor Hermann Müller's request for emergency powers to approve the budget, forcing the latter to resign. He was replaced by Heinrich Brüning, a right-wing Centre Party politician who agreed to head a minority administration supported by the main bourgeois parties and the moderate wing of the DNVP only.[11]

However, the immediate cause of the fall of the grand coalition was perhaps less important than its consequence, for it presented Hindenburg with an opportunity to realise his long-term goal of moving from a parliamentary to an authoritarian form of government 'above parties'.[12] Indeed the President and his close circle of military advisers, including most notably the head of the *Ministeramt* (political office) of the Reichswehr, General Kurt von Schleicher, had never really got over their mistrust of the SPD and were anxious to exclude the party from power wherever possible. Brüning, an ex-army officer with monarchist leanings, suited their purposes well because, lacking a parliamentary majority, he became, in effect, a 'presidential Chancellor', increasingly dependent on Hindenburg as head of state to approve laws using the extraordinary powers invested in him under Article 48 of the constitution. This became even more obvious after the 14 September 1930 Reichstag election, in which the Communists and Nazis both made gains at the expense of the moderate republican parties, making a parliamentary majority for Brüning even less likely.

In many ways Brüning was also trapped by his dependency on Hindenburg, particularly as the President's inner circle of advisers now had a de facto veto over government policy. Yet Brüning himself cannot be considered blameless in this process. As a conservative traditionalist and advocate of a vague form of corporatist state in partnership with the Christian trade unions, he had always distrusted republicanism and preferred 'unpolitical' solutions to political problems.[13] In 1930 he willingly took on emergency powers under Article 48 of the Weimar constitution which had been refused to his Social Democrat predecessor, Hermann Müller, and introduced a series of deflationary economic policies, including cuts in welfare spending and public sector wages, which he knew would not command majority support in the Reichstag. Already in the spring of 1929, before the

TABLE 6.1 Results of the Reichstag election, 14 September 1930

	No. of votes (millions)	% of votes cast	No. of seats
NSDAP	6.409 (+5.599)	18.3 (+15.7)	107 (+95)
DNVP	2.458 (−1.923)	7.0 (−7.2)	41 (−32)
DVP	1.578 (−1.101)	4.5 (−4.2)	30 (−15)
DDP/Staatspartei	1.322 (−0.183)	3.8 (−1.1)	20 (−5)
Zentrum	4.127 (+0.415)	11.8 (−0.3)	68 (+6)
BVP	1.005 (+0.06)	3.0 (−0.1)	19 (+3)
SPD	8.577 (−0.576)	24.5 (−5.3)	143 (−10)
KPD	4.592 (+1.328)	13.1 (+2.5)	77 (+23)
Other parties	4.888 (+0.614)	14.0 (−)	72 (+21)
Total	34.956 (+4.203)	100.0 Turnout =	577 (+86)
	+0.268 invalid votes	82.0% (+6.4%)	

Source: Eberhard Kolb, *The Weimar Republic*, 2nd edn (London: Routledge, 2005), p. 225.

economic and political crisis precipitated by the Wall Street Crash, he had held meetings with various Reichswehr representatives aimed at finding ways of removing the SPD from power in Prussia and the Reich, or at least minimising its ability to frustrate the Reichswehr's plans for secret rearmament and the reintroduction of conscription.[14] In July 1930, when his new budget was voted down, he deliberately made use of Hindenburg's right under Article 25 of the constitution to dissolve the Reichstag and announce fresh elections, even though all the indications were that this would only benefit the Nazis and not the pro-government or centre-right parties.[15]

Even so, recent historiography has challenged the notion that Brüning's own aim between 1930 and 1932 was a restoration of the monarchy, an impression which he gave, somewhat incongruously, in his memoirs published in 1970.[16] Matters were more complex than this. Certainly his political views were authoritarian, and his long-term ambition was to make the Weimar state more independent of parties and parliament. Yet, as Richard Evans suggests, his actual day-to-day decisions were governed more by 'short-term imperatives' which in practice ruled out the development of any consistent strategy for a reformed Reich.[17] Thus at times he tried to make his policies more acceptable to the SPD and the Free Trade Unions, in order to lessen his dependence on the parties of the right. He was also hamstrung by his respect for the idea of the *Rechtsstaat*, the rule of law, which during his term in office led him to reject any plans to depose the SPD-led government in Prussia by means of a *coup d'état*.[18] There is even some evidence to suggest that Brüning would have preferred to have kept the Müller government in power in March 1930 for at least another six months, had Hindenburg been willing to grant it emergency powers with which to approve a budget.[19]

When, in spite of this, the Müller government did fall and Brüning came to office at the head of a minority 'Hindenburg' cabinet, his first priority was to deal with the fiscal consequences of the economic Depression, i.e. falling tax revenues, record numbers of bankruptcies, and higher welfare costs. His austerity budgets of July and December 1930, together with rising levels of unemployment and new tariffs on food imports, alienated large sections of the left and extreme right, and earned him the title of 'Hunger Chancellor'. To make matters worse, his attempts to decrease government spending were hampered by some of his government's own backers, i.e. the Reichswehr's insistence that the military budget remain immune from cuts, and the agrarian lobby's demands for a programme of debt and tax relief for impoverished landowners in the east, known as *Osthilfe* (eastern aid).[20] Even so, the requests made by leading employers for an end to state labour arbitration were rejected; instead the government imposed wage reductions but also insisted that industrialists and rural producers pass on the benefits of reduced costs to consumers. In this way, some attempt was made to win over 'moderate' trade union support for the austerity measures.[21] The SPD was likewise persuaded to 'tolerate' Brüning after October 1930, albeit more out of fear of the Nazis or civil war than genuine regard for his policies.[22]

A second part of Brüning's strategy for German economic recovery lay in the sphere of foreign policy. From the end of 1930, facing the need for further budget cuts, he resolved to use the Depression as a means of enhancing Germany's ability to wrest substantial new concessions from the Allies. At home, both he and his Labour Minister Adam Stegerwald insisted that the best way to improve standards of living and employment rates in the future was to create a substantial export surplus which would force foreign governments to take a fresh look at the reparations question. This meant accepting wage and price reductions in the present.[23] On the international stage he combined a policy of fulfilling the terms of the Young Plan with an insistence on Germany's inability to pay reparations and a greater emphasis on other demands, such as territorial revisions of the Treaty of Versailles and 'parity of rights' in respect to arms.[24]

This new assertiveness ended in the debacle of the proposed Austro-German customs union of spring 1931, which failed due to opposition from the Western powers and was made all the worse by a series of financial shocks including the collapse of the Viennese Credit-Anstalt bank on 11 May and a run on the German banks in early July.[25] In essence France now held all the advantages as a result of its stockpile of gold reserves and its ability to accentuate the panic-driven flight of investors from the Austrian Schilling and the German Mark into 'safer' currencies. The spectre of the head of the Reichsbank, Hans Luther, being forced to go to London, Paris and Basel to beg for financial help was in turn a serious humiliation for Germany, and the mission failed when the French government insisted on attaching political conditions to any loan.[26] The Hoover moratorium of 20 June 1931, which suspended all debt payments for a year, and the growing sympathy for Germany's predicament in America and Britain, were minor successes in comparison. As with the Young Plan in 1929–30, although this time on a more extreme level, foreign policy issues thus proved capable of stirring up political divisions and inciting nationalism. When the International Court at The Hague finally ruled in September 1931 that a customs union with Austria would be a breach of Germany's treaty obligations, the only thing left for the Foreign Minister Julius Curtius to do was resign in a futile attempt to deflect criticism from the government as a whole.[27]

Brüning's final aim was to 'tame' the radical right and eventually bring it into government as a means of ridding himself of the need for 'toleration' by the SPD. However, this was difficult to match with his foreign policy ambitions, which were still focused on ending reparations by negotiation rather than confrontation.[28] It was during the Reichstag election of 14 September 1930 that the Nazis made their first electoral breakthrough, coming from almost nowhere to reach 18.3 per cent of the vote on the propagandistic slogan: 'For or against the Young Plan?'[29] Worse still, in the presidential elections of March–April 1932 Hitler won 36.8 per cent in the second round, compared to 53.0 per cent for the incumbent, Hindenburg. Political violence had reached unprecedented levels, with Communists and Nazis battling for control of the streets in the major cities on an almost daily basis. In October 1931 the Nazis had also temporarily reunited with Hugenberg and the monarchist Stahlhelm to form the Harzburg Front, with the express aim of creating a 'National Opposition' based on all 'patriotic' forces opposed to the existing state and its 'weak-kneed' foreign policy. Even though this new alliance soon collapsed, rumours of a possible right-wing coup, to be led by the almost 400,000-strong Nazi paramilitary organisation, the SA, remained rife throughout the early months of 1932.[30]

Against this background, Brüning and his Defence and Interior Minister Wilhelm Groener moved to dissolve the SA on 13 April 1932, shortly after the presidential elections were over. This annoyed right-wing elements in Hindenburg's entourage, who were angered that no parallel move had been made against the Reichsbanner, the republican defence organisation close to the SPD. In the event of a Nazi putsch attempt or civil war, there was by now no question of the Reichswehr working with the Reichsbanner to defend the republic itself. Rather, the army claimed to represent its own idea of the eternal German state 'above politics'. Furthermore, in spite of the official ban on political activity in the armed forces, there were many Nazi sympathisers within the officer corps, including at the most senior levels.[31]

In late April 1932 Groener, himself a former member of the general staff and ally of Friedrich Ebert in November 1918, was the first target of a new Reichswehr-led conspiracy organised by his one-time protégé, Schleicher. The conspirators' aim, which was shared by Groener, was the reintroduction of conscription as a prelude to substantial rearmament, but now they no longer believed that he could implement this step for them. The ban on the SA was the final straw: in their view, it indicated that the Reich government was following pressure from the SPD-led Prussian government to rein in the rowdies and stick slavishly to the terms of the Treaty of Versailles. Groener was forced to resign as Defence Minister on 12 May 1932, after being told that he no longer had the confidence of the army. Schleicher, with the agreement of Hindenburg, now drew up plans to lift the prohibition on the SA as a prelude to the formation of a new government well to the right of Brüning. The losses suffered by the moderate parties in the Prussian Landtag election on 24 April 1932 were a further indication, in his view, that the time was ripe for doing away with this final bastion of SPD power.[32]

The man chosen to perform these tasks was the Catholic aristocrat Franz von Papen, still nominally a member of the Centre Party but willing to abandon his former colleagues for the sake of wresting the Chancellorship from Brüning. Together he and Schleicher discussed ways of winning over the Nazis for a programme of constitutional reform which would place Germany on a more authoritarian footing without handing full powers to Hitler. Brüning himself was now also the subject of a vicious campaign by members of the old Prussian *Junker* class, who attacked his new proposals for land reform in the east as 'agrarian bolshevism' and increasingly had the ear of the ailing President. The Chancellor held on for two more weeks, but finally fell on 30 May 1932, when Hindenburg withdrew his confidence in him.[33]

As Anthony Nicholls and others have convincingly argued, Brüning's dismissal 'marked a real turning-point' in the fall of Weimar and the concomitant rise of the Nazis.[34] Certainly in comparison with his immediate successor, Franz von Papen, who instigated the long-expected coup against the Prussian government in July 1932 and then paved the way for Hitler's takeover some six months later, Brüning was a staunch upholder of constitutional principles. Yet under him, the drift towards authoritarianism was undeniable. For instance, parliament was increasingly sidelined, losing its ability to scrutinise government decisions, and censorship was tightened.[35] The Reichstag itself met for only 94 days in 1930, falling to 42 in 1931 and a mere 13 in 1932. The number of government bills passed under Article 48 (i.e. without parliamentary approval) meanwhile increased from 5 in 1930 to 44 in 1931 and 66 in 1932.[36]

Perhaps the strongest criticism of Brüning, however, is that he was prepared to allow unemployment to rise to politically unacceptable levels for the sake of his domestic and foreign policy objectives, namely the trimming back of the welfare state and the abolition of reparations.[37] This shortsightedness prevented him from taking up some of the schemes suggested by his own ministers for economic growth and job creation at home after the immediate prospect of a banking collapse had passed in July 1931. It also led him to underestimate the threat from the Nazis, who he saw as a temporary phenomenon and even as a useful lever with which to gain further concessions from the Allies.[38] Brüning's later claim that he had been dismissed 'a hundred metres short of the finishing line' – a reference to the final cancellation of reparations at the Lausanne Conference of June–July 1932 – is true, but somewhat beside the point, given the damage which his earlier decisions had already caused. By the beginning of 1932 it was clear to everyone that the reparations offensive alone could not solve the problem of domestic political extremism and the slide towards civil war. Nor could it provide the material and political foundations for a sound economic recovery.[39]

The failure of anti-fascism

After the fall of Brüning, the only means of staving off a victory for the extreme right over the whole of Germany was the combined strength of the major left-wing parties, the SPD and the KPD. Indeed, both of these parties saw themselves as anti-fascist, and carried direct messages in their electoral propaganda warning of the dangers of a Nazi takeover, especially for ordinary working-class people. Between them, they had hundreds of thousands of members and could rely on millions of voters at election times. In the September 1930 Reichstag election the SPD still scored 24.5 per cent of the vote, and the KPD 13.1 per cent, compared to 18.3 per cent for the Nazis (see Table 6.1). The left-wing parties, in other words, formed a sizeable bloc in the Reichstag and in many state parliaments, and completely dominated the trade union movement. Yet in spite of this, they remained divided as ever on ideological questions, and went on to develop entirely different strategies for defeating fascism. This could be seen when the KPD refused to join the SPD-led Iron Front (*Eiserne Front*), a republican defence organisation founded at the end of 1931 and consisting of Social Democrats, the Free Trade Unions (ADGB), the workers' sports associations and the Reichsbanner.[40] Instead, it persisted with its own attempts to build an illegal mass 'armed-defensive struggle' (*wehrhafter Kampf*) from below, based around the Red Front Fighters' League and its willingness to take on the Nazi SA at street level whenever the latter invaded 'red' neighbourhoods.[41] Meanwhile, in the presidential elections of March–April 1932 the SPD and the Iron Front supported Hindenburg against Hitler, much to the former's discomfort, while the KPD put up its own candidate, party leader Ernst Thälmann, whose vote fell from 13.2 per cent in the first round to just 10.2 per cent in the second and final round.[42]

In part, the divisions on the left reflected the different social compositions of the two parties. Thus the KPD had become during the Depression a party of the unemployed, with 78 per cent of its members out of work by the end of 1931, and 85 per cent by April 1932.[43] By contrast, the SPD was still predominantly a party of the male, unionised, skilled worker, with only 30 per cent of Social Democrats claiming unemployment benefits in 1932 against a national average of over 40 per cent for male wage earners as a whole.[44] The KPD also had an extremely fluid membership in the early 1930s, with an annual turnover rate of up to 80 per cent, whereas the SPD had an older and more stable base of supporters who were more likely to stick with the party through thick and thin and pay their subscription dues on time.[45]

At the same time, the split between the SPD and the KPD also reflected genuine ideological differences in the political outlook of their respective leaderships, even if both parties had common roots in Marxism. Thus the SPD still saw itself as part of the Weimar system, and believed that its mission was to deliver gradual reforms through state and national parliaments which would be beneficial to the working class and which would eventually lead to socialism. In order to defend the constitution and avoid civil war, it was prepared to work with the bourgeois parties, either directly, in government, or indirectly, through toleration and moderate opposition.[46] Yet it was also adamantly opposed to any deal with Hitler's National Socialists, whom it rightly identified as a major threat to the republic. Instead, wherever it formed part of the ruling coalition at *Land* level in the period after September 1930, namely in Prussia, Baden, Hamburg and Hesse, it sought to use its executive power to purge active Nazis from public sector and civil service posts, a policy which met with little support from the Reich government of Heinrich Brüning.[47]

The KPD, by contrast, stood against the republic and parliamentary democracy, and instead followed the 'class against class' line laid down by the Comintern in 1928, which dictated that Communists should regard Social Democrats as the 'main enemy' of the revolutionary working class.[48] After September 1930, indeed, the party's targets included both Social Democrats in government (in August 1931 the KPD supported a referendum campaign organised by the NSDAP, the Stahlhelm and the German Nationalists which called for the immediate dissolution of the SPD-led administration in Prussia and the calling of fresh elections); and left-wing social democrats in the trade unions and parliaments who advocated common action with the KPD against fascism. The latter, known as 'left social fascists' were considered a particular threat as they undermined the KPD's claim to a monopoly on anti-fascism, and because their very existence blurred the important doctrinal distinctions between social democrats and communists as laid down by the Comintern in 1928.[49]

The Prussian government, for its part, survived the attempt to force a referendum in August 1931, and Otto Braun remained in office as Minister-President.

However, after suffering a catastrophic defeat at the hands of the Nazis in the Landtag election held on 24 April 1932, Braun's SPD-Centre Party-DDP coalition had to continue as a minority administration, and much of its legitimacy had evaporated. Elements in the army – alongside the new Reich Chancellor from 1 June, Franz von Papen – were already plotting to bring Prussia under the control of the Reich as a whole.[50] Right-wing figures within the Catholic Centre Party were also contemplating ditching their Social Democrat allies in Prussia in favour of a deal with the Nazis or the DNVP or both.[51] Meanwhile, on the left wing of the SPD, voices were growing in support of closer cooperation with the KPD and a programme which would bring about the immediate introduction of a socialist-style economy. Implicitly this would mean abandoning the Iron Front and joining the Communist-dominated 'united front from below'. For younger party activists in particular, the social democrat variant of anti-fascism looked like it was on its last legs, with the Communists, or left-wing splinter parties like the SAPD (Socialist Workers' Party, founded 1931) offering the only hope of genuine proletarian resistance against the Nazis and 'Hunger Chancellor' Brüning.[52]

In spite of these setbacks, the Iron Front revived itself in June 1932 with a strong campaign aimed at 'reclaiming the Republic' through adopting a more militant stand against fascism. Indeed, if the SPD had 'tolerated' Brüning it was completely opposed to the new authoritarian government of Franz von Papen. *Vorwärts*, the main SPD newspaper, dubbed it the 'cabinet of barons', in reference to the large number of ministers from aristocratic backgrounds. The Iron Front also began to distance itself from the cold, austere slogans it had used in March and April 1932 in support of Hindenburg as the only candidate who could defeat Hitler. Instead, following the ideas of the Hessian Social Democrat Carlo Mierendorff and the Soviet émigré Sergei Chakhotin, its campaigning became more direct and punchier, with an emphasis on style and delivery as a means of repositioning itself within an increasingly competitive political market.[53]

Thus in the run up to the 31 July 1932 Reichstag election, the SPD and ADGB leadership agreed to Mierendorff's proposals to engage the Nazis in a 'symbols war' in an attempt to mobilise support for the republic on an emotional level. This involved, among other things, the adoption of a closed fist 'freedom salute' at Iron Front meetings, to counter the Nazi Hitler salute, and the use of a new three-arrow motif to symbolise the Iron Front's three main principles – *Einigkeit, Aktivität, Disziplin* (unity, action, discipline) – against its three enemies – *Kapitalismus, Faschismus, Reaktion* (capitalism, fascism, reaction).[54] It also meant deliberately adopting nationalist rhetoric, especially in connection with the reparations question and the so-called

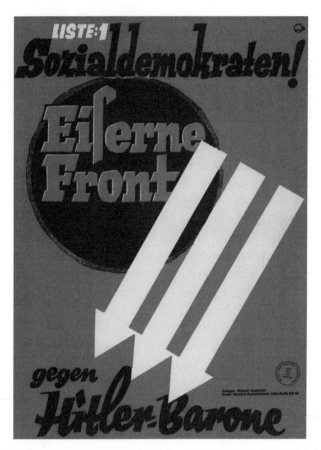

PLATE 6.1 The Iron Front against the 'Hitler barons'. SPD poster for the July 1932 Reichstag election campaign.

Source: Archiv der sozialen Demokratie der Friedrich-Ebert-Stiftung, Bonn, Germany

'war guilt lie'. The Nazis, meanwhile, were referred to as the 'Hitler-Barone' in order to associate them with the reactionary policies of Papen's 'cabinet of barons'.[55]

Yet still, the SPD, as the moderate wing of the socialist movement, and as the leading coalition partner in Prussia, Hamburg, Hesse and Baden, could not adopt the 'class against class' programme or extreme nationalist slogans of its main rivals, the communists and the Nazis. Nor could it effectively combat the welfare cuts introduced by Brüning and then Papen. Instead, it remained wedded to the compromise with the moderate bourgeois parties which had prevented civil war in the years 1917 to 1920, and to the principle of constitutional legality. This policy, as Hans Mommsen notes, was 'based on the belief that the working class had no need for revolutionary action as long as the democratic framework for working-class political advance was intact and not threatened by counter-revolution'.[56] In other words, the SPD wished to defend what was left of the democratic system for the time being, in the belief that the current popularity of the Nazis was a temporary phenomenon which would soon pass with the ending of the Depression. In the long term, the SPD could be confident of the victory of socialism so long as the chosen means – free elections and the rule of law – remained in force.[57]

Two events in July 1932 demonstrated that this strategy was no longer capable of saving the republic. The first was the so-called *Preussenschlag* of 20 July. Using the excuse of communist–Nazi violence in Altona on 17 July ('Bloody Sunday'), the Reich government of Franz von Papen, backed by the President and the Reichswehr, finally instituted a coup in Prussia, replacing the minority government of Otto Braun with a special Reich Commission led by Papen himself. Martial law was declared in Berlin and Brandenburg province, and the SPD police chief Albert Grzesinski and his deputy Bernhard Weiss were both temporarily held in custody.[58] Without support from the bourgeois parties, and with the strike weapon effectively neutered by mass unemployment, the SPD was, in contrast to 1920, powerless to act. Instead, it sought redress through the constitutional court in Leipzig, which failed to rule decisively against the coup in October 1932.[59]

The second event was the Reichstag election of 31 July, deliberately called by Papen in the full knowledge that the Nazis would be the main beneficiaries. Indeed, when the results were known, the SPD had come a poor second to the NSDAP, with only 21.6 per cent compared to 37.3 per cent of the popular vote. Worse still, between them the Nazis and the communists (the latter on 14.3 per cent) had a 'negative majority' in the Reichstag which they could use to block any attempts to create a democratic alternative to Papen. With barely more than one in five seats in the new Reichstag, the SPD's notion of a parliamentary road to socialism seemed well and truly dead.

While the SPD put its faith in the ballot box and the eventual triumph of rationalism, the KPD's main source of power lay in the millions of unemployed Germans whom it sought to mobilise in local taverns, tenements and labour exchanges. All of these public spaces were regarded as sites of what had become both a real and an imagined civil war by the summer of 1932, as the struggle against fascism and its supposed ally, social democracy, moved from the factory and the shopfloor to the working-class neighbourhoods.[60] Furthermore, in addition to organising rent strikes and demonstrations outside welfare offices, and engaging in violent physical confrontations

TABLE 6.2 Results of the Reichstag election, 31 July 1932

	No. of votes (millions)	% of votes cast	No. of seats
NSDAP	13.745 (+7.336)	37.3 (+19.0)	230 (+123)
DNVP	2.177 (−0.281)	5.9 (−1.1)	37 (−4)
DVP	0.436 (−1.142)	1.2 (−3.3)	7 (−23)
DDP/Staatspartei	0.371 (−0.951)	1.0 (−2.8)	4 (−16)
Zentrum	4.589 (+0.462)	12.5 (+0.7)	75 (+7)
BVP	1.192 (+0.187)	3.2 (+0.2)	22 (+3)
SPD	7.959 (−0.618)	21.6 (−2.9)	133 (−10)
KPD	5.283 (+0.691)	14.3 (+1.2)	89 (+12)
Other Parties	1.130 (−3.758)	3.0 (−11.0)	11 (−61)
Total	36.882 (+1.926) +0.280 invalid votes	100.0 Turnout = 84.1% (+2.1%)	608 (+31)

Source: Eberhard Kolb, *The Weimar Republic*, 2nd edition (London: Routledge, 2005), p. 225.

with the SA in places like Berlin, Munich and Hamburg-Altona, the KPD was also much better than the SPD at fighting the so-called 'symbols war'. One striking example of this would be the July 1932 election poster, *Schluss mit diesem System!* (Smash the System!), featuring a red proletarian giant with his fist clenched in readiness for a final act of revolutionary violence which would sweep away the old republic of militarists, traitors and fascists, and instead usher in a 'Soviet Germany'.[61]

In the meantime, the communists were also not above using extreme nationalist slogans in a bid to out-do the Nazis and other political opponents. This can be seen in particular in their August 1930 'Declaration on the national and social liberation of the German people', which denounced all other parties as fascists or lackeys of international capital, and later in Ernst Thälmann's address to the party Central Committee on 19 February 1932. Here we find once again a reiteration of the Comintern's 'class against class' line:

Our strategy directs the main blow against social democracy, without thereby weakening the struggle against Hitler fascism; our strategy creates the very preconditions of an effective opposition to Hitler's fascism precisely in its direction of the main blow against social democracy. This strategy is only to be understood once one has understood clearly the role of the proletariat as the only class that will carry the revolution through to the end.[62]

In electoral terms, the KPD was the only party whose support grew at every Reichstag election between May 1928 and November 1932, reaching a high point of 16.9 per cent, or nearly six million votes, a feat largely achieved at the expense of the SPD (see Table 6.7 below). The party also received an

PLATE 6.2 'Smash the System!' KPD poster for the July 1932 Reichstag election campaign.   Source: Deutsches Historisches Museum, Berlin

unexpected boost in September 1932 when the newly elected Nazi president of the Reichstag, Hermann Goering, permitted a division on a Communist motion of no confidence in the Papen government, which was carried by an overwhelming majority of 512 to 42 with five abstentions.[63] Yet in many ways these successes were deceptive, for they disguised the more general failure of the KPD to win over the majority of the industrial working class to its cause. Instead, the left-wing vote remained split between the KPD and the SPD, to both parties' disadvantage.

Meanwhile, on the streets demoralisation was setting in, as the SA, revived by the lifting of the ban in June 1932, and by the Nazis' great electoral success of July 1932, grew in size and confidence, and as long-term unemployment gradually undermined what was left of feelings of proletarian solidarity and 'industrial muscle' in working-class communities.[64] From late July 1932 onwards, indeed, the SA were making serious encroachments into 'red' neighbourhoods in cities like Hamburg, Altona and Berlin, taking over pubs and meeting halls which could no longer afford to rely on their former, largely communist- or SPD-supporting clientele.[65] At one point, the Nazis and the KPD even collaborated in the short-lived Berlin transport strike of early November 1932, which collapsed after five days.[66] But soon after this they went back to fighting each other in the streets, and in general they remained absolute enemies with incompatible visions of what should become of Germany after the expected collapse of the republic.

The rise of the Nazis

While the SPD represented skilled workers and the KPD was the 'party of the unemployed par excellence',[67] the NSDAP developed a much broader base of support in the early 1930s, becoming, in the words of Jürgen Falter, a 'people's party of protest' (*Volkspartei des Protests*).[68] By July 1932, indeed, 13.75 million Germans were voting for this party, including people of all social classes and backgrounds. As Eberhard Kolb writes, summarising the work of Falter and others in a big statistical project on voting patterns undertaken in the 1980s:

It is assumed that, in 1930, every third DNVP voter, every fourth DVP or DDP voter, every seventh non-voter and every tenth SPD voter of 1928 switched their allegiance to the NSDAP . . . In the July election in 1932, every second voter from the [right-wing] splinter parties . . . every third from [the DNVP, DVP and DDP], every fifth non-voter and every seventh SPD voter of 1930 transferred to the NSDAP . . .[69]

Even former supporters of the Catholic Centre Party, the BVP and the KPD showed some tendency to move over to the NSDAP, albeit on a significantly smaller scale. This can also be illustrated by means of Table 6.3 (see below).

What, then, were all these voters protesting about? According to Heinrich August Winkler, in the first instance they were registering their disquiet at the deflationary policies of the Brüning government and the record levels of unemployment. In this sense, the NSDAP was helped by the SPD's 'toleration' of Brüning, which had indirectly tied the main workers' party to supporting welfare cuts and a whole range of unpopular fiscal and foreign policy measures. Indeed, between October 1930 and May 1932 the Nazis could pose as the only political force to the right of the KPD which could legitimately be described as an 'opposition party', and at the same time as an

TABLE 6.3 Defections from other parties to the NSDAP between the May 1928, September 1930 and July 1932 Reichstag elections

Transfer of votes	KPD to NSDAP (%)	SPD to NSDAP (%)	Centre and BVP to NSDAP (%)	DVP and DDP to NSDAP (%)	DNVP to NSDAP (%)	Others (splinter parties) (%)	NSDAP to NSDAP (%)	Non-voters (%)
May 1928 to Sept. 1930	5	10	9	26	31	11	38	14
Sept. 1930 to July 1932	5	16	10	36	33	49	85	19

Source: Jürgen Falter, *Hitlers Wähler* (Munich: C. H. Beck, 1991), p. 111.

anti-Marxist movement which represented the 'national' interest above class and sectional differences. Nazism, in other words, was a 'pseudo-democratic populism of the right' which mobilised masses of voters against the government and the left-wing, 'anti-national' parties.[70]

Viewing the National Socialists' electoral success in this way has a number of important implications. Firstly, it has caused historians to look again at Theodor Geiger's notion that the NSDAP was primarily a *Mittelstandspartei*, a party of the lower middle-class. At least for the period after 1928, Nazism, it now seems, appealed to people of all classes, not just the petit-bourgeoisie. Upper middle-class voters, for instance, account for an extremely large portion of Nazi support in the early 1930s, especially in relation to their overall representation in the population. For them, the main attraction of National Socialism was its determination to smash the Communist party and restore 'law and order' to the streets, as well as its increasingly vocal opposition to Brüning's policy of ordering cuts in civil service salaries and pensions in order to balance the Reich budget.[71] In many small towns, the Nazis were also successful in winning over conservative notables, newspaper proprietors and the leaders of established civic and voluntary organisations, enabling them to combine populism with bourgeois 'respectability'.[72]

More controversially, Falter's figures, backed by other findings, suggest that in each Reichstag election from May 1928 to November 1932, the Nazis relied on working-class supporters for 39–40 per cent of their total vote.[73] This is significant, because, at least superficially, it supports the contention that the NSDAP had become a 'catch-all party' by 1932, claiming support across the different social classes and occupational groups.[74] In one or two industrial areas, moreover, such as Halle-Merseburg, Chemnitz-Zwickau,

North Bavaria, East Prussia and Upper and Lower Silesia, the Nazis were even able to make some headway at the expense of both the major left-wing parties, with an additional 60,000 urban workers joining the party between 1930 and 1932 (compared to 180,000 who joined the KPD).[75] If one also includes here consideration of the membership of Nazi specialist organisations like the SA, which likewise 'served as a major vehicle for Nazi urban working-class recruitment', then it is clear that National Socialism was something more than a movement of middle-class protest.[76] Indeed, most of the Nazis arrested by the police for politically motivated acts of violence in the years 1930 to 1932 came from wage-earning, proletarian backgrounds.[77]

Even so, the notion of a substantial working-class contribution to Nazism should still be treated with some caution. For instance, non-propertied 'wage earners and their adult dependants' – who made up at least 45–50 per cent of the electorate, according to the census of 1933[78] – were still slightly under-represented among Nazi voters as a whole, as Table 6.4 suggests. By contrast, approximately 60 per cent of the party's votes came from the old and new Mittelstand, who between them accounted for only around 43 per cent of the electorate:

TABLE 6.4 The social composition of the Nazi electorate in Reichstag elections from 1928 to 1932

	May 1928 (%)	Sept. 1930 (%)	July 1932 (%)	Nov. 1932 (%)
Working Class	40	40	39	39
New Mittelstand	22	21	19	19
Old Mittelstand	37	39	42	41

Source: Detlef Mühlberger, *The Social Bases of Nazism* (Cambridge: Cambridge University Press, 2003), p. 76.

The nationwide figures for rank and file party membership are even more striking here, with only 31.5 per cent of paid-up NSDAP members describing themselves as 'workers' in January 1933, compared to 57.9 per cent designating themselves as middle-class.[79] Furthermore, few workers made it into the higher ranks of the party or the SA; rather, as Tim Mason argues, 'the social composition of local leadership groups read like a roll-call of bourgeois occupations – government officials, school teachers, doctors, clerks, self-employed businessmen, salesmen, retired officers, engineers, students'.[80] On top of this, the Nazi 'trade union', the NSBO, was a flop, receiving little funding from the party until 1932 and claiming at best 300,000 members by January 1933 compared to 5.8 million manual and white-collar workers in the Free Trade Unions, the Christian Trade Unions and the (Communist) Red Trade Unions combined.[81]

The Geiger thesis thus still holds in part; or as Falter puts it, the NSDAP was a 'people's party with a middle-class belly' (*Volkspartei mit Mittelstandsbauch*).[82] Furthermore, even if one were to accept that the working class made up a substantial and unignorable portion of Nazi supporters and voters, it is important to distinguish very clearly between different sections of that class, rather than treating it as an undifferentiated whole. Thus it is clear that the NSDAP did particularly well among rural labourers and tradesmen, and among unorganised workers engaged in traditional crafts and cottage industries, especially in small town and village settings.[83] However, it performed less well in towns and cities with populations of over 100,000, where unemployment tended to be at its highest, and where the NSBO found it all but impossible to win over an industrial labour force which was traditionally well-integrated into class-based politics through trade unions, workers' cooperatives and the strong presence of the SPD and KPD.[84]

This was particularly the case, as Richard Hamilton has shown, in some of the major industrial centres in the Rhine-Ruhr region, such as Dortmund, Duisburg and Essen, where in July 1932 the Nazis performed considerably below their average vote of 37.3 per cent, and where the SPD and KPD showed a greater tendency to work together against fascism (see Table 6.5).[85] In addition, as Dick Geary points out, where pockets of working-class support for the Nazis did exist in the Ruhr, this was usually in politically conservative areas with a tradition of voting for parties like the DVP or the DNVP rather than the left. In this part of Germany, then, voters who did switch parties tended to stay within their particular milieu, with some SPD voters transferring to the KPD in the elections of September 1930 and July 1932 and a larger number of DVP and DNVP voters moving to the NSDAP.[86]

A similar pattern was also discovered by Claus-Christian Szejnmann in his study of the rise of the Nazis in 'Red' Saxony, where again the degree of support for Nazism in particular regions was dependent on existing patterns of integration into socialist or bourgeois milieu. In his own words:

Because of the deep-rooted socialist traditions [in Saxony] workers here were relatively immune to the appeal of National Socialism, and remained so for a longer period than in the rest of Germany, including during the 1930 election. Even after this, the success of the NSDAP varied from region to region, depending on various social and cultural factors. Thus while the National Socialists made considerable headway in South West Saxony, they faced a much harder task in many areas of North West and Central Saxony. These were also the main strongholds of the German labour movement.[87]

TABLE 6.5 Germany's largest cities by population (1933); religion (1933) and NSDAP share of the vote (July 1932)

City	Population	Protestant (%)	Catholic (%)	Jewish (%)	Without affiliation (%)	NSDAP percentage (national average = 37.3%)
Berlin	4,242,501	71.1	10.4	3.8	14.2	29
Hamburg	1,129,307	77.4	5.3	1.5	15.6	33
Cologne	756,605	19.6	75.3	2.0	2.9	24
Munich	735,388	15.2	81.1	1.2	1.3	29
Leipzig	713,470	77.9	3.6	1.6	14.3	32
Essen	654,461	40.9	54.0	0.7	4.2	24
Dresden	642,143	83.7	5.9	0.7	8.7	38
Breslau	625,198	59.6	31.5	3.2	4.8	43
Frankfurt/M	555,857	57.2	33.1	4.7	4.4	39
Dortmund	540,875	53.6	40.0	0.8	5.3	20
Düsseldorf	498,600	31.5	61.2	1.0	6.1	29
Hanover	443,920	80.9	10.6	1.1	6.3	40
Duisburg	440,419	42.7	51.7	0.6	4.8	27
Stuttgart	415,028	74.6	20.2	1.1	3.9	27
Nuremberg	410,438	62.7	32.1	1.8	1.6	38
Wuppertal	408,602	70.1	20.3	0.6	8.8	43
Chemnitz	350,734	86.0	3.7	0.7	9.1	42
Gelsenkirchen	332,545	47.6	47.9	0.5	3.9	23
Bremen	323,331	84.7	6.6	0.4	7.3	30
Königsberg	315,794	91.3	5.2	1.0	2.3	44

Source: Richard F. Hamilton, *Who Voted for Hitler?* (Princeton, NJ: Princeton University Press, 1982), p. 485.

Finally, in Germany's two biggest cities, Berlin and Hamburg, the Nazis also underperformed in comparison with their national average, and in both cases there were also notable differences between the working-class communities of the inner-city and the middle-class suburbs. True, some of the larger Protestant industrial towns such as Hanover, Wuppertal, Chemnitz and Königsberg, saw an overall vote of 40 per cent or more for the Nazis in July 1932, but Catholic cities, like Cologne, Düsseldorf and Munich – the birthplace and headquarters of the NSDAP – were again marked by a relative (although by no means absolute) immunity to Nazism and by strong support for the Catholic Centre Party or the BVP.

Overall, then, confession as well as class continued to have an important impact in determining a region's susceptibility to Nazism. The best results for the NSDAP were still in the rural Protestant areas of north-west and north-east Germany, and especially in those regions with virtually no Catholics and a relatively small number of industrial workers. They did markedly less well in rural Catholic districts, such as Koblenz-Trier and Upper and Lower Bavaria, and in urban settings where there was a larger than average percentage of Catholics (as in the case of Düsseldorf and Cologne) and/or industrialised workers with a strong tradition of voting SPD/USPD (for instance in Leipzig, Stuttgart and Bremen). Yet by far the worst results for the party came in KPD strongholds with high levels of unemployment, including the mining districts of the Ruhr and the poorest inner-city areas of Berlin and Hamburg.[88]

Three other points can also be made on the basis of recent research. Firstly, it has often been suggested that many young first-time voters, and those who had previously not bothered to vote, decided to cast their ballots in favour of the Nazis in the early 1930s. This assumption is backed both by the increasing turnout at election time and the steady growth in the size of the electorate between 1928 and 1933. Yet Falter's analysis suggests that in both the September 1930 and the July 1932 Reichstag elections only a relatively small proportion of the NSDAP's support came from former non-voters. In other words, first-time voters cannot account for the overall rise in the electoral popularity of the Nazis; a much more important role was played by people transferring from other parties.[89] Furthermore, while many young voters backed the National Socialists, so did many older voters – and wherever statistics can yield evidence, they suggest a positive correlation between support for the Nazis and the proportion of middle-aged and retired people living within a particular electoral district.[90] None of this, of course, should detract from the general finding that the NSDAP was a party of protest which clearly benefited from the collapse in support for other parties – and in particular for the DNVP, DDP, DVP and the various right-wing splinter parties (see Table 6.3).[91]

Secondly, at least until July 1932 the Nazis were largely a party of male protest. Indeed, in spite of claims from a number of different quarters after 1933 that women had somehow 'brought Hitler to power',[92] they remained under-represented among Nazi voters and members throughout the period 1928 to 1933.[93] By contrast, Hindenburg owed his re-election as President in March–April 1932 to the support of women, and would have been able to claim victory in the first round had women been the only voters.[94] Right-wing women also seemed to prefer the established anti-Marxist parties like the DNVP and the DVP to the more radical and rowdy Nazis.[95] Only in the Reichstag elections of July and November 1932 did the NSDAP begin to make progress towards closing this 'gender gap', especially in the Protestant regions of Germany.[96] In Catholic areas such as Cologne, however, women showed a much greater propensity to stick with the Centre Party or the BVP than did men, even if here, too, the gender gap was becoming slightly smaller by the second half of 1932 (Table 6.6).

TABLE 6.6 Nazi share of the vote in Cologne, 1930–1932, by gender

	Men (%)	Women (%)	Difference
Reichstag election 14 September 1930	19.8	15.5	−4.3
Presidential election 13 March 1932	21.7	16.7	−5.0
Presidential election 10 April 1932	26.2	19.7	−6.5
Reichstag election 31 July 1932	26.4	22.8	−3.6
Reichstag election 6 November 1932	21.8	19.2	−2.6

Source: Gabriele Bremme, *Die politische Rolle der Frau in Deutchsland* (Göttingen: Vandenhoeck & Ruprecht, 1956), p. 74.

Finally, in spite of their success in mobilising hundreds of thousands of members and millions of supporters, it is vital to note that the Nazis were not elected into office and never won an absolute majority in the Reichstag. The July 1932 result, with 37.3 per cent of the popular vote, remained their best score in a nationwide election held under democratic auspices. Yet when Hitler was appointed (rather than elected) as Reich Chancellor some six months later, on 30 January 1933, the party was in a much weaker position. In the first instance, it had lost two million votes and 34 seats in the November 1932 Reichstag election, while the KPD had actually gained 700,000 votes and 11 seats. True, the NSDAP remained the largest party, but without an overall majority: indeed, two in every three electors had voted against it. Moreover, its tactic of attacking the 'reactionary' cabinet of von Papen as well as the left had clearly backfired, with a small but significant number of middle-class voters clearly deciding to return to the more 'respectable' right-wing parties like the DNVP and the DVP.[97]

TABLE 6.7 Results of the Reichstag election, 6 November 1932

	No. of votes (millions)	% of votes cast	No. of seats
NSDAP	11.737 (−2.008)	33.1 (−4.2)	196 (−34)
DNVP	2.959 (+0.782)	8.3 (+2.4)	52 (+15)
DVP	0.661 (+0.225)	1.9 (+0.7)	11 (+4)
DDP/Staatspartei	0.336 (−0.035)	1.0 (−)	2 (−2)
Zentrum	4.230 (−0.359)	11.9 (−0.6)	70 (−5)
BVP	1.095 (−0.097)	3.1 (−0.1)	20 (−2)
SPD	7.248 (−0.711)	20.4 (−1.2)	121 (−12)
KPD	5.980 (+0.697)	16.9 (+2.6)	100 (+11)
Other Parties	1.225 (+0.095)	3.4 (+0.4)	12 (+1)
Total	35.471 (−1.411) +0.287 invalid votes	100.0 Turnout = 80.6% (−3.5%)	584 (−24)

Source: Eberhard Kolb, *The Weimar Republic*, 2nd edition (London: Routledge, 2005), p. 225.

On top of this, the NSDAP was now effectively bankrupt, having had to fight a two-round Presidential election, two Reichstag elections, and several state elections in the space of less than twelve months. Fears also grew that the 400,000-strong SA might collapse, or be vulnerable to communist subversion, following reports that some units were being deserted by their members, and that others were falling victim to infighting between rival left- and right-wing factions.[98] Most analysts agreed that support for the Nazis had peaked and that they would only lose more votes if fresh elections were called and, as if to reinforce this, on 8 December 1932 Gregor Strasser, the head of the party organisation, publicly resigned following a series of disagreements with Hitler over strategy, a move which was clearly designed to embarrass the party leadership at a time of growing uncertainty as to its future.[99]

In order to understand why, in spite of these setbacks, the Nazis were eventually able to assume power in Germany at the end of January 1933, we need to move beyond an exploration of the social foundations of their support to examine the changing relationship between Hitler and the forces of traditional anti-republican conservatism in Germany, especially after Hindenburg appointed Franz von Papen as Reich Chancellor on 1 June 1932.

Hitler, Hindenburg and the end of Weimar

The behind-the-scenes negotiations which led to Hitler's appointment as Reich Chancellor on 30 January 1933 have been investigated down to the finest detail and do not need exhaustive treatment here.[100] The importance of particular individuals, including the reactionary Catholic aristocrat Franz von Papen; his one-time Defence Minister and subsequently successor as Reich Chancellor, General Kurt von Schleicher; the head of the President's Office Otto Meissner; the President's son, Oskar von Hindenburg; and a range of other personalities, is now beyond dispute. Between them, these men conspired to create a 'government of national concentration' based on forces to the right of the Catholic Centre party but also involving an element of popular support from the masses.

More controversial is the role of particular institutions and pressure groups, such as the Reichswehr, the landowning lobby, the government bureaucracy and big business, not least because – contrary to some of the cruder versions of Marxist historiography – these groups did not form an indivisible 'ruling class' and rarely acted together.[101] Nonetheless, Hans-Ulrich Wehler's contention that Hitler 'could . . . never have climbed into

the saddle' if these 'traditional power elites' had not been willing to 'hold up
the stirrups' for him, seems essentially correct, at least in the negative sense
that their opposition could have blocked his path to power.[102] It was because
they had run out of other options for creating a stable anti-leftist government, and in particular because they distrusted Schleicher, Hitler's immediate predecessor, that they were finally willing to take the risk of tolerating a
Hitler-led administration. At the same time they clearly underestimated
Hitler and his determination to put the most extreme parts of his programme into practice.[103]

One individual whose role has come under more scrutiny recently, however, is Hindenburg himself. Conventional accounts have usually depicted
him as having been reluctant to hand power to Hitler, the 'Austrian lance
corporal' – largely because of the class differences between them – but he is
now seen as having been much more proactive in the process of 'levering'
the Nazi leader into power.[104] His motive here seems to have been the desire
to restore the putative 'national community' or 'inner unity' of 1914,[105]
albeit shorn of all 'socialist' and republican elements, and instead upheld by
'an alliance of Nazis and nationalistic conservatives that would suppress the
leftist parties once and for all'.[106]

Since 1918, and especially during his two successful campaigns for the
Reich Presidency in 1925 and 1932, Hindenburg had built on his reputation
as a military hero (victor of Tannenberg) and as a healer of Germany's
domestic wounds to forge an image as father of the nation. The key ingredient in this Hindenburg myth, which appealed to voters across the political
spectrum, from right-wing anti-republicans to 'patriotic' elements within
the SPD, was the notion of a 'special bond' tying the German people to the
man who had become their national saviour in 1914 and who understood
and embodied their disappointment at losing the war in spite of so much
heroism and sacrifice.[107] As if to underline this, the Tannenberg memorial,
built in 1927 on the site of the famous battle in East Prussia, had as its purpose not the commemoration of the war dead (too divisive an issue in the
late 1920s) but rather the celebration of Germany's – and in particular
Hindenburg's – 'historic' victory over the Russians in August 1914.[108]

Yet although Hindenburg assiduously promoted his image as a soldier
'above politics', engaged in 'selfless service' to the nation, many of his
actions were in fact profoundly political and partisan in nature. Thus
already in November 1919 he had given encouragement to right-wing conspiracy theorists by declaring, before the Reichstag Commission of Inquiry,
that the German army had not been defeated in the field, but was 'stabbed
in the back' by traitors at home.[109] Although he swore an oath to uphold the

republican constitution upon taking office as Reich President in May 1925, he remained a monarchist at heart and, in line with this, always mistrusted the SPD on defence matters.[110] This undoubtedly influenced his insistence on the retention of General Wilhelm Groener as Defence Minister after the appointment of the grand coalition government in June 1928.[111] Equally it guided his decision to allow the fall of the Müller government in March 1930, and to dissolve the Reichstag in July 1930 in the hope of obtaining a working anti-socialist majority. From late 1931 he favoured a sharp shift to the Right in terms of government policy, a complete '*Entparlamentarisierung* of the political system' and a 'realignment' of Prussia with the Reich, ambitions which eventually brought him to the fateful decision to hand the Chancellorship to Hitler in January 1933.[112]

The first step down the path to disaster was the dismissal of Brüning in May 1932. Hindenburg was partly influenced here by the landowning lobby's opposition to the government's very mild proposals for agrarian reform, as mentioned above, but he was equally furious with Brüning for allowing him to be re-elected as President in April 1932 on the back largely of Catholic, liberal and SPD voters. This is because it made him indebted to Otto Braun and other republican politicians, and undermined his determination to be seen as a President of national unity 'above parties' and even above the constitution itself.[113] His displeasure at the ban on the SA on 13 April (which he felt should go hand in hand with an equal ban on the republican Reichsbanner), and his willingness to sacrifice Groener, and then Brüning to further his political aims should also be seen in this light.[114]

Franz von Papen, Brüning's replacement, was willing to act in accordance with Hindenburg's thinking by making moves towards persuading the Nazis to enter into a 'government of national concentration'.[115] As a first step, the Reichstag was dissolved on 4 June 1932 and the ban on the SA lifted on 16 June. The immediate result was a huge increase in political violence, with 99 people killed in street battles in various parts of Germany between 14 June and 18 July.[116] When, as expected, the Nazis made huge gains in the election held at the end of that month, becoming the largest single party in the Reichstag, Hindenburg was willing to offer Hitler a role in government, as Vice-Chancellor under Papen, but was unwilling at this stage to grant him the post of Chancellor. At a tense meeting on 13 August 1932, he also told the Nazi leader that 'he could not answer before God, his conscience and the Fatherland if he handed over the entire power of government to a single party, and one which was so intolerant to the views of others'.[117] The meeting ended in failure, and Papen had to continue without Nazi support in the Reichstag. Worse still, as we have seen, Hitler took revenge on Papen, instructing Goering to allow the KPD-sponsored vote of no confidence in the government to go ahead when the Reichstag met on 12 September 1932. In the weeks that followed, the Nazis not only attacked Papen and his 'cabinet of barons' as reactionary, but also hinted at the possibility of an anti-Papen 'black-brown' coalition with the Catholic Centre Party after the 6 November election.[118] In reality, though, Hitler was only interested in power for his own party, not in coalitions, and so turned down a renewed offer from Hindenburg on 21 November either to join Papen's government of national concentration or to form his own administration with a parliamentary majority. Hindenburg, for his part, refused for a second time Hitler's request to be appointed head of a presidential cabinet.[119]

With only a tiny number of DNVP and DVP deputies willing to support his government in the Reichstag, and with even a majority in his own cabinet against him, Papen was forced to resign on 2 December 1932. Yet although he had been a complete failure as Reich Chancellor, Hindenburg had been reluctant to dismiss him and almost immediately regretted having done so. Here issues of personality came into play, for Hindenburg now found Papen's successor, General Kurt von Schleicher, much less palatable and had already decided to get rid of him by early January 1933. One reason for this was Schleicher's abrupt manner of speaking to the President; another was his apparent pursuit of an alternative strategy for breaking the political stalemate in Germany by appealing to 'patriotic' elements in the trade union movement and renegade members of the Nazi party like Gregor Strasser to unite behind a package of economic reforms and job creation projects.[120] In fact, as the late Henry Ashby Turner Junior has shown, Schleicher's alternative *Querfront* strategy almost certainly did not exist; it was a myth behind which still lurked his long-term goal of bringing the Nazis into an authoritarian right-wing government by invoking a sacred sense of duty to the Reich and by making concessions to some of their policy demands.[121] After these efforts failed when Hitler 'broke definitively'[122] with him in late January 1933, and knowing that he faced certain defeat in a vote of no confidence in the Reichstag on 31 January, Schleicher appealed to Hindenburg for permission to declare parliament dissolved before it had even met. Yet Hindenburg refused.[123]

In the meantime, Papen had begun plotting against his former mentor Schleicher, holding a secret meeting with Hitler at the house of the pro-Nazi banker Baron Kurt von Schroeder near Cologne on 4 January, and following this up with further discussions at a property owned by Joachim von Ribbentrop in Berlin later that month. Both Hindenburg and Schleicher were almost immediately made aware that these meetings had taken place;

but Hindenburg personally sanctioned Papen to continue his discussions with Hitler, while Schleicher chose to believe Papen's protestations that he was not intriguing against him. In the meantime, by 22 January Papen himself had come to the conclusion that the only way of getting rid of Schleicher was to give way to Hitler's demands for the Chancellorship, albeit with certain conditions attached.[124]

The final turning point came on 28 January, when Schleicher resigned and Hindenburg instructed Papen to 'offer' Hitler the Chancellorship in a presidential cabinet which would also include Hugenberg's DNVP and the monarchist Stahlhelm organisation. Papen himself would be Vice Chancellor, with an independent line of communication to the President, and several other non-party figures would continue in the same offices they had held under Papen and Schleicher. Intriguingly, one cabinet position, that of Justice Minister, was also left open to give the impression that the Catholic parties might still be persuaded to join the government, thus giving it a parliamentary majority. But none of the people involved seriously intended to make the kind of concessions needed to attract the Centre Party or the BVP into taking up this offer.[125] In the meantime, the anti-Schleicher conspirators, who essentially had Hindenburg's backing, were able to hurry things along by concocting the spurious line that Schleicher was intending to launch a military coup, confining the President to his country estate and installing himself as dictator. On the morning of 30 January 1933 Hindenburg swore Hitler in as Reich Chancellor, having first made sure that his own nominee, the non-party aristocrat Werner von Blomberg, had replaced Schleicher as Defence Minister.[126]

What, then, had changed between August and November 1932, and January 1933, to make Hindenburg willing to appoint Hitler as Chancellor? And why did he agree to the Nazi leader's request for an immediate dissolution of parliament, with elections set for 5 March,[127] when he had refused this to Schleicher?

One theory is that representatives of the old landowning elite, who distrusted Schleicher, persuaded the ageing President to agree to a Hitler-led government. Certainly it is true that Hindenburg was always willing to lend a sympathetic ear to representatives of the East Prussian landowner class, to which he himself belonged. It is also true that the RLB, whose representatives met with the President and Chancellor on 11 January 1933 to complain about the lack of state aid for the depressed agriculture of the east, had swung firmly behind the Hitler movement, but there is no proof that either of these factors were decisive. In fact, shortly after the 11 January meeting, Hindenburg broke off the government's relations with the RLB, claiming that they had acted in bad faith by publishing an article attacking official agrarian policy behind his (and Schleicher's) back.[128] Perhaps a greater influence on Hindenburg were the views of his neighbour in East Prussia, the elderly and ultra-conservative aristocrat Elard von Oldenburg-Januschau, who believed that the strong DNVP presence in the cabinet would bar Hitler from establishing a one-party dictatorship.[129] Yet here too there is no evidence that Hindenburg could be swayed by Oldenburg-Januschau alone; in fact, the two men had temporarily fallen out in March 1932 when Oldenburg-Januschau supported the DNVP's candidate, Theodor Duesterberg, against the incumbent, Hindenburg, in the first round of the presidential elections.[130]

Other theories are that Hindenburg was somehow tricked on 29–30 January into believing that he was appointing Hitler to head a parliamentary government also backed by the Centre Party and the BVP,[131] or that he was browbeaten by elements in the Reichswehr who believed that the NSDAP's participation in government was the only means of avoiding civil war.[132] However, neither of these explanations holds much water on its own. Certainly Hindenburg was looking for a way out of continuing the policy of presidential cabinets, as he believed this was damaging to his personal image as a head of state 'above parties', but the solution he was looking for did not run in the direction of a return to parliamentarism, still less in the direction of military dictatorship, since he was always anxious to keep the Reichswehr 'above politics'.[133] The clue here lies in his insistence on personally appointing the new Defence Minister while conceding Hitler's nomination of Wilhelm Frick as Reich Interior Minister and Hermann Goering as Prussian Interior Minister, giving the latter full power over policing in Germany's largest state.[134]

A third theory, and undoubtedly the most plausible, is that Hindenburg really wanted Papen back at the helm, as both Reich Chancellor and Reich Commissioner for Prussia, with Hitler 'contained' by being granted a subordinate position within a new cabinet of the conservative and nationalist Right.[135] However, Papen had made himself so unpopular – even with the army, which feared civil war if he were reappointed – that the President finally agreed to a Hitler-led government as the next best option. By this stage, he would also perhaps have believed – as did his advisers – that Hitler was weakened by the two million votes lost in November 1932 and by the defection of Strasser in December 1932. This would make him more controllable – or, as Papen put it, 'Within two months we will have pushed Hitler so far into a corner that he'll squeak.'[136]

Nonetheless, by agreeing to a Hitler Chancellorship – a step for which he carried the ultimate responsibility – and worse still, by granting Hitler's

PLATE 6.3 NSDAP poster for the March 1933 Reichstag election campaign featuring both Hindenburg and Hitler. The caption reads: 'The Reich will never be divided if we remain true and united'.   Source: Deutsches Historisches Museum, Berlin

request to dissolve the Reichstag, Hindenburg had in effect betrayed the millions of Catholic, Social Democrat, liberal and non-party Germans who had voted for him as President some nine months earlier, in the belief that he would protect the constitution and uphold the rule of law.[137] He had also moved well beyond what he had been willing to contemplate in August 1932, namely a deal bringing the Nazis into government but without conceding Hitler's demand for 'full leadership of the state' (*die Staatsführung in vollem Umfange*).[138] Hindenburg was fully conscious of the implications of dissolving the Reichstag on 1 February (and the Prussian Landtag on 6 February), for it meant agreeing to elections in which the Nazis would be able to call upon his name and his myth in support of their calls for the destruction of Marxism and parliamentarism through the passing of an

Enabling Act. In this way, the constellation of 1932, Hindenburg versus Hitler, had been transformed into a virtually undefeatable alliance: Hindenburg with Hitler.[139]

On 5 March 1933 the Nazis and their DNVP allies won a narrow majority in semi-free elections in which the ruling parties were able to monopolise all media outlets and political opponents of the new government were harassed by the police and the SA. Further intimidation of opposition parties took place on 23 March 1933 to ensure the two-thirds majority in the Reichstag necessary to pass the Enabling Act, which gave Hitler dictatorial powers for four years and brought to an end the period of presidential cabinets. The Reichstag fire of 27 February, for which the Communists were blamed, had lent further legitimacy to the Nazi dictatorship, and allowed it to introduce a range of new emergency laws 'for the protection of people and state' without, for the time being, having to negotiate a formal ban on the KPD.[140] Yet it was Hindenburg's politically motivated decision to appoint Hitler as Reich Chancellor on 30 January, and to dissolve parliament two days later, which marked the true end of the Weimar Republic. The saviour of the German nation in 1914, the would-be embodiment of the 'spirit of 1914' and the self-appointed guardian of its legacy, had become its betrayer in 1933.

Notes

1 The best study is Wright, *Stresemann*. See also Peter Krüger, *Die Aussenpolitik der Republik von Weimar* (Darmstadt, 1985).

2 Evans, *The Coming of the Third Reich*, p. 212.

3 Clavin, *The Great Depression*, pp. 92–3.

4 Ibid., p. 112; Richard Overy, *The Nazi Economic Recovery, 1932–1938*, 2nd edition (Cambridge, 1996), p. 24.

5 Eve Rosenhaft, 'The Unemployed in the Neighbourhood: Social Dislocation and Political Mobilisation in Germany 1929–33', in Richard J. Evans and Dick Geary (eds), *The German Unemployed. Experiences and Consequences of Mass Unemployment from the Weimar Republic to the Third Reich* (London, 1987), pp. 194–227 (here p. 207).

6 Rosenhaft, *Beating the Fascists?*, pp. 41–2; Clavin, *The Great Depression*, p. 112.

7 Tim Mason, 'National Socialism and the Working Class, 1925 to May 1933', in Mason, *Social Policy in the Third Reich. The Working Class and the 'National Community'* (Oxford, 1993), pp. 41–87 (here p. 81).

8 Fischer, *The Rise of the Nazis*, p. 187.

9 Helen Boak, 'The State as an Employer of Women in the Weimar Republic', p. 88.

10 Harold James, *The German Slump. Politics and Economics 1924–1936* (Oxford, 1986), pp. 272–6.

11 Mommsen, *The Rise and Fall of Weimar Democracy*, p. 287.

12 For further details see Wolfram Pyta, *Hindenburg. Herrschaft zwischen Hohenzollern und Hitler* (Berlin, 2007), pp. 555–75.

13 Karl Dietrich Bracher, 'Brünings unpolitische Politik und die Auflösung der Weimarer Republik', *Vierteljahrshefte für Zeitgeschichte*, 19/2 (1971), pp. 113–23 (here p. 115).

14 Karl Dietrich Bracher, *Die Auflösung der Weimarer Republik. Eine Studie zum Problem des Machtverfalls in der Demokratie*, 5th edition (Villingen, 1971) [1955], pp. 243–53; Carsten, *The Reichswehr and Politics*, pp. 306–8.

15 Evans, *The Coming of the Third Reich*, p. 255.

16 Heinrich Brüning, *Memoiren, 1918–1934*, edited by Claire Nix and Theoderich Kampmann (Stuttgart, 1970). Cf. William L. Patch Jr., *Heinrich Brüning and the Dissolution of the Weimar Republic* (Cambridge, 1998).

17 Evans, *The Coming of the Third Reich*, p. 251.

18 Patch, *Brüning*, pp. 15, 94 and 110–12 and 118–19.

19 Ibid., pp. 60–71; Kolb, *The Weimar Republic*, p. 207.

20 Patch, *Brüning*, pp. 78–9; James, *The German Slump*, pp. 272–6.

21 Patch, *Brüning*, pp. 109–11.

22 Harsch, *German Social Democracy*, p. 95.

23 Patch, *Brüning*, pp. 76, 85–7 and 120.

24 Krüger, *Die Aussenpolitik*, pp. 512–16.

25 For further details see Aguado, 'The Creditanstalt Crisis', esp. pp. 207–18.

26 James, *The German Slump*, pp. 312–14; Theo Balderston, *Economy and Politics in the Weimar Republic* (Cambridge, 2002), pp. 85–6.

27 Krüger, *Die Aussenpolitik*, p. 535.

28 Wolfram Pyta, *Die Weimarer Republik* (Opladen, 2004), pp. 114–5, 126–7 and 132–3.

29 Patch, *Brüning*, p. 102; James, *A German Identity*, p. 133.

30 Kershaw, *Hitler, 1889–1936*, p. 365.

31 Carsten, *The Reichswehr and Politics*, pp. 319–21 and 338.

32 Ibid., pp. 339–50; Patch, *Brüning*, pp. 247–56.

33 Patch, *Brüning*, pp. 265–71; Bracher, *Die Auflösung*, pp. 449–62.

34 Nicholls, *Weimar*, p. 161.

35 Evans, *The Coming of the Third Reich*, pp. 251–2.

36 Kolb, *The Weimar Republic*, p. 121.

37 This is the argument put forward, among others, by Carl-Ludwig Holtfrerich, 'Economic Policy Options and the End of the Weimar Republic', in Ian Kershaw (ed.), *Weimar: Why Did German Democracy Fail?* (London, 1990), pp. 58–91 (esp. pp. 71–4).

38 Krüger, *Die Aussenpolitik*, pp. 516–7; Balderston, *Economics and Politics*, p. 92.

39 Carl-Ludwig Holtfrerich, 'Comment on Harold James' Paper', in Kershaw (ed.), *Weimar: Why did Germany Democracy Fail?*, pp. 155–9 (here p. 159). See also Kolb, *The Weimar Republic*, pp. 209–10.

40 On the Iron Front, see Donna Harsch, 'The Iron Front: Weimar Social Democracy between Tradition and Modernity', in Barclay and Weitz (eds), *Between Reform and Revolution*, pp. 251–74.

41 Rosenhaft, *Beating the Fascists?*, p. 96; Fischer, *The German Communists*, pp. 152–3.

42 Harsch, *German Social Democracy*, p. 180.

43 Hermann Weber, *Die Wandlung des deutschen Kommunismus. Die Stalinisierung der KPD in der Weimarer Republik* (Frankfurt/M, 1969), p. 243.

44 Dick Geary, 'Unemployment and Working-Class Solidarity: The German Experience 1929–33', in Evans and Geary (eds), *The German Unemployed*, pp. 261–80 (here p. 267).

45 Ibid., p. 275; Weber, *Die Wandlung des deutschen Kommunismus*, pp. 243–4.

46 Winkler, 'Choosing the Lesser Evil', p. 214.

47 See Wolfram Pyta, *Gegen Hitler und für die Republik. Die Auseinandersetzung der deutschen Sozialdemokratie mit der NSDAP in der Weimarer Republik* (Düsseldorf, 1989), esp. pp. 303–72 and 510–13.

48 Hermann Weber, 'The Stalinization of the KPD: Old and New Views', in Norman Laporte, Kevin Morgan and Matthew Worley (eds), *Bolshevism, Stalinism and the Comintern. Perspectives on Stalinization, 1917–53* (Basingstoke, 2008), pp. 22–44 (here p. 26).

49 Weber, *Die Wandlung des deutschen Kommunismus*, p. 241.

50 Carsten, *The Reichswehr and Politics*, p. 368.

51 Winkler, 'Choosing the Lesser Evil', p. 214; Detlev Junker, *Die Deutsche Zentrumspartei und Hitler 1932/3* (Stuttgart, 1969); Richard F. Hamilton, *Who Voted for Hitler?* (Princeton, NJ, 1982), p. 256.

52 Hans Mommsen, 'Social Democracy on the Defensive: The Immobility of the SPD and the Rise of National Socialism', in Mommsen, *From Weimar to Auschwitz* (Cambridge, 1991), pp. 39–61 (esp. pp. 55–7).

53 Harsch, 'The Iron Front', esp. pp. 258–69.

54 Gerhard Paul, 'Krieg der Symbole. Formen und Inhalt des symbolpublizistischen Bürgerkrieges 1932', in Kerbs and Stahr (eds), *Berlin 1932*, pp. 27–55 (here p. 52).

55 Wolfgang Wippermann, '"Falsch gedacht und nicht gehandelt". Der 20. Juli 1932 und das Scheitern des sozialdemokratischen Antifaschismus', in ibid., pp. 131–42 (here pp. 132–3), Harsch, 'The Iron Front', p. 266.

56 Mommsen, 'Social Democracy on the Defensive', p. 47.

57 Pyta, *Gegen Hitler und für die Republik*, p. 507; Harsch, *German Social Democracy*, pp. 193–5.

58 Clark, *Iron Kingdom*, pp. 645–6.

59 Ibid., p. 647.

60 Evans, *The Coming of the Third Reich*, p. 238; Rosenhaft, *Beating the Fascists?*, esp. pp. 128–66; idem., 'Working-Class Life and Working-Class Politics: Communists, Nazis and the State in the Battle for the Streets of Berlin, 1928–1932', in Richard Bessel and E. J. Feuchtwanger (eds), *Social Change and Political Development in Weimar Germany* (London, 1981), pp. 207–40; Anthony McElligott, 'Street Politics in Hamburg, 1932–3', *History Workshop Journal*, 16/1 (1983), pp. 83–90; Fischer, *The German Communists*, esp. pp. 138–61; Pamela Swett, *Neighbors and Enemies. The Culture of Radicalism in Berlin, 1929–1933* (Cambridge, 2004). On the 'imagined' civil war as constructed in the press and public discourse see also Dirk Blasius, *Weimars Ende. Bürgerkrieg und Politik 1930–1933* (Göttingen, 2005).

61 Cf. Paul, 'Krieg der Symbole', pp. 39–40.

62 Ernst Thälmann, address to the plenary session of the Central Committee of the Communist Party of Germany, 19 February 1932. Reproduced in Kaes *et al.* (eds), *The Weimar Republic Source Book*, pp. 327–8 (here p. 328).

63 Winkler, *Weimar*, p. 523; Evans, *The Coming of the Third Reich*, pp. 297–8.

64 Geary, 'Unemployment and Working-Class Solidarity', esp. pp. 272–4.

65 McElligott, 'Street Politics in Hamburg', pp. 85–6; Rosenhaft, 'The Unemployed in the Neighbourhood', pp. 208–9.

66 Klaus Rainer Röhl, 'Fünf Tage im November. Kommunisten, Sozialdemokraten und Nationalsozialisten und der BVG-Streik vom November 1932 in Berlin', in Kerbs and Stahr (eds), *Berlin 1932*, pp. 161–77.

67 Evans, *The Coming of the Third Reich*, p. 237.

68 Falter, *Hitlers Wähler*, p. 364.

69 Kolb, *The Weimar Republic*, p. 216.

70 Winkler, 'Choosing the Lesser Evil', p. 224.

71 Jane Caplan, 'Speaking the Right Language: The Nazi Party and the Civil Service Vote in the Weimar Republic', in Thomas Childers (ed.), *The Formation of the Nazi Constituency, 1919–1933* (London, 1986), pp. 182–201.

72 This was shown most famously in William Sheridan Allen's case study, *The Nazi Seizure of Power. The Experience of a Single German Town, 1930–1935* (Chicago, 1965). For more recent studies which make the same point see Fritzsche, 'Weimar Populism and National Socialism', esp. pp. 294–304; and Art, *The Politics of the Nazi Past*, pp. 206–7.

73 Cf. Detlef Mühlberger, *The Social Bases of Nazism, 1919–1933* (Cambridge, 2003), pp. 75–6.

74 Thomas Childers, *The Nazi Voter. The Social Foundations of Fascism in Germany, 1919–1933* (Chapel Hill and London, 1983), p. 268. Childers is less happy to call the NSDAP a 'people's party', however, describing its claims here as 'tenuous at best'.

75 Conan Fischer, 'Class Enemies or Class Brothers? Communist-Nazi Relations in Germany, 1929–33', *European History Quarterly*, 15/3 (1985), pp. 259–79 (here p. 265); idem., 'The KPD and Nazism: A Reply to Dick Geary', *European History Quarterly*, 15/4 (1985), pp. 465–71 (here p. 466).

76 Fischer, 'The KPD and Nazism', p. 466. For the broader debate on the class composition of the SA, see the competing interpretations offered by Conan Fischer, *Stormtroopers. A Social, Economic and Ideological Analysis, 1929–35* (London, 1983), esp. pp. 25–81, and Richard Bessel, *Political Violence and the Rise of Nazism. The Storm Troopers in Eastern Germany* (New Haven and London, 1984), esp. pp. 33–9.

77 Mason, 'National Socialism and the Working Class', p. 68.

78 Ibid., p. 53; Falter, *Hitlers Wähler*, p. 198.

79 Bessel, *Political Violence and the Rise of Nazism*, p. 33; Mühlberger, *The Social Bases*, pp. 11–12.

80 Mason, 'National Socialism and the Working Class', pp. 49–50.

81 Ibid., p. 65.

82 Falter, *Hitlers Wähler*, pp. 371–2.

83 Ibid, p. 199; Dick Geary, 'Nazis and Workers', *European History Quarterly*, 15/4 (1985), pp. 453–64 (here p. 459).

84 Geary, 'Nazis and Workers', p. 458; Childers, *The Nazi Voter*, p. 266.

85 Hamilton, *Who Voted for Hitler?*, pp. 156–98.

86 Dick Geary, 'Employers, Workers and the Collapse of Weimar', in Kershaw (ed.), *Weimar: Why did German Democracy Fail?* pp. 92–119 (here p. 109).

87 Szejnmann, *Vom Traum zum Alptraum*, p. 121. Cf. Szejnmann, *Nazism in Central Germany. The Brownshirts in 'Red' Saxony* (Oxford, 1999), pp. 243–4.

88 Geary, 'Workers and Nazis', p. 454; Falter, *Hitlers Wähler*, p. 215; Jeremy Noakes and Geoffrey Pridham (ed.), *Nazism, 1919–1945. A Documentary Reader. Vol 1: The Rise to Power, 1919–1934* (Exeter, 1983), p. 83; Hamilton, *Who Voted for Hitler?*, pp. 78 and 111.

89 Falter, *Hitlers Wähler*, pp. 98–101.

90 Ibid., pp. 151–4. Cf. Falter, 'The National Socialist Mobilisation of New Voters, 1928–1933', in Thomas Childers (ed.), *The Formation of the Nazi Constituency* (London, 1986), pp. 202–31.

91 Cf. Jones, 'The "Dying Middle"', passim; Peukert, *The Weimar Republic*, pp. 156–7.

92 Annemarie Tröger, 'Die Dolchstoßlegende der Linken: "Frauen haben Hitler an die Macht gebracht"', in *Frauen und Wissenschaft. Beiträge zur Berliner Sommeruniversität für Frauen* (West Berlin, 1976), pp. 324–55.

93 For an overview of historiographical trends on this issue see Falter, *Hitlers Wähler*, pp. 136–46; and Stibbe, *Women in the Third Reich*, pp. 26–9.

94 Helen Boak, 'Mobilising Women for Hitler: The Female Nazi Voter', in Anthony McElligott and Tim Kirk (eds), *Working Towards the Führer. Essays in Honour of Sir Ian Kershaw* (Manchester, 2003), pp. 68–92 (here p. 84).

95 Scheck, *Mothers of the Nation*, pp. 157–74.

96 Boak, 'Mobilising Women for Hitler', p. 82; Falter, *Hitlers Wähler*, pp. 143–5; Kershaw, *Hitler, 1889–1936*, pp. 408–9.

97 Kershaw, *Hitler, 1889–1936*, pp. 389–90.

98 Fischer, *Stormtroopers*, pp. 210–11.

99 Kershaw, *Hitler, 1889–1936*, pp. 396–404.

100 For three of the best accounts see Henry Ashby Turner Jr, *Hitler's Thirty Days to Power: January 1933* (London, 1996); Kershaw, *Hitler, 1889–1936*, pp. 379–427; and Evans, *The Coming of the Third Reich*, pp. 289–308.

101 Kershaw, *Hitler, 1889–1936*, p. 379.

102 Wehler, *The German Empire*, p. 231.

103 Mason, 'National Socialism and the Working Class', p. 84.

104 See in particular Wolfram Pyta's recent study, *Hindenburg*. The phrase 'levered into power' comes from Kershaw, *Hitler, 1889–1936*, pp. 379–427.

105 Pyta, *Hindenburg*, pp. 506 and 800.

106 Turner, *Hitler's Thirty Days*, p. 44.

107 Menge, 'The *Iron Hindenburg*', p. 357.

108 Mosse, *Fallen Soldiers*, p. 97; Berger, *Germany*, p. 138.

109 Pyta, *Hindenburg*, pp. 406–9.

110 Turner, *Hitler's Thirty Days*, p. 116.

111 Mommsen, *The Rise and Fall of Weimar Democracy*, p. 248.

112 Pyta, *Hindenburg*, pp. 711–12 and 800; Kershaw, *Hitler, 1889–1936*, p. 366.

113 Pyta, *Hindenburg*, p. 681.

114 Ibid., p. 688.

115 Ibid., p. 701.

116 Harsch, *German Social Democracy*, p. 189.

117 Kershaw, *Hitler, 1889–1936*, p. 373.

118 Stibbe, *Women in the Third Reich*, p. 24.

119 Kershaw, *Hitler, 1889–1936*, pp. 394–5; Pyta, *Hindenburg*, p. 792.

120 Turner, *Hitler's Thirty Days*, pp. 79–108.

121 Turner, 'The Myth of Chancellor von Schleicher's *Querfront* Strategy', passim.

122 Ibid., p. 680.

123 Ibid., p. 151; Kershaw, *Hitler, 1889–1936*, p. 418.

124 Turner, *Hitler's Thirty Days*, p. 112.

125 Ibid., p. 151; Kershaw, *Hitler, 1889–1936*, p. 423; Pyta, *Hindenburg*, pp. 793–4.

126 Turner, *Hitler's Thirty Days*, pp. 144–5, 153–4; Carsten, *The Reichswehr and Politics*, p. 394.

127 Kershaw, *Hitler, 1889–1936*, p. 439.

128 Pyta, *Hindenburg*, pp. 791–2.

129 Turner, *Hitler's Thirty Days*, p. 143.

130 Pyta, *Hindenburg*, p. 695.

131 Turner, *Hitler's Thirty Days*, pp. 150–1; Mommsen, *The Rise and Fall of Weimar Democracy*, pp. 527–8.

132 Carsten, *The Reichswehr and Politics*, pp. 392–3.

133 Pyta, *Hindenburg*, p. 798; Kershaw, *Hitler, 1889–1936*, p. 422.

134 Evans, *The Coming of the Third Reich*, p. 307; Turner, *Hitler's Thirty Days*, p. 150.

135 Kershaw, *Hitler, 1889–1936*, pp. 394 and 419.

136 Evans, *The Coming of the Third Reich*, p. 308.

137 Turner, *Hitler's Thirty Days*, p. 182.

138 Kershaw, *Hitler, 1889–1936*, p. 373.

139 Pyta, *Hindenburg*, p. 795; Peter Fritzsche, *Life and Death in the Third Reich* (Cambridge, MA, 2008), p. 45.

140 Kershaw, *Hitler, 1889–1936*, pp. 459–60.

Conclusion

In February 1934, just over twelve months after Hitler's appointment as Chancellor, the Nazi newspaper the *Völkischer Beobachter* published an article drawing a direct parallel between the heroism and sacrifices of the war dead of 1914–18 and the politics of the new Third Reich:

Fallen comrades, the world war was not fought in vain! Blood flowed and hunger reigned for a purpose, you sacrificed your lives for a cause. Your spirit lives on today more than ever. It inspires the youth, the nation, the Reich. Your death created the foundations for our revolution of 1933.[1]

Furthermore, the article continued, this 'front spirit' or 'spirit of 1914' – which the republic had supposedly tried to bury or destroy – was not just the property of veterans, but rather of the whole German people, including those who had served on the home front or who had spent the war in enemy captivity:

The front experience is not just a distant memory for us, it first helped to convey an idea, and then grew beyond this into a source of strength and unity which today shapes the life and existence of the entire German nation.[2]

Only those 'cowardly' Jews and Marxists who had been responsible for the 'Ungeist' or 'demonic' collapse of November 1918, the article suggested, were excluded from the honour which surrounded the fallen heroes. Here the 'divisive' Weimar Republic was indeed held up as the direct opposite of the youthful enthusiasm of the *Frontkämpfer* or front-line soldier. Or as Hitler himself proclaimed in a speech in northern Bavaria in 1927:

There was one place in Germany where there was no class division. That was at the front . . . Why could one do it at the front? Because the enemy lay opposite us, because one recognised the danger. Thus, if I want to bring our people together, to unite them, I have first to build a new front, which has a common enemy, so that everyone knows: we have to be united, then this enemy is our common enemy.[3]

This book too has looked for continuities between 1914 and 1933, but not quite in the same way as the Nazis and their supporters intended. After all, as we have seen, the 'spirit of 1914' to which so many right-wing and conservative critics of the Weimar Republic referred was more myth than reality. It was a slogan and battle cry which came to mean more in retrospect than it did at the time. Indeed, those studies which have examined the views and experiences of ordinary soldiers and civilians during the First World War have stressed resignation and fatalism over enthusiasm for battle.[4] In truth there was no miraculous 'inner unity' in 1914, and no healing of past divisions and past wounds through a shared 'August experience' or putative 'community of the trenches'.[5]

More generally, any crude attempt to draw a direct line from 1914 to 1933 runs the risk of lending too much importance to the Nazi world view at the expense of understanding the colour and diversity of Weimar politics. As Donna Harsch rightly points out, many important lines of continuity were actually broken in Germany after 1933. Among them would be a significant number of progressive middle-class cultures (including pacifism, feminism and liberal forms of Protestantism, Catholicism and Judaism) and at least three different working-class cultures (Social Democrat, Catholic and Communist), all of which were invigorated and reinforced by the First World War, and all of which encompassed ambiguous and overlapping attitudes towards the republic and its institutions.[6] The same could also be said for the different movements in the arts and literature, where, as we have seen, the challenge of modernism created its own tensions and uncertainties, both inside Germany and beyond.[7] On top of this there were generational conflicts between the young and old, and political divisions within social classes, for instance between the old and the new Mittelstand, between town and countryside, or between heavy industry and high finance.[8] It was only the calamity of the Great Depression that allowed the Nazis to pose as the champions of a spurious 'national unity' above the divisions of class, party and confession, and even above the state itself. Or, to quote Ian Kershaw, had it not been for the global economic downturn of the early 1930s and its peculiarly harsh effects on Germany, 'the Nazi Party may well have broken up and faded into oblivion, remembered essentially as a passing phenomenon of the post-war upheaval'.[9]

Even so, I would maintain that 1914 is still an important starting point for an understanding of some of the key problems and challenges facing the Weimar Republic itself. This can be seen at the level both of structures and of mentalities. In terms of structures, the decision of the SPD parliamentary fraction to approve war credits on 4 August 1914 in many ways fore-shadowed the Ebert-Groener Pact of November 1918, which had catastrophic consequences for the future of democratic republican rule. In particular it led to a disastrous split on the left, made worse by the murders of Liebknecht and Luxemburg in January 1919 and the virtual civil war between government troops and workers in the Ruhr district in 1919–20.[10] Of course there are more positive aspects to the SPD's political strategy dur-ing these years, including its adherence to the Reichstag Peace Resolution in July 1917, its decision to enter coalition governments with bourgeois parties after 1919 in Prussia and in the Reich, and its strong support for the foreign policy of Gustav Stresemann between 1923 and 1929. The party's preference for a deal with the bourgeois parties instead of with the Independent social-ists and the Communists was, as Heinrich August Winkler says, a precondi-tion for the foundation and medium-term stability of the Republic.[11] Yet it also determined that the SPD would put 'nation' above proletarian unity, and fear of civil war above commitment to radical overhaul of existing sociopolitical structures. This proved fatal for the long-term survival of democratic institutions and values, as became all too evident during the crisis period of the early 1930s.[12]

Secondly, in terms of mentalities, the fact that the SPD and the moderate bourgeois parties had voted for war credits in August 1914 made it difficult for them, after 1918, to make a clear 'moral break with the Kaiserreich'.[13] Instead, the violence of war, against enemy civilians and soldiers, and against women on the home front, was denied even by those who partici-pated in the revolution of November 1918. This was the true meaning of Ebert's speech welcoming the troops home in December 1918 ('I salute you, who return unvanquished from the field of battle'), for instance, and of the repeated failure of successive republican governments to conduct an honest and open inquiry into German atrocities committed during the war.[14] The returning soldiers were regarded as undefeated heroes, in other words, and as victims of Allied lies and propaganda.

More to the point, many republican politicians remained trapped 'under the spell of their own August experience', as Stefan Berger puts it, rendering them unable to accept that the war had been fought for anything other than defensive purposes.[15] 'You do not return defeated and beaten', declared the revolutionary government of Baden on 16 November 1918 to the troops arriving home. 'You have defended our homeland against a world of enemies.'[16] The power of this myth was indeed so great that it even survived the calamities of the Second World War, to become a central theme in the memoirs of 'patriotic' Social Democrats exiled during the Nazi era, like Friedrich Stampfer,[17] and in the political writings of conservative-liberal academics who opposed National Socialism, like Friedrich Meinecke. The latter, for instance, wrote in 1946 of the need for a 'radical break with [Germany's] military past' but still clung on defiantly to his own positive recollections of the year 1914:

The exultation of spirit experienced during the August days of 1914, in spite of its ephemeral character, is one of the most precious, unforgettable memories of the highest sort. All the rifts which had hitherto existed in the German people, both within the bourgeoisie and between the bourgeoisie and the working classes, were suddenly closed . . . And more than that, one perceived in all camps that it was not a matter merely of the unity of a gain-seeking partnership, but that an inner renovation of our whole state and culture was needed. We genuinely believed that this had already commenced and that it would progress further in the common experiences of the war, which was looked upon as a war of defence and self-protection.[18]

Given this refusal to let go of the 'mythology of August 1914',[19] it is perhaps not surprising that few Germans were willing to challenge the army leadership's version of events in 1918 ('betrayal' by the home front) publicly and fewer still were willing to concede that German troops had behaved unheroically by committing violence against POWs and unarmed civilians in occupied territories. Yet some did so in private or within their own specific sociopolitical milieu. Thus as one front-line veteran and member of the republican Reichsbanner organisation put it in an unpublished memoir in 1926:

The [November 1918] armistice was the hour of liberation from the terrible sufferings and deprivations of war, but also from the yoke of Prussian militarism . . . Had it not come, we would have been driven across the Rhine, and the Entente would have transformed our beloved Rhineland into a wasteland, in order to make us feel the same pain as those who lived in the occupied territories. Since what the people in the territories occupied by us went through and suffered during the war is something that those [Germans] who stayed at home are completely unaware of.[20]

For some left-wing, anti-war veterans, then, it was possible to admit that Germany had emerged relatively unscathed from the war. Indeed, the German home front between 1914 and 1918 had experienced neither military occupation (except East Prussia, very briefly, in 1914), nor civilian

casualties on a large scale, nor forced labour, nor devastation of agriculture and
industry. No bombs had been dropped on the capital, Berlin, and no towns
and villages had been ransacked or looted by maurading enemy soldiers. [21]
The separatist movements that did exist were too weak to pose a serious
threat to the unity of the Reich. Complete collapse and subjugation had
been averted by the military surrender in November 1918, when German
troops still stood on French and Belgian soil. In spite of the terrible food
shortages, which continued well into 1919, there was no famine. Yet paradoxically, avoidance of the worst enabled wealthier Germans to concentrate
on the smaller things that they had lost: economic security, freedom from
crime and public disorder, a smoothly functioning bureaucracy, a sense of
national pride, an overseas empire, Alsace-Lorraine, the 'bleeding borders' in
the East, the certainties of the old class and gender order.[22] Or, to put it
another way, middle-class Germans were unable or unwilling to attribute
blame for the defeat on the old regime, as French men and women had done
after 1871, or even on the enemy. Instead they turned inwards, against the
republic itself. To cite the same Reichsbanner representative again:

The senior military figures, higher state officials, big landowners, and small and
big industrialists all lived out the war in the rear areas and on the home front,
but today the same people cannot proclaim their patriotism loudly enough. In my
own home town I know several of these 'heroes' who seize every opportunity to
raise the [old Imperial] black-white-and-red flag and proclaim themselves to be
'national' men, although they have never committed a patriotic act in the whole
of their lives. The long suffering front-line fighter, on the other hand, who gave
his all to protect the German people against the threat of foreign occupation . . .
but who today wants nothing more than to live an upright and peaceful life, is
immediately branded a traitor [ein vaterlandsloser Geselle] as soon as he joins
the Reichsbanner. Of course, it would take a rational being only a moment of
consideration to work out who the real patriots are . . .[23]

How was it, then, that the Reichsbanner veteran, who had done his soldierly
duty in defending the fatherland against external enemies and returning
home in good order, could be denigrated as a traitor? Why was he held
responsible for the collapse of 1918, whereas those whose nerves had really
failed during the last weeks of the war, the Hindenburgs and Ludendorffs
at general headquarters, and the armchair patriots at home, were now
honoured as past and future saviours of the fatherland?

One answer provided by Wolfgang Schivelbusch is that the middle
classes, who in reality had capitulated without a fight in 1918, projected
their own 'patriotic shortcomings' during the war onto the representatives

of the new republican political order. In private, many middle-class Germans had come to hate the war, and to deplore the Imperial government's mishandling of the food situation in particular. Like the Social Democrats, they recognised that the strikes of 1917–18 and the sudden collapse of morale at the front in the summer of 1918 were the result of hunger and individual exhaustion on a mass scale, rather than political radicalisation. They too were relieved when the fighting stopped and the soldiers were able to come home, becoming angry only when the precise terms of the peace settlement became known. Yet even after Allied troops arrived to occupy part of the Rhineland, they demonstrated a profound aversion to organised or even personal resistance, remaining silent and passive in 1918–19 (and again during the Ruhr invasion in 1923) in order to save their jobs and their wealth. As good patriots they accepted the army's explanation that the collapse had come from within rather than on the battlefield. However, in order to deflect responsibility from the home front as a whole it became necessary to blame the revolution alone for causing military defeat.[24]

The sense of shame attached to November 1918 in turn deprived the Weimar Republic of what it most needed, namely a 'legitimising foundational myth' which rooted the new regime in terms of longer historical continuities or traditions of heroic social and political struggle on behalf of the German nation and people.[25] Instead the tone was set by Friedrich Ebert himself, who on 3 August 1924 – the first and only occasion on which the outbreak of the war was officially commemorated in Weimar Germany – delivered a speech which clearly privileged the fallen soldiers over the revolutionaries of 1918. What was needed, the President declared, was for the 'spirit of the dead [to] remain alive in our people, so that it can be born once again: the free Germany'. The war would always be associated with their memory, while the republic and the Weimar constitution, neither of which was mentioned in Ebert's speech, would be forever sullied by images of downfall and betrayal, humiliation and 'enslavement'.[26]

To be fair, Ebert also claimed to be speaking for the entire German nation, including the millions who had lost loved ones on the battlefield. Feelings were still very raw on this subject, making the celebration of anniversaries connected with the 1914–18 conflict fraught with political difficulties. In short, it was impossible to please everybody. True, in the year 1924 members of the newly formed Reichsbanner still hoped that the majority of Germans would eventually come to accept their view that the 1918 revolution had freed Germany from the threat of tyranny, military dictatorship or foreign invasion, while preserving – through a new democratic constitution – the unifying, state-building and peace-loving traditions of the old Reich.[27] Yet after Paul von Hindenburg was elected Reich President in April 1925, the chances for the creation of a strong republican narrative based on a symbolic link between wartime sacrifices and the promulgation of a people's constitution became even slimmer. This is not to say that the Hindenburg view of the war – the stab-in-the-back legend – now came to predominate; in fact it was probably less accepted after 1925 than it had been before. But it did mean that the richness and multifarious nature of Weimar culture did not give rise to a genuine political pluralism based on a common understanding of the democratic process and respect for the views of others. Instead, to cite Donna Harsch, 'cultural values became the banners of political armies engaged in battles over the very nature of the state'.[28] And the disputed territory, for Communists, Nazis, nationalists and republicans alike, was more often than not the war itself, the way it was fought and the manner in which it was remembered.

The effects of this 'brutalisation of politics', as George Mosse calls it, [29] are still being investigated. One thing we do know is that it was quite compatible with anti-war feeling, which was still very much alive in Germany in the early 1920s.[30] It was also quite compatible with support for Franco-German reconciliation and greater European integration, as seen in the Locarno Pact of 1925. Yet one of the chief weaknesses of the Weimar Republic was its failure to shake off the poisonous enmities which the 1914–18 conflict had given rise to, and its inability to demobilise in a cultural sense, even during the honeymoon period of the Locarno era.[31] The fact that the different veterans' organisations could not agree on the best way to commemorate the fallen on the battlefield, even though they co-operated on other issues to do with ex-soldiers' welfare rights and pensions, would be a case in point. In this context Rainer Pöppinghege is surely right to speak of a 'fracturing of war memory' (*Fraktionierung der Kriegserinnerung*), with competing discourses used to mobilise new emotions and hatreds in the increasingly divided society of the late 1920s.[32]

Two further aspects of this failure of cultural demobilisation are especially important. The first is the growth of misogony – hatred of women – which has been a theme running throughout this book. After 1918 female emancipation was blamed for all manner of things, from the supposed evils of consumerism and Americanisation to the falling birth rate and the misery of mass male unemployment in the early 1930s. True, the Weimar political parties all competed for women's support at election times, but ultimately they treated female voters and politicians with contempt or worse.[33] This applied as much to the republican left as it did to the nationalist, anti-republican right. The Social Democrat Theodor Geiger's false assumption that women were especially responsible for the rise in support for the Nazis after 1930 because their 'greater emotional sensitivity' made them 'more receptive to radicalism', is a good example here.[34] Indeed, in many ways the claim of the SPD to be engaging in rational political discourse reflected its only reluctant acceptance of the presence of women in political life. Certainly it failed wholeheartedly to embrace the new opportunities this presented.[35]

Secondly, the shadow of 1914 and the war pushed the SPD and various allied organisations – the trade unions, the Reichsbanner and the Iron Front – into a defensive position in which upholding the mere trappings, as opposed to the spirit, of democratic constitutionalism became the main priority.[36] Above all, the party was imprisoned by the belief that it could only defend the cause of democracy by aligning itself 'with existing national symbols' rather than by championing and pushing forward the important political, social and cultural advances which had taken place on all fronts since 1918.[37] Often it seemed to agree with the Right that it was not the institutions of the republic but the authority of the state that should be upheld in the face of political extremism, thus staking its reputation on its claim to being law-abiding and patriotic.[38] 'We are the true party of the state' (*Wir sind die staatspolitische Partei*), proclaimed the senior Social Democrat Rudolf Breitscheid in the Reichstag in April 1930, hoping thereby to distance the SPD from the anti-constitutional manoeuvres of the minority Brüning government.[39] Yet as the main state party the SPD had palpably failed to create the unifying myths and symbols necessary to construct a lasting, stable political system which appealed to the majority of the German people. Instead, to use the words of Stefan Berger, it 'stood on the sidelines, watching events unfold rather than actively shaping them'.[40]

Having said this, a much bigger responsibility for the step by step dismantlement of republican rule between 1930 and 1933 lies with the German industrialists and bourgeois parties who, from July 1930 at the latest, systematically withdrew from their side of the bargain forged in 1918 (and tentatively renewed during the 'inflation consensus' of 1919–21 and the 'rationalisation consensus' of 1924–30), namely the notion that parliamentary democracy, to survive, required a readiness to compromise with the representatives of labour.[41] In this they saw eye to eye with Hindenburg, who was already looking for ways of sidelining the SPD from government in 1929/30. But they also fell out of line with the real spirit of the *Burgfrieden*, the spirit forged by Bethmann Hollweg in July–August 1914, which had sought to integrate the SPD and the trade unions into the state, not to exclude the masses of social democrat voters (and veterans) from the 'national community' and from a share in government.[42]

The first formal breach of this bargain was seen at the Reich level in July 1930, when Brüning, in an act of 'breathtaking irresponsibility',[43] requested the dissolution of the Reichstag rather than seeking an informal compromise with the SPD on budgetary questions. The undermining of the Weimar constitution and the parliamentary system was then deepened further in 1932 when in different ways both Brüning and Papen, and behind them the major right-wing parties, sought to entice the NSDAP into an authoritarian, 'anti-Marxist' coalition in Prussia and in the Reich as a whole. It was this coalition, backed by the Reichswehr, the Stahlhelm, the SA, and above all by President Hindenburg, which finally destroyed the republic by agreeing to the formation of a new government led by Adolf Hitler in January 1933.

Notes

1 'Ihr seid nicht umsonst gefallen! Gedanken eines Frontsoldaten zum Heldengedenktag', *Völkischer Beobachter*, 25–26 February 1934. Reproduced in Ulrich and Ziemann (eds), *Krieg im Frieden*, pp. 141–2.

2 Ibid., p. 142.

3 Verhey, *The Spirit of 1914*, p. 216.

4 See Nonn, 'Oh what a lovely war?', *passim*; and Ziemann, *War Experiences, passim*.

5 Berger, *Germany*, p. 140; Schivelbusch, *The Culture of Defeat*, p. 206.

6 Harsch, *German Social Democracy*, p. 14.

7 For the broader perspective see Peter Gay's excellent new study *Modernism: The Lure of Heresy. From Baudelaire to Beckett and Beyond* (London, 2007).

8 See also Peukert, *The Weimar Republic*, pp. 14–18 and 147–63.

9 Kershaw, *Hitler, 1889–1936*, p. 259.

10 Volker Ullrich, 'Die Noske-Pabst-Connection', *Die Zeit*, 15 January 2009, p. 51.

11 Winkler, *Weimar*, p. 595.

12 Berger, *Social Democracy*, p. 102.

13 Winkler, 'Choosing the Lesser Evil', p. 223.

14 Horne and Kramer, *German Atrocities*, p. 338. For Ebert's speech see James, *A German Identity*, p. 116.

15 Berger, *Germany*, p. 128.

16 Schivelbusch, *The Culture of Defeat*, p. 203.

17 Friedrich Stampfer, *Erfahrungen und Erkenntnisse: Aufzeichnungen aus meinem Leben* (Cologne, 1957), pp. 165–71.

18 Friedrich Meinecke, *The German Catastrophe. Reflections and Recollections* (Boston, MA, 1950), p. 25.

19 Peukert, *The Weimar Republic*, p. 23.

20 Fritz Einert, 'Gedanken eines Reichsbannermannes auf Grund von Erlebnissen und Erfahrungen', unpublished memoirs, 1926. Reproduced in Ulrich and Ziemann (eds), *Krieg im Frieden*, pp. 94–5.

21 Schivelbusch, *The Culture of Defeat*, p. 191.

22 Richard Bessel, 'Catastrophe and Democracy: The Legacy of the World Wars in Germany', in Anthony McElligott and Tim Kirk (eds), *Working Towards the Führer* (Manchester, 2003), pp. 15–40 (here p. 19).

23 Einert, 'Gedanken eines Reichsbannermannes' (as note 20 above). Reproduced in Ulrich and Ziemann (eds), *Krieg im Frieden*, pp. 117–18.

24 Schivelbusch, *The Culture of Defeat*, p. 207.

25 Ibid., p. 204; Art, *The Politics of the Nazi Past*, p. 17.

26 Verhey, *The Spirit of 1914*, pp. 208–9.

27 Ullrich, 'Mehr als Schall und Rauch', pp. 196–7.

28 Harsch, *German Social Democracy*, p. 14.

29 Mosse, 'The Brutalization of German Politics', *passim*.

30 Verhey, *The Spirit of 1914*, p. 210.

31 On cultural demobilisation see also John Horne, 'Introduction: Démobilisations culturelles après la grande guerre', and 'Locarno et la politique de démobilisation culturelle, 1925–1930' both in *14/18 aujourd'hui today heute* 5 (2002), pp. 45–53 and 72–87 respectively.

32 Pöppinghege, ' "Kriegsteilnehmer zweiter Klasse?" ', p. 392.

33 Sneeringer, *Winning Women's Votes*, *passim*.

34 Falter, *Hitlers Wähler*, p. 136.

35 Thönnessen, *The Emancipation of Women*, esp. pp. 107–39.

36 Mommsen, 'Social Democracy on the Defensive', pp. 43–4.

37 Verhey, *The Spirit of 1914*, pp. 207–8.

38 Mosse, 'The Brutalization of German Politics', p. 172.

39 Breitscheid's speech before the Reichstag, 1 April 1930. Reproduced in Longerich (ed.), *Die Erste Republik*, pp. 423–5 (here p. 423).

40 Berger, *Social Democracy*, p. 102.

41 Mommsen, *The Rise and Fall of Weimar Democracy*, p. 220; idem., 'Social Democracy on the Defensive', pp. 39–40; Mosse, 'The Brutalization of German Politics', p. 161.

42 Kruse, *Krieg und nationale Integration*, *passim*.

43 Kershaw, *Hitler, 1889–1936*, p. 324.

Glossary

ADGB   *Allgemeiner Deutscher Gewerkschaftsbund* (General Association of German Trade Unions). Umbrella organisation representing the Free Trade Unions in Weimar Germany. Allied to the SPD and the Reichsbanner

Article 48   Article 48 of the Weimar constitution of August 1919 granted the Reich President the right to suspend the constitution, dissolve or set aside state governments or the Reichstag, and rule by emergency decree in situations where public order and security were seriously 'endangered', a mechanism used on several occasions by Presidents Ebert (1919–25) and Hindenburg (1925–34)

BDF   *Bund Deutscher Frauenvereine* (League of German Women's Associations). Umbrella organisation representing the mainstream bourgeois feminist movement in Germany. Founded in 1894, closely linked with the DDP in the Weimar period, dissolved by the Nazis in 1933

BNV   *Bund Neues Vaterland* (New Fatherland League). Pacifist organisation, founded in October 1914, banned in February 1916

BVP   *Bayerische Volkspartei* (Bavarian People's Party), founded in November 1918. Largest party in Bavaria in the 1920s and early 1930s, with authoritarian Catholic leanings. Although loosely allied to the Catholic Centre Party in the rest of Germany, it was in practice somewhat to the right of it

Burgfriede(n)   Wartime civil truce between the political parties in the Reichstag, proclaimed in August 1914

Central Powers   Germany and Austria-Hungary, later joined by Turkey and Bulgaria, were known as the Central Powers during the First World War

Centre Party   The *Zentrum* or Catholic Centre Party, was founded in 1875 to represent the Catholic interest in Germany. It was strong in the Rhineland, Westphalia and Baden, but had little support in Protestant areas

Comintern   The Comintern, or Communist International, was established in Moscow in March 1919 as a body which claimed to organise and represent all pro-communist parties throughout the world. It was committed to achieving revolution in Germany and elsewhere through violent means, and included the KPD as one of its key members

DDP   *Deutsche Demokratische Partei* (German Democratic Party). Founded in November 1918 as successor to the old left-liberal parties, with a firm commitment to parliamentary democracy and a republican constitution. Turned to the right after 1930 and renamed itself the *Deutsche Staatspartei* (German State Party)

DHV   *Deutschnationaler Handlungsgehilfenverband* (German-National Commercial Employees' Union). Right-wing white-collar workers association, founded in 1893. During the 1920s it displayed strong anti-socialist and anti-feminist tendencies; many of its members supported the NSDAP after 1930

DNVP   *Deutschnationale Volkspartei* (German National People's Party) – right-wing nationalist, anti-republican party, founded as successor to the old German Conservative Party in December 1918 and led from 1928 by Alfred Hugenberg who helped Hitler into power in 1933

DVFP   *Deutschvölkische Freiheitspartei* (German Völkisch Freedom Party). Founded in north Germany in late 1922 as an extreme right-wing, anti-Semitic breakaway from the DNVP. Many members left to join the Nazis in 1927

DVP   *Deutsche Volkspartei* (German People's Party) – centre-right pro-business party, founded in December 1918 as successor to the old National Liberal Party and initially opposed to the Weimar constitution. Led by Gustav Stresemann, a late convert to democratic politics, until his death in October 1929

DVSTB   *Deutschvölkischer Schutz- und Trutzbund* (German Völkisch Defence and Defiance League). Extreme right-wing group

with racist and anti-Semitic leanings. Established in
September 1918 in Hamburg, banned in most parts of
Germany in July 1922

Hindenburg Peace   Slogan adopted by opponents of the Reichstag Peace
Resolution in 1917 to signify the idea of a peace imposed
on the enemy through victory on the battlefield
(as opposed to a negotiated peace)

KPD   *Kommunistische Partei Deutschlands* (German Communist
Party), founded 30 December 1918, led by the Stalinist
Ernst Thälmann from 1925, opposed to the Weimar
Republic and in favour of a Soviet-style proletarian
dictatorship in Germany

Landtag   Name for a provincial or state parliament. During the
Weimar Republic all eighteen German states (*Länder*) had
their own democratically-elected parliaments or *Landtage*.
The largest of these was the Prussian Landtag, the
parliament for the state of Prussia

MSPD   *Mehrheitssozialdemokratische Partei Deutschlands* (Majority
Social Democratic Party). Official name for the SPD
between 1917 and 1920, when it was used to distinguish
the majority party from the anti-war Independents or
USPD (see below)

NSDAP   *Nationalsozialistische Deutsche Arbeiterpartei* (National
Socialist German Workers' Party – the Nazi Party), founded
in Munich in 1919. Led by Adolf Hitler from 1921

OHL   *Oberste Heeresleitung* (German Supreme Command during
the First World War). In August 1916 Hindenburg and
Ludendorff were appointed to head the third OHL,
following on from Helmuth von Moltke (1914) and Erich
von Falkenhayn (1914–16)

Reichsbanner   A pro-republican militia, founded in 1924 and closely
linked to the SPD

Reich Chancellor   The title given to the head of the government of the
German Reich from 1871 onwards. Until 1918 the Reich
Chancellor was chosen by the Kaiser and was not
responsible to the Reichstag; under the Weimar
constitution the Reich Chancellor could be recalled by a
vote of no confidence in the Reichstag, but was still

	appointed by the President and could be kept in office without a parliamentary majority under Article 48 (see above)
Reichstag	German Parliament, elected by universal manhood suffrage from 1871 to 1918, and by universal suffrage after 1918
Reichstag Peace Resolution	Resolution passed by a majority in the Reichstag on 19 July 1917 calling on the government to open talks with the enemy with a view to obtaining a negotiated end to the war
Reichswehr	The official name for the German armed forces during the Weimar Republic; renamed the Wehrmacht by Hitler in 1935
RFB	*Roter Frontkämpferbund* (Red Front Fighters' League), founded in 1924 as the paramilitary wing of the KPD – often known simply as the Red Front
RJB	*Reichsbund jüdischer Frontsoldaten* (Reich Federation of Jewish War Veterans), founded in 1919, dissolved by the Nazis in 1938
RLB	*Reichslandbund* (Reich Land League); founded in 1921 as a farming and protectionist lobby and as the successor to the old Agrarian League. Allied in political terms to the anti-republican DNVP
SA	*Sturm-Abteilungen* (Stormtroopers or Brown shirts), paramilitary wing of the NSDAP, founded in 1921
SAPD	*Sozialistische Arbeiterpartei Deutschlands* (Socialist Workers' Party), founded in late 1931 by young left-wing radicals inside the SPD dissatisfied with the party leadership's somewhat passive stance towards the rise of fascism
Schlieffen Plan	German General Staff's overall strategic plan for winning a war on two fronts, against Russia in the east and France in the west. Named after its original author, the chief of the general staff Count Alfred von Schlieffen (1891–1906), it envisaged devoting the first six weeks of the war to delivering a knock-out blow against France through a deliberate violation of neutral Belgian territory. Schlieffen's successor, Helmuth von Moltke the younger (1906–14) made a number of modifications to the original plan

	which, in the view of at least some military historians, weakened it to the point of failure in September 1914.
SPD	*Sozialdemokratische Partei Deutschlands* (German Social Democratic Party), the main centre-left party in Germany, founded in 1875
Stahlhelm, Bund der Frontsoldaten	Right-wing, semi-monarchist paramilitary organisation, founded in December 1918. Loosely linked to the DNVP and briefly allied with Nazis in 1931, but banned by Hitler after 1933
STIs	Sexually transmitted infections
USPD	*Unabhängige Sozialdemokratische Partei Deutschlands* (Independent German Social Democratic Party), founded in 1917 as a breakaway anti-war faction from the SPD, played a major role in the November 1918 revolution and in the councils' movement of 1918/19, wound up in 1920/22, with members going into the KPD or back to the SPD
ZAG	*Zentralarbeitsgemeinschaft* (Central Working Association). A consultative body established after the revolution in November 1918 to bring employers and trade unions together to agree on basic issues such as wages and conditions
Zentrum	See Centre Party above

The Political Spectrum in Weimar Germany

Left				Centre			Right
KPD	USPD	SPD	DDP	Zentrum/ Catholic Centre Party	DVP	DNVP	NSDAP

Bibliography

Collections of Documents

Afflerbach, Holger (ed.), *Kaiser Wilhelm II. als Oberster Kriegsherr im Ersten Weltkrieg. Quellen aus der militärischen Umgebung des Kaisers 1914–1918* (Munich, 2005)

Hohorst, Gerd, Kocka, Jürgen and Ritter, Gerhard A. (eds), *Sozialgeschichtliches Arbeitsbuch: Materialien zur Statistik des Kaiserreiches, 1871–1914* (Munich, 1975)

Kaes, Anton, Jay, Martin and Dimendberg, Edward (eds), *The Weimar Republic Sourcebook* (London, 1994)

Lane, Barbara Miller and Rupp, Leila J. (eds), *Nazi Ideology Before 1933. A Documentation* (London, 1978)

Longerich, Peter (ed.), *Die Erste Republik. Dokumente zur Geschichte des Weimarer Staates* (Munich, 1992)

Materna, Ingo and Schreckenbach, Hans-Joachim (eds), *Dokumente aus geheimen Archiven, vol. 4: Berichte des Berliner Polizeipräsidenten zur Stimmung und Lage der Bevölkerung in Berlin, 1914–1918* (Weimar, 1987)

Noakes, Jeremy and Pridham, Geoffrey (eds), *Nazism, 1919–1945. A Documentary Reader. vol. 1: The Rise to Power, 1919–1934* (Exeter, 1983)

Sauder, Gerhard (ed.), *Die Bücherverbrennung: Zum 10. Mai 1933* (Munich, 1983)

SED-Institut für Marxismus-Leninismus (ed.), *Dokumente und Materialien zur Geschichte der deutschen Arbeiterbewegung, vol. 1: Juli 1914 – Oktober 1917* (East Berlin, 1958)

Ulrich, Bernd and Ziemann, Benjamin (eds), *Frontalltag im Ersten Weltkrieg. Wahn und Wirklichkeit* (Frankfurt/M, 1994)

—— *Krieg im Frieden. Die umkämpfte Erinnerung an den Ersten Weltkrieg* (Frankfurt/M, 1997)

Witkop, Philipp (ed.), *German Students' War Letters*, translated by A. F. Wedd, with a foreword by Jay Winter (Philadelphia, 2002) [1916/1929]

Diaries, Memoirs and Journalistic Writings

Blücher, Princess Evelyn, *An English Wife in Berlin* (London, 1920)

Brüning, Heinrich, *Memoiren 1918–1934*, edited by Claire Nix and Theoderich Kampmann (Stuttgart, 1970)

David, Eduard, *Das Kriegstagebuch des Reichstagsabgeordneten Eduard David 1914 bis 1918*, edited by Erich Matthias and Susanne Miller (Düsseldorf, 1966)

Gay, Peter, *My German Question. Growing up in Nazi Berlin* (London, 1998)

Görlitz, Walter (ed.), *The Kaiser and His Court. The Diaries, Note Books and Letters of Admiral Georg Alexander von Müller, Chief of the Naval Cabinet, 1914–1918*, translated from the German by Mervyn Savill (London, 1961) [1959]

Howard, Elizabeth F. *Across Barriers* (London, 1941)

Kessler, Count Harry, *The Diaries of a Cosmopolitan, 1918–1937*, translated from the German and edited by Charles Kessler (London, 1971)

Meinecke, Friedrich, *The German Catastrophe. Reflections and Recollections*, translated from the German by Sidney B. Fay (Boston, MA, 1950) [1946]

Pogge von Strandmann, Hartmut (ed.), *Walther Rathenau. Industrialist, Banker, Intellectual and Politician. Notes and Diaries, 1907–1922*, translated from the German by Caroline Pinder-Cracraft (Oxford, 1985) [1967]

Roth, Joseph, *What I Saw. Reports from Berlin, 1920–33*, translated and introduced by Michael Hofmann (London, 2003)

Stampfer, Friedrich, *Erfahrungen und Erkenntnisse: Aufzeichnungen aus meinem Leben*, (Cologne, 1957)

Books, articles and essays

Abrams, Lynn, 'From Control to Commercialization: The Triumph of Mass Entertainment in Germany, 1900–1925?', *German History*, 8/3 (1990), pp. 278–93

Afflerbach, Holger, *Falkenhayn: Politisches Denken und Handeln im Kaiserreich* (Munich, 1994)

—— 'Wilhelm II as Supreme Warlord in the First World War', *War in History*, 5/4 (1998), pp. 427–49

Aguado, Iago Gil, 'The Creditanstalt Crisis of 1931 and the Failure of the Austro-German Customs Union Project', *Historical Journal*, 44/1 (2001), pp. 199–221

Allen, Ann Taylor, *Women in Twentieth-Century Europe* (London, 2008)

Allen, William Sheridan, *The Nazi Seizure of Power. The Experience of a Single German Town, 1930–1935* (Chicago, 1965)

Angress, Werner T., 'Das deutsche Militär und die Juden im Ersten Weltkrieg', *Militärgeschichtliche Mitteilungen*, 19/1 (1976), pp. 77–146

Appignanesi, Lisa, *Cabaret. The First Hundred Years* (London, 1975)

Art, David, *The Politics of the Nazi Past in Germany and Austria* (Cambridge, 2006)

Ashworth, Tony, *Trench Warfare, 1914–1918. The Live and Let Live System* (London, 1980)

Bailey, Stephen, 'The Berlin Strike of January 1918', *Central European History*, 13/2 (1980), pp. 158–74

Baker, Mark, 'The War and Revolution', in Martel (ed.), *A Companion to Europe*, pp. 243–58

Balderston, Theo, *Economy and Politics in the Weimar Republic* (Cambridge, 2002)

Baranowski, Shelly, *The Sanctity of Rural Life. Nobility, Protestantism and Nazism in Weimar Prussia* (New York, 1995)

Barclay, David E., and Weitz, Eric D. (eds), *Between Reform and Revolution. German Socialism and Communism from 1840 to 1990* (Oxford, 1998)

Barth, Boris, *Dolchstosslegenden und politische Desintegration: das Trauma der deutschen Niederlage im Ersten Weltkrieg, 1914–1933* (Düsseldorf, 2003)

Becker, Annette, *Oubliés de la grande guerre. Humanitaire et culture de guerre. Populations occupées, déportés civils, prisonniers de guerre* (Paris, 1998)

Beetham, David, *Marxists in Face of Fascism* (Manchester, 1983)

Berger, Stefan, *Social Democracy and the Working Class in Nineteenth- and Twentieth-Century Germany* (London, 2000)

—— *Inventing the Nation: Germany* (London, 2004)

Berghahn, Volker, *Der Stahlhelm. Bund der Frontsoldaten 1918–1935* (Düsseldorf, 1966)

Berliner Geschichtswerkstatt (ed.), *August 1914: Ein Volk zieht in den Krieg* (West Berlin, 1989)

Bessel, Richard, *Political Violence and the Rise of the Nazis: The Stormtroopers in Eastern Germany, 1925–34* (New Haven and London, 1984)

—— *Germany after the First World War* (Oxford, 1993)

—— 'Germany from War to Dictatorship', in M. Fulbrook (ed.), *Twentieth-Century Germany* (London, 2001), pp. 11–35

—— 'Demobilmachung', in Hirschfeld, Krumeich and Renz (eds), *Enzyklopädie Erster Weltkrieg* (Paderborn, 2003), pp. 427–30

—— 'Catastrophe and Democracy: The Legacy of the World Wars in Germany', in McElligott and Kirk (eds), *Working Towards the Führer*, pp. 15–40

Biddis, Michael Denis, *The Age of the Masses. Ideas and Society in Europe since 1870* (London, 1977)

Bieber, Hans-Joachim, 'The Socialist Trade Unions in War and Revolution', in R. Fletcher (ed.), *Bernstein to Brandt*, pp. 74–85

Blackbourn, David and **Eley, Geoff**, *The Peculiarities of German History. Society and Politics in Nineteenth Century Germany* (Oxford, 1984)

Blasius, Dirk, *Weimars Ende. Bürgerkrieg und Politik 1930–1933* (Göttingen, 2005)

Boak, Helen, 'The State as an Employer of Women in the Weimar Republic', in W. R. Lee and Eve Rosenhaft (eds), *State, Social Policy and Social Change in Germany, 1880–1994*, revised edition (Oxford, 1997), pp. 64–101

—— 'Mobilising Women for Hitler: The Female Nazi Voter', in Anthony McElligott and Tim Kirk (eds), *Working Towards the Führer*, pp. 68–92

Bookbinder, Paul, *Weimar Germany. The Republic of the Reasonable* (Manchester, 1996)

Bosetzky, Horst, *Die Bestie vom Schlesischen Bahnhof. Dokumentarischer Roman aus den 20er Jahren* (Berlin, 2004)

Bowlby, Chris, 'Blutmai 1929. Police, Parties and Proletarians in a Berlin Confrontation', *Historical Journal*, 29/1 (1986), pp. 137–58

Bracher, Karl Dietrich, *Die Auflösung der Weimarer Republik. Eine Studie zum Problem des Machtverfalls in der Demokratie*, 5th edition (Villingen, 1971) [1955]

—— 'Brünings unpolitische Politik und die Auflösung der Weimarer Republik', *Vierteljahrshefte für Zeitgeschichte*, 19/2 (1971), pp. 113–23

Braunthal, Julius, *History of the International, vol. 2: 1914–1943*, translated from the German by J. Clark (London, 1967)

Bremme, Gabriele, *Die politische Rolle der Frau in Deutschland. Eine Untersuchung über den Einfluß der Frauen bei Wahlen und ihre Teilnahme in Partei und Parlament* (Göttingen, 1956)

Bridenthal, Renate, ' "Professional" Housewives. Stepsisters of the Women's Movement', in Renate Bridenthal, Atina Grossmann and Marion Kaplan (eds), *When Biology Became Destiny. Women in Weimar and Nazi Germany* (New York, 1984), pp. 153–73

—— 'Organized Rural Women and the Conservative Mobilization of the German Countryside in the Weimar Republic', in Jones and Retallack (eds), *Between Reform, Reaction and Resistance*, pp. 375–405

Bridenthal, Renate and **Koonz, Claudia**, 'Beyond *Kinder, Kirche, Kuche*: Weimar Women in Politics and Work', in Bridenthal *et al.* (eds), *When Biology Became Destiny*, pp. 33–65

Bullivant, Keith, 'The Conservative Revolution', in Anthony Phelan (ed.), *The Weimar Dilemma. Intellectuals in the Weimar Republic* (Manchester, 1985), pp. 47–70

Burke, Peter, *What is Cultural History?* (Cambridge, 2004)

Carr, E. H., *What is History?* (London, 1961)

Carsten, Francis L., *The Reichswehr and Politics, 1918–1933* (London, 1968)

—— *Revolution in Central Europe, 1918–1919* (London, 1972)

—— *A History of the Prussian Junkers* (London, 1989)

Chickering, Roger, *Imperial Germany and the Great War, 1914–1918*, 2nd edition (Cambridge, 2004) [2000]

—— *The Great War and Urban Life in Germany. Freiburg, 1914–1918* (Cambridge, 2007)

Childers, Thomas, *The Nazi Voter. The Social Foundations of Fascism in Germany, 1919–1933* (Chapel Hill, NC and London, 1983)

—— (ed.), *The Formation of the Nazi Constituency, 1919–1933* (London, 1986)

Clark, Christopher, *Kaiser Wilhelm II. Profiles in Power* (London, 2000)

—— *Iron Kingdom. The Rise and Downfall of Prussia, 1600–1987* (London, 2006)

Clavin, Patricia, *The Great Depression in Europe, 1929–1939* (London, 2000)

Craig, Gordon A., *The Politics of the Prussian Army, 1640–1945* (Oxford, 1955)

Crew, David F., 'The Ambiguities of Modernity: Welfare and the German State from Wilhelm to Hitler', in Eley (ed.), *Society, Culture and the State*, pp. 319–44

—— *Germans on Welfare. From Weimar to Hitler* (Oxford, 1998)

—— 'A Social Republic? Social Democrats, Communists and the Weimar Welfare State, 1919 to 1933', in Barclay and Weitz (eds), *Between Reform and Revolution*, pp. 223–49

Daniel, Ute, *The War From Within. German Working-Class Women in the First World War*, translated from the German by Margaret Ries (Oxford, 1997) [1989]

—— idem., 'Frauen', in Hirschfeld, Krumeich and Renz (eds), *Enzyklopädie Erster Weltkrieg*, pp. 116–34

Davies, Peter, 'Transforming Utopia: The "League for the Protection of Mothers and Sexual Reform" in the First World War', in Fell and Sharp (eds), *The Women's Movement in Wartime*, pp. 211–26

Davis, Belinda J., 'Reconsidering Habermas, Gender and the Public Sphere: The Case of Wilhelmine Germany', in G. Eley (ed.), *Society, Culture and the State in Germany*, pp. 397–426

—— *Home Fires Burning. Food, Politics and Everyday Life in World War I Berlin* (Chapel Hill, NC and London, 2000)

—— 'Food, Politics and Women's Everyday Life during the First World War', in Hagemann and Schüler-Springorum (eds), *Home/Front*, pp. 115–37

—— 'Experience, Identity and Memory. The Legacy of World War I', *Journal of Modern History*, 75/1 (2003), pp. 111–31

Deist, Wilhelm, 'Censorship and Propaganda in Germany During the First World War', in Jean-Jacques Becker and Stéphane Audoin-Rouzeau (eds), *Les sociétés européenes et la guerre de 1914–1918* (Paris, 1990), pp. 199–210

—— 'Kaiser Wilhelm II. als Oberster Kriegsherr', in J. C. G. Röhl (ed.), *Der Ort Kaiser Wilhelms II.*, pp. 25–42

Domansky, Elizabeth, 'Militarization and Reproduction in World War I Germany', in Eley (ed.), *Society, Culture and State*, pp. 427–63

Dorpalen, Andreas, *German History in Marxist Perspective. The East German Approach* (London, 1985)

Eksteins, Modris, *The Limits of Reason. The German Democratic Press and the Collapse of Weimar Democracy* (Oxford, 1975)

—— 'War, Memory and Politics: The Fate of the Film *All Quiet on the Western Front*', *Central European History*, 13/1 (1980), pp. 60–82

—— *Rites of Spring. The Great War and the Birth of the Modern Age* (London, 1989)

Eley, Geoff, 'The SPD in War and Revolution, 1914–1919', in Fletcher (ed.), *Bernstein to Brandt*, pp. 65–74

—— 'Conservatives and Radical Nationalists in Germany: The Production of Fascist Potentials, 1912–1928', in Martin Blinkhorn (ed.), *Fascists and Conservatives: The Radical Right and the Establishment in Twentieth-Century Europe* (London, 1990), pp. 50–70

—— (ed.), *Society, Culture and State in Germany, 1870–1930* (Ann Arbor, MI, 1996)

—— 'Cultural Socialism, the Public Sphere and the Mass Form: Popular Culture and the Democratic Project, 1900 to 1934', in Barclay and Weitz (eds), *Between Reform and Revolution*, pp. 315–40

Erger, Johannes, *Der Kapp-Lüttwitz Putsch. Ein Beitrag zur deutschen Innenpolitik 1919/20* (Düsseldorf, 1967)

Evans, Richard J., *Rituals of Retribution. Capital Punishment in Germany, 1600–1987* (London, 1996)

—— *The Coming of the Third Reich* (London, 2003)

Evans, Richard J. and **Geary, Dick** (eds), *The German Unemployed. Experiences and Consequences of Mass Unemployment from the Weimar Republic to the Third Reich* (London, 1987)

Falter, Jürgen, 'The National Socialist Mobilisation of New Voters, 1928–1933', in Childers (ed.), *The Formation of the Nazi Constituency*, pp. 202–31

—— *Hitlers Wähler* (Munich, 1991)

—— 'The Social Bases of Political Cleavages in the Weimar Republic, 1919–1933', in Jones and Retallack (eds), *Elections, Mass Politics and Social Change*, pp. 371–97

Farquharson, J. E., *The Plough and the Swastika. The NSDAP and Agriculture in Germany, 1928–45* (London, 1976)

Feldman, Gerald, *Army, Industry and Labor in Germany, 1914–1918* (Princeton, NJ, 1966)

—— 'The Origins of the Stinnes-Legien Agreement: A Documentation', *Internationale wissenschaftliche Korrespondenz zur Geschichte der deutschen Arbeiterbewegung*, 19/20 (1972), pp. 45–102

—— *Iron and Steel in the German Inflation, 1916–1923* (Princeton, NJ, 1977)

—— *The Great Disorder. Politics, Economics and Society in the German Inflation, 1914–1924* (Oxford, 1993)

—— *Hugo Stinnes: Biographie eines Industriellen 1870–1924* (Munich, 1998)

Fell, Alison F. and **Sharp, Ingrid** (eds), *The Women's Movement in Wartime. International Perspectives* (Basingstoke, 1997)

Ferguson, Niall, *The Pity of War* (London, 1998)

—— 'Max Warburg and German Politics. The Limits of Financial Power in Wilhelmine Germany', in Geoff Eley and James Retallack (eds), *Wilhelminism and Its Legacies. German Modernities, Imperialism and the Meanings of Reform, 1890–1933. Essays for Hartmut Pogge von Strandmann* (Oxford, 2003), pp. 185–201

—— 'Prisoner Taking and Prisoner Killing in the Age of Total War. Towards a Political Economy of Military Defeat', *War in History*, 11/2 (2004), pp. 148–92

Fischer, Conan, 'Class Enemies or Class Brothers? Communist-Nazi Relations in Germany, 1929–33', *European History Quarterly*, 15/3 (1985), pp. 259–79

—— 'The KPD and Nazism: A Reply to Dick Geary', *European History Quarterly*, 15/4 (1985), pp. 465–71

—— *The German Communists and the Rise of Nazism* (London, 1991)

—— *The Rise of the Nazis*, 2nd edition (Manchester, 2002) [1995]

—— *The Ruhr Crisis, 1923–1924* (Oxford, 2003)

—— 'A Very German Revolution? The Post-1918 Settlement Re-Evaluated', *Bulletin of the German Historical Institute London*, XXVIII/2 (2006), pp. 6–32

Fischer, Fritz, *Germany's Aims in the First World War*, translated from the German by W. W. Norton (London, 1967) [1961]

—— *War of Illusions. German Policies from 1911 to 1914*, translated from the German by Marian Jackson (London, 1975) [1969]

—— *From Kaiserreich to Third Reich. Elements of Continuity in German History, 1871–1945*, translated from the German by Roger Fletcher (London, 1986) [1979]

—— 'Theobald von Bethmann Hollweg', in Sternburg (ed.), *Die deutschen Kanzler*, pp. 87–114

Fletcher, Roger (ed.), *Bernstein to Brandt: A Short History of German Social Democracy* (London, 1987)

Föllmer, Moritz, 'Der "kranke Volkskörper": Industrielle, hohe Beamte und der Diskurs der nationalen Regeneration in der Weimarer Republik', *Geschichte und Gesellschaft*, 27 (2001), pp. 41–67

—— 'Was Nazism Collectivistic? Redefining the Individual in Berlin, 1930–1945', forthcoming in *Journal of Modern History*, 82 (2010)

Fowkes, Ben, *Communism in Germany under the Weimar Republic* (London, 1984)

Frank, Mario, *Walter Ulbricht. Eine deutsche Biografie* (Berlin, 2001)

Frevert, Ute, *Women in German History. From Bourgeois Emancipation to Sexual Liberation*, translated from the German by Stuart McKinnon-Evans in association with Terry Bond and Barbara Norden (Oxford, 1998) [1989]

Fritzsche, Peter, *Rehearsals for Fascism: Populism and Political Mobilization in Weimar Germany* (Oxford, 1990)

—— 'Breakdown or Breakthrough? Conservatives and the November Revolution', in Jones and Retallack (eds), *Between Reform, Reaction and Resistance*, pp. 299–328

—— 'Weimar Populism and National Socialism in Local Perspective', in Jones and Retallack (eds), *Elections, Mass Politics and Social Change*, pp. 287–306

—— 'Landscape of Danger, Landscape of Design: Crisis and Modernism in Weimar Germany', in Thomas W. Kniesche and Stephen Brockmann (eds), *Dancing on the Volcano. Essays on the Culture of the Weimar Republic* (London, 1994), pp. 29–46

—— 'Did Weimar Fail?', *Journal of Modern History*, 68/3 (1996), pp. 629–56

—— *Germans into Nazis* (Cambridge, MA, 1999)

—— *Life and Death in the Third Reich* (Cambridge, MA, 2008)

Fromm, Erich, *The Fear of Freedom*, new edition (London, 1991) [1942]

Führer, Karl Christian, 'Auf dem Weg zur Massenkultur? Kino und Rundfunk in der Weimarer Republik', *Historische Zeitschrift*, 262 (1996), pp. 739–81

Führer, Karl Christian and **Ross, Corey** (eds), *Mass Media, Culture and Society in Twentieth-century Germany* (Basingstoke, 2006)

Fulbrook, Mary (ed.), *Twentieth-Century Germany. Politics, Culture and Society, 1918–1990* (London, 2001)

Fussell, Paul, *The Great War and Modern Memory* (London, 1975)

Gay, Peter, *Weimar Culture. The Outsider as Insider*, Penguin edition (London, 1974) [1968]

—— *Modernism: The Lure of Heresy. From Baudelaire to Beckett and Beyond* (London, 2007)

Geary, Dick, 'Nazis and Workers', *European History Quarterly*, 15/4 (1985), pp. 453–64

—— 'Unemployment and Working-Class Solidarity: The German Experience 1929–33', in Evans and Geary (eds), *The German Unemployed*, pp. 261–80

—— 'Employers, Workers and the Collapse of Weimar', in Kershaw (ed.), *Weimar: Why did German Democracy Fail?*, pp. 92–119

—— 'Arbeiter', in Hirschfeld, Krumeich and Renz (eds), *Enzyklopädie Erster Weltkrieg*, pp. 142–54

Geiger, Theodor, 'Panik im Mittelstand', *Die Arbeit* 7 (October 1931), pp. 638–53

—— *Die soziale Schichtung des deutschen Volkes. Soziographischer Versuch auf statistischer Grundlage* (Stuttgart, 1932)

Geyer, Martin H., *Verkehrte Welt. Revolution, Inflation und Moderne. München, 1914–1924* (Göttingen, 1998)

Gilbert, Martin, *The First World War* (London, 2004)

Gluckstein, Donny, *The Nazis, Capitalism and the Working Class* (London, 1999)

Goenner, Hubert, *Einstein in Berlin 1914–1933* (Munich, 2005)

Grossmann, Atina, 'Abortion and Economic Crisis: The 1931 Campaign Against Paragraph 218', in Bridenthal *et al.* (eds), *When Biology Became Destiny*, pp. 66–86

—— *Reforming Sex: The German Movement for Birth Control and Abortion Reform, 1920–1950* (Oxford, 1995)

Grotefeld, Stefan, *Friedrich Siegmund-Schultze. Ein deutscher Ökumeniker und christlicher Pazifist* (Gütersloh, 1995)

Grunberger, Richard, *Red Rising in Bavaria* (London, 1973)

Gunn, Simon, *History and Cultural Theory* (Harlow, 2006)

Gutsche, Willibald, *Aufstieg und Fall eines kaiserlichen Reichskanzlers. Theobald von Bethmann Hollweg 1856–1921. Ein politisches Lebensbild* (East Berlin, 1973)

—— 'Monarchistische Restaurationsstrategie und Faschismus. Zur Rolle Wilhelms II. im Kampf der nationalistischen und revanchistischen Kräfte um die Beseitigung der Weimarer Republik', in Röhl (ed.), *Der Ort Kaiser Wilhelms II.*, pp. 287–96

—— *Ein Kaiser im Exil. Der letzte deutsche Kaiser Wilhelm II. in Holland* (Berlin, 1991)

Hackett, Amy, 'Helene Stöcker: Left-Wing Intellectual and Sex Reformer' in Bridenthal *et al.* (eds), *When Biology Became Destiny*, pp. 109–30

Haffner, Sebastian, *Die verratene Revolution. Deutschland 1918/19* (Bern, 1969)

Hagemann, Karen and **Schüler-Springorum, Stefanie** (eds), *Home/Front. The Military, War and Gender in Twentieth-Century Germany* (Oxford, 2002)

—— 'The Military, Violence and Gender Relations in the Age of the World Wars', in ibid., pp. 1–41

Hagenlücke, Heinz, *Deutsche Vaterlandspartei: Die nationale Rechte am Ende des Kaiserreichs* (Düsseldorf, 1997)

Hamilton, Nigel, *The Brothers Mann. The Lives of Heinrich and Thomas Mann, 1871–1950 and 1875–1955* (London, 1978)

Hamilton, Richard F., *Who Voted for Hitler?* (Princeton, NJ, 1982)

Hardtwig, Wolfgang (ed.), *Politische Kulturgeschichte der Zwischenkriegszeit 1918–1939* (Göttingen, 2005)

Harsch, Donna, *German Social Democracy and the Rise of Nazism* (Chapel Hill, NC and London, 1993)

—— 'The Iron Front: Weimar Social Democracy between Tradition and Modernity', in Barclay and Weitz (eds), *Between Reform and Revolution*, pp. 251–74

Harvey, Elizabeth, 'Private Fantasy and Public Intervention. Girls' Reading in Weimar Germany', in Jennifer Birkett and Elizabeth Harvey (eds), *Determined Women. Studies in the Construction of the Female Subject* (London, 1991), pp. 38–67

—— *Youth and the Welfare State in Weimar Germany* (Oxford, 1993)

—— 'The Failure of Feminism? Young Women and the Bourgeois Feminist Movement in Weimar Germany, 1918–1933', *Central European History*, 28/1 (1995), pp. 1–28

—— 'Culture and Society in Weimar Germany: The Impact of Modernism and Mass Culture', in Fulbrook (ed.), *Twentieth-Century Germany*, pp. 58–76

—— 'Pilgrimages to the "Bleeding Border". Gender and Rituals of Nationalist Protest in Germany, 1919–1939', *Women's History Review*, 9/2 (2000), pp. 201–28

—— 'National Icons and Visions of Modernity. Asserting and Debating Gender Identities in New National Contexts', in Johanna Gehmacher, Elizabeth Harvey and Sophia Kemlein (eds), *Zwischen Kriegen. Nationen, Nationalismen und Geschlechterverhältnisse in Mittel- und Osteuropa, 1918–1939* (Osnabrück, 2004), pp. 305–15

Hausen, Karin, 'Mothers Day in the Weimar Republic', in Bridenthal *et al.* (eds), *When Biology Became Destiny*, pp. 131–52

—— 'The German Nation's Obligations to the Heroes' Widows of World War I', in Margaret Randolph Higonnet, Jane Jenson, Sonya Michel and Margaret Collins Weitz (eds), *Behind the Lines. Gender and the Two World Wars* (New Haven and London, 1987), pp. 126–40

Heid, Ludger, *Oskar Cohn: Ein Sozialist und Zionist im Kaiserreich und in der Weimarer Republik* (Frankfurt/M, 2002)

Heinsohn, Kirsten, 'Im Dienste der deutschen Volksgemeinschaft: Die "Frauenfrage" und konservative Parteien vor und nach dem Ersten Weltkrieg', in Planert (ed.), *Nation, Politik und Geschlecht*, pp. 215–33

Herbert, Ulrich, *A History of Foreign Labor in Germany, 1880–1980. Seasonal Workers/Forced Laborers/Guest Workers*, translated from the German by William Templer (Ann Arbor, MI, 1990) [1985]

—— 'Generation der Sachlichkeit. Die völkische Studentenbewegung der frühen zwanziger Jahre' (1991), reproduced in U. Herbert, *Arbeit, Volkstum, Weltanschauung. Über Fremde und Deutsche im 20. Jahrhundert* (Frankfurt/M, 1995), pp. 31–58

Herf, Jeffrey, *Reactionary Modernism. Technology, Culture and Politics in Weimar and the Third Reich* (Cambridge, 1984)

Hermand, Jost and **Trommler, Frank**, *Die Kultur der Weimarer Republik* (Munich, 1978)

Herrmann, Ursula, 'Sozialdemokratische Frauen in Deutschland im Kampf um den Frieden vor und während des Ersten Weltkriegs', *Zeitschrift für Geschichtswissenschaft*, 33/3 (1985), pp. 213–30

Hertzman, Lewis, *DNVP. Right-Wing Opposition in the Weimar Republic, 1918–1924* (Lincoln, NE, 1963)

Hinz, Uta, 'Die deutschen "Barbaren" sind doch die besseren Menschen. Kriegsgefangenschaft und gefangene "Feinde" in der Darstellung der deutschen Publistik, 1914–1918', in Rüdiger Overmans (ed.), *In der Hand des Feindes. Kriegsgefangenschaft von der Antike bis zum Zweiten Weltkrieg* (Cologne, 1999), pp. 339–61

—— *Gefangen im Großen Krieg. Kriegsgefangenschaft in Deutschland 1914–1921* (Essen, 2006)

Hirschfeld, Gerhard, Krumeich, Gerd and **Renz, Irina** (eds), *Enzyklopädie Erster Weltkrieg* (Paderborn, 2003)

Hirschfeld, Magnus, (ed.), *Sittengeschichte des Weltkrieges*, 2 Vols. (Leipzig and Vienna, 1930)

—— *Sittengeschichte der Nachkriegszeit*, 2 Vols. (Leipzig and Vienna, 1932)

Holtfrerich, Carl-Ludwig, *The German Inflation 1914–1923. Causes and Effects in International Perspective* (West Berlin and New York, 1986)

Hong, Young-Sun, 'World War I and the German Welfare State. Gender, Religion and the Paradoxes of Modernity', in Eley (ed.), *Society, Culture and the State*, pp. 345–69

Horne, John (ed.), *State, Society and Mobilization During the First World War* (Cambridge, 1997)

—— 'Introduction: Mobilizing for "Total War", 1914–1918', in ibid., pp. 1–17

—— 'Introduction: Démobilisations culturelles après la grande guerre', *14/18 aujourd'hui today heute* 5 (2002), pp. 45–53

—— 'Locarno et la politique de démobilisation culturelle, 1925–1930', *14/18 aujourd'hui today heute* 5 (2002) pp. 72–87

—— 'Masculinity in Politics and War in the Age of Nation-States and World Wars, 1850–1950', in Stefan Dudink, Karen Hagemann and John Tosh (eds), *Masculinities in Politics and War. Gendering Modern History* (Manchester, 2004), pp. 22–40

—— 'Kulturelle Demobilmachung 1919–1933. Ein sinnvoller historischer Begriff?', in Hardtwig (ed.), *Politische Kulturgeschichte der Zwischenkriegszeit*, pp. 129–50

Horne, John and **Kramer, Alan**, 'War Between Soldiers and Enemy Civilians, 1914–1915', in Roger Chickering and Stig Förster (eds), *Great War, Total War. Combat and Mobilization on the Western Front, 1914–1918* (Cambridge, 2000), pp. 153–68

—— *German Atrocities, 1914. A History of Denial* (New Haven and London, 2001)

Hull, Isabel V., "Persönliches Regiment"', in Röhl (ed.), *Der Ort Kaiser Wilhelms II.*, pp. 3–23

—— 'Military Culture, Wilhelm II, and the End of the Monarchy in the First World War', in Mombauer and Deist (eds), *The Kaiser*, pp. 235–58

Iggers, Georg, *The Social History of Politics. Critical Perspectives in West German Historical Writing since 1945* (Leamington Spa, 1985)

Jaeger, Hans, *Unternehmer in der deutschen Politik (1890–1918)* (Bonn, 1967)

Jahr, Christoph, 'Policing Anti-Semitic Crime in Weimar Germany', in Gerard Oram (ed.), *Conflict and Legality. Policing Mid-twentieth Century Europe* (London, 2003), pp. 64–77

James, Harold, *The German Slump. Politics and Economics, 1924–1936* (Oxford, 1986)

—— *A German Identity, 1770–1990*, revised edition (London, 1990) [1989]

Jarausch, Konrad, *The Enigmatic Chancellor. Bethmann Hollweg and the Hubris of Imperial Germany* (New Haven and London, 1973)

Jefferies, Matthew, *Contesting the German Empire, 1871–1918* (Oxford, 2008)

Jentsch, Harald, *Die KPD und der 'Deutsche Oktober' 1923* (Rostock, 2005)

Jochmann, Werner, 'Die Ausbreitung des Antisemitismus in Deutschland 1914–1923', in Jochmann, *Gesellschaftskrise und Judenfeindschaft in Deutschland 1870–1945* (Hamburg, 1988), pp. 99–170

John, Jürgen, 'Das Bild der Novemberrevolution 1918 in Geschichtspolitik und Geschichtswissenschaft der DDR', in Winkler (ed.), *Weimar im Widerstreit*, pp. 43–84

Joll, James, *The Origins of the First World War*, 2nd edition (London, 1992)

Jones, Elizabeth Bright, 'A New Stage of Life? Young Farm Women's Changing Expectations and Aspirations about Work in Weimar Saxony', *German History*, 19/4 (2001), pp. 549–70

—— *Gender and Rural Modernity. Farm Women and the Politics of Labor in Germany 1871–1933* (Farnham, 2009)

Jones, Heather, 'The Enemy Disarmed. Prisoners of War and the Violence of Wartime. Britain, France and Germany, 1914–1920', Ph.D. dissertation, Trinity College, Dublin, 2005

—— 'Encountering the "Enemy": Prisoner of War Transport and the Development of War Cultures in 1914', in P. Purseigle (ed.), *Warfare and Belligerence*, pp. 133–62

—— 'A Missing Paradigm? Military Captivity and the Prisoner of War, 1914–18', *Immigrants and Minorities*, 28/1–2 (2008), pp. 19–48

Jones, Larry Eugene, 'The "Dying Middle": Weimar Germany and the Fragmentation of Bourgeois Politics', *Central European History*, 5/1 (1972), pp. 23–54

—— '"Between the Fronts": The German National Union of Commercial Employees from 1928 to 1933', *Journal of Modern History*, 48/3 (1976), pp. 462–82

—— 'Catholic Conservatives in the Weimar Republic: The Politics of the Rhenish-Westphalian Aristocracy, 1918–1933', *German History*, 18/1 (2000), pp. 60–85

Jones, Larry Eugene and **Retallack, James** (eds), *Elections, Mass Politics and Social Change in Modern Germany. New Perspectives* (Cambridge, 1992)

—— *Between Reform, Reaction and Resistance. Studies in the History of German Conservatism from 1789 to 1945* (Providence, RI, 1993)

Kater, Michael H., *The Nazi Party. A Social Profile of Members and Leaders, 1919–1945* (Oxford, 1983)

Kellogg, Michael, *The Russian Roots of Nazism. White Emigrés and the Making of National Socialism, 1917–1945* (Cambridge, 2005)

Kerbs, Diethart and **Stahr, Henrick** (eds), *Berlin 1932. Das letzte Jahr der Weimarer Republik* (Berlin, 1992)

Kershaw, Ian, *Popular Opinion and Political Dissent in the Third Reich. Bavaria 1933–1945* (Oxford, 1983)

—— (ed.), *Weimar: Why Did German Democracy Fail?* (London, 1990)

—— *Hitler, 1889–1936: Hubris* (London, 2000)

Kienitz, Sabine, *Beschädigte Helden. Kriegsinvalidität und Körperbilder 1914–1923* (Paderborn, 2008)

Klein, Fritz, 'Between Compiègne and Versailles: The Germans on the Way from a Misunderstood Defeat to an Unwanted Peace', in Manfred F. Boemeke, Gerald D. Feldman and Elisabeth Glaser (eds), *The Treaty of Versailles. A Reassessment After 75 Years* (Cambridge, 1998), pp. 203–20

—— 'Versailles und die deutsche Linke', in Krumeich with Fehlemann (eds), *Versailles 1919*, pp. 314–22

Klein, Fritz, Gutsche, Willibald and **Petzold, Joachim**, *Deutschland im Ersten Weltkrieg*, 3 vols (East Berlin, 1968–9)

Kocka, Jürgen, 'The First World War and the "Mittelstand": German Artisans and White-Collar Workers', *Journal of Contemporary History*, 8/1 (1973), pp. 101–23

—— *Facing Total War. German Society, 1914–1918*, translated from the German by Barbara Weinberger (Oxford, 1984) [1973]

Kolb, Eberhard, *Die Arbeiterräte in der deutschen Innenpolitik* (Düsseldorf, 1962)

—— *The Weimar Republic*, translated from the German by P. S. Falla and R. J. Park, 2nd edition (London, 2005) [1988]

Kramer, Alan, 'Kriegsrecht und Kriegsverbrechen', in Hirschfeld, Krumeich and Renz (eds), *Enzyklopädie Erster Weltkrieg*, pp. 281–92

—— *Dynamic of Destruction. Culture and Mass Killing in the First World War* (Oxford, 2007)

Kranzfelder, Ivo, *George Grosz, 1893–1959* (Cologne, 1999)

Krause, Hartfrid, *USPD: Zur Geschichte der Unabhängigen Sozialdemokratischen Partei Deutschlands* (Frankfurt/M and Cologne, 1975)

Krüger, Peter, *Die Aussenpolitik der Republik von Weimar* (Darmstadt, 1985)

Krumeich, Gerd with Fehlemann, Silke (eds), *Versailles 1919. Ziele – Wirkung – Wahrnehmung* (Essen, 2001)

Kruse, Wolfgang, *Krieg und nationale Integration. Eine Neuinterpretation des sozialdemokratischen Burgfriedensschlusses 1914/15* (Essen, 1993)

Kuczynski, Jürgen, *Der Ausbruch des ersten Weltkrieges und die deutsche Sozialdemokratie. Chronik und Analyse* (East Berlin, 1957)

Lademacher, Horst, 'Philipp Scheidemann', in von Sternburg (ed.), *Die deutschen Kanzler*, pp. 161–75

Lange, Silvia, *Protestantische Frauen auf dem Weg in den Nationalsozialismus: Guida Diehls Neulandbewegung 1916–1935* (Stuttgart, 1998)

Langewiesche, Dieter, *Liberalism in Germany* (London, 2000)

Laqueur, Walter, *Weimar: A Cultural History 1918–1933* (London, 1974)

—— *Generation Exodus. The Fate of Young Jewish Refugees from Nazi Germany* (Hanover and London, 2001)

Large, David Clay, *Where Ghosts Walked. Munich's Road to the Third Reich* (London, 1997)

—— '"Out with the Ostjuden": The Scheunenviertel Riots in Berlin, November 1923', in Christhard Hoffmann, Werner Bergmann and Helmut Walser Smith (eds), *Exclusionary Violence. Antisemitic Riots in Modern German History* (Ann Arbor, MI, 2002), pp. 123–40

Leopold, J. A., *Alfred Hugenberg. The Radical Nationalist Campaign Against the Weimar Republic* (New Haven and London, 1977)

Lieberman, Ben, 'Testing Peukert's Paradigm: The "Crisis of Classical Modernity" in the "New Frankfurt", 1925–1930', *German Studies Review*, 17/2 (1994) pp. 287–303

Liulevicius, Vejas Gabriel, *War Land on the Eastern Front. Culture, National Identity and German Occupation in World War I* (Cambridge, 2000)

Lohalm, Uwe, *Völkischer Radikalismus. Die Geschichte des Deutschvölkischen Schutz- und Trutzbundes 1918–1923* (Hamburg, 1970)

MacMillan, Margaret, *Paris 1919. Six Months that Changed the World* (New York, 2003)

Major, Patrick, '"Smut and Trash". Germany's Culture Wars Against Pulp Fiction', in Führer and Ross (eds), *Mass Media, Culture and Society*, pp. 234–50

Martel, Gordon (ed.), *A Companion to Europe 1900–1945* (Oxford, 2006)

Mason, Tim, 'Women in Germany, 1925–1940: Family, Welfare and Work', *History Workshop Journal* (1976), Part I, pp. 74–113

—— 'National Socialism and the Working Class, 1925 to May 1933', in Mason, *Social Policy in the Third Reich. The Working Class and the 'National Community'* (Oxford, 1993), pp. 41–87

Matthews, William Carl, 'The Rise and Fall of Red Saxony', in Barclay and Weitz (eds), *Between Reform and Revolution*, pp. 293–313

Maurer, Trude, *Ostjuden in Deutschland 1918–1933* (Hamburg, 1986)

May, Ernest R., *The World War and American Isolation, 1914–1917* (Cambridge, MA, 1959)

McDermott, Kevin, 'Hermann Webers Konzept der "Stalinisierung" der KPD und der Komintern. Eine kritische Bewertung', *Jahrbuch der Historischen Kommunismusforschung* (2008), pp. 197–206

McDermott, Kevin and Agnew, Jeremy, *The Comintern. A History of International Communism from Lenin to Stalin* (Basingstoke, 1996)

McElligott, Anthony, 'Street Politics in Hamburg, 1932–3', *History Workshop Journal*, 16/1 (1983), pp. 83–90

—— 'Mobilising the Unemployed: The KPD and the Unemployed Workers' Movement in Hamburg-Altona during the Weimar Republic', in Evans and Geary (eds), *The German Unemployed*, pp. 228–60

—— 'Introduction', in McElligott (ed.), *Weimar Germany* (Oxford, 2009), pp. 1–25

McElligott, Anthony and Kirk, Tim (eds), *Working Towards the Führer. Essays in Honour of Sir Ian Kershaw* (Manchester, 2003)

McPhail, Helen, *The Long Silence. Civilian Life under the German Occupation of Northern France, 1914–1918* (London, 1999)

Menge, Anna, 'The *Iron Hindenburg*: A Popular Icon of Weimar Germany', *German History*, 26/3 (2008), pp. 357–82

Mergel, Thomas, 'Führer, Volksgemeinschaft und Maschine. Politische Erwartungsstrukturen in der Weimarer Republik und dem Nationalsozialismus 1918–1936', in Hardtwig (ed.), *Politische Kulturgeschichte der Zwischenkriegszeit*, pp. 91–127

Michel, Marc, 'Intoxication ou "brutalisation"? Les "represailles" de la grande guerre', *14–18 aujourd'hui today heute*, 4 (2001), pp. 175–97

Miller, Susanne, *Burgfrieden und Klassenkampf: Die deutsche Sozialdemokratie im Ersten Weltkrieg* (Düsseldorf, 1974)

Moeller, Robert G., *German Peasants and Agrarian Politics, 1914–1924. The Rhineland and Westphalia* (Chapel Hill, NC and London, 1986)

Möller, Horst, *Die Weimarer Republik. Eine unvollendete Demokratie*, new edition (Munich, 2004)

Mombauer, Annika, *The Origins of the First World War. Controversies and Consensus* (London, 2002)

Mombauer, Annika and Deist, Wilhelm (eds), *The Kaiser. New Research on Wilhelm II's Role in Imperial Germany* (Cambridge, 2003)

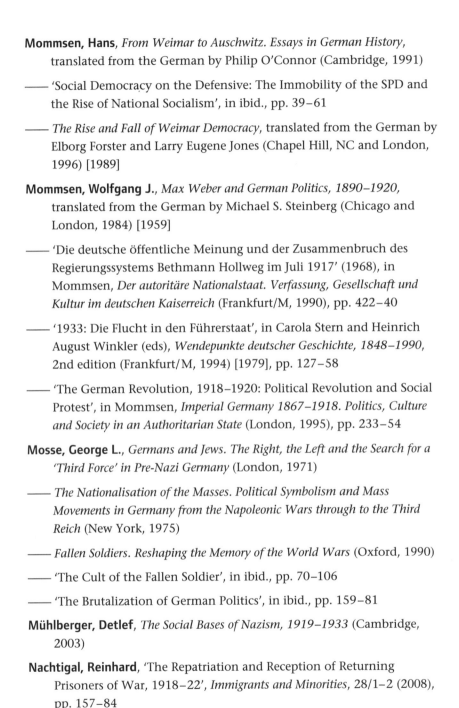

Mommsen, Hans, *From Weimar to Auschwitz. Essays in German History*, translated from the German by Philip O'Connor (Cambridge, 1991)

—— 'Social Democracy on the Defensive: The Immobility of the SPD and the Rise of National Socialism', in ibid., pp. 39–61

—— *The Rise and Fall of Weimar Democracy*, translated from the German by Elborg Forster and Larry Eugene Jones (Chapel Hill, NC and London, 1996) [1989]

Mommsen, Wolfgang J., *Max Weber and German Politics, 1890–1920*, translated from the German by Michael S. Steinberg (Chicago and London, 1984) [1959]

—— 'Die deutsche öffentliche Meinung und der Zusammenbruch des Regierungssystems Bethmann Hollweg im Juli 1917' (1968), in Mommsen, *Der autoritäre Nationalstaat. Verfassung, Gesellschaft und Kultur im deutschen Kaiserreich* (Frankfurt/M, 1990), pp. 422–40

—— '1933: Die Flucht in den Führerstaat', in Carola Stern and Heinrich August Winkler (eds), *Wendepunkte deutscher Geschichte, 1848–1990*, 2nd edition (Frankfurt/M, 1994) [1979], pp. 127–58

—— 'The German Revolution, 1918–1920: Political Revolution and Social Protest', in Mommsen, *Imperial Germany 1867–1918. Politics, Culture and Society in an Authoritarian State* (London, 1995), pp. 233–54

Mosse, George L., *Germans and Jews. The Right, the Left and the Search for a 'Third Force' in Pre-Nazi Germany* (London, 1971)

—— *The Nationalisation of the Masses. Political Symbolism and Mass Movements in Germany from the Napoleonic Wars through to the Third Reich* (New York, 1975)

—— *Fallen Soldiers. Reshaping the Memory of the World Wars* (Oxford, 1990)

—— 'The Cult of the Fallen Soldier', in ibid., pp. 70–106

—— 'The Brutalization of German Politics', in ibid., pp. 159–81

Mühlberger, Detlef, *The Social Bases of Nazism, 1919–1933* (Cambridge, 2003)

Nachtigal, Reinhard, 'The Repatriation and Reception of Returning Prisoners of War, 1918–22', *Immigrants and Minorities*, 28/1–2 (2008), pp. 157–84

Nathans, Eli, *The Politics of Citizenship in Germany. Ethnicity, Citizenship and Nationalism* (Oxford, 2004)

Natter, Wolfgang G., *Literature at War, 1914–1940. Representing the 'Time of Greatness' in Germany* (New Haven and London, 1999)

Nelson, Keith L., 'The "Black Horror on the Rhine". Race as a Factor in Post-World War I Diplomacy', *Journal of Modern History*, 42/4 (1970), pp. 606–27

Nelson, Robert L., 'German Comrades – Slavic Whores: Gender Images in the German Soldier Newspapers of the First World War', in Hagemann and Schüler-Springorum (eds), *Home/Front*, pp. 69–86

—— '"Ordinary Men" in the First World War? German Soldiers as Victims and Participants', *Journal of Contemporary History*, 39/3 (2004), pp. 425–35

Nicholls, A. J., *Weimar and the Rise of Hitler*, 4th edition (New York, 2000) [1968]

Niewyk, Donald L., *The Jews in Weimar Germany* (Manchester, 1980)

Noakes, Jeremy, *The Nazi Party in Lower Saxony, 1921–1933* (Oxford, 1971)

Nolte, Ernst, *Die Weimarer Republik. Demokratie zwischen Lenin und Hitler* (Munich, 2006)

Nonn, Christoph, 'Oh What a Lovely War? German Common People and the First World War', *German History*, 18/1 (2000), pp. 97–111

Offer, Avner, 'The Blockade of Germany and the Strategy of Starvation, 1914–1918', in Roger Chickering and Stig Förster (eds), *Great War, Total War. Combat and Mobilization on the Western Front, 1914–1918* (Cambridge, 2000), pp. 169–88

Oltmer, Jochen, 'Zwangsmigration und Zwangsarbeit – Ausländische Arbeitskräfte und bäuerliche Ökonomie im Ersten Weltkrieg', *Tel Aviver Jahrbuch für deutsche Geschichte*, 27 (1998), pp. 135–68

—— *Migration und Politik in der Weimarer Republik* (Göttingen, 2005)

—— *Migration im 19. und 20. Jahrhundert* (Osnabruck, 2008)

Orlow, Dietrich, *Weimar Prussia, 1918–1925. The Unlikely Rock of Democracy* (Pittsburgh, PA, 1986)

Overy, Richard, *The Nazi Economic Recovery, 1932–1938*, 2nd edition (Cambridge, 1996)

—— 'The German Economy, 1919–1945', in Panikos Panayi (ed.), *Weimar and Nazi Germany. Continuities and Discontinuities* (London, 2001), pp. 33–73

Patch, William L. Jr, *Heinrich Brüning and the Dissolution of the Weimar Republic* (Cambridge, 1998)

Paul, Gerhard, 'Krieg der Symbole. Formen und Inhalt des symbolpublizistischen Bürgerkrieges 1932', in Kerbs and Stahr (eds), *Berlin 1932*, pp. 27–55

Peukert, Detlev J. K., *The Weimar Republic. The Crisis of Classical Modernity*, translated from the German by Richard Deveson (London, 1991) [1987]

Phelps, Reginald, 'Before Hitler Came. Thule Society and *Germanenorden*', *Journal of Modern History*, 25/3 (1963), pp. 245–61

Picht, Clemens, 'Zwischen Vaterland und Volk. Das deutsche Judentum im Ersten Weltkrieg', in Wolfgang Michalka (ed.), *Der Erste Weltkrieg. Wirkung, Wahrnehmung, Analyse* (Munich, 1994), pp. 736–55

Pipes, Richard, *Communism. A Brief History* (London, 2001)

Planert, Ute (ed.), *Nation, Politik und Geschlecht. Frauenbewegungen und Nationalismus in der Moderne* (Frankfurt/M, 2000)

Plant, Robert, *The Pink Triangle. The Nazi War Against Homosexuals* (New York, 1986)

Pommerin, Reiner, 'Die Ausweisung von "Ostjuden" aus Bayern 1923. Ein Beitrag zum Krisenjahr der Weimarer Republik', *Vierteljahrshefte für Zeitgeschichte*, 34/3 (1986), pp. 311–40

Pöppinghege, Rainer, '"Kriegsteilnehmer zweiter Klasse"? Die Reichsvereinigung ehemaliger Kriegsgefangener 1919–1933', *Militärgeschichtliche Zeitschrift*, 64/2 (2005), pp. 391–423

—— *Im Lager unbesiegt. Deutsche, englische und französische Kriegsgefangenen-Zeitungen im Ersten Weltkrieg* (Essen, 2006)

Porter, Patrick, 'New Jerusalems: Sacrifice and Redemption in the War Experiences of English and German Military Chaplains', in Purseigle (ed.), *Warfare and Belligerence*, pp. 101–32

Pulzer, Peter, *The Rise of Political Anti-Semitism in Germany and Austria*, 2nd edition (London, 1988) [1964]

Purseigle, Pierre (ed.), *Warfare and Belligerence. Perspectives in First World War Studies* (Leiden, 2005)

—— '"A Wave on to our Shores": the Exile and Resettlement of Refugees from the Western Front, 1914–1918', *Contemporary European History*, 16/4 (2007), pp. 427–44

Purseigle, Pierre and **Macleod, Jenny**, 'Introduction: Perspectives in First World War Studies', in Jenny Macleod and Pierre Purseigle (eds), *Uncovered Fields. Perspectives in First World War Studies* (Leiden, 2004), pp. 1–23

Pyta, Wolfram, *Gegen Hitler und für die Republik. Die Auseinandersetzung der deutschen Sozialdemokratie mit der NSDAP in der Weimarer Republik* (Düsseldorf, 1989)

—— *Die Weimarer Republik* (Opladen, 2004)

—— *Hindenburg. Herrschaft zwischen Hohenzollern und Hitler* (Berlin, 2007)

Reagin, Nancy R., *A German Women's Movement. Class and Gender in Hanover, 1880–1933* (Chapel Hill, NC and London, 1995)

—— *Sweeping the Nation. Domesticity and National Identity in Germany, 1870–1945* (Cambridge, 2007)

Rees, Laurence, *The Nazis: A Warning from History* (London, 1997)

Rietzler, Rudolf, *'Kampf in der Nordmark'. Das Aufkommen des Nationalsozialismus in Schleswig-Holstein* (Neumünster, 1982)

Ritter, Gerhard, *Die Tragödie der Staatskunst. Bethmann Hollweg als Kriegskanzler (1914–1917)* (Munich, 1964)

Röhl, John C. G. (ed.), *Der Ort Kaiser Wilhelms II. in der deutschen Geschichte* (Munich, 1991)

—— *Wilhelm II: Die Jugend des Kaisers, 1859–1888* (Munich, 1993)

—— *The Kaiser and his Court. Wilhelm II and the Government of Germany* (Cambridge, 1996)

—— *Wilhelm II: Der Aufbau der persönlichen Monarchie, 1888–1900* (Munich, 2001)

—— *Wilhelm II: Der Weg in den Abgrund, 1900–1941* (Munich, 2008)

Röhl, Klaus Rainer, 'Fünf Tage im November. Kommunisten, Sozialdemokraten und Nationalsozialisten und der BVG-Streik vom November 1932 in Berlin', in Kerbs and Stahr (eds), *Berlin 1932*, pp. 161–77

Rosenhaft, Eve, 'Working-Class Life and Working-Class Politics: Communists, Nazis and the State in the Battle for the Streets of Berlin, 1928–1932', in Richard Bessel and E. J. Feuchtwanger (eds), *Social Change and Political Development in Weimar Germany* (London, 1981), pp. 207–40

—— *Beating the Fascists? The German Communist Party and Political Violence, 1929–1933* (Cambridge, 1983)

—— 'The Unemployed in the Neighbourhood: Social Dislocation and Political Mobilisation in Germany 1929–33', in Evans and Geary (eds), *The German Unemployed*, pp. 194–227

Ruge, Wolfgang, *Weimar – Republik auf Zeit* (East Berlin, 1969)

Rürup, Reinhard, 'Friedrich Ebert und das Problem der Handlungsspielräume in der deutschen Revolution 1918/19', in Rudolf König, Hartmut Soell and Hermann Weber (eds), *Friedrich Ebert und seine Zeit. Bilanz und Perspektiven der Forschung* (Munich, 1991), pp. 69–87

Sabrow, Martin, *Der Rathenau-Mord. Rekonstruktion einer Verschwörung gegen die Republik von Weimar* (Munich, 1994)

Sachse, Carole, *Industrial Housewives. Women's Social Work in the Factories of Nazi Germany*, introduced and edited by Jane Caplan (London, 1987)

—— *Siemens, der Nationalsozialismus und die moderne Familie. Eine Untersuchung zur sozialen Rationalisierung in Deutschland im 20. Jahrhundert* (Hamburg, 1990)

Saldern, Adelheid von, *Auf dem Wege zum Arbeiter-Reformismus. Parteialltag in sozialdemokratischer Provinz Göttingen (1870–1920)* (Frankfurt/M, 1984)

—— 'Latent Reformism and Socialist Utopia: The SPD in Göttingen, 1890 to 1920', in Barclay and Weitz (eds), *Between Reform and Revolution*, pp. 195–221

Sauer, Bernhard, 'Vom "Mythos eines ewigen Soldatentums". Der Feldzug deutscher Freikorps im Baltikum im Jahre 1919', *Zeitschrift für Geschichtswissenschaft*, 43/10 (1995), pp. 869–902

Scheck, Raffael, *Alfred von Tirpitz and German Right-Wing Politics, 1914–1930* (Atlantic Highlands, NJ, 1997)

—— 'German Conservatism and Female Political Activism in the Early Weimar Republic', *German History*, 15/1 (1997), pp. 34–55

—— 'Women against Versailles. Maternalism and Nationalism of Female Bourgeois Politicians in the Early Weimar Republic', *German Studies Review*, 22/1 (1999), pp. 21–42

—— *Mothers of the Nation. Right Wing Women in Weimar Germany* (Oxford, 2004)

Schiefel, Werner, *Bernhard Dernburg, 1865–1937. Kolonialpolitiker und Bankier im wilhelminischen Deutschland* (Zurich, 1974)

Schildt, Axel, *Konservatismus in Deutschland. Von den Anfängen im 18. Jahrhundert bis zur Gegenwart* (Munich, 1998)

Schivelbusch, Wolfgang, *The Culture of Defeat. On National Trauma, Mourning and Recovery*, translated from the German by Jefferson Chase (London, 2003) [2001]

Schönwälder, Karen, 'Akademischer Antisemitismus. Die deutschen Historiker in der NS-Zeit', *Jahrbuch für Antisemitismusforschung*, 2 (1993), pp. 200–29

Schröder, Anette, *Vom Nationalismus zum Nationalsozialismus. Die Studenten der Technischen Hochschule Hannover von 1925 bis 1938* (Hanover, 2003)

Schulze, Hagen, *Weimar: Deutschland 1917–1933* (West Berlin, 1982)

Schwabe, Klaus, *Woodrow Wilson, Revolutionary Germany and Peacemaking, 1918–1919: Missionary Diplomacy and the Realities of Power* (Chapel Hill, NC and London, 1985)

Scruton, Roger, *A Dictionary of Political Thought* (London, 1982)

Seligmann, Matthew S. and **McLean, Roderick R.**, *Germany from Reich to Republic, 1871–1918* (London, 2000)

Sharp, Ingrid, 'Blaming the Women: Women's "Responsibility" for the First World War', in Fell and Sharp (eds), *The Women's Movement in Wartime*, pp. 67–87

—— 'The Debate on "Surplus Women" in Post-First World War Germany', in Ingrid Sharp and Matthew Stibbe (eds), *Aftermaths of War. Women's Movements and Individual Activists, 1918–1923* (forthcoming)

Siebrecht, Claudia, 'The *Mater Dolorosa* on the Battlefield – Mourning Mothers in German Women's Art of the First World War', in Heather Jones, Jennifer O'Brien and Christoph Schmidt-Supprian (eds), *Untold War. New Perspectives in First World War Studies* (Leiden, 2008), pp. 259–91

Sieferle, Rolf Peter, *Die konservative Revolution. Fünf biographische Skizzen* (Frankfurt/M, 1995)

Siegmund-Schultze, Friedrich, *Die Wirkungen der englischen Hungerblockade auf die deutschen Kinder* (Berlin, 1919)

Sigel, Robert, 'Die Lensch-Cunow-Haenisch Gruppe. Ihr Einfluss auf die Ideologie der deutschen Sozialdemokratie im Ersten Weltkrieg', *Internationale wissenschaftliche Korrespondenz zur Geschichte der deutschen Arbeiterbewegung*, 11 (1975), pp. 421–36

Smid, Marijke, 'Protestantismus und Antisemitismus 1930–1933', in Jochen-Christoph Kaiser and Martin Greschat (eds), *Der Holocaust und die Protestanten. Analysen einer Verstrickung* (Frankfurt/M, 1988), pp. 38–72

Smith, Jeffrey R., *A People's War. Germany's Political Revolution, 1913–1918* (Lanham, M, 2007)

Sneeringer, Julia, *Winning Women's Votes. Propaganda and Politics in Weimar Germany* (Chapel Hill, NC and London, 2002)

Sösemann, Bernd, 'Der Verfall des Kaisergedankens im Ersten Weltkrieg', in Röhl (ed.), *Der Ort Kaiser Wilhelms II.*, pp. 145–70

Speed III, Richard B., *Prisoners, Diplomats and the Great War. A Study in the Diplomacy of Captivity* (New York, 1990)

Speier, Hans, *German White-Collar Workers and the Rise of Hitler*, new edition (New Haven, CT and London, 1986) [1932]

Sperber, Jonathan, 'The Social Democratic Electorate in Imperial Germany', in Barclay and Weitz (eds), *Between Reform and Revolution*, pp. 167–94

Stahr, Henrick, '"Erst Essen – dann Miete!" Mieterkrawalle, Mieterstreiks und ihre bildliche Repräsentation', in Kerbs and Stahr (eds), *Berlin 1932*, pp. 90–114

Stark, Gary D., *Entrepreneurs of Ideology: Neo-Conservative Publishers in Weimar Germany* (Chapel Hill, NC and London, 1981)

—— 'All Quiet on the Home Front: Popular Entertainments, Censorship and Civilian Morale in Germany, 1914–1918', in Frans Coetzee and Marilyn Shevin-Coetzee (eds), *Authority, Identity and the Social History of the Great War* (Oxford, 1995), pp. 57–80

Steakley, James D., *The Homosexual Emancipation Movement in Germany* (New York, 1975)

Steinweis, Alan, 'Weimar Political Culture and the Rise of National Socialism: The *Kampfbund für deutsche Kultur*', in *Central European History*, 24/4 (1991), pp. 402–23

Stephenson, Jill, *Women in Nazi Germany* (London, 2001)

Stern, Fritz, *The Politics of Cultural Despair. A Study in the Rise of the Germanic Ideology* (Berkeley, CA, 1961)

—— 'Bethmann Hollweg and the War: The Bounds of Responsibility' (1968), reproduced in Stern, *The Failure of Illiberalism. Essays on the*

Political Culture of Modern Germany, new edition (New York, 1992), pp. 77–118

Sternburg, Wilhelm von (ed.), *Die deutschen Kanzler. Von Bismarck nach Kohl*, new edition (Frankfurt/M, 1994) [1985]

Stibbe, Matthew, *German Anglophobia and the Great War, 1914–1918* (Cambridge, 2001)

—— 'Anti-Feminism, Nationalism and the German Right, 1914–1920: A Reappraisal', *German History*, 20/2 (2002), pp. 185–210

—— *Women in the Third Reich* (London, 2003)

—— 'Germany's "last card". Wilhelm II and the Decision in Favour of Unrestricted Submarine Warfare in January 1917', in Mombauer and Deist (eds), *The Kaiser*, pp. 217–34

—— 'The First World War: Aims, Strategy and Diplomacy', in Martel (ed.), *A Companion to Europe*, pp. 228–42

—— 'Prisoners of War during the First World War', *Bulletin of the German Historical Institute London*, XXVIII/2 (2006), pp. 47–59

—— 'Elisabeth Rotten and the "Auskunfts- und Hilfsstelle für Deutsche im Ausland und Ausländer in Deutschland", 1914–1919', in Fell and Sharp (eds), *The Women's Movement in Wartime*, pp. 194–210

—— *British Civilian Prisoners of War in Germany. The Ruhleben Camp, 1914–1918* (Manchester, 2008)

—— 'Civilian Internment and Civilian Internees in Europe, 1914–20', *Immigrants and Minorities*, 28/1–2 (2008), pp. 49–81

—— 'Fighting the First World War in the Cold War: East and West German Historiography on the Origins of the First World War, 1945–1961', in Andrew Plowman, Tobias Hochscherf and Christoph Laucht (eds), *Divided but not Disconnected. German Experiences of the Cold War* (Oxford, 2010) (forthcoming)

Stieg, Margaret F., 'The 1926 German Law to Protect Youth against Trash and Dirt: Moral Protectionism in a Democracy', *Central European History*, 23/1 (1990), pp. 22–56

Streubel, Christiane, *Radikale Nationalistinnen. Agitation und Programmatik rechter Frauen in der Weimarer Republik* (Frankfurt/M, 2006)

—— 'Raps Across the Knuckles: How Right-Wing Women Showed "True National Behaviour" in German Newspapers', in Ingrid Sharp and

Matthew Stibbe (eds), *Aftermaths of War. Women's Movements and Individual Activists, 1918–1923* (forthcoming)

Striesow, Jan, *Die Deutschnationale Volkspartei und die Völkisch-Radikalen 1918–1922*, 2 vols (Frankfurt/M, 1981)

Süchting-Hänger, Andrea, 'Die Anti-Versailles-Propaganda konservativer Frauen in der Weimarer Republik – Eine weibliche Dankesschuld?', in Krumeich with Fehlemann (eds), *Versailles 1919*, pp. 302–13

Swett, Pamela, *Neighbors and Enemies. The Culture of Radicalism in Berlin, 1929–1933* (Cambridge, 2004)

Szejnmann, Claus-Christian W., *Nazism in Central Germany. The Brownshirts in 'Red' Saxony* (Oxford, 1999)

—— *Vom Traum zum Alptraum. Sachsen in der Weimarer Republik* (Leipzig, 2000)

Tatar, Maria, *Lustmord. Sexual Murder in Weimar Germany* (Princeton, NJ, 1995)

Theweleit, Klaus, *Male Fantasies*, 2 vols, translated from the German by Stephen Conway in collaboration with Erica Carter and Chris Turner (Cambridge, 1987–9) [1980]

Thiel, Jens, *'Menschenbassin Belgien'. Anwerbung, Deportation und Zwangsarbeit im Ersten Weltkrieg* (Essen, 2007)

Thimme, Annelise, *Flucht in den Mythos. Die Deutschnationale Volkspartei und die Niederlage von 1918* (Göttingen, 1969)

Thönnessen, Werner, *The Emancipation of Women. The Rise and Decline of the Women's Movement in German Social Democracy, 1863–1933*, translated from the German by Joris de Bres (London, 1973) [1969]

Thoß, Bruno, 'Nationale Rechte, militärische Führung und Diktaturfrage in Deutschland 1913–1923', *Militärgeschichtliche Mitteilungen*, 42/1 (1987), pp. 27–76

Travers, Tim, 'The War in the Trenches', in Martel (ed.), *A Companion to Europe*, pp. 213–27.

Tröger, Annemarie, 'Die Dolchstoßlegende der Linken: "Frauen haben Hitler an die Macht gebracht"', in *Frauen und Wissenschaft. Beiträge zur Berliner Sommeruniversität für Frauen* (West Berlin, 1976), pp. 324–55

Turner, Henry Ashby Jr, *Hitler's Thirty Days to Power: January 1933* (London, 1996)

—— 'The Myth of Chancellor von Schleicher's *Querfront* Strategy', *Central European History*, 41/4 (2008), pp. 673–81

Ullrich, Sebastian, 'Mehr als Schall und Rauch: Der Streit um den Namen der ersten deutschen Demokratie 1918–1949', in Moritz Föllmer and Rüdiger Graf (eds), *Die 'Krise' der Weimarer Republik: Zur Kritik eines Deutungsmusters* (Frankfurt/M, 2005), pp. 187–207

Ullrich, Volker, *Kriegsalltag. Hamburg im ersten Weltkrieg* (Cologne, 1982)

Ulrich, Bernd, *Die Augenzeugen: Deutsche Feldpostbriefe in Kriegs- und Nachkriegszeit 1914–1933* (Essen, 1997)

Urbschat, Kerstin, 'Mecklenburg-Schwerin in den letzten Jahren der Weimarer Republik', in Frank Bajohr (ed.), *Norddeutschland im Nationalsozialismus* (Hamburg, 1993), pp. 83–98

Usborne, Cornelie, '"Pregnancy is the Woman's Active Service": Pronatalism in Germany during the First World War', in Richard Wall and Jay Winter (eds), *The Upheaval of War. Family, Work and Welfare in Europe, 1914–1918* (Cambridge, 1988), pp. 389–416

—— *The Politics of the Body in Weimar Germany* (London, 1992)

—— 'The New Woman and Generational Conflict. Perceptions of Young Women's Sexual Mores in the Weimar Republic', in Mark Roseman (ed.), *Generations in Conflict. Youth Revolt and Generation Formation in Germany, 1770–1968* (Cambridge, 1995), pp. 137–63

—— 'Wise Women, Wise Men and Abortion in the Weimar Republic: Gender, Class and Medicine', in Lynn Abrams and Elizabeth Harvey (eds), *Gender Relations in German History* (London, 1996), pp. 143–76

—— *Cultures of Abortion in Weimar Germany* (Oxford, 2007)

Verhey, Jeffrey, *The Spirit of 1914. Militarism, Myth and Mobilization in Germany* (Cambridge, 2000)

Vincent, C. Paul, *The Politics of Hunger. The Allied Blockade of Germany, 1915–1919* (Athens, OH and London, 1985)

Wachsmann, Nikolaus, 'Between Reform and Repression: Imprisonment in Weimar Germany', *Historical Journal*, 45/2 (2002), pp. 411–32

Walter, Dirk, 'Scheunenviertel Pogrom', in Richard S. Levy (ed.), *Antisemitism. A Historical Encyclopaedia of Prejudice and Persecution* (Santa Barbara, CA, 2005), p. 641

Walzer, Anke, *Käthe Schirmacher. Eine deutsche Frauenrechtlerin auf dem Wege vom Liberalismus zum konservativen Nationalismus* (Pfaffenweiler, 1991)

Watson, Alexander, *Enduring the Great War. Combat, Morale and Collapse in the German and British Armies, 1914–1918* (Cambridge, 2008)

Watt, Richard M., *The Kings Depart: The German Revolution and the Treaty of Versailles, 1918–1919*, Penguin edition (London, 1973) [1968]

Weber, Hermann, *Die Wandlung des deutschen Kommunismus. Die Stalinisierung der KPD in der Weimarer Republik* (Frankfurt/M, 1969)

—— 'The Stalinization of the KPD: Old and New Views', in Norman Laporte, Kevin Morgan and Matthew Worley (eds), *Bolshevism, Stalinism and the Comintern. Perspectives on Stalinization, 1917–53* (Basingstoke, 2008), pp. 22–44

Wehler, Hans-Ulrich, *The German Empire, 1871–1918*, translated from the German by Kim Traynor (Leamington Spa, 1985) [1973]

—— *Deutsche Gesellschaftsgeschichte. Vol. 4: Vom Beginn des Ersten Weltkriegs bis zur Gründung der beiden deutschen Staaten 1914–1949* (Munich, 2003)

Weindling, Paul, *Health, Race and German Politics between National Unification and Nazism, 1870–1945* (Cambridge, 1989)

Weisbrod, Bernd, *Die Schwerindustrie in der Weimarer Republik* (Wuppertal, 1978)

Weitz, Eric D., *Creating German Communism, 1890–1990* (Princeton, NJ, 1997)

—— 'Communism and the Public Spheres of Weimar Germany', in Barclay and Weitz (eds), *Between Reform and Revolution*, pp. 275–91

—— *Weimar Germany. Promise and Tragedy* (Princeton, NJ, 2007)

Wheeler, Robert F., *USPD und Internationale: Sozialistischer Internationalismus in der Zeit der Revolution* (Frankfurt/M, 1975)

Widdig, Bernd, *Culture and Inflation in Weimar Germany* (London, 2001)

Wildenthal, Lora, 'Mass-Marketing Colonialism and Nationalism: The Career of Else Frobenius in the "Weimarer Republik" and Nazi Germany', in Planert (ed.), *Nation, Politik und Geschlecht*, pp. 328–45

Willett, John, *Art and Politics in the Weimar Period. The New Sobriety, 1917–1933* (New York, 1978)

Williams, Raymond, *Culture and Society, 1780–1950*, Penguin edition (London, 1963) [1958]

Winkler, Heinrich August, *Von der Revolution zur Stabilisierung: Arbeiter und Arbeiterbewegung in der Weimarer Republik, 1918 bis 1924* (Bonn, 1984)

—— 'Choosing the Lesser Evil: The German Social Democrats and the Fall of the Weimar Republic', *Journal of Contemporary History*, 25/2 (1990), pp. 205–27

—— *Weimar, 1918–1933. Die Geschichte der ersten deutschen Demokratie* (Munich, 1993)

—— (ed.), *Weimar im Widerstreit. Deutungen der ersten deutschen Republik im geteilten Deutschland* (Munich, 2002)

Winter, Jay, *Sites of Memory, Sites of Mourning. The Great War in European Cultural History* (Cambridge, 1995)

—— 'Surviving the War: Life Expectation, Illness and Mortality Rates in Paris, London and Berlin, 1914–1919', in Jay Winter and Jean-Louis Robert (eds), *Capital Cities at War. Paris, London, Berlin, 1914–1919* (Cambridge, 1997), pp. 487–523

Winter, Jay and **Prost, Antoine**, *The Great War in History. Debates and Controversies, 1914 to the Present* (Cambridge, 2005)

Wippermann, Wolfgang, '"Falsch gedacht und nicht gehandelt". Der 20. Juli 1932 und das Scheitern des sozialdemokratischen Antifaschismus', in D. Kerbs and H. Stahr (eds), *Berlin 1932*, pp. 131–42

Witt, Peter-Christian, *Friedrich Ebert: Parteiführer, Reichskanzler, Volksbeauftragter, Reichspräsident* (Bonn, 1987)

Wittek, Thomas, *Auf ewig Feind? Das Deutschlandbild in den britischen Massenmedien nach dem Ersten Weltkrieg* (Munich, 2005)

Wright, Jonathan, *Gustav Stresemann. Weimar's Greatest Statesman* (Oxford, 2002)

Wulf, Peter, *Hugo Stinnes: Wirtschaft und Politik, 1918–1924* (Stuttgart, 1976)

Zamoyski, Adam, *Warsaw 1920. Lenin's Failed Conquest of Europe* (London, 2008)

Ziemann, Benjamin, 'Republikanische Kriegserinnerung in einer polarisierten Öffentlichkeit. Das Reichsbanner Schwarz-Rot-Gold als Veteranenbund der sozialistischen Arbeiterschaft', *Historische Zeitschrift*, 267 (1998), pp. 357–98

—— 'Germany after the First World War – A Violent Society? Results and Implications of Recent Research on Weimar Germany', *Journal of Modern European History*, 1 (2003), pp. 80–95

—— 'Geschlechterbeziehungen in deutschen Feldpostbriefen des Ersten Weltkrieges', in Christine Hämmerle and Edith Saurer (eds), *Briefkulturen und ihr Geschlecht. Zur Geschichte der privaten Korrespondenz vom 16. Jahrhundert bis heute* (Vienna, 2003), pp. 261–82

—— *War Experiences in Rural Germany, 1914–1923*, translated from the German by Alex Skinner (Oxford, 2007) [1997]

Zwach, Eva, *Deutsche und englische Militärmuseen im 20. Jahrhundert. Eine kulturgeschichtliche Analyse des gesellschaftlichen Umgangs mit dem Krieg* (Münster, 1999)

Novels and Plays

Brecht, Bertolt, *The Threepenny Opera* [1928], translated from the German and introduced by Ralph Manheim and John Willett (London, 1979)

Döblin, Alfred, *Berlin Alexanderplatz: The Story of Franz Biberkopf* [1929], translated from the German by Eugene Jolas, Penguin edition (London, 1978)

Isherwood, Christopher, *Goodbye to Berlin* [1939], Penguin edition (London, 1945)

Mann, Thomas, *The Magic Mountain* [1924], translated by H. T. Lowe-Porter, Penguin edition (London, 1960)

Remarque, Erich Maria, *All Quiet on the Western Front* [1929], translated by A. W. Wheen (London, 1929)

Index